Luminos is the open access monograph publishing program from UC Press. Luminos provides a framework for preserving and reinvigorating monograph publishing for the future and increases the reach and visibility of important scholarly work. Titles published in the UC Press Luminos model are published with the same high standards for selection, peer review, production, and marketing as those in our traditional program. www.luminosoa.org

STUDIES OF THE WEATHERHEAD EAST ASIAN INSTITUTE,
COLUMBIA UNIVERSITY

The Studies of the Weatherhead East Asian Institute of Columbia University were inaugurated in 1962 to bring to a wider public the results of significant new research on modern and contemporary East Asia.

For a select list of books in the series, see page 308.

Imperial Genus

ASIA PACIFIC MODERN

Takashi Fujitani, Series Editor

1. *Erotic Grotesque Nonsense: The Mass Culture of Japanese Modern Times*, by Miriam Silverberg

2. *Visuality and Identity: Sinophone Articulations across the Pacific*, by Shu-mei Shih

3. *The Politics of Gender in Colonial Korea: Education, Labor, and Health, 1910–1945*, by Theodore Jun Yoo

4. *Frontier Constitutions: Christianity and Colonial Empire in the Nineteenth-Century Philippines*, by John D. Blanco

5. *Tropics of Savagery: The Culture of Japanese Empire in Comparative Frame*, by Robert Thomas Tierney

6. *Colonial Project, National Game: A History of Baseball in Taiwan*, by Andrew D. Morris

7. *Race for Empire: Koreans as Japanese and Japanese as Americans during World War II*, by T. Fujitani

8. *The Gender of Memory: Rural Women and China's Collective Past*, by Gail Hershatter

9. *A Passion for Facts: Social Surveys and the Construction of the Chinese Nation-State, 1900–1949*, by Tong Lam

11. *Redacted: The Archives of Censorship in Transwar Japan*, by Jonathan E. Abel

12. *Assimilating Seoul: Japanese Rule and the Politics of Public Space in Colonial Korea, 1910–1945*, by Todd A. Henry

13. *Working Skin: Making Leather, Making a Multicultural Japan*, by Joseph D. Hankins

14. *Imperial Genus: The Formation and Limits of the Human in Modern Korea and Japan*, by Travis Workman

Imperial Genus

The Formation and Limits of the Human in Modern Korea and Japan

Travis Workman

UNIVERSITY OF CALIFORNIA PRESS

University of California Press, one of the most distinguished university presses in the United States, enriches lives around the world by advancing scholarship in the humanities, social sciences, and natural sciences. Its activities are supported by the UC Press Foundation and by philanthropic contributions from individuals and institutions. For more information, visit www.ucpress.edu.

University of California Press
Oakland, California

© 2016 by The Regents of the University of California

This work is licensed under a Creative Commons CC BY-NC-ND license. To view a copy of the license, visit http://creativecommons.org/licenses.

Suggested citation: Workman, Travis. *Imperial Genus: The Formation and Limits of the Human in Modern Korea and Japan*. Oakland: University of California Press, 2016. doi: http://dx.doi.org/10.1525/luminos.9

Library of Congress Cataloging-in-Publication Data

Workman, Travis, 1979- author.
    Imperial genus : the formation and limits of the human in modern Korea and Japan / Travis Workman.
        pages cm. — (Asia Pacific modern ; 14)
    Includes bibliographical references and index.
    ISBN 978-0-520-28959-8 (cloth : alk. paper) — ISBN 0-520-28959-5 (cloth : alk. paper) — ISBN 978-0-520-96419-8 (ebook) — ISBN 0-520-96419-5 (ebook)
       1. Korea—History—Japanese occupation, 1910-1945. 2. Essentialism (Philosophy) 3. Korean literature—20th century—History and criticism. 4. Japanese literature—20th century—History and criticism. 5. Japan—Cultural policy—History—20th century. 6. Japan—Politics and government—1912-1945. 7. Korea—Colonial influence.
   I. Title. II. Series: Asia Pacific modern ; 14.
   DS916.54.W67 2016
   951.9'03—dc23

                                                           2015029804

24 23 22 21 20 19 18 17 16 15
10 9 8 7 6 5 4 3 2 1

CONTENTS

Acknowledgments   *vii*

   Introduction   *1*
   The Japanese Empire and Universality   *1*
   The Logic of Genus-Being   *6*
   From Civilization to Culture in Imperial Rule, 1895–1919   *13*
   Practice, Pragmatics, and Norming Space   *18*
   The Limits of the Human   *22*

1. Culturalism and the Human   *26*
   Culturalism and Cultural Policy   *26*
   Morality, Life, and the Person: Kuwaki Gen'yoku   *31*
   Political Economy and Cultural Economy: The Limit Concept in Sōda Kiichirō   *41*
   Translating the Human, Communicating Concepts, National Language   *49*
   Japan's Area Studies: Korea as Cultural and Literary Region   *56*

2. The Colony and the World: Nation, Poetics, and Biopolitics in Yi Kwang-su   *62*
   Cultural Reconstruction   *66*
   Forming Life for Humanity   *70*
   Cosmopolitan Sentiment and the Role of Literature   *80*
   Finitude and the Allegorical Novel   *84*
   Critiques of Cultural Personhood   *92*

3. Labor and *Bildung* in Marxism and the Proletarian Arts   98
    An Uncertain International: Nakano Shigeharu and Im Hwa   102
    Soviet Debates: Unevenness, Anthropology, and Culture   108
    Proletarian *Bildung* in East Asia: The Cultural Formation of a National Proletariat   113
    Economic Stages of Genus-Being: Paek Nam-un   128
    Proletarian Culture and the East Asian Community   132

4. Other Chronotopes in Realist Literature   134
    Chronotope and Humanism   134
    Allegory and Realism in Fiction and Criticism   139
    Ch'oe Sŏ-hae: Migration, Letters, and Death   153
    Countryside, City, Primitive Accumulation   160

5. World History and Minor Literature   167
    The World-Historical State   167
    Osmotic Expression   176
    Ch'oe Chae-sŏ and People's Literature: The Crisis of Modern Humanism   180
    Translation as Tactic   191
    Acting Human: The Minor Literature of Kim Sa-ryang and Kim Nam-ch'ŏn   196
    Ambiguous Identities: "Into the Light"   208

6. Modernism without a Home: Cinematic Literature, Colonial Architecture, and Yi Sang's Poetics   213
    Modernist Temporality and Imperialism   214
    The Ecstatic Time of Cinematic Literature: Ch'oe Chae-sŏ and Yokomitsu Riichi   219
    Culturalism and Architectural Space: Korea and Architecture   229
    Yi Sang's Cinepoetic Space: "Blueprint for a Three-Dimensional Shape"   240

Notes   249
Appendix   271
    Opening an Umbrella on Yokohama Pier/Im Hwa   271
    Blueprint for a Three-Dimensional Shape/Yi Sang   273
Selected Bibliography   277
Index   293

ACKNOWLEDGMENTS

In the decade I have been working on this project, I have received help and support from a number of teachers, colleagues, students, and institutions. I was blessed to have Brett de Bary as a dissertation adviser. She patiently helped me to work through my ideas and to chart a manageable path during my years at Cornell. She also gave me important advice and comments about writing in the early stages of the dissertation, which I carried with me all the way until the completion of this book. The influence of Naoki Sakai's thinking and the effects of his teaching are apparent throughout this work and I was very fortunate to have the opportunity to be immersed in philosophy, translation, and political discussion in the context of his seminars. He has an enviable ability to pinpoint the crux of a theoretical or historical problem, and at multiple points his responses to what I had done so far led me in new and fruitful directions. In addition to their individual contributions to my growth as a scholar, they, along with J. Victor Koschmann, created a transnational environment for comparative historical and literary studies that I was extremely lucky to enter into as a young graduate student in East Asian studies. Michael D. Shin introduced me to the field of Korean studies and generously shared with me his knowledge of colonial period intellectual history, as well as many of the specific discoveries he had made in his archival research. Without the connections he made between Yi Kwang-su and Japanese culturalism, this project would have been impossible.

Harry Harootunian's work has affected my own for quite some time and he also kindly gave me guidance concerning publishing. Other professors who had a strong impact on me through their teaching are Susan Buck-Morss and Peter Hohendahl. Many of the central ideas in the book were developed during a summer at Cornell's School of Criticism and Theory, where I was fortunate to take a seminar with Robert J. C. Young.

I could not have hoped for a better cohort in graduate school and many of my peers ended up being my teachers as well; Takeshi Kimoto, Pedro Erber, Gavin Walker, Annmaria Shimabuku, John Namjun Kim, Yoshiaki Mihara, Judy Park, Sean Franzel, and Josh Dittrich all contributed ideas and necessary distractions. Sun Min Oh steered me toward very useful texts and helped me to connect with scholars in South Korea. With great generosity and kindness, Go Mi-sook, Yi Jin-kyung, and Goh Byeong-gwon welcomed me to research, study, eat, cook, and occasionally pluck away at a piano at their commune in Seoul. It inspired me to think that intellectual pursuits could still be meaningful and transformative in practice. Thanks also to Tobias Liefert, Emilia Wojtasik, Maija Brown, and David Olson, and to Pia Vogler for her encouragement.

This project grew up quite a bit during my time as a postdoctoral fellow at the University of California, Los Angeles. The program directors, Shu-mei Shih and Françoise Lionnet, created and developed a truly remarkable environment for both scholarship and friendship and I am indebted to them. I thank my fellow fellows in the program, Sonali Pahwa, Greg Cohen, Maya Boutaghou, Sarah Valentine, Joseph Bauerkemper, Marcela Fuentes, Sze-wei Ang, Jeannine Murray-Román, and Fatima El-Tayeb, for both their keen intellects and their senses of humor.

Many people in Korean studies welcomed me, despite my late arrival. Jin-kyung Lee, Janet Poole, Sonia Ryang, Steven Chung, Kyung Hyun Kim, Immanuel Kim, Dafna Zur, Jinsoo An, Kyeong-Hee Choi, Christopher Hanscom, Michelle Cho, Baek Moonim, and Youngmin Choe have all enabled me at some point to carve out a place in the field. Jie-Hyun Lim was kind enough to invite me to present in Seoul. Theodore Hughes and Michael Robinson have done a great deal to move my career along with their advocacy of my work.

It was in Santa Cruz, California, as an undergraduate that I first realized that publishing a book like this was what I wanted to do. There, Professors Christopher Connery and Earl Jackson, Jr. enlivened my dedication to a life of reading, writing, and thinking. Dave Youssef, Zen Dochterman, Manuel Schwab, Kinneret Israel, Alexei Nowak, and Morgan Adamson have become lifelong friends and continue to impact my academic work. In Los Angeles, I met Erin Trapp, who became an invaluable contributor to the project, reading and commenting on every chapter. Rei Terada and Eyal Amiran went out of their way to provide friendship and support. Numerous discussions with Duy Lap Nguyen and Duncan Yoon on philosophical and historical topics allowed me to deepen my argument and clarify its contours.

My mother, Monica George-Halling, and my father, Jay Workman, have always been in my corner, no matter what I have decided to do, and I love them for it. My brother Brandon and my sister Hana are inspirational in their talents and their ability to endure. Bill Halling and Angela and John Guy made me more adventurous early on. Bob, Eva, Micah, Roman, Mark, Steven, Daniel, Chris, Tracy, and the rest of the Trapp family have taken an interest in and bolstered this project in various ways.

The colleagues in my department, Asian Languages and Literatures at the University of Minnesota, have been tremendously supportive. It is difficult to create an atmosphere that is both congenial and intellectually engaging, but they have done so despite all of the usual pressures. Jason McGrath has been a wonderful mentor when it comes to university matters and a good friend when it comes to food, drinks, and music. I will miss the wit and kindness of my former office neighbor, Simona Sawhney. It has been instructive sharing ideas on humanism and ecology with Christine Marran. As a junior faculty member navigating a new university and a new city, I am lucky to have had Paul Rouzer and Joseph Allen as department chairs and Maki Isaka as a senior colleague. Suvadip Sinha and Baryon Posadas have brought magnificent energy to the department. Hangtae Cho has built a strong and enduring Korean-language program that is inimitable in its support of my own teaching and research. I owe a lot to him and to his large undertaking.

Matthias Rothe is a precious colleague and friend, and my many discussions with him about both Foucault and German thought improved this book immensely. He also read and provided detailed commentary on the introduction and chapter 1. My reading groups and discussions with Hoon Song stimulated new thinking on Marx and deconstruction. Hiromi Mizuno's work building Asian studies at the university has been crucial. The argument of the introduction was advanced greatly through a graduate seminar on the colonial construction of Asia and the West. Thank you to the graduate student participants. Sejung Ahn has done superb research work for me and also kindly tracked down the cover photo. Minhwa Ahn and Saena Dozier were excellent teaching and research assistants. I am also grateful to Matt Sumera, Aaron McKain, and Michael Gallope for our musical endeavors.

The Weatherhead East Asian Institute at Columbia University was instrumental in getting the manuscript reviewed and eventually published. In particular I would like to acknowledge Ross Yelsey for his timely and friendly assistance at all stages of the process. I would also like to thank Carol Gluck for supporting publication and for finding the right press and series. Takashi Fujitani was not just a supportive series editor; his work on biopolitics in the Japanese empire contributed in fundamental ways to the rearticulation of my argument between the dissertation and the book. It was a pleasure and a privilege to have Reed Malcolm of UC Press as an editor. Stacy Eisenstark kept everything on track and kept me reassured by fielding my many questions. Two reviewers provided very useful and spot-on commentary that allowed me to improve the manuscript significantly. Robert Demke did a masterful job of copyediting and Alexander Trotter created a superb index.

The Korea Foundation supported my time in Korea with its Korean Language Training Fellowship, as well as my position at the University of Minnesota. A McKnight Land-Grant Professorship from the University of Minnesota supported the latter stages of the writing process. Part of chapter 5 first appeared as "Locating Translation: On the Question of Japanophone Literature," *PMLA* 126, no. 3 (May 2011): 701–8. It is reprinted by permission of the copyright owner, the Modern Language Association of America. Thank you to the YoungIn Museum of Literature for their permission to use the cover photo.

A number of texts that I began working with at the dissertation stage have now been translated into English and published, particularly in the case of Korean texts. Unless an English source is cited in the notes, translations from Korean, Japanese, and German are my own. If an English source is cited, I have used that translator's translation.

Finally, I dedicate this book to Erin, Philomena, and Imogen, who not only sustained me emotionally through the long process of writing, but also gave this life's project a meaning that I never would have found on my own.

Introduction

THE JAPANESE EMPIRE AND UNIVERSALITY

In an essay from 1920 titled "On the Notion of 'Japanese,'" published as part of *Culturalism and Social Problems,* the philosopher Kuwaki Gen'yoku discusses his attendance at a Berlin production of Giacomo Puccini's *Madame Butterfly* during his time as a student in Germany. He recounts how reluctant he was to attend the opera, because he could not bear to watch the various historical and cultural inaccuracies in this kind of Orientalist production:

> Once in Berlin I saw and heard the opera *Madame Butterfly.* At that time I was going to plays, opera, and musical theater quite often, but I did not have any desire to go see Japanese things. However, I had a change of heart and ended up going because it was my only opportunity to see Geraldine Farrar, who had returned from the United States after a long time. This was a useless justification that I made to myself. Really I wanted to show that I did not appreciate this kind of play. Why did I not appreciate it? One reason was that I did not have time for that sort of thing, because I was researching Western cultural artifacts for only a brief time and with limited means; however, the main reason was that I could not bear to see the frequent mistakes made in such a play.[1]

In his response to the play, Kuwaki is particularly critical of the depiction of the subservient Cho Cho and thinks that modern Japanese women could not identify with such a character. He points out that a man in a Chinese hat appears at a Japanese inn from an indefinite time period and that time and place are generally out of joint. He also discusses that he felt embarrassment when the audience members were watching this depiction of Japan, because the habits and behaviors of lower-class peasants and merchants were used to epitomize Japanese national culture. As a matter of time, money, and academic interest—or perhaps as a quiet mode of resistance—he would have refused to go entirely, if not for the chance to see one of the greatest opera and silent film stars in the world at the time, Geraldine Farrar. Unfortunately, it was difficult to appreciate the talent of the actress due to the character she portrayed. In Kuwaki's account, Cho Cho is an American and European fantasy of a timeless and feminized Japan of the past that bears little resemblance to the reality of that past or, certainly, to the Japan of Kuwaki's present.

Such passages recounting a personal experience are very rare in Kuwaki's works, which are mostly dedicated to interpretations of ancient Greek philosophy and the German philosophical tradition, including the life philosophy *(Lebensphilosophie)* and neo-Kantian cultural science that were prominent in the early twentieth century. He recounts the experience not in a diary, but rather to make a conceptual point in the middle of a political tract, one of two attempts he made around 1920 to address the social problems of his day through the "philosophy of culturalism" *(bunkashugi no tetsugaku)*.[2] Having suffered through the historical and cultural inaccuracies of *Madame Butterfly*, he describes how he came away even more convinced that those concerned about the meaning and value of the idea of Japan should not cede them to the false observations and representations of American and European Orientalists.

Kuwaki does not primarily seek to correct the historical inaccuracies of such representations, as if Orientalism only needs to improve its content, to give a better accounting of the materials it uses to construct national and continental essences. He rather uses *Madame Butterfly* as a case in point for the need to challenge the transcendental rules of the human sciences, in which Europe is positioned on the side of the subject and Japan on the side of the anthropological object. He states that an indexical notion of Japan, or the "remarkable illusion" of pointing to a cultural artifact and stating "This is Japan!" is unacceptable, because it lacks "universal validity" *(fuhen-teki datōsei)*.[3] In another formulation, he states that such an indexical notion of Japan "confuses the contingent characteristics of culture with its essential characteristics."[4] Taking up the neo-Kantian concern for the transcendental rules governing knowledge formation, he argues that the truth of "Japanese" *(nihon-teki)* should not be sought in experience at all, but rather in an a priori *(senten-teki)* concept arrived at through an internal critical philosophy: "It is really a huge mistake to make imported thought the standard for establishing the 'a priori' quality of 'Japanese' or theorizing 'Japanese' through critical philosophy. That which determines the 'a priori' through critical philosophy is 'Japaneseness' itself performing a criticism of 'Japanese.'"[5] Kuwaki gives an a priori rather than a posteriori meaning to the signifier "Japanese," taking the meaning of "Japan" out of the realm of the experience of phenomena and into the realm of noumenal concepts that precede experience, effectively dismantling the structure of Orientalist representation.

What did it mean for Kuwaki to take Japanese out of the realm of experience and make it the object of critical philosophy, of a Kantian attempt to establish transcendentally the conceptual conditions of possibility for experience? Modern narratives of the emergence of the European subject or the West—from Immanuel Kant's statements on history and anthropology to postwar US modernization theory—have told the story of this kind of scientific separation of the human subject from the chaotic manifold of experience as a culturally specific possibility with an identifiable origin in Europe.[6] Defining this cultural specificity of the transcendental subject, as well as priming it for colonial export, was a process concomitant with the figuring of the non-West as an object of empirical knowledge, particularly through the discipline of anthropology.[7] How, then, can one read Kuwaki's critique, which breaks from the construction of Japan as an empirical object of the anthropological gaze? How can his work, and the innumerable humanist works of the Japanese empire that articulated political and cultural positions according to the standard of universal validity, be read as an element of their time and place without falling back into the very historical, cultural, and anthropological constructions of the non-West that Kuwaki rightfully questions?

It might seem adequate to analyze Kuwaki's call for Japaneseness to critique Japanese as a straightforward ethnic nationalist response to the coding of universality as a particularly European possibility, but this reading cannot account for how he changes the meaning of both Japaneseness and Japanese such that they no longer immediately refer to a shared ethnic tradition. In a discussion of the "perpetual development" of history in his philosophy of history, Kuwaki pointed out that once the human being becomes the object of a priori scientific knowledge, there is no point in historical or human scientific development when the cosmopolitan purpose of history will have been completely fulfilled in the actual world.[8] Likewise, in the nationalist language of *Culturalism and Social Problems,* when Japanese is posed as the object of transcendental critique, there will be no point in history when it has been exhaustively conceptualized or understood. If Japaneseness is the subject that performs such an internal critique, then the perpetual development of history also entails the constant reconfiguration of the anthropological concepts that one uses to define the essence of this subject. The empirical identity of this subject will be constantly transformed in history. In other words, once the anthropological category of Japanese is understood not as an object of experience, but rather as a transcendental idea, it will not be possible for national identity to be constructed by an atavistic turn to a stable past of the ethnic nation; this identity can only be a future constantly iterated and reimagined.

This view of the nation and national history, based on a modernizing notion of universal history and the scientific requirement of universal validity, had very important political and social consequences. Kuwaki wrote *Culturalism and Social Problems* one year after the March First independence movement in Korea, a nationwide popular uprising met with a great deal of violence by the Japanese colonial authorities and then by the governor-general of Korea's shift to cultural policy *(bunka seiji)*. Kuwaki's discussions of Japanese as an object of critique rather than observation and Japaneseness as a historical subjectivity constantly transformed were suitable to the flexible notion of nationality that was becoming necessary for the new discourses of assimilation in the colonies. However, there is another important aspect to such a turn to universality and universal history in the philosophy and literature of the Japanese empire in the 1920s. Along with the more flexible notions of the nation and national borders that were created by the idea of Japanese as an object of perpetual internal critique and development, there was also the figure of the human being itself, through which Kuwaki and other culturalists situated Japan within a larger cosmopolitan project of uniting humanity through "general culture" and "absolute values."[9] Kuwaki and other culturalists translated Kant's grounding of the universal in morality in order to present culturalism not simply as a project for national development, but as an equally interminable mission to create a moral cosmopolitan community.

In his early short fiction, the Korean novelist and philosopher Yi Kwang-su also recounted experiences of being reduced to an unconscious object through the depiction of Korean foreign exchange students living in Tokyo whose lack of interiority or purpose leads them to unrequited love and suicide.[10] However, he was a student of Kuwaki's at Waseda University in the 1910s and took up the philosophy of culturalism in order to argue that self-consciousness *(chagak)* and value philosophy should be foundational for the development of Korean national character. He came to see Korea as a population that had to become capable of applying transcendental, cosmopolitan values to its empirical circumstances before it could hope to be part of human history, much less regain nation-state sovereignty. Furthermore, just as Kuwaki's assertion of the transcendental human subject influenced and was intertextual with Marxism, the proletarian arts, and imperial nationalist philosophies, Yi's turn to the universality of self-consciousness, and the allegorical literature he wrote from this philosophical position, introduced new modes of comparison that affected nearly every intellectual and writer in colonial Korea.

The primary purpose of this book is to trace how this kind of cosmopolitan thinking related in various explicit and implicit ways to Japan's imperial project, as well as to trace simultaneously how anthropological universals, and the figure of the human being in general, allowed for new critical modes of thinking about the singularity of capitalist modernity. Kuwaki's and Yi's notions of internal, transcendental critique ended up reverting to a colonial logic when they were applied as elements of cultural policy. However, they also opened up, albeit in a very idealist fashion, the possibility for a common plain on which Europe and Japan, and also Japan and Korea, could be considered temporally coeval. Although their models for modernity and capitalism became developmental, the original insight that modernity is fundamentally about possible futures, rather than a position from which to index the past of the anthropological other, includes a claim to universality not immediately reducible to an imperialist position. In order to analyze their discourses as imperial discourse, therefore, it is necessary to see their universalisms as comparatively as they themselves saw them, while also locating where these universalisms instituted anthropologically defined colonial, gender, and class hierarchies. Their philosophies of the human, and by extension of empire, were both a transformative translation of the universalism of neo-Kantian thought and maneuvers comparable to other instances when the human being has been invoked politically as a figure of both sameness and difference, of the transcendental and the empirical, and of the universal and the particular.

In order to understand how anthropological universals were situated and translated within the Japanese empire, and to see the extent of their political and historical effects, I have chosen to compare philosophical, social-scientific, and literary discourses in Japan proper and colonial Korea, roughly between 1910 and 1945. This comparison is in some respects meant to challenge the structure of universality and particularity that governed Cold War knowledge about East Asia, as well as ethnic nationalist readings of the Japanese empire in postwar Japan, South Korea, and North Korea.[11] During the Cold War, US modernization theory and cultural anthropology ethnicized knowledge about East Asia, discussing tradition and modernity as matters of collective psychology and ethnic national identity.[12] These discourses treated Japan and Korea as discrete and organic national spheres, thereby forging an interpretation of the significance of universalist humanisms in the colonial policy and practices of assimilation of the Japanese empire. With their concern for both historical convergence and the maintenance of ethnic-cultural differences, modernization theory and cultural anthropology repeated many of the problems in the humanist discourses of the Japanese empire. However, in doing so unconsciously, they came to assume that views of the human being in the Japanese empire must have been antimodern, traditionalist, ethnocentric, and semifeudal.[13]

In a different but complicit way, the formation of ethnic nationalism in Japan, South Korea, and North Korea after 1945 meant that the question of Japanese imperial rule would be framed as a matter of one identifiable nation's exploitation of another identifiable nation. Discussions of collective war guilt or collective innocence on the political right defined the debate on historical memory in Japan. The category of "pro-Japanese" allowed for South Korean ethnic national identity to be solidified despite uncomfortable connections with the Japanese imperial past. In North Korea, the landlord class was branded as antinational and complicit with the Japanese and US empires. Those intellectuals who had been patriotic Japanese only years earlier struggled to remain politically or economically relevant to a regime whose political ideology was founded on anti-Japanese guerrilla struggle.[14]

Most texts from the period of the Japanese empire, particularly in the textual traffic between Japan and Korea, suggest something different from this dichotomous Cold War view of warring ethnic nationalisms. Universalist claims about humanity were central to Japanese imperial rule, responses to that rule, and the conflicted mediation between these. They also became embedded in postwar discourse in, for example, the continuation of culturalist notions of the cosmopolitan in postwar Japan, in the violent humanist critique of communism employed at the founding of the Republic of Korea (particularly in the work of An Hosang), and in the Juche thought of North Korea (whose humanist aspect was developed by Hwang Changyŏp, and which proclaims that "man is the master of all things").[15] In order to understand the workings of the Japanese empire and its postcolonial legacies, this book recognizes the universalist dimension of those modern humanist discourses that facilitated the political and economic processes of primitive accumulation, assimilation, and identification with empire, opening up the epistemological and other representational problems in that context to comparison with other situations of modern imperialism (including the historical present of late US empire). It also examines the limits of these universalist concepts, which appear as they come into contact with located practices of thinking, writing, and representing. In this respect, I take seriously Kuwaki's assertion of the coevalness of Japanese empire, including colonial Korea, with the modern world at large, while questioning the specific ways that the transcendental and universal notion of humanity posited by the philosophy of culturalism was employed to identify and to regulate the political, social, and cultural differences internal to the imperial nation-state.

How can the universalism of anthropocentric knowledge continually be translated and particularized, despite the acts of norming and exclusion that it also enables? That is the guiding question of this book.

THE LOGIC OF GENUS-BEING

Culturalism *(bunkashugi)* was the hegemonic "-ism" of the Japanese empire in the 1920s. It refers generally to the cosmopolitan ethos of Taishō democracy, to the idea that culture in Japan belonged to the general culture of global liberal society. Wilhelm Windelband, Heinrich Rickert, and others in the Southwest Baden School of Neo-Kantianism first developed cultural science *(Kulturwissenschaft)*, which became, through the works of Kuwaki Gen'yoku, Sōda Kiichirō, and others, the dominant philosophical articulation of the culturalist ethos in the Japanese empire in the 1920s.[16] Rickert and Windelband opposed the human, spiritual, historical, and cultural sciences to natural science and established different methodologies for the study of nature and the study of the human. In Rickert's formalized version of cultural science, he states that natural science studies the objective laws of nature, but must limit itself to nature when questions of human will, individuality, and history enter the picture.¹⁷ Rickert's cultural science studies how cultural values and cultural value formation determine historical events and their understanding. Cultural science was central to the establishment of various anthropocentric epistemologies in early-twentieth-century Japan, particularly those organized around a concept of human generality. The philosophies of culturalism of Kuwaki, Sōda, and Yi Kwang-su can be understood as the politicization of cultural science, and they each claimed that liberal society required the cultural integration of the individual, the nation, and the world.

The concept of proletarian culture served a similar purpose for Marxism and the proletarian arts as general culture did for the philosophy of culturalism. It reintroduced anthropological content into the formal concept of productive labor as the general determination of the modern human. For the various exploited classes of the empire to be unified under the banner of the proletariat, the most historically advanced subject in world history, proletarian culture had to intervene, guided by the vanguard, in order to provide the masses with purposive consciousness. Otherwise, the merely spontaneous and natural acts of revolt against capitalism and colonialism could never actualize the necessary transition of humanity to the stage of socialism, enacted by a unified national-international subject, the proletariat. Quantifiable productive labor differentiated the industrial proletariat, the proper political subject of modernity, from those social classes whose form of labor and class consciousness belonged to the premodern past and were trapped in nature, spontaneity, and mechanism.

For imperial nationalists of the 1930s and 1940s, individuals who lacked a nation-state, or rather failed to identify with a nation-state, were not properly modern, because they had no means to connect their individuality to the generally human within the imperialist competition called *world history*. Multiethnic Japanese national culture was called upon to mediate between the world-historical imperial state and the as-yet stateless individuals, particularly those belonging to colonial and ethnic minority communities. The idea of culture was again employed at the intersection of the universal and the particular, this time between the world-historical state and its various anthropologically defined, internal others. National or regional culture performed an integrative and mediatory function as a means of liberating the individual from previous ethnic, class, or local affiliations. This culture also allowed for the representation of a dynamic and culturally differentiated relation between the various ethnic nations internal to the world-historical state. The world-historical state was the unity of individual moral actions. However, these actions were not undertaken solely for the state and by state subjects, because the world-historical state was the concrete, earthly mediation between the individual and *general humanity*, or what the philosopher Tanabe Hajime referred to as *rui*, or "genus."[18]

In these shifting references to culture as the site for the actualization of a proper subject of modernity, it becomes clear that modern anthropological universals cannot remain empty signifiers detached from history, but must be related to actual people through concepts that reference the human being's active and practical construction of the world (concepts like culture). Universal claims about the human being require a concept of general human activity and practice that can mediate between transhistorical anthropological universals and particular historical conjunctures. In the German intellectual tradition, this mediation is the *genus-being (Gattungswesen)*— that formal generality and mode of practice through which the specific characteristics, content, and differences within the genus *homo* might disappear and the human world might become unified. The genus-being is not the existing state of the human being, but its practical mode of actualizing a future in which significant differences will no longer exist within it. In this sense, the genus-being is radically temporal, but only insofar as it is historical; it is a presence that is never entirely present in the present. It is not a quality that defines the essence of the human being taxonomically upon an ahistorical table of representation. It is not human nature. It is rather the generic existence and practice of the human that distinguish it from other animals and govern its development over the long duration of its history.[19]

In the philosophy, literature, and social science of culturalism in early-twentieth-century Japan and Korea, the genus-being of the human is *self-legislated morality*. In Marxism and the proletarian arts, it is *productive labor*. In imperial nationalism, it is *nation-state subjectivity*. These definitions of the genus-being of the human were each in their own way caught up in the language of Japan's imperial project and in colonial Korean intellectuals' fraught efforts to respond to it. With the institution of cultural policy in Korea (1919–31), culturalist concepts of moral personhood transformed the way that both metropolitan and colonial intellectuals discussed the individual, the nation, and the world, making bourgeois cosmopolitanism into a universalist discourse of empire. As Marxism and the proletarian arts critiqued the abstractions and moral didactics of culturalism (1923–35), they defined labor and productive relations as the genus-being of the human, a redefinition that often entangled them in another kind of universalizing imperialist discourse. Finally, with the formulation of ideas of multiethnic empire (1932–45), intellectuals began to articulate the Japanese nation-state as a specific and worldly representative of the human genus, employing narratives of world history to explain how the idea of general humanity now required a concrete nation-state community if it was to be more than an abstract and ahistorical idea of cosmopolitanism. In each of these discourses, the imperial project sought to unmoor existing social relations and reconstruct humanity around and through an idea of genus-being.

Statements about the human genus-being get entangled with imperialism, because governing a multiplicity requires some definition of the generic standards or rules that can unify the one and the many. Imperialism is an ideology of state and capital expansion that must assimilate new subjects while also justifying inequality (or much worse) between nations, classes, genders, races, and ethnicities. It requires knowledge that empties the human being of any particular content, while also regulating and differentiating humanity according to flexible categories and hierarchies. Knowledge centered on a claim about the human's genus-being is particularly adept at performing these dual roles. In positing the essential historical being of the human in order to evacuate humanity of differences, ideas of the genus-being attempt to integrate all of humanity into a single system of knowledge. Ideas of the genus-being also code the internal differences of humanity according to a normative ideal and therefore can be employed for the pragmatic and technological construction of the human being. Formal concepts of the genus-being contribute to the assimilatory function of imperialism because they can empty the human of any other content while at the same time reorganizing any residual differences around an ideal type (the moral subject, the proletariat, the National Subject). Nonetheless, in the use of the concept of general culture for colonial purposes, in the schematic way Marxists conceptualized the national proletariat as an embodiment of productive man, and in the way imperial nationalists thought the Japanese state should represent the generally human, the genus-being is clearly the site of an ongoing political contestation. The notion that the generally human mediates between the universal and the particular is not necessarily imperial, just as the dominant concepts of "culture" cannot remain uncontested. As Marx argued in his critique of the ahistorical aspect of Ludwig Feuerbach's concept of genus-being, this generality is not a figure that will resolve the conflicts and disagreements of history, but rather the site of sensuous activity and the alienation of labor into production, and therefore a site of political contestation.[20] There is nothing inherently imperialist about concepts of the genus-being, but through the contestation over the meaning of the generally human one possibility is the employment of genus-being for the purposes of empire. This was no doubt the case in the Japanese empire.

Admittedly, not all of the texts I will discuss use the philosophical terminology of the genus, but each is concerned with some etymological or conceptual variant on the idea that the human being has a regulative, historical essence that guides the spatiotemporal process of cultural and social development. These variants include the idea of a moral general culture *(ippan bunka)* or world culture *(sekai bunka)* in culturalism and the concept of human productive labor in Marxism and the proletarian arts. Those who translated the philosophical terminology of the genus-being most directly were philosophers such as Tanabe Hajime in Japan and Sŏ In-sik in Korea. They drew from Hegel to argue that the human genus in the abstract could no longer be thought of as a universal immediately unifying individuals, nations, and the world, as culturalism had claimed. Rather, an imperial nation-state, or species *(shu)*, was required in order to mediate "absolutely" between the individual *(ko)* and the genus within world history. This species was not representative of an ethnic nation, but rather a mediator between general humanity and the individual (in other words, nation-state subjectivity was no longer tied to ethnic origin, but rather became a kind of genus-being).[21] Although these precise discussions of the changing status of the concept of the human genus in a time of interimperial warfare did not solidify until the mid-1930s, the problem of genus-being and generality was significant in philosophy, social science, and literature beginning in the late 1910s, coinciding with the acceleration of Japanese imperialism and the political need for universalist anthropocentric epistemologies. Tanabe's and Sŏ's discussions of the genus most clearly show how cosmopolitan ideas about the generally human could be appropriated for an intellectual justification for the imperial state, but the underlying premises that genus-being is the teleological purpose of historical development and that imperialism is a pragmatic means to achieve this purpose were present in important ways in both culturalism and Marxism.

In each case, a concept of the generally human tended to revert to a specific identity. Symptomatic of this tendency for concepts of the genus-being to return to determined anthropological identities, Marx's *Gattungswesen* was mistranslated in English for decades as "species-being." The translation "species-being" coded "genus-being" as a transcendental essence of the human species, something inhering in every human transhistorically and a specific difference between the human and other animals. Peter Osborne and Simon Skempton have argued convincingly that "species-being" is a misleading translation for an understanding of the status of the general in Marx's works.[22] I agree with their readings of Marx, particularly the important distinction between labor as genus-being and production as estranged labor in industrial capitalism. However, in analyzing the historical body of Marxist thought in Japan and Korea, I would rather see the "mistranslation" of *Gattung* as "species" as symptomatic of a tension between the formal concept of a human being with no specific content and the figuration of this possibility of a contentless human in specific historical types like the industrial worker. This is particularly important for understanding the colonial dimension of Marxism and the proletarian arts, particularly at a time when Marxism was taken up not just as an analytic of capitalism, but for modernizing projects in peripheral areas that were concerned with the reformation of consciousness along with economy in ways that conceived of productive labor not primarily as estranged labor, but rather as a necessary step in the process of entering human history.

The ambiguity about whether *Gattung* refers to something specific or to something general comes through in the coexistence in Japanese and Korean of a distinction between anthropology (人類学) and ethnology (人種学)—one of which suggests general humanity and the other specific ethnic communities—and the compound 種類, which combines the specific and the general into a single term approximating "type." The confluence of generality and specificity under concepts of the genus-being is deeply related to typology (類型学), which in Japanese and Korean contains the character for "genus." "Type" can at once refer to a specific group and an abstract ideal such as the moral person, the productive laborer, or the loyal national subject. In the case of Japanese and Korean, we also have to consider the term *ningen* or *in'gan* (人間), which is certainly a generality, but also connotes both a proper human being in the normative sense and a situated, specific, and relational being. Because I am locating and analyzing the historical and political effects of a broad discursive formation of humanism in the Japanese empire, it will not be possible in this book to take account of every nuance of translation involved in the transnational discussion of the human. However, in the background of all of my uses of the term "human," I have in mind a problem that emerged in Japanese philosophical discourse in 1925 with Miki Kiyoshi's Pascalian reading of the human as *ippansha*, or "concrete generality," and continued in 1934 with Watsuji Tetsurō's parsing of *ningen* (human) as ethical relationality—the human is a liminal figure that mediates problematically and politically between the infinite and the finite, the universal and the particular, and the transcendental and the empirical.[23]

Furthermore, because the discourses I analyze sought to reconcile or overcome this liminal status of the human, their concepts of the genus-being often do not remain expressions of a contentless, purely formal generality, but tend to collapse into a species within the genus, a species that is universalizable. Therefore, when Tanabe and Sŏ wrote of the imperial state, that species that represents in concrete world history the abstract principles of humanity in general, they were referring, in particular, to the universality of the Japanese state or the East Asian Community. There will be numerous other examples in this book of this movement of modern thought from genus-being to such a universalization of the particular and particularization of the universal, processes that Naoki Sakai, Etienne Balibar, and Takashi Fujitani have all identified as fundamental to twentieth- and twenty-first-century nationalism and racism.[24]

The translation of *Gattung* as both "species" and "genus" points to the problematic way that concepts of the human genus must at once differentiate humanity from other species of animal while also regulating humanity's internal variations. In the European context, Carl von Linné's eighteenth-century system of binomial taxonomy set the stage for the modern discussions of the genus-being of the human, even though the taxonomy quickly became too rigid and ahistorical for modern anthropocentric knowledge. In Linné's *Systema Naturae,* the human, or *homo,* became a genus unto itself for the first time.[25] Linné introduced a concept of multiple historical species belonging to the genus *human* (*homo sapiens, homo erectus,* and so on). He also made possible various elaborations on sentience (*sapiens*) that later took on a social-scientific connotation in modernity. Beginning in the mid-eighteenth century, binomial terms such as *homo aestheticus* (Goethe), *homo oeconomicus* (Smith and Ricardo), and *homo loquens* (Herder) began to proliferate, each attempting to give *homo* a defining nature. In Linné's system, the specific difference *sapiens* distinguished *homo sapiens* from other animals, but *sapiens* as a specific difference within the human genus also allowed Linné's more historically minded successors, such as Kant, to connect the defining characteristics of the modern human (sentience and morality) to a historical model that placed the white race and Europe at the origin and telos of history and the yellow, black, and reddish-brown races at differing degrees of cultural development in relation to whiteness.[26]

Therefore, by the time of the nineteenth century, the era of universal history, the racial varieties of mankind were not thought to be unified by their shared human nature, but were rather organized hierarchically by their nearness to the genus-being of historical practice and the supposedly empirical category "white." According to Michel Foucault in *The Order of Things,* Linné's continued dependence on the table of representation and an idea of the world as the Great Chain of Being gave way to the modern notion that the human exists in History.[27] In Linné's system *homo sapiens* was still one being on a taxonomic table of beings, not the finite historical being around which the entirety of an *episteme* (the modern) was soon to be organized. Foucault argued convincingly that Linnaean binomial taxonomy belongs to the prehistory of modern thought, and that the eighteenth-century European debates about human nature signal that the human itself had not yet become the historical subject-object of knowledge it would become in modernity.[28] In my argument, with the emergence of modern thought, human nature was rearticulated as genus-being, as a historical essence that would be both general to the species, in the sense that every proper human being must have or seek to have this trait, and specific to the genus, in the sense that this trait differentiates the human species from other animals. The question as to whether genus-being is a purely formal concept of the generally human or a concept that delineates a specific difference is not solely one of accuracy in translation, but is inherent in the way that the generally human tends to fall back upon specific, empirical, and anthropological categories, including racial and national identity.

Because of the prominence of this movement of modern thought from genus-being to particular empirical features of the human, one should take into account, in an analysis of Japanese empire, not only the empirical anthropology that racialized or ethnicized the colonial Other, but also the transcendental claims about the human through which such a racializing and ethnicizing regime could be instituted as a regime of truth, as well as translated into the colony and into colonial modernization projects on the part of the colonized. Culturalism, Marxism, and imperial nationalism were all formulated through an unstable intersection between anthropological universals, formal truth claims about the genus-being, and anthropological identities in the empirical world. Culturalism's metaphysical assertions about the moral genus-being of the human intersected with anthropological theories concerning the cosmopolitan-national individual (the person) and the "natural human." Marxism's genus-being of productive labor intersected with the class identity of the national proletariat, articulated through social science and distinguished abstractly from the subalterns, the peasants, and, often, women. While imperial nationalists discussed the Japanese state as a completely inclusive and universal political body empty of any specific anthropological content, they nonetheless continued to connect it to anthropologically defined national, racial, regional, and continental identities, such as Japan, the yellow race, East Asia, and Asia.

Such an intersection between universality and its ideal type or exemplar in the phenomenal world is a structural feature characteristic of modern thought. In this book I analyze this structural feature through figures and concepts of the generally human, because it is in these figures and concepts where the tensions between universal and particular come to light, especially when anthropological universals are a matter of imperialism, colonization, and responses to them. Concepts of the genus-being and the practice of the genus-being in the Japanese empire are regulative not only because they allow knowledge to imagine a human being empty of any specific content, but also because they organize all the empirical differences around a regulative identity that is phenomenal, experienced, and constructed as a fact in history. In order to construct this identity, modernity has to be presented as a unilinear and sudden passage from another state of being to the genus-being, from nature to culture, from peasant to industrial worker, or from stateless individual to nation-state subjectivity. In each case, anthropological otherness is not something external to the modern subject, like the colonial Other, but is rather accorded differentially, by the relative distance of *someone* from the genus.

FROM CIVILIZATION TO CULTURE IN IMPERIAL RULE, 1895–1919

How can one historicize in a reading of texts of the Japanese empire the emergence of formal concepts of the human genus-being? Through Foucault's convincing archaeology, in the context of nineteenth-century Europe we find a transition from the genus *homo* as it appeared on the table of representation to modern, historical, and anthropocentric thought. However, the dissemination and translation of knowledge are extremely uneven and we should not assume that Foucault's archaeology of the human sciences is either entirely consistent internally within Europe or applicable globally. Nonetheless, something important did happen to knowledge in the late 1910s in modern Korea and Japan. I would hesitate to think of it as a complete "epistemic break" in any way subsumable into Foucault's local archaeology of the human sciences, but the analogies are certainly sufficient to make comparative reference to Foucault's insights into the emergence of the human being as the subject and object of modern thought. Between the Meiji and Taishō periods in Japan (ca. 1912), and between the end of the Korean empire and Japan's institution of cultural policy in Korea (ca. 1905–19), a dramatic shift occurred in knowledge from a model of civilization and enlightenment to a model of culturalism, which corresponded to the emergence of new connections between ideas of the genus-being and the imperial project. These conceptual relations were between the individual, the nation, and the world in the case of the moral genus-being of culturalism, between social class, modernization, and culture in the case of the productive genus-being of Marxism and the proletarian arts, and between the individual, the imperial state, and world history in the theories of nation-state subjectivity in imperial nationalism.

There were differences and continuities between the humanist discourses of the Japanese empire of the 1920s and 1930s and those of previous decades, both in their content and in how they functioned for Japan's imperial project. Previous to the philosophies of culturalism, the March First Movement in Korea (1919), and Japan's institution of cultural policy, the most significant translation of knowledge between Japan and Korea had occurred from the First Sino-Japanese War (1895–96) until Japan made Korea a protectorate in 1905. This period of translation corresponds to the years of the Korean empire, when intellectuals, political leaders, and journalists in Korea took up the early Meiji slogan of "civilization and enlightenment" *(bunmei kaika, munmyŏng kaehwa)* for the purposes of their own nation-building project.[29] The first ten years of Japanese colonial rule (1910–19) were particularly brutal, and the violent effort to nationalize the people of the Korean peninsula created enough popular animosity that upward of two million people participated in the anticolonial rebellion of 1919. By the time widespread Korean-language publication emerged again with the institution of cultural policy in 1919, the intellectual and political landscape had changed considerably in the Japanese empire and globally.

The most obvious difference between the two periods was that Korea was no longer a politically independent empire in respect to international recognition, which greatly transformed the way that intellectuals approached the nation-building project. As the historian Andre Schmid has shown, the proponents of civilization and enlightenment in the Korean empire, while increasingly wary of Japan's rising power in continental Asia and in many ways subordinate to its interests, were able to appropriate many of the themes of Meiji thought and use them to think through the Korean situation.[30] These themes included the concept of civilization, which organized the nations and societies of the world temporally according to their level of material and spiritual progress. In this regard, the writers of *Independent News* and *Capital News* often emphasized the need to become independent from China and to catch up with the West and Japan technologically and culturally. At the same time, some intellectuals, particularly at *Capital News*, delinked the concept of civilization from the geographic West and argued for the civilizational possibilities of Pan-Asia, Pan–East Asia, or the yellow race, a prospect that was increasingly troubled by Japan's imperial hegemony in the region. Social Darwinism (the account of history as the gradual weeding out of weaker nations and peoples) greatly affected the views of civilization and enlightenment that appeared in these newspapers.

What was translated between Meiji Japan and the intellectuals of the Korean empire, then, was a particular model of nation-building in which a peripheral country, racialized and marginalized at the global level, attempted to rise to the level of civilizational progress of the West by invigorating and modernizing existing institutions. The teleology of this development, the moment of convergence between Korea, the West, and Japan, would be an imperial state, a shared national language, and a civilized population of citizens governed by benevolent elites. This nation-building project, like that of the Meiji state, integrated the modernization of government institutions, sovereignty centered on an imperial figurehead, and nationalization of the citizens and their language. The universalism of this model lay in the unilinear view of the progress of civilizations and a Social Darwinist perspective that warned of the potential to lose out in the competition between empires, national economies, and state formations.

Some have argued that the institution of cultural policy in 1919 marked a return to the ideas of civilization and enlightenment in the mediation of Japan-Korea relations, but this book argues that it was not so simple.[31] Those Korean intellectuals and writers who studied abroad in Japan in the late Meiji and Taishō periods confronted a very different political situation, in which Korea had lost the possibility to establish national sovereignty due to Japan's colonization and the Japanese empire's agreements with other empires (for example, the Taft-Kastura agreement of 1905).[32] Furthermore, academic discourse in Japan was no longer dominated by civilization and enlightenment, but rather by epistemologies that emphasized the cultural unity of humankind and later, with the influx of Marxism, the unity of humanity through the stages of economic development. In Kuwaki's distinction between "progress" and "development," he marked civilization's difference from culture, stating that history should be imagined not as a straight line to a defined end point, but as a perpetual process of human cultivation and development guided by moral universality and the idea of world culture. This development required a "purpose" *(mokuteki)*, but the precise material and technological content of this purpose could not be defined entirely beforehand by a fixed image of civilization.[33] In this distinction between progress and development, the turn to culture as the totality of expressions of human will came to the fore and transformed the idea of empire from one of imperial sovereignty and unilinear progress to one of the perpetual cultivation of the generally human. Therefore, in 1925, the governor-general of Korea, Saitō Makoto, used a metaphor of personal cultural development when he called for the "cultivation of state power" as a means of contributing to world culture.[34]

The distance from Meiji and the reality of Japan's aggressive imperialist expansion transformed perspectives on both culture and history. Yoshino Sakuzō and others would not formally establish the Research Group on Meiji Culture until 1924.[35] However, when Yi Kwang-su was a student at Waseda University in the late 1910s, Yoshino had published his *mimponshugi* theory for Taishō democracy and was criticizing the militarism of Japan's imperial project, which was obvious in the aftermath of the Sino-Japanese and Russo-Japanese wars. Yoshino's response to Japan's military mode of imperialism was to highlight the cultural achievements of the Meiji period, especially the cultural contributions of great individuals, while critiquing militarist slogans like "rich country, strong military" *(fukoku kyōhei)*.[36] He extended this criticism of Meiji imperialism to Japan's colonial rule in Korea, and after visiting Korea he wrote positively about the March First Movement.[37] At the same time, his political philosophy and his Christian cosmopolitanism provided a humanist political discourse to Korean intellectuals such as Yi Kwang-su, a discourse that facilitated their turn away from anticolonial revolution toward a gradualist cultural nationalism.

In his political theory, Yoshino parsed the cultural aspects of imperialism from its military aspects. His reading of this division and his later attempts to recuperate Meiji culture from the excesses of Meiji imperialism reflect a different concept of sovereignty and national subjectivity than Meiji civilizational rhetoric. As is well known in Japanese intellectual history, Yoshino differentiated between *minshushugi*, a notion of democracy that asserted the direct sovereignty of the people, and *mimponshugi*, which asserted that sovereignty remains with the emperor, but that the emperor and his representatives in the Diet and the bureaucracy were morally obligated to govern in the interests of the mass of people, who were at the foundation of society. In Yoshino's theory we find an attempt to reconcile imperial sovereignty with popular sovereignty through a moral philosophy based on the capacity for great individuals, or persons *(jinkaku)*, to act for the greater good of Japan's imperial subjects and humanity at large. The sign of modern subjectivity and enlightenment is in the capacity of the self to legislate moral universals, which requires the cultural and spiritual cultivation of the self into a cosmopolitan-national individual. The gradual turn away from the rhetoric of civilization to the rhetoric of culture reflected this shift from the idea of the globe as organized according to levels of technological, educational, and nation-state development to a more explicitly humanist model that Sōda Kiichirō, for example, articulated as the individual human's development from natural, physiological being, to the psychological ego, to "transindividual general consciousness."[38] The model of the progress of civilizations and empires in competition with one another was displaced by a model based on the internal spiritual development of the human individual toward general consciousness and general culture.

In culturalism, nations are not neatly bordered civilizations in military, technological, and spiritual competition with other civilizations, but rather anthropological, cultural, and moral entities with their own life, language, and internally constituted organic form. In "On the Reconstruction of the Nation" (1922), Yi Kwang-su took up both Yoshino and Kuwaki, completely deemphasizing the issue of sovereignty—which for him resided in human reason alone—and reinterpreting the Wilson Doctrine not as a call for self-determination in the sense of popular sovereignty, but rather as a call for Koreans and other stateless people to seek a more fundamental transformation of their individual and national characters and their everyday lives, a transformation that would transcend the mundane, natural changes of technological and civilizational progress.[39] In this way, the genus-being of self-legislated morality, and its linking up with cultural anthropology, became essential to the working of empire under cultural policy, because it conveyed that in modernity there was another, entirely secular and human realm in which the sovereignty of emperors and the international recognition of nation-states were relatively minor affairs compared to the cultural and moral improvement of the individual, the biopolitical reformation of life, and the formation of a national community.

With the new authority accorded to neo-Kantian cultural science and the philosophy of culturalism, the idea of culture came to mediate between freedom and determination, the universal and the particular, the transcendental and the empirical, change and identity. As Terry Eagleton points out, the idea of culture includes such seemingly contradictory meanings.[40] This mediatory function of culture is connected in my reading to the logic of genus-being. In its colonial usage, culture promises to liberate the colonized from previous social formations and reform them according to a process that is general to humanity, but at the same time culture can determine specific spheres of ethnic and racial difference that continue to racialize the colonized. This distinction is reflected in the difference in early-twentieth-century anthropology between culture and Culture, a difference that was not fixed in the malleable and myriad ways that the terms *munhwa* and *bunka* were used in modern Korea and Japan. In the interstice between particular culture and general culture, the human becomes the object of its own self-consciousness and self-cultivation. For the modern idea of culture, nature is the raw material, or the seed to be cultivated, but without the improvements of culture, the natural element remains inorganic, mechanistic, and ultimately inconsequential to universal history. Therefore, the divide between nature and culture functions to distinguish the purely human realm of will and freedom from the mechanism of nature, but this does not mean that culture is then transformed into something purely subjective. In the pragmatic application of the idea of culture, the human becomes an object of empirical anthropological knowledge. As the idea of cosmopolitan culture became integral to the Korean nation-building project under Japanese colonial rule, it became a cultural and anthropological project rather than one of gaining popular national sovereignty. Through this project, the idea of culture was also employed to ethnicize the population of the Korean peninsula into a single, anthropologically defined nation *(minjok)*, to which a number of empirical characteristics could be attached, not as stagnant essences, but as historically mutable traits.

The discourses of culturalism, Marxism, and imperial nationalism were more complexly political than the earlier rhetoric of civilization and enlightenment in Meiji Japan and fin de siècle Korea. The notion of the world in culturalism was a hypothetical spiritual unity of humanity to be attained at some point in the future, one that was dependent neither upon the official establishment of national sovereignty nor upon a particular degree of technological, civilizational progress. Despite the colonial dimension of culturalism, which is blatant in the statements of Japanese colonial officials in the 1920s, many Korean intellectuals were seduced by culturalism precisely because it provided a new discourse of civilization in which internal matters of subjectivity and life practices—moral values, spiritual cultivation, the cultural refinement of the senses—were more significant for politics and history than the mundane concerns of technological advancement, sovereignty, natural rights, or equality in the distribution of material goods. By discussing the genus-being of the human in moral and spiritual terms, both colonial administrators and Korean nationalists found a way to circumvent, or actually to rearticulate, the political and economic problem of imperialism.

PRACTICE, PRAGMATICS, AND NORMING SPACE

Perhaps to confront the autonomy of practice in modernity, a whole network of discussions concerning practice developed in the Japanese empire of the 1920s. Concepts of the genus-being—of morality, productive labor, and nation-state subjectivity—are essentially concepts of practice belonging to ideologies of practice. However, they are also pragmatic concepts applied to the practices of the human as the *object* of knowledge and technology, which is an aspect, at least, of what Foucault meant by "governmentality."[41] In order to analyze how, at the level of practice, cosmopolitanism became exclusionary, Marxism became schematically organized around the national proletariat, and a supposedly "deethnicized" imperial state continued to rely on regulative anthropological categories, it is necessary to locate in these discourses the formal genus-being around which they are organized. Furthermore, it is necessary to understand how these formal concepts of genus-being boomerang back to the empirical to regulate and norm practice, as well as the space and time of practice. The genus-being as a concept of practice should be read in relation to the fundamental problem in modern anthropocentric thought: in modernity, the human being becomes the legislator of knowledge and history and at the same time an enigma at the center of the world in constant need of decoding through empirical observation. This was Foucault's watershed insight into the place of the human in modern thought: "Man, in the analytic of finitude, is a strange empirico-transcendental doublet, since he is a being such that knowledge will be attained in him of what renders all knowledge possible."[42] It is this rendering of knowledge that became the focus of concepts of the genus-being in the Japanese empire, because in the anthropological observation of practices it was supposed to be detectable which actors were proper subjects of this rendering, capable of applying the transcendental pragmatically to their empirical conditions. Insofar as the philosophy of culturalism and cultural policy in Korea were founded on the anthropological principle of the subject as citizen of the world, this figure of the human as self-legislating but also empirically observable became directly related to colonial governmentality.

In the preface to *Anthropology from a Pragmatic Point of View*, Kant set the stage for the structure of the empirico-transcendental doublet.[43] He also suggested the way that anthropology would become enmeshed in practices of governmentality that seek the pragmatic formation of the human, particularly in culturalist discourses of empire such as Japan's cultural policy in Korea or postwar US modernization theory and cultural anthropology. Kant states that the move from theoretical knowledge to pragmatic knowledge is a matter of applying knowledge to the human, who is the centerpiece and the only proper object for knowledge about the world. This is the conflation of knowledge of man *(Menschkenntnis)* with knowledge of the world *(Weltkenntnis)*, the anthropocentric view of world history from which Foucault began his archaeology of the human sciences.[44] Kant writes in the preface:

> All cultural progress, by means of which the human being advances his education, has the goal of applying this acquired knowledge and skill for the world's use. But the most important object in the world to which he can apply them is the human being: because the human being is his own final end.—Therefore, to know the human being according to his species as an earthly being endowed with reason especially deserves to be called *knowledge of the world*, even though he constitutes only one part of the creatures on earth.[45]

In the Kantian epistemology, the human is free; it conceptualizes the laws of nature, but it also distinguishes itself from nature as the legislator of the laws of freedom, as a being with the capacity for morality.[46] In this passage, the human is the only animal capable of recognizing others as ends rather than means, in other words, the only animal capable of morality. When Kant turns to the pragmatic application of theoretical knowledge through anthropology, he states that science should take the free-acting, willful human being as the only object of knowledge through which the totality of the world should be understood. In his dissertation on Kant's *Anthropology*, Foucault discusses how this pragmatic view of anthropology differs from the physiological anthropology from which Kant also drew, because it is "not a description of what man is but what he can make of himself" in the process of his education or *formation (Bildung)*.[47] The human being becomes the object of pragmatic anthropology precisely because it is a free being defined by its moral practice, a being capable of making something of itself. Kant creates a confluence between practice in the universal sense and the pragmatic transformation of cultural practices through the generality of the human being and the anthropology he developed to study it.

Kant's privileging of the human as the sole object of pragmatic knowledge had to be given time and space if it were to have actual historical effects. Giving time and space to this metaphysical and largely transhistorical concept of the human became normative and racialized. Modern thought has often negotiated the relation between the inside and outside of humanity, and therefore the inside and outside of the world, through ideas of cultural and moral practice. Charles Mills, having traced the tradition of spatializing and racializing ethics in European social contract theories, states that white supremacist discourse, including Kant's own moral philosophy, "norms space" through ideas of cultural and moral practice.[48] By linking the capacity or incapacity for self-legislated morality to anthropologically defined spaces, modern moral philosophy polices the borders between the human, the subhuman, and the nonhuman, including and excluding according to the norms of the metaphysics of morals and a racialized spatiality. This turn from the transcendental and regulatory claims of practical reason, or the "interiority" of the proper human subject, to the empirical register of anthropocentric thought, including races and nations, is expressed in the title of part 2 of Kant's *Anthropology*: "Anthropological Characteristic: On the Way of Cognizing the Interior of the Human Being from the Exterior."[49] The first half of the *Anthropology* is concerned primarily with inner sense, moods, affects, and practical reason, but in the second part these concerns give way to a cognizing of such interior states through the observation of the exterior. Ideas about the proper unity to give to the human's interior life are connected to external, empirical traits like race, national character, and geographic origin. Therefore, Kant connected his conception of the human genus quite directly to race, in many ways inaugurating the problems of nation, race, and universalism that would develop in the late nineteenth and early twentieth centuries. This problem of the empirico-transcendental doublet of the human was explicitly centered on the genus-being of the human and whether or not it has an identifiable origin. He argued in "On the Different Races of Man" that the white, brunette race, which historically inhabited the Old World between the thirty-first and fifty-second parallels, was an ancient "stem-genus" *(Stammgattung)* from which all other racial variations of the human genus derived (*Stamm* meaning "stem" or "trunk," but also "tribe").⁵⁰ His project of European cosmopolitanism was as much a project of reconstituting this stem-genus as it was a theory of the cultural and moral progress of humanity as a whole. Although clearly a historical fallacy and a construct of both the nascent human sciences and eighteenth-century race theory, the mythical stem-genus of Europe was a hypothetical figure that served as an image for the shared origins of the cosmopolitan, secular human.

Kant's conception of the human in the *Anthropology* was very influential in the philosophical discourse of the Japanese empire, from the neo-Kantian philosophy of culturalism in the 1920s to Kyoto School texts by Watsuji Tetsurō, Tanabe Hajime, and others. In *Ethics as the Study of the Human* (1934), Watsuji Tetsurō writes, "Kant's moral philosophy—in other words, his philosophy of practice—is the most originary anthropology; it is the 'study of the total determination of the human.'"⁵¹ As Watsuji discusses in his reading of Kant's *Anthropology*, his own "study of the human" *(ningen no gaku)* is not physiological, but rather pragmatic.⁵² It has little to do with the natural historical, empirical, or structuralist study of "primitive" or "exotic" social formations—it is rather concerned with what the human being can make of itself through its practical reason. Kant's critique of practical reason is the foundation for a more originary anthropology because it grounds itself in the metaphysics of morals. When Watsuji defined the object of his study, he sought its universality in ethics and its generality in culture. This moral philosophy allowed Watsuji to map the world not simply according to culturally and geographically determined customs, the object of his *Climate and Culture,* but also according to a normative ethical universality that he associated anthropologically with Japan proper.⁵³ In interpreting Kant, Watsuji shifted the precise location of the ground for "originary anthropology" from Europe to Japan, but maintained the basic logical structure of Kant's intersection of moral universality and the stem-genus.

Watsuji's trajectory suggests the kinds of connections between moral philosophy, anthropology, and the norming of space that Charles Mills analyzes in his reading of the racial contract. Because such humanism begins with a generic definition—self-legislated morality—intellectuals in Japan could appropriate Kant while ignoring or reworking his claims to white racial superiority and their connections to his Eurocentric view of geography and history. Likewise, colonial intellectuals in Korea could appropriate "originary anthropology" and its practice of norming space for their own nationalization project, even though humanist philosophers like Watsuji often made overt claims to ethnic superiority when they wrote about Japan's colonies.⁵⁴ Again, the primary question of this book: how can the universalism and transcendentality of anthropocentric knowledge continually be translated and particularized, despite the acts of norming and exclusion that it also enables?

I return to Foucault's early work on cultural-historical thinking in his dissertation on Kant and in *The Order of Things* because I see it as an important aspect of his understanding of governmentality, and one that we might hesitate to apply to intellectual discourse if we imagine that governmentality is solely a matter of welfare institutions, prisons, colonial policy, and technology. By linking Foucault's later themes of biopolitics and governmentality to his archaeology of the human sciences, it becomes possible to read philosophy, literature, and social science as embedded in a network of political relations mediated by normative understandings of the human and human practice. In some respects, this urge to connect governmentality to Foucault's analysis of culture in *The Order of Things* is an effect of the historical instance of Japan's "cultural policy," which demands an investigation into the ways philosophers and writers have theorized the citizen of the world and how this cosmopolitanism can become a technology of colonial rule. Or less ambitiously, at least this connection helps to explain how and why Yi Kwang-su's controversial essay from 1922 on the anthropological "reconstruction" of Korean national character begins with a reference not to the loss of national sovereignty, but rather to the need for a more fundamental reconstruction of the human, thought and felt by all citizens of the world *(segyein)*.[55]

THE LIMITS OF THE HUMAN

Although a good deal of this book is concerned with tracing different iterations of the problem of the human in imperial discourse, I am also concerned with tracing the limits of the structure of the empirico-transcendental doublet, or the modern confluence of genus-being and particular identities, facts, or subjectivities. Specifically, I look for the places in texts and historical situations where philosophy, in becoming spatiotemporal, gives way to the nonidentity of the subject to itself, where, in literature, writing practices push language toward the nonrepresentable, or where the ethico-political construction of a human community fails to come to completion. In locating the limits of modern anthropocentric thought, I have tried to move between (rather than within) the areas of Korea, Japan, Europe, and the North American academy, with the hope of disrupting the repetition of the structure of the empirico-transcendental doublet and the patterns of knowledge it has produced. Rather than discussing the dynamics of self and other in colonial discourse as dynamics between two established and assumable identities, I focus instead on three limits to the formation of the human, limits that modern thought constantly confronts and attempts to resolve: a *semiotic* limit, a *spatiotemporal* limit, and an *existential* limit.

The semiotic limit to humanism is related to the metaphysics of national language, because it emerges out of the way that philosophers and writers discussed national language not only in empirical anthropological terms, but also as the means of grounding the transcendental subject of modernity within a local territory. In chapters 1 and 2, I show how culturalist thinkers such as Sōda Kiichirō, Kuwaki Gen'yoku, and Yi Kwang-su turned to the idea of national language at various points in order to ground the transcendental subject and its self-legislated morality in a local anthropological identity. Sōda, for example, argued (in German, paradoxically) that Japanese had to become a "generally understood world language of science" for Japanese and Asian cultural scientists to properly study their own past.[56] He also argued that the limits of what the philosophy of culturalism could know were not real limits to the capacity of the human sciences to represent the totality of human life (or the world). The existence of limits to anthropocentric knowledge rather required the positing of general cultural values as transcendental limit concepts that governed morally and teleologically the development of anthropocentric knowledge and the cosmopolitan human. The formation of the national language allowed for both the recognition of the limits of knowledge and the internalization of that difference within the cosmopolitan-national subject. National language provided a ground for the national subject within a bordered cultural area, but it was also the mediation that allowed one to translate communicatively between the concepts of the generally human and new, as-yet unincorporated territories. Likewise, in Korea Yi Kwang-su and Ch'oe Nam-sŏn wrote, respectively, of the future and prehistoric unity of the modern Korean language, not solely out of nationalism, but in order to make the case that a moral and cultural cosmopolitanism could find its local grounding in Korean national self-consciousness.[57] Bilingual writers such as Arai Tetsu (Uchino Kenji), a migrant from Japan proper to Korea, and Kim Sa-ryang, an ethnically Korean Japanophone writer, were both very immersed in culturalism, but they also formulated different interfaces between languages that disrupted the idea of a cosmopolitan totality created through the communicative function of national languages.

The spatiotemporal limit of humanism emerges out of the way that historical models of world history tend to homogenize the differences between and within spatial locales in order to make them subject to the historical model. At the spatiotemporal limit of humanism, the chronotopes of representation break with the logics and narratives of the genus-being. In chapter 3, I examine the stage theory of history in both economics and cultural theory, a theory founded in a concept of the genus-being as productive labor. In stage theory, a form of labor and division of labor determines the stage—tribal, slave, feudal, capitalist, socialist, and communist. In the debates on Japanese capitalism, as well as in the stagist histories of Korea developed by Paek Nam-un, space and time are reduced to the nation form and the historical stages of its developing economy. Likewise, the chronotope of the nation form, as it appeared, for example, in Nakano Shigeharu's essays on the proletarian arts and Im Hwa's dialectical and Hegelian reading of the development of modern Korean literature, greatly affected how fiction, poems, and literary criticism represented the spatiotemporal divides between metropole and colony, and between the city and the countryside. It also came to require a theory of cultural modernization, or what I call proletarian *Bildung*, through which the peripheries of the exploited groups of humanity could be formed into a universal class subject, the national proletariat. However, as I show in chapter 4, through chronotopes that broke with historical modeling, realist literature and anthropological texts were able to critique the notion that art should be an allegory of the historical process of universal history as defined by the dominant Marxist social science. The result was more complex chronotopes that were more revealing of the content of social relations, because they did not adhere to the formalistic intersection between universal history and national history. In the anthropology and fiction of Nakanishi Inosuke and Kobayashi Takiji in Japan and Ch'oe Sŏ-hae, Kang Kyŏng-ae, and Yi Ki-yŏng in Korea, we find examples of different chronotopic imaginaries that are equally critical of imperialism and capitalism, but do not attempt to regulate the limits of the formation of the human by reducing spatial and temporal differences to differences within a nation's diachronic-synchronic history.

The existential limit concerns how the ontology of the living human always exceeds the pragmatism of anthropological discourse and the technologies of humanist imperial rule. Leo Ching writes about the period of imperial subjectification (1939–45), "Cultural representations under *kōminka* [imperial subjectification] displaced the concrete problematic of the social and replaced it with the ontology of the personal."[58] As I discuss in chapter 5, Ch'oe Chae-sŏ and other colonial Korean advocates of a multiethnic Japanese national literature welcomed this displacement of the social into an ontology of the personal, because it promised to create a new subject position out of which the contradictions of colonial modernity might be overcome. By writing from the people's standpoint and in the Japanese national language, Korean writers could reunite the level of consciousness with the level of existence, which had, Ch'oe assumed, been separated through the abstract cosmopolitanism of culturalism and the trivial mass culture of the proletarian arts. Other Korean writers, such as Kim Sa-ryang and Kim Nam-ch'ŏn, explored the existential limits to the project of Japanese national literature. By showing that the ontology of the personal demanded by imperial nationalist discourse remained a highly precarious venture in the interiority of the colonial subject, they exposed an existential limit to the demand that the colonials transform themselves into subjects of the Japanese state. In other words, they refused or complicated the function that imperialist thinkers had assigned to national culture—the mediator between ethnic difference and the subjectivity of the world-historical state.

Although the semiotic, spatiotemporal, and existential limits of the human appear through all of the counterdiscursive strategies that I examine, chapter 6 touches explicitly on each. This chapter is concerned with how aesthetic modernism relates to the imperial project, both through its valid critiques of anthropological notions of the generally human and in the ways that this critique can easily revert back, through conservative ideas about social space, to notions of culture and subjectivity that are in concert with fascist politics and the imperial state. I am particularly interested in the status of "ecstatic temporality" in modernist writings, and the way that time as the constant projection of the human being outside of itself, and therefore as the condition for the human's self-alienation, was related in the early twentieth century to the advent of cinema and cinematic space-time. I approach ecstatic temporality through a reading Ch'oe Chae-sŏ's earlier work and also the works of the New Sensationist Yokomitsu Riichi. I show how and why in each case the ecstasis of the modernist view of the human being enabled a particular kind of turn to a fascist political perspective. I then move on to the poetry and fiction of Yi Sang, who also used cinematic poetic images to figure the human being as an ecstatic subject constantly projected outside of itself, but perhaps offering another possibility to at once undo the anthropological epistemology of culturalism, while also keeping in motion a cinepoetic subject that never becomes identical to itself again by returning to a spatial origin. In my reading of Yi Sang, I first analyze the culturalist spatial imaginary present in the colonial architecture journal *Korea and Architecture* and then show how Yi's poetry in that journal drew from the theory of relativity and cinematic space to critique the journal's culturalist understanding of space and time. It also shows how this subversion of culturalism differs from the Hegelian dialectic of Tanabe Hajime, which was based on an osmotic rather than intensive mode of expression. The chapter ends by asking whether or not Yi Sang's cinematic notion of "vision," not as a total perspective, but rather as a network of singular, temporal points around which space curves, might offer another possibility for a genus-being without subject, objects, or individuals.

1

Culturalism and the Human

He who is not oriented toward cultural value is only a natural human; personhood can only exist in a cultural human.
—SŌDA KIICHIRŌ

CULTURALISM AND CULTURAL POLICY

In March 1919, there were nationwide protests in colonial Korea against Japanese imperialism, leading up to the proclamation of a declaration of independence by leading intellectuals. Following the March First Movement, the governor-general of Korea shifted its policy from military policy to cultural policy. Cultural policy was not simply a euphemism for colonial exploitation, but a set of policies and discourses based on particular ideas of culture. At the same time as cultural policy was instituted in Korea, culturalism became a dominant intellectual orientation in Japan proper and in the colonies. As culturalism became the dominant intellectual orientation and cultural policy the mode of government in the colonies, ideas of culture were gradually linked to political domination. The rational organization of education, populations, aesthetic practices, and social space became connected in various manners to ideas of culture.

Cosmopolitanism and the cultural unity of humanity were central themes in statements by liberal Japanese reformers and governors in colonial Korea in the aftermath of the March First Movement. These reformers' appropriation of metropolitan cosmopolitan ideas and their translation of them into the colonial context had profound effects on governing practices and colonial politics, as well as intellectual discourse in Korea. In 1925, six years into cultural policy, the governor-general of Korea, Saitō Makoto, wrote the following sentimental statement about the prospects for the development of world culture, coprosperity between the imperial countries, and a mutual love shared by humanity:

International relations between each nation in the alliance have become more and more congenial; each is employing its power for the development of world culture; the spirit of coexistence and coprosperity is spreading; we can see a trend toward actualizing the ideal of a mutual love shared by all of humanity; in order to achieve this, the greatest purpose of our times, we take the cultivation of state power, in both name and fact, to be the primary principle.[1]

Considering the imperialist expansion of Japanese capital, the policing of politics, and the cultural erasure that was ongoing in colonial Korea, such statements seem blind to colonial violence, or even constructed cynically to shroud the realities of colonialism in a veil of triumphal, idealist History. In its banal humanism, it moves vaguely but assertively from the idea of world culture, to humanity's shared sentiment of mutual love, to the power of the state, giving it the equivocation typical of colonial proclamations. Despite its blatant obfuscations of the violence of colonialism, the statement is nonetheless revealing if we consider it as part of a broader discursive formation in its intertextuality. It contains, in condensed form, many of the questions and solutions that arose as universalist claims about humanity became integral to both culturalist thinking and Japan's colonial project.

Saitō was concerned with how to imagine and to manage a multiethnic and assimilatory state, while still maintaining social hierarchies between colonizer and colonized. In order to resolve the tension between the universality and inclusiveness of the state and its regulation and subjugation of Korean colonial subjects, Saitō turns to the idea of development, presented within a cultural-historical framework, asserting the formation of a world culture and a universal sentiment of love shared by humanity as the greatest purpose of history. For the Japanese empire to contribute to this project of cosmopolitanism—understood as the unification of humanity through cultural-historical development—the power of the colonial state in Korea must be "cultivated" *(kanyō suru)*, in an anthropomorphizing turn of phrase. The governor-general's frequent demand that Korea contribute to this cosmopolitan project offered Koreans a means to enter the development of universal history by assimilating to its local representative, Japan, but it also differentiated Koreans ethnically and politically by figuring them as a people internal to the nation who were not yet national and not yet cosmopolitan.

Saitō's statement echoes the more serious philosophical concerns of prominent culturalists and cultural scientists in Germany, Japan, and colonial Korea. In the aftermath of World War I, neo-Kantian philosophers, who had constituted one dominant strain of academic philosophy in Germany since the 1880s, became more directly concerned with the political ramifications of the ethnic nationalist response to modernity that had led to the war and began to think about the philosophical system of the cultural sciences as the potential departing point for a cosmopolitan-national community with a transcendental and universal, rather than particularistic, foundation. Many liberals in Germany, particularly the neo-Kantians who focused on the cultural and human sciences, were asking how an individual, postimperial nation-state could take on a cosmopolitan purpose and how through this nation-state national subjects could overcome their ethnic chauvinism. Japanese philosophers and social scientists such as Kuwaki Gen'yoku and Sōda Kiichirō, both of whom studied in Germany for long periods, engaged with the German philosophical discourse of the time and also created their own epistemologies for the study of culture. In developing Kantian and neo-Kantian thought into a culturalist program for the reformation of society, or what they called "the philosophy of culturalism," they shared with the German neo-Kantians a critique of ethnic nationalism, a concern with finding a transcendental and universal foundation for the nation-state, and a belief in the formation of a united world and world culture as the ultimate historical purpose of humanity. The significant difference between the philosophy of culturalism and the German context, however, was that Japan had neither participated extensively nor suffered defeat in World War I. It remained an imperial power with growing colonial holdings. Under these conditions, what was imagined as a cultural mode of reconstructing the German nation-state along cosmopolitan lines was able to transform into a colonial discourse that demanded that Korean colonial subjects overcome their ethnocentrism and enter universal history and world culture through the mediation of the Japanese colonial state.

In the philosophy of culturalism, the formal essence of the human (or its genus-being) is self-legislated morality, the capacity of the cosmopolitan-national individual to autonomously and freely determine how to act in the interest of the public good. Kantian liberals of the 1920s understood the moral universality of Kant's categorical imperative in historical terms—seeds of goodness exist in all humans, but these seeds have to be cultivated over time through education and culture. Compared to civilizational claims and claims about human nature, such a historical and cultural claim to humanity was more easily tailored to the flexible and differential mode of colonial rule developed through cultural policy, because individuals and groups could be categorized according to their relative distance from the regulative, historical, and general idea of the perfected moral person. When Saitō wrote of "mutual love" between the more developed states, he did not assume that every human felt this love due to his or her nature, but rather considered this sentiment to be something developing historically, through individual and collective cultivation. Therefore, he repeatedly demanded that Koreans contribute to world culture by cultivating their inner sense of correct action and their dedication to both the empire and its world-historical mission. In combining the rhetoric of cultural cosmopolitanism with a moral justification for colonial rule, colonial officials and the intellectuals who informed their discourse articulated a national economy and a colonial-imperial state formed through normative practices of inclusion and exclusion, through that combination of universalist humanism and ethnic discrimination that characterized assimilation.

The moral concept of general humanity was in part a critical response to the unbridled individualism associated with economic liberalism. The relation between economic self-interest and universal moral sentiment remained problematic in the expanding Japanese empire. In the statement "The Primary Mission of the Nation" (1924), Japan's Inspector General of Political Affairs in Korea, Ariyoshi Chūichi, makes more explicit the two tendencies in thought with which cultural policy's idea of the moral human is meant to compete. Referring to World War I, Ariyoshi discusses forging a new, more sustainable relation between the individual and the human collectivity, one that improves upon both individualism and collectivism:

> The majority of world humanity, having suffered the wounds of the Great War, and having experienced much anguish in thought, economics, and politics, wonders whether the calamity of war will end with this period or will continue onward indefinitely; we could say that God has given humanity a great test. The majority of the world senses the huge significance of this test, supports the ideas of justice and charity, is endeavoring to advance the welfare of the human community, and believes that the current mission to which humanity should devote itself is to escape from the anguish of the present and accept a world of peace and happiness. However, with the aim of actualizing such a world, each person makes himself the standard, swaggering about and displaying an extreme individualism; in order to create a new, noble period of humanity, this is certainly not the path to be taken.
>
> It seems that an extreme collectivism is called for, but the situation in Russia shows clearly that in the present state of humanity such collectivism does not offer happiness, but rather terrible suffering. Among those who have returned from a tour of Euro-America, there are some who have the impression that individualism is accepted there, but the majority of conscientious observers agree with the perspective that Euro-America, while wary of today's extreme individualism, sees in the Russian situation the harm of extreme collectivism, and feels acutely the need to reinvigorate the state. From this example, it can be hypothesized that no great development can be accomplished by acting as though the self is the only standard or by being partial to extreme collectivism.[2]

Ariyoshi states that humanity has a shared sense of mission that defines its history, particularly in the aftermath of the ethnic national conflicts of World War I. In articulating cultural cosmopolitanism for the colony, he emphasizes that an overly individualistic liberalism does not recognize the need for society and social conscience, whereas the extreme collectivism of the Soviet Union threatens the bourgeois state and the individuality that it grants to its subjects. He goes on to discuss the primary mission of cultural policy as the creation of a new moral connection and sense of mission shared by the individual, the nation, and the world. He appropriated the neo-Kantian idea of culture, with its tones of civility and moral cultivation, to articulate a new relation between the individual and the totality, a new kind of liberalism that would be a third way between the asocial individualism of unrestrained capitalism and the destruction of the bourgeois state in revolutionary Russia.

In speaking of the cultivation of the state and the contribution of the state and its colonial subjects to world culture, Saitō and Ariyoshi were borrowing from a prominent intellectual and public discourse, culturalism, and putting it to use for colonial rule. This chapter discusses how in culturalist thinking, ideas of moral universality and personhood became connected to empirical anthropological claims about national character, origins, behaviors, and ethnic worldviews. The developmental understanding of cultural phenomena, derived from the neo-Kantian interpretation of Kant, involved Kuwaki and Sōda in the conceptual problem of the limit and the limit concept. In casting Japan, its culture, and its national economy as a priori ideas rather than empirical entities, they were forced to ask how this transcendental Japan could be translated into a territory governed by the Japanese state but marked as anthropologically different (Korea). This is where the *supplementarity* of the binary signs of the cultural human (the person) and the natural human came into play for the human scientific system to be presented as a total system determinant of both the world and the nations making up the world. In arguing that general cultural values served as the regulative principles for cultural historical development, and that the capacity to attain these values distinguished the cultural human from the natural human, Kuwaki and Sōda transformed the limits of knowledge about the human into the very guiding principles for this knowledge. In order to try to overcome the question of the limits of the transcendental knowledge of the human in the actual historical existence of humanity, they used the concept of the world to refer to both the totality of humanity and the nations belonging to this totality. The relationship between the totality of the world and its nations became biopolitical, because transforming the nation to suit the cosmopolitan order required bringing life under the rule of the categorical imperative through the human's attainment of its genus-being, self-legislated morality.

In this turn to a cosmopolitan-national framework for humanist knowledge, culturalist thinkers in Japan proper and Korea confronted a semiotic limit to the attempt to guide knowledge of the human by the limit concept of general values and by the binary of cultural humans and natural humans. At marginal moments of epistemological crisis—when culture and nature, freedom and necessity, and transcendental and empirical threatened to blur into one another unsystematically—culturalists turned to the idea of a communicative and spiritual national language as the ground for the transcendental subject within local spheres of difference. In the final part, I show how area studies knowledge about Korea, produced and compiled largely by Japanese migrants to the colony, reiterated in popular form many of the precepts of the philosophy of culturalism. I also discuss how some texts, such as the poetry of Arai Tetsu, both participated in culturalist discourse and articulated differently the semiotic limit to the culturalist idea of the human.

MORALITY, LIFE, AND THE PERSON: KUWAKI GEN'YOKU

Kuwaki Gen'yoku and Sōda Kiichirō were the two thinkers most responsible for establishing the anthropocentric philosophies of neo-Kantianism and culturalism as the most powerful liberal ideologies of the Japanese empire of the late 1910s and early 1920s. Kuwaki taught at Waseda University and had a strong impact upon Yi Kwang-su and other cultural nationalists in Korea. Sōda was a banker and finance capitalist whose integration of the philosophy of culturalism with political economy became a central social-scientific discussion of liberal society in the 1920s. Each of these philosophers defined the essence of the human being as the capacity for self-legislated morality, a capacity that had its origins in nature but had to be cultivated self-consciously through the use of reason. The human's self-conscious cultivation of its knowledge and its practical reason was a historical process; therefore, they referred to general consciousness as the telos of the development of the individual psyche and general culture as the telos of the development of everyday cultural life. They argued that just as the human is not an effect of nature, its cultural life is not determined by natural factors, but rather governed by metaphysical cultural values. In the work of Kuwaki and Sōda, most of the central issues presented by culturalism and cultural policy are brought together into a philosophical system—the regulation of life by ideas, the primacy of spirit over matter, a political economy centered on money and finance capital, and a theory of moral action as the actualization of general cultural value (Sōda) or absolute cultural value (Kuwaki).

Drawing from French and German legal concepts, Inoue Tetsujirō and others had developed philosophies of personhood in late-nineteenth-century Japan, long before culturalism.[3] However, the culturalist concept of personhood was somewhat unique in that it utilized a neo-Kantian philosophy of history to posit a completely moral human world, or Kant's "kingdom of ends," as the utopian culmination and telos of cultural value formation.[4] The capacity to govern one's own practical activity, or to act morally, was that essential quality that differentiated the human from other animals; it also organized the empirical differences of humanity regulatively and historically. The philosophy of culturalism did not consider all humans to be moral, but it did assert that the development of humankind and knowledge about this development both ought to be governed by the idea of the moral human, visible in the actual world in the form of the person. In this sense, the person was the actual-ideal figure for the genus-being of morality, the ideal actor and effect of all human cultural and moral development.

One primary concern of neo-Kantians was to arrive at a concept of moral action that saw it not as an effect of a heteronomous law of divinity or nature, but rather as an expression of human freedom that therefore requires an internal spiritual and cultural life to guide it. In Kuwaki's and Sōda's texts, morality is free individual activity, but it is also what connects the individual, however conflictually, to both the laws of the state and the rules of society. Therefore, the moral law should not be merely an individual sense of right and wrong, but should also be able to serve as a potentially universal law that can ground a community of free individuals, or the nation-state. Just as Kant turned to moral philosophy when the transcendental realm of human knowledge seemed hermetically closed off from its objects, Kuwaki arrived at a moral philosophy of the person at that ambiguous point of intersection between transcendental reflection and the elusiveness of experience (indicated in the following passage by his reference to the person as the thing-in-itself).

In *Kant and Contemporary Philosophy* (1917), Kuwaki writes,

> A human *(hito)* is more elevated than the self, and Kant has given this human a name, person *(jinkaku)*. Through the person, the ground for the transcendental elements was established in the practical field. A factual thing *(jibutsu)* that is heteronomic and necessary is a means employed for the use of another, but because something *(mono)* autonomous and free is only employed for the use of its self, its end is itself. A means has only a price, but an end has value and dignity; we call the former an article *(Sache)* and the latter a person *(Person)*. The moral law must be established by taking the human to be free, a thing-in-itself, and a person.[5]

The figure through which the universal moral law should be established in actuality is the autonomous actor who is employed only for its own use, or the free person understood as end rather than means. On the one hand, Kuwaki is concerned with the noninstrumental treatment of others, at least within the limited sphere of subjects who are capable of morality. On the other hand, in order to belong to the kingdom of ends, the acting subject must be autonomously capable of applying the moral law to itself through self-legislated morality. The person must be capable of legislating morality autonomously and freely, but also universally, or it risks being reduced to a mere factual thing *(jibutsu)*, or even an article with a price. Finally, in a neo-Kantian transformation of the meaning of the "thing-in-itself" from its reference to the unknowable in Kant's own system, this subject of self-legislated morality is also the final end and object of epistemological inquiry, of cultural science as a transcendental and empirical study of the nonnatural, anthropocentric world. In a structure akin to the empirico-transcendental doublet diagnosed by Foucault, the person is the actual-ideal figure through which a philosophy and science of human culture can unite transcendental inquiry about culture with culture as a possible object of experience; or, in the simpler formulations of culturalism, the ideal figure of the person brings the Culture of what ought to be *(Sollen)* to bear on the culture of what is *(Sein)*. Sōda Kiichirō discussed this passage from *Sein* to

Sollen as a "leap" *(hiyaku)* whereby one would come to determine all particular and contingent cultural values by the limit concept of general cultural value.⁶

Kuwaki connects self-legislated morality and its autonomy from the unconscious mechanism of nature directly to nation-state formation when he argues that "if humans that are their own ends gather together and make a country, then it is in contradiction with a country belonging to nature; therefore, in the social state that unites people, a meaning outside of nature emerges."⁷ In this turn from the moral universal to a kind of social contract between proper subjects of culture, what Charles Mills calls the "norming of space" through the racial contract finds a subtle articulation.⁸ The implication is that this country's boundaries will not be vertical lines drawn on a map, but rather will be inscribed into society through the binary of culture and nature, which will be applied differentially within social space according to the ideal standard of the person. In that case, "countries belonging to nature" could be any group or space internal to the "social state" that is marked, through customs, practices, or physiological features, as remaining in the state of nature. Somewhat paradoxically, considering the inevitable violent discrimination implied by the distinction between cultural and natural nations, it is also through this kind of agreement between moral subjects and their collective contradiction with the peoples belonging to nature that self-legislated morality will not devolve into a destructive individualism.

Therefore, just as Ariyoshi argues in his official statement that extreme individualism could threaten the world community of nations as easily as extreme collectivism, Kuwaki thought of the difference between natural and cultural countries as analogous to the difference between a country comprising individualists and a country comprising moral persons treating one another as ends rather than means. Again stating this difference in terms of a difference between empiricism and the transcendental, Kuwaki writes,

> Individualism has at its foundation an empirical theory, but if personalism does not depart from an a priori theory then it has no meaning. Therefore, it is absolutely a mistake to conflate individualism and personalism. However, if we are to articulate a collectivism that opposes individualism in a complete way, we must make personalism the foundation. Because a collective that is simply an aggregation of people only has an empirical significance and does not have universal validity, we cannot recognize in it any kind of authority; in other words, the collective obtains its transcendental foundation first in the person.⁹

If a philosophical origin for cultural policy in Korea can be located in any meaningful way, it is in this kind of attempt to create a transcendental concept of the social contract, a kingdom of ends in which individuals are at once free and autonomous from external determinations and also cultivated and educated enough to apply the universal rules of practice. In thinking of Kant as a modern philosopher, Kuwaki was addressing the problem of the lack of a heteronomous foundation for ethics in modernity. In Ariyoshi's appropriation of the logic of the categorical imperative for the colonial state, the capacity for self-legislated morality also became a demand placed on colonial subjects as a mark of their entrance into modernity through the cultivation of their capacity for moral personhood.

In this respect, self-legislated morality was a formal concept of the human's genus-being, the norm through which the differences within humanity would disappear. However, Kuwaki connected this formal concept to a pragmatic anthropological project immersed in and transformative of human life. Like all neo-Kantians, Kuwaki distinguished between natural science and cultural science by distinguishing their objects of inquiry: natural science studies the laws of nature and cultural science studies the historical and cultural world of the human being. Furthermore, by thinking of cultural science as a philosophy of life (*jinsei tetsugaku, Lebensphilosophie*), he made human life the subject and object of cultural history. This separation of the human from nature required an epistemological distinction between human cultural life and "nature" understood as mechanism. Yet this distinction between human cultural life and nature actually allowed for the inclusion of the bios of the human being within culture, as something malleable and transformable. Giorgio Agamben has discussed this distinction and this inclusion as marking philosophy's turn to the biopolitical.[10]

Outline of Philosophy: The Thing and the I (1929) is a work that spans the history of European philosophy and Kuwaki's own research and teaching career, discussing a number of topics through the basic philosophical problem of the subject's relation to the object. In the chapter titled "The I and Action," Kuwaki presents his own perspective on the problem of the subject and object. It emphasizes the human being's moral autonomy from objects and the way that human life (*jinsei*) unifies moral action into a total system. The chapter opens with some reflections on the relationship between human life and proper conduct, through which Kuwaki articulates in culturalist terms the connection between the governing of oneself, the governing of things, and the governing of the population, or what Foucault names "governmentality."[11] Kuwaki discusses this confluence with the concepts of conduct, the thing, and life:

> Interpreted analytically, "knowing" is a phenomenon that emerges when the I receives the operation of the Thing. However, insofar as the I is independent from the Thing, the I reacts against the Thing. This is called action or Conduct.[12] Of course, making such a clear distinction between the I and the Thing is not proper, but for the convenience of explanation we can state it this way. Just as individual knowing accumulates to form knowledge or learning, individual actions accumulate to form human life. Here the philosophy of life must be established alongside the philosophy of knowledge. However, in order to establish this philosophy we must determine if we should first ascertain the concept of life, or, assuming there must be something that unifies conduct, if we should ask what this unifying principle might be.[13]

Kuwaki turns to the problem of conduct at the point where the I transcends or is independent from things. This is the problem of the free will of the human being, which distinguishes itself from the necessity of nature through its free conduct. Two problems emerge from this separation. What is the rule or law that unifies or should unify various individual actions? If human life is the accumulation of individual actions, should we analyze human life first or rather analyze what unifies the actions that constitute human life? In this situation of aporia between human life and its transcendental determination, Kuwaki turns to an organicist theory of general culture, because culture conceived this way can unify and be unified by the moral universal as practiced by individuals. Because human life and individual conduct taken as empirical objects appear too dispersed and differentiated, the philosophy of human life must turn to the transcendental if it proposes to arrive at a unity that could be properly called Culture in the global sense. This is how he was able to differentiate his theory of culture and cultural activity from the empirical study of customs, traditions, or the minutiae of modern styles and behaviors emerging in the social sciences and literature of the time.[14]

In the full formulation of the relationship between morality and life, Kuwaki turns to Kant's categorical imperative: "act only in accordance with that maxim through which you can at the same time will that it become a universal law."[15] Kuwaki makes the further assertion that because the categorical imperative constitutes the substance of morality and unifies conduct in the actual cultural world, a total system can be founded on its universality. This despite the trace of the hypothetical in the formulation "as if." The subject and object of this unification of the moral law are human life, which therefore becomes the subject and object of a pragmatic application of the transcendental:

> If we take the substance of the moral law to be the purely formal categorical imperative, then it becomes the transcendental element of morality, the substance of morality, or the transcendental and formal element of conduct, thereby becoming a ground and, in the case of knowledge, something like a category. If we interpret conduct and morality in this way, then a unity for each conduct emerges for the first time; a unity exists for the totality of conducts and a single system is formed. In the case of knowledge, each individual understanding synthesizes and becomes something like learning. If we give to the system of conduct the name "human life," then we must say that human life is that which takes morality and makes it a unified principle, or an "a priori."[16]

Human life unifies morality under the rules of the transcendental, becoming cultural life *(bunka seikatsu)*. Morality, in turn, forms a system of conducts through its substantive universality. At this point, Kuwaki's discourse collapses into the structure of the empirico-transcendental doublet, because the human being and human life unify morality in the material world while the material world comes to reflect the unity of moral universality ascertained transcendentally. This is where

Kuwaki turns to the concepts of culture and cultural value, which refer to both the conducts that constitute the unity of human life and the transcendental values through which they are unified.

For Kuwaki, because cultural value connects particular histories to a developing universal history, it is not an interpretive practice directed primarily toward the past, but rather the foundation for historical development. History is a history of the ongoing passage from nature as merely contingent incident to Culture as the unity of consciously and freely enacted historical events (what he calls, quoting Kant, the "history of freedom"). Kuwaki emphasizes that the historical perspective of culturalism, or his version of "historicism," must not be solely a conservative look to the past, but must be both modern and modernizing: "People name the turn to history 'historicism' and take this to mean that historicism must venerate only the past; however, speaking about the essence of history, historicism must not grasp development in the future by simply understanding the laws of development of the past; in other words, it cannot be simple conservative thinking."[17]

In addition to this differentiation of culturalist historicism from cultural conservatism, Kuwaki associates history as simply a "written record of the past" with an outmoded naturalist idea of causality, for which each event appears as an effect of preceding events and as a cause for subsequent events.[18] In opposition to cultural conservatism and naturalist views of history, Kuwaki proposes a perpetual historical development that must have a purpose, but whose purpose cannot be fully formulated outside of historical time. Development is the transformation of human life according to universal moral law, but this development is continuous and its own end.[19] In discussing history as perpetual development, culture is figured as radically temporal. What ought to be never completely becomes what is through the unity of cultural life. The idea of unifying human life according to cultural values was in this sense a symptom of modernity and a response to modernity. Despite his primary concern with unifying humanity under moral universals, Kuwaki could not locate a fixed substance for morality, but only the generally human capacity to individually arrive at the moral universal. In history he recognized an eternal process that can never find its final resting point. In this sense, the person as the ideal center of moral and cultural life would always be in the process of actualizing and being actualized—history would be the history of cultivating the individual and the totality of individuals, or, in the language of nation-state building, Saitō's "cultivation of state power."[20]

This understanding of culture and cultural values was very political. As texts engaged with popular understandings of the political present, *Culturalism and Social Problems* (1920) and *Culture and Reconstruction* (1922) discuss philosophy in a more everyday language that reveals some of the underlying social circumstances motivating Kuwaki's turn to culture. He opposes the philosophy of culturalism to various materialist and natural scientific views of society, including Social Darwinism, naturalized ethnic nationalisms (including that of the colonized), and, increasingly, Marxism and the historical materialist view of history. Cultural science is no longer solely a matter of epistemological or philosophical truth, but is intended to be the foundation for a new cosmopolitan ethos for Taishō democracy and its imperial missions. We also discover in *Culturalism and Social Problems* that Kuwaki's experiences as a student in Germany did not solely provide him with a philosophical education. His confrontation with European Orientalism turns out to have been a significant motivation for his search for a science of culture governed by a priori values. In the passages quoted at the beginning of this book, Kuwaki argues against the type of historical thinking that informed Orientalism, which was one motivation for claiming in modern fashion that the historical future is necessarily open and therefore allows for the perpetual development of the cultural human. Edward Said describes the method of Orientalism as a haphazard piecing together of fragments into an illusory representation of Oriental society. It is a discourse of experience that follows no identifiable rules except to objectify the past of the Other as the present of the Other, from the position of the informed expert.[21] According to Kuwaki, Puccini's opera brings together fragments of the Asian past and presents them as the essence of Japanese things. In turning to Kantian critical philosophy, Kuwaki uses *Madame Butterfly* as a sign of the need for an internal critique that will define the true essence of Japaneseness in an a priori manner.

However, once Kuwaki identified cultural values as the guiding force of historical development, and the human being as the subject and object of this development, he was very much working within the structure of the empirico-transcendental doublet that he identified as the primary problem in European representations of Asia. Positing the unity of human life under absolute values reintroduced anthropology into Kuwaki's system, particularly an understanding of national character, which Kant differentiated from the natural racial variations—white, black, yellow, reddish-brown—that he had picked up from eighteenth-century racial science. This national characterological rather than explicitly racial confusion of the transcendental and the empirical, posited at the level of culture and cultural practice, comes through in a section of *Kant and Contemporary Philosophy,* "Kant's View of Japan." Kuwaki works through Kant's dubious reflections on national character in the *Anthropology,* including the reference to the Japanese as the English of Asia. Kuwaki states that for Kant Japan was "neither utopia nor an uncivilized land."[22] He also discusses Voltaire, Marco Polo, and other European views of Japan. His final conclusion is that despite Kant's prejudices, we can assume from the content of Engelbert Kaempfer's *The History of Japan* (1727)—the primary European source on the country in eighteenth-century Europe—that "the Japan that appeared to Kant, in a certain sense, would have been a country that understands *das Primat der praktischen Vernunft* (the primacy of practical reason)."[23] In opposition to Puccini's pastiche of Japanese and Asian culture, Kuwaki fantasizes that in gazing on the unity called "Japan" Kant would have recognized that unity as an effect of its collective formation under the rule of the universal, and therefore as a national character (a confusion of the transcendental and the empirical that is particular to the neo-Kantian understanding of cultural value formation as a cosmopolitan-national process). If the unity of the transcendental in the practical realm happens through culture and moral values, these values will be not only cosmopolitan, but also formative of national character, and therefore observable as a custom, a behavior, or even a physical feature.

This doubling of subject/object, universal/particular, transcendental/empirical affected Kuwaki's discussions of Korea and the problem of cultural reform in the colonies. His perspectives on Korea were not Orientalist in the same way as Puccini's opera, but the idea of world history as the ideal unity of humanity was still an ethnicized idea that maintained an anthropological boundary between the cultural spheres of Japan and Korea. His culturalist view of the world returned to empirical anthropology when he spoke of the discrete national worlds that made up the cosmopolitan world. In an essay titled "The Korean World of Ideas," Kuwaki writes of Korea as a unified "world of ideas" both integrated within and distinct from "our world of ideas." He puts Koreans in the position of students who need to regain faith in values-centered thought, and to overcome, along with their Japanese teachers, the Meiji period's false application of natural-scientific principles to culture and society:

> I see that Korean thinkers' faith is shaken because of scientific research (particularly the knowledge of evolutionary theory).... Biology is the science that developed most remarkably in the nineteenth century and evolutionary theory inspired the minds of numerous cultivated men. Herbert Spencer's philosophy of evolution, which confused Darwin's evolutionary biology for a methodology, entered our country on the heels of English and American utilitarianism at the beginning of the Meiji period.... The secrets of psychology, law, economics—all of the human sciences[24]—could supposedly be revealed through the principle of evolution....
>
> The theory of evolution is an explanation of facts and does not provide a standard for the evaluation of facts.... One thing that I myself tried to assert strongly during the aforementioned public lecture was the intent of critical philosophy and the questions that I received afterward confirm the degree to which the theory of evolution, psychologism, and the superficial and polarizing metaphysics that so easily combines with them have become the foundation for our world of ideas; they confirmed the fact that very few people really understand logicism and critical philosophy. From this I can say that the Korean world of ideas, even in its large tendencies, resembles the world of ideas of our own society. In this we must feel the need to clarify the true meaning of criticalism.[25]

Kuwaki employs the fact/value dichotomy of neo-Kantianism in order to critique Social Darwinism and utilitarianism, which had been very powerful in East Asia,

Meiji Japan, and the Korean empire. By distinguishing between the facts of nature and the values of the human sciences, Kuwaki shifts the discussion of the nation and the world from one of struggle, adaptation, and potential extinction, to one of culture, spirit, and the metaphysics of morals. He interprets the power of materialist and natural science epistemologies in Korea as a sign that the culturalist view of history, as well as the unity of Japanese and Korean culture within general Culture, has yet to take hold sufficiently. In the statements of Saitō and Ariyoshi we can see how liberal reformers of the colonial state saw political potential in this argument, because it demanded the negation of present factual conditions while making the capacity to evaluate facts morally and self-reflexively a condition for modernity shared by individuals in both Japan and Korea.

What Kuwaki calls "the evaluation of facts" requires critique, or the ethos of what he calls "criticalism." In turn this critique requires the capacity for moral judgment and a sense of historical and cosmological purpose. Prefiguring the colonial versions of culturalism that would emerge in the years to come, Kuwaki saw the problem of separating the purpose and methods of the human sciences from natural science as the central intellectual and social problem of the whole Japanese empire. For him, Social Darwinist accounts of history justified both world war and anticolonial nationalism, and the assertion of cosmopolitan community against any materialist philosophy functioned at once as a call for peace and reconstruction and as a justification of Japan's colonial rule in Asia. Culturalism purported to reform the Japanese and Korean "worlds" into one world of ideas based on a universalist concept of moral genus-being and *homo culturalis,* but it at the same time continued to demarcate national variations of humanity according to their relative distance from the teleological form of the human (the person). Prefiguring late-twentieth-century area studies paradigms, Kuwaki asserted the generality of culture and the transcendental status of the idea of Japan while at the same time using the concept of the world at cross-purposes—to refer simultaneously to the "world of ideas" of the colonized people and to the world at large that could potentially unify the lives of colonizer and colonized under the rules of absolute cultural values (or what postwar US modernization theorists, in their concern with the "non-economic factors of growth," called "convergence").[26]

Therefore, when Kuwaki wrote of the difference between natural facts and cultural values, he was not situating all Koreans in the sphere of natural objects, but he was warning both the colonizer and the colonized of the dire historical effects of remaining natural humans and a natural nation. He was concerned with separating the realm of freedom of the human individual, as well as the entire process of human historical progress, from the causality of natural laws. Values are the a priori ideas that are actualized through the moral and cultural practice of individuals who make up a society and they therefore belong to an entirely different causal order from nature. By emphasizing the autonomy of the human being from natural laws, he could claim that left labor activists as well as Korean ethnic nationalists both had too materialist an understanding of the human being as a laboring machine, as the owner of natural rights, or as a member of a nation with a foundation in nature.[27] The power of the cosmopolitan humanism of culturalism derived from this metaphysical claim that all philosophies that situated the human being in nature—as a primarily material being or as a being endowed with rights from nature—stripped the human of its moral freedom and the spontaneity it required to actualize what ought to be.

The concept of the world as both the totality of life and the discrete national spheres that make it up transformed Korea into an integrated cultural object of pragmatic anthropology, a place where ideas and worldviews could be actively transformed and molded. In this project, Korea actually resembles Japan, although the difference of its world is always reiterated through the imaginary boundary between our world and Korea. Through this structure, Korea can signify for Kuwaki an anxiety about a time lag between the cosmopolitan world of general values and the Japanese national subject who will enter that world by becoming a self-conscious, reasoning, and moral subject. Kuwaki suggests both that the Korean world is particularly steeped in the outdated epistemologies of the Meiji past and that Korean intellectuals' reluctance to enter the purely human time of cosmopolitan history indicates the weakness of criticism in "our world" (Japan proper) as well.

In this dualist world of cosmopolitan and natural nations, Koreans will eventually join cultural humanity, but it is impossible that the ideal person could be found first in Korea, because Korea's development will always be a reflection of the advancements made by its teacher. The notion of teacher and student is at the foundation of this mode of assimilation and discrimination. As part of the project of Japaneseness critiquing Japanese self-consciously, Kuwaki also took up the social mission to educate Koreans by drawing them away from natural-scientific epistemologies and politicized materialist philosophies (that is, Marxism). Yet, as the case of Korean cultural nationalism shows, the most powerful ideas of assimilation and discrimination in the Japanese empire were such humanist ones, because they posited a realm of freedom belonging to all of humanity at the same time as they ethnicized and normed space. These two moves were appealing to cultural nationalists in Korea who were interested in the project of national enlightenment and, in the 1940s, to those Korean intellectuals who thought that becoming Japanese was a condition for belonging to humanity and world history. Kuwaki's simultaneous distinction between and conflation of "our world of ideas" and the "Korean world of ideas" also reflect how an ethnicized cultural border was necessary in order to posit the unity of world humanity suitable to colonial governmentality. Later in this chapter I will analyze how this border can be regulative in a universal sense and differentiating in an anthropological sense only through another notion of the border, which is the communicative translation between nations and national languages. The idea that communicative translation between national languages can serve as the foundation for the transmission of the transcendental subject is intimately related to the biopolitics of culturalism, to its other assertion that regulative general values allow its transcendental epistemology to give organic unity to cultural life.

POLITICAL ECONOMY AND CULTURAL ECONOMY: THE LIMIT CONCEPT IN SŌDA KIICHIRŌ

Despite its claims to have risen above politics through its focus on morality and spirit, culturalism was obviously very political, not least of all because culturalists proclaimed it to be a form of democracy superior to the shared sovereignty of and natural equality between all people. Culturalists developed theories of democratic society based on cosmopolitan cultural values and other anthropological criteria, a social contract whose utopian image was akin to Kant's kingdom of ends rather than a contract guaranteeing natural rights. For Kant, "A rational being belongs as a *member* to the kingdom of ends when he gives universal laws in it but is also himself subject to these laws. He belongs to it as *sovereign* when, as lawgiving, he is not subject to the will of any other."[28] Therefore, one can only belong to the state and live under the laws of the state if one is capable of legislating one's morality universally for the public good; the benefits and responsibilities of living under the laws of the state are not given by nature. Along these lines, Sōda Kiichirō criticized Voltaire and the socialist political economist Anton Menger for arguing that both political rights and a portion of the social product were guaranteed to individuals solely because they were *Gattungsexemplar* (or one natural instance of the human genus), and he organized his culturalist political and economic philosophy around self-legislated morality as *Gattungswesen* (or genus-being).[29] In his culturalist theory of political conduct, no one is human in the given sense of natural rights, but everyone must try nonetheless to belong to the moral general culture, the kingdom of ends, through the proper use of their freedom.

Because culturalist imperialism was an economic venture overlaid with the discourses of general culture and moral practice, political economy underwent a transformation into cultural economy. The intersection between the transcendental and empirical aspects of culturalism occurred most concretely in Sōda's field of "national economy studies" *(Volkswirtschaftslehre, kokumin keizaigaku)*. In this discipline, the transcendental philosophy of value became social science. The image of the national economy it presents is an imperialist one in which the limits of the national economy are precisely where cosmopolitan values must be asserted, where humanization and culturalization must improve upon nature, transforming the natural human into the cultural human through the pragmatic institution of abstraction and exchange, and through the teleological image of an organic totality of proper human subjects living under the rule of ideas (that is, general values). While working as a banker, Sōda Kiichirō wrote a number of significant texts in national economy studies, as well as essays in culturalist philosophy.[30] He wrote many works on more strictly economic topics, such as the credit system, Adam Smith's and David Ricardo's criticisms of mercantilism, and critiques of the economic theories of syndicalists and socialists.[31] However, like Smith before him, Sōda put a great deal of philosophical reflection into the question of the subjectivity that could sustain a well-functioning world market. His work in political economy was concerned with how the formation of the national and world economies could be reconsidered as problems of culture. Sōda's reading of the national economy in culturalist terms provides an image of the society that culturalists desired to create. His defense of this image of society required a rearticulation of the limits of culturalist epistemology—or what may not be known about (other) humans—as the very site where humanism's regulative principles come to govern the world anthropologically and pragmatically.

During his time living abroad in Germany, Sōda published, in German, two major texts in economics, *Money and Value* (1909) and *The Logical Nature of Economic Laws* (1912).[32] In each of these texts, Sōda applied perspectives on epistemology and logic garnered from neo-Kantian cultural science to questions of money, value, and economic laws. He attempted to synthesize this cultural and moral genus-being with a cruder utilitarian one: *homo economicus,* or the human as self-interested, rational economic actor. In the introduction to *Money and Value,* Sōda explains that the cultural cosmopolitanism that had been asserted in German understandings of culture since the late eighteenth century came to influence his research into economics:

> I want to return, in my research concerning the essence of money and value, to the German classical period and, in general, to the fountain of youth of German culture. National economy studies are no longer to me a mere "bread-and-butter issue," but rather a huge cultural question for all of mankind. I am especially thankful to the German sciences for having given me this conviction.[33]

By 1909 Sōda was reading political economy through his appreciation for Goethe, Kant, and others in the pantheon of "German thought," and had come to consider economic problems to be problems of cultural life. Sōda's return to the "fountain of youth" of German thought resulted in the application of Kantian philosophy to the field of economics. Such an application has been rare, and Simmel's *Philosophy of Money* is probably one of the only works still read widely from this convergence at the turn of the century.[34] In both Simmel's work and Sōda's reading of it, series of financial and commodity exchanges in capitalism make up a manifold of experiences that must be unified under an idea. For Simmel, money is both ideal and material. As the quintessential sign for the idea of exchangeability, it brings together the manifold of exchanges under the rule of the transcendental; however, as a thing in the material world, it unifies these manifold experiences in actuality, not solely in the realm of noumenal concepts.[35] At the same time, what makes things equal is the human subject of judgment, the economic actor who determines according to his aesthetic and cultural judgment that a certain object is rightly considered exchangeable with another.

Many significant lapses and dead ends in transcendental philosophy become clear when it is explicitly displaced into the field of political economy in this manner. The version of national economy studies that Sōda undertook was a liberal alternative to the increasingly powerful socialist and communist movements in Germany and the rest of Europe. The works of the economists that Sōda cites in *Money and Value*—Carl Johannes Fuchs, Georg Simmel, and so on—tend to ignore the labor theory of value and focus mostly on money, exchange, and consumption. Even in the realm of exchange, there were problems that emerged when trying to read money through transcendental philosophy, problems that are very related to the semiotic limits of the philosophy of culturalism. The philosophy of culturalism was Sōda's attempt to solve the ethical issues presented by Simmel's formulation that money is the form that governs and rules all the various experiences and transactions occurring in the capitalist system. Just as Kuwaki's discussion of the person was an attempt to transform questions of material inequalities into spiritual and moral questions, Sōda recognized that if money is the sole value governing exchanges in society, then human agency is reduced to the mechanical acting out of a principle external to itself. In developing a culturalist understanding of the human subject, in which general cultural values are what govern the formation of the national economy, he tried to improve on the instrumental understanding of money, value, and causality. He made the issue of exploitation and surplus value that Marx located in the movement of Money-Commodity-Money into an issue of morality and personhood. The limit of capitalism, Sōda thinks, is not the incapacity to fully transform surplus value into profit, as Marx theorized. Rather than recognize that incapacity as the limit to capital accumulation and expansion, Sōda developed a moral philosophy of the limit, asserting an anthropological distinction between the properly cultural agent of the national economy and those humans who remained trapped in the mechanism of natural phenomena. This maneuver in his moral philosophy racialized and gendered, through cosmopolitan rhetoric, the borders of the national economy.

Sōda's philosophy of culture and cultural value is quite complex, but I would like to focus on three main aspects: his understanding of the causality in history, his introduction of the "limit concept" into cultural science, and the way that he used anthropological distinctions in order to present the "system of cultural values" as an organic system with no clear distinction between itself and an outside, but rather an internal border constituted through the figuration of the national language and its others, as well as the binary between cultural and natural humans.

Sōda's rejection of the narrative logic of chronology proper to positivist historical science is explicit in his criticism of the application of what Kant called the "schema of succession" to the causality of historical events.[36] Rather than given causes producing given effects in history, history is rather the realm of individual freedom, but a freedom that should be guided by morality and purpose. He states in "The Logic of Individual Causality" that in order to differentiate between cause and effect there must be an ethical position from which this real distinction is made—the division of material into cause and effect never occurs autonomously from the subject's actualization of general values.[37] Because he defines positions according to the "purpose of knowledge" to which they are dedicated, the epistemological subject is essentially practical and teleological (that is, moral in the sense of Kantian universal self-legislation). He argues that science establishes a position whenever it is oriented toward its final purpose, and only through this purpose can the epistemological subject define historical events and their causal relations. Causality does not occur mechanically, with one event or value producing a certain effect; rather, the cultural scientist can decide what causes an event only retrospectively by way of the final purpose for interpreting the event. For Sōda, the human was divided between the lived experience of individual life and the transcendental conditions under which he experienced history, and connecting these two realms of individual life was the purpose of the interpretations made by cultural science. This was a matter of reason applying what ought to be *(Sollen)* to the study and formation of what is *(Sein)*. Nonmechanistic time as the basis for historical thought and action intervened in both the empirical and transcendental registers of human life. What gave form and purpose to these two registers of human life was not the categories and laws of nature, including the law of mechanical causality, but rather a historical process of natural humans developing into a morally and politically liberated human genus.

Within this dualism, how did Sōda arrive at limit concepts as the teleology of cultural science and the person as the teleology of daily cultural life? Sōda dedicated *Cultural Value and the Limit Concept* to Heinrich Rickert, but he was critical of certain aspects of Rickert's theory of value formation. "The process of the actualization of cultural value" remains central to his philosophy of culturalism, but he disagrees with Rickert that values are categories of actuality *(Wirklichkeitskategorie)*, or characteristics of an object that precede our experience of it (for example, characteristics belonging to quantity, quality, unity, and modality).[38] Sōda claims that values do not structure historical experience in this way. Values are not so closely related to the categories of natural science, but are pure concepts with no relation to experience; in other words, they are ideas. In order to explain this difference, he turns to the second half of the *Critique of Pure Reason*, which deals with transcendental philosophy and reason's attempt to regulate itself through regulative ideas. He refers to these regulative ideas as "limit concepts," concepts that define the teleological purpose of fields of knowledge beyond the categories through which the understanding comprehends nature. Limit concepts are ideas with no relation to cultural experiences of otherness, or any experience at all; they are pure concepts through which the subject can imagine the complete rationality of the system of cultural values. This wholeness, this organic unity, is not given in nature, but actualized through the effort of individuals free from nature's mechanical causality.

Paul Natorp, in his neo-Kantian rereading of the thing-in-itself, situated the limit concept where Kant himself asserted a more fundamental and uncrossable divide, or "block," between the transcendental and the empirical.[39] By rearticulating the thing-in-itself as a limit concept, or in Kant's terms a "regulative principle" for science, Natorp argued that even if it is never cognized fully, the thing-in-itself nonetheless remains the goal of scientific pursuits, and can therefore serve as the teleology of scientific progress.[40] In *Kant and Contemporary Philosophy*, Kuwaki posited the person as the thing-in-itself, making the formation of a perfectly moral subject the teleology of a continuous cultural development.[41] The figure of the person was always present, but only as an absent ideal, a lack in the existing human. Sōda also appropriated the limit concept for cultural science, displacing it into the human sciences, so that the formation of the cosmopolitan individual became the teleological purpose of the whole realm of human activity referred to as culture. In *Cultural Value and the Limit Concept*, Sōda displaces the limit concept from the natural sciences into the cultural sciences, discussing general values as values that guide human development toward the telos of "transindividual general consciousness" (or, in moral rather than epistemological terms, the person). In the natural sciences of the time, the limit concept represented an admission that there are physical and natural phenomena beyond the conceptual grasp of the human being. It was also expressive of a kind of scientific sublime, a feeling that the human subject can potentially comprehend the chaos of nature and conceive it as a totality, despite the incongruency of concept and reality.[42]

In discussing "general values" as the limit concepts for the philosophy of culturalism, limit concepts that should guide the cultural and moral development of the national economy, Sōda similarly transformed the external limits of the social system into internal limits; the limit at which the "system of cultural values" *(bunka kachi no taikei)* was incomplete in its comprehension of reality was rearticulated as this system's very teleology, its regulative principle. Therefore, Sōda discussed the limit concepts governing the economic system—particularly money and general cultural values—not as contradictory concepts partially inadequate to the "thing-in-itself" of the real economic and cultural system, but rather as the very signs that would allow for cultural life and cultural science to undergo their proper formations. As I show in the next part, this transformation of external limits into internal limits was made possible by the idea of the national language and its formation into a world-scientific language. It also required a moral binary between natural humans and cultural humans; the system of cultural values could only be presented as an organic whole by supplementing it with an external element, the natural human, and a master-signifier (the person).

Just as Foucault pointed out that Kant's anthropology belonged to the realm of transcendental philosophy, Sōda's philosophy of the limit concept was anthropological precisely because it was transcendental. Once reason regulates itself with concepts that have no relation to a possible experience, but rather are simply teleological concepts that allow one to imagine that the conditions of possibility for experience have been fulfilled, then the question arises: what is the identity of the being that is capable of regulating its own reason in this manner? Therefore, in order to ground his transcendental philosophy of culture, and to give it a wholeness and systematicity, Sōda simultaneously relied on an anthropological distinction between the person and the natural human that maintained an empirical dimension. The anthropological side of Sōda's transcendental philosophy of culture is most apparent in the models he provided for the human's cultivation out of nature toward his genus-being, his cultural and moral subjectivity. His discussion of historical interpretation described a split subject of culture that appeared in the empirical as a historical individual and projected itself in the transcendental as the interpreter of history.

In "Cultural Value as Limit Concept," Sōda describes the metamorphosis of the subject from a mere physiological being, to a psychological being, to general consciousness as a process of the natural raw material of the human developing toward its ideal form:

> For example, let us take the Ought *(Sollen)* of general consciousness. In the transition from the physiological ego to the psychological ego, and from judgmental consciousness to transindividual general consciousness, general consciousness serves as an ideal (Ideal). Therefore, in its content, general consciousness is a singular idea. When a direction is given to the transition from the physiological self to the psychological self, the rise toward the extreme point of this direction must arrive at the ideal of transindividual general consciousness, or the "limit concept" of this transition.[43]

If culture is regulated by cultural values as limit concepts, as well as the teleology of cultural-historical development, the development of the subject is governed by the regulative principle of its most ideal form. For Sōda, the Ought of subjectivity is general consciousness, a subject whose thoughts and values are generally valid for all of humanity. Again, transcendental philosophy turned to the empirical philosophy of anthropology to discuss how the transcendental could take objective form, because the human being was the only possible object of experience once nature was bracketed as unfree mechanism.

How, then, was Sōda able to present this anthropocentric system of cultural values as an organic totality? In his teleological and prescriptive version of cultural science, the purpose of the process of the actualization of cultural value (the person) was linked to an ideal organization of social life, as a kind of second nature of modern capitalist society, rather than to Kant's image of nature as intelligent design. As the final purpose of culture, the person could not be related to any other conditions of possibility. Culture was to serve as the foundation for the actualization of this teleological principle: "Culture is the location in which the teleological principle of the person should be actualized."[44] The teleological judgment of the interpreter of cultural history could recognize the ideal organization of the material world, and the market of cultural objects, as the products of intention. Neither this rational organization nor the subjects who created it were subject to natural laws. Rather, the organization was reflective of, and reflected in, the intentionality of the individual persons who were free actors upon its surface. In turn, the realm of culture was where individuals could progress toward their complete individuation as persons, and toward the ideal identity between their historical individuality and general consciousness.

Sōda's understanding of final purpose and intentionality was entirely anthropocentric. The objectification of the ideal cultural system was a result of human rather than divine intentionality. Nonetheless, there is a clear reference to Kant's teleological view of nature in the relationship between form and intentionality in Sōda's image of the ideal social system:

> Cultural goods [including technology, morality, law, and economy] are the products of a single effort occurring in the background of cultural life. These goods serve various individual purposes, working collectively and supplementing the actualization of a defined norm. Putting it in more conventional terms, these goods have an organic organization. We call this organization "the unity of cultural goods," and we name this unity "culture." Only when we view culture as a process of the actualization of value does it gain its complete significance, which it must have as a force opposed to nature. Cultural value is the Ought *(Sollen)* that creates culture, and carries with it the direction and purpose of culture. A person recognizes his own individual significance by seeking to preserve his own value in the process of realizing cultural value and to avoid being replaced by others (in other words, by promoting his own importance and value through contact with the products and creations of culture). Cultural value is the object that includes immanently its own logic and the person is the subject who gives it meaning. There can be no cultural value without persons and no persons without cultural value. He who is not oriented toward cultural value is only a natural human; personhood can only exist in a cultural human. Therefore, culturalism seeks the following: that each person is an individual in the process of the realization of value, but is not buried beneath the surface of the process; that each person ensures its individual position on the surface and that persons are assembled by one obligation, one law, and one order; that cultural values emerge as norms and

purposes, and, moreover, that their logical and universal validity is actualized in content and in fact, in accordance with the person. In other words, culturalism is "humanism" and personalism, which attempt to understand, on the basis of a philosophy of cultural value, a person and a culture.[45]

In describing the cultural system that cultural science was to produce and understand, Sōda developed an image of a national economy in which the whole of the system was reflective of the intentions of individual actors. He endowed the surface of identical cultural value with real existence through a teleological argument. Though he considered the ideal subjects and objects of culture—persons and values—to be ends in themselves, and therefore cultural phenomena free from external conditions, he simultaneously claimed that culture organized social life into an organic organization that resembled a natural phenomenon. The *organon* of culture confronted and improved upon nature, and brought individuals out of their stagnancy as natural humans; it also reified the human subject by placing it within the "organization of cultural goods." As organic products of the intentionality of individual actors, society, the national economy, and the world economy were analogous to organic natural phenomena that grew naturally toward their ultimate cosmopolitan purpose. This notion of the "second nature" of capitalism, articulated through Kantian teleology, situated Sōda within the liberal tradition of naturalizing capitalist social relations.

Sōda does not examine the problem of surplus value or connect the concept of value to labor power (he almost completely ignored the labor theory of value in either the Ricardian or the Marxian version). Instead, he displaces the production process into the "process of the actualization of cultural value," and seeks the essence of money as a nonquantifying determinant of value. The bourgeois notion of individual freedom in exchange, regulated by the concept of money and the subjective valuation of objects, was the starting point and end point of Sōda's economics. Political economy was one primary field in which concepts (for example, money) were to regulate the process of rationalization, and thus draw the cultural system and cultural community into an organic organization. The historical uncertainty of politics and economy, epitomized by the often chaotic movements of capital, seems to have demanded that his political economy not rely on the mechanical causality of natural science, but also that it be able to overcome, through regulative principles and a theory of moral practice, the potential chaos that might be exposed through the pure individuation of phenomena. The infinite substitution of cultural values came to require limit concepts at the level of epistemology and teleology at the level of the sign. In her reading of Kant's teleology, Gayatri Spivak points out that the process of making-whole within the Kantian system, or supplementation *(Ergänzung),* comes to require the binary signs of God and Man in the Raw, as well as a moral and aesthetic but ultimately anthropological distinction between those who experience the sublime and those who cannot.[46] In the more secular discourse of the philosophy of culturalism, this supplementation occurred with the person and the natural human as the two axes. In order to establish the national economy as an object of knowledge, Sōda made the external internal through epistemology (the limit concept articulates the boundary as a norm) and supplementarity (the whole is made such by the insertion of a master-signifier that both belongs to the system and is outside it—the person, the fully constituted moral subject, in that contradictory position where God had once been).

As in Kuwaki's theory of the social state, both of these maneuvers required anthropology and the negative figure of the natural human in order to present culture as an organic system. This transformation of an external border (the limit of the system) into an internal border (the limit concept, or norm for the system) also became a matter of national language as the universalizing medium that allowed for the localization of the transcendental, moral subject of general culture. Kuwaki's idea of a unified world of humanity made up of various national worlds required a poetics of national language and a communicative notion of translation, as did Sōda's internalization of the external, or the transformation of the limits of knowledge into the very foundation for rationality.

TRANSLATING THE HUMAN, COMMUNICATING CONCEPTS, NATIONAL LANGUAGE

Culturalism was characterized by an abstract and schematic mode of historical interpretation. Its transcendental method resulted in the subjection of history to philosophical logic, an organicist understanding of social totality, and a view of historical time as universal, developmental, and form-giving. Despite these idealist foundations, culturalism was also highly pragmatic, and its abstractions were transformed into strategies, as the case of cultural policy attests. One powerful means of connecting the abstract logic and teleology of cultural history to the historical present and to the everyday was through ideas of national language. If culturalism's ideas for a universal human community seemed out of reach in history, national subject formation and national language formation could serve as prosthesis, and were often perceived as a means toward ascending to "general consciousness" within a particular territory.

Rickert, Sōda, and Yi Kwang-su all argued that a communicative national language could maintain and invigorate the spirit of culture, as well as the subject who studies and lives general culture. Although cultural science attempted to study culture through a generally valid methodology and by way of cultural values, it also encountered the limits of the conceptual determination of cultural life. Concepts seemed to lose their universality in the face of radical spatial, historical, and linguistic differences within the generally human. At the margins of their texts, culturalists proposed the unifying power of national language, and the possibility of communicative translation between national languages, as the means of grounding the concepts of the transcendental subject within a local sphere of anthropological difference.

The question of the role of national language for science, as well as the semiotic limits to a scientific understanding of the human, did not emerge for Sōda in a language that he thought of as his own. Language was not an important part of Sōda's philosophy of culture. However, in the introduction to *Money and Value*, addressed to his mentor Carl Johannes Fuchs, he makes a significant mention of the "mother tongue," which takes a tone similar to Kuwaki's critique of Orientalism. He implicitly questions Fuchs's Orientalism and, as in Kuwaki's response to *Madame Butterfly*, he asserts the need for Japanese science to take its place in the pantheon of human generality. Writing in German, he argues for the power of the mother tongue to communicate or transmit the concepts of this science across Asia and to the world:

> As I submit this work, I would not only like to express personal gratitude for letting me experience during the past four years both directly and indirectly, both socially and scientifically, unlimited and indefatigable support and unwavering friendship, but also like to take the opportunity to give due expression to my acknowledgment of the wonderful inspiration that I have received from the German spirit generally. I am fully aware that you are an admirer and an aficionado of the art of our ancestors, the ancient Japanese, and that you might miss that old beauty in this work, the product of a "modern Japanese." To build something on our own Japanese, or even Asian, science alone—which has not yet received significant acknowledgment from European scholars and which appears to me to be a sleeping giant that must only be woken, and is, despite various prejudicial opinions, a rare and extraordinarily refined cultural product of humankind in general—that is only a task for the future. However, if I once have the pleasure to be able to claim for myself a small fraction of your own appreciation for ancient Japanese art, my scholarly hope that I hold as a member of this people, whose mother tongue has not yet been accepted as a generally understood world language of science, would have been fulfilled even within my generation.[47]

This text, written by an "Asian" student whose modern subjectivity seems to have been in question by his professor, subordinates the past to science and implicitly to the German language's status as a world-scientific language. German allows the intellectual a capacity for applied aesthetic judgment, and it is this capacity that Sōda wants to secure for his mother tongue and its "Japanese or even Asian science." He implies that German has already developed to the degree that it allows the subject to appreciate the artwork of the Japanese past, whereas such an appreciation can only occur for him when his language becomes properly scientific. The potential collapse of the concepts of cultural science occurs at the level of language; Sōda suggests that the underdevelopment of the mother tongue threatens to render aesthetic judgment mute and somnolent. However, the rescue of science, or the awakening of science, also occurs through the universalizing power of language, because the development of the mother tongue could potentially enliven and ground a Japanese science (or, in a turn of linguistic imperialism, "Asian science"). This new scientific language would allow Sōda's generation to determine the value of the artifacts of its own past and the Asian past more generally. It is in this way that cultural scientists posited national language as a universalizing medium.

Sōda's assertion of national language as the basis for a scientific understanding of the national cultural past is given in part as a response to the Orientalist fascination of Fuchs with ancient Japanese art. This Orientalism is apparent not in the mere fact of Fuchs's aesthetic taste, but rather in Sōda's intimation that Fuchs will be disappointed to read a book of economic theory written by a "modern Japanese," because it lacks the "ancient beauty" of Japanese art. Sōda's mother tongue remains outside of the sphere of scientific communicability called "Europe," which is contrasted to its other, "Asia." Japan will become scientific as scientists and intellectuals develop the mother tongue to the point where it too can properly communicate scientific concepts and methods. Sōda expressed this desire for his mother tongue to become a "world language of science" only three years after the institution of compulsory Japanese-language education at normal schools in Korea (1906).[48] This timing was not coincidental, as the enlivening of a native Asian and Japanese science through the Japanese national language entailed the production of native and nonnative speakers and the unification of the national language through its (colonial) pedagogical formation.

The significance of the Europe/non-Europe distinction, and its linguistic determination, is apparent also in the following quotation by Rickert, which appears in the introduction to *The One, the Unity, and the Oneness* (dedicated to "my Japanese colleagues").[49] Rickert sought an objective relationship between individuals and values that were generally valid. His tautological view of society ascribed general validity to the everyday representations that formed individuals' relationships to singular events; however, the dependency of this general validity upon a communicative notion of human culture, and therefore of translation, becomes apparent at the margins of his texts. He writes in this introduction,

> As for the matters that have been important in my exchanges with Japanese researchers, there is a particular point to be emphasized. In Germany today one has, in philosophy, lost the belief in an "object" *(Sache)* that exists independently from the composition of an individual man, and that approaches him as something impersonal. One thinks that in "worldviews" *(Weltanschauung)* everything depends on either the individual or the historical and national conditions under which groups live. "Objective" science, therefore, cannot provide the objects *(Sache)* for philosophy and occasionally—and this is only "consequent"—one would like to know nothing more, in general, from science. Our "youth" . . . view different national and historical

cultures in their totality as forms, which emerge and dissolve like mere creatures, and between them there is to be found no overlapping, objective community that realizes, through various peoples and times, a continuous development of a "general human" culture. There are, one says, many sciences that come and go, but not a single, permanent science, least of all in philosophy. One calls it "relativism" and it appears—despite Plato's *Theatatus*—very "evident."

In this regard, exchanges with my Japanese colleagues have been very instructive. In them we are confronted with agents of a culture that not only originates in a locale far removed spatially, but also is one whose differences in content are more drastic than those between the European cultures with which we are acquainted. The difficulties of mutual understanding must be greater than those that standardly exist between the various nations of Europe. Nonetheless, as I "experienced" it, these colleagues were sooner or later brought, not only in the realm of logic (quickly overcome), but also in questions of aesthetics, ethics, and even religious philosophy, to a common and purely objective realm, such that discussions of national and historical differences no longer played an essential role.[50]

In this introduction, Rickert is addressing the cultural relativists in Germany, whose ethnic nationalism was already beginning (in 1924) to undermine the cosmopolitan idea of culture that was at the foundations of cultural science. In the face of these worldview philosophies, Rickert tried to reestablish an objective relationship between the individual subject and the matters of philosophical inquiry. In exhibiting an admiration of his Japanese colleagues, he was criticizing the rise of ethnic nationalism in Germany, whose historical basis lay in World War I, as well as in colonialism in Africa and, to a lesser extent, Asia.[51] Therefore, his academic interactions with students from Japan became a test case for the universality of German cosmopolitanism. Just as Sōda saw Europe as a separate unity from Japan and Asia, Rickert thought of the agents of Japanese culture as representatives of a homogeneous people from outside Europe. Cultural and linguistic distinctions allowed for the demarcation of Europe and non-Europe. He asserted the capacity of world culture to overcome ethnic nationalism within the nation and the continent of Europe more broadly. However, Rickert failed to notice a certain compatibility between the ethnic nationalisms he criticized and his idea of an "overlapping, objective community" that could be established through a historical development that would "move through the multiplicity of peoples and times." His idea that there did exist, or should exist, an objective unity to global community instituted a homogeneity of historical time that conflated the cosmopolitan and the national. Through logic quite similar to ideas of assimilation in colonial Korea, Rickert marked his Japanese colleagues as both cultural outsiders to Europe and tremendous assimilators, anthropological proof of the power of the German language and German philosophy to mediate the communications of the general cosmopolitan community and not just a single ethnos.

While the German state had yet to reassert its imperial ambitions in the mid-1920s, questions of national language and translation in culturalism are rendered more complex by the history of culturalism's place within the Japanese imperial project. The figuration of dominant and subordinate languages was not precisely the same for colonized intellectuals, such as the subject of the next chapter, the Korean novelist Yi Kwang-su. However subordinated Japanese science was to European science for Sōda, and however reminiscent Rickert's views on culture are of Japan's assimilation policies, the relationship between their societies was not precisely colonial. Historians in South Korea have traced the educational policies of the Japanese colonial state's Department of Education following the Treaty of Portsmouth of 1905 and the Japan-Korea Annexation Treaty of 1910. In her informative study of education policy, Kim Kyŏng-mi emphasizes the centrality of Japanese-language education in policies for middle school–aged children.[52] The Department of Education justified the emphasis on language education in normal schools by claiming that knowledge of the Japanese language was common knowledge necessary in everyday life. In this way, the spread of Japanese was meant to expand the sphere of communicability between national subjects to the colony. The idea of necessary common knowledge initially served the instrumental needs of the colonial state in its expansion of Japanese national education into the colony. It was the colonial aspect of the process of Japanese becoming what Sōda calls a "generally understood world language of science." As Kim points out, as Japanese became regarded as the language of science and commerce, and a means toward upward mobility, acquiring knowledge of Japanese could lead to the improvement of one's economic and social standing (although she also discusses the problem of overeducation and unemployment).[53]

The ease with which the Department of Education bureaucrats posited the unity of Japanese in their theories of colonial education is striking. Since the 1980s, there has been a great deal of scholarly work on the *genbun itchi* (unification of speech and writing) movements of the late Meiji period. Karatani Kojin historicized this movement as part of Japan's nation-building project in the late nineteenth century, and compared it to other national language projects, from Dante's use of the Italian vernacular to earlier discussions of language in Japan's Tokugawa-period national studies *(kokugaku)*.[54] Considering that the debates on the unification of speech and writings had reached their apex only a couple decades earlier, it is significant that the Department of Education documents that Kim cites refer to "Japanese" and "the spread of Japanese" without any uncertainty concerning the unity of the language or the identity of its spoken and written forms. As Gauri Viswanathan first showed in relation to British imperialism in India, the national language and the national literary tradition were only canonized and organized through colonial education.[55] Likewise, intellectuals and bureaucrats declared the complete unification of speech and writing and the self-identity of the speaking subject of Japanese—in other words, the formation of the national language—contemporaneously with the institution of colonial education and the figuration of Taiwanese and Koreans as nonnative speakers.

In the 1920s, under cultural policy, the governor-general did not place an outright ban on the use of the Korean language in schools or eliminate *han'gŭl* publication, even as Japanese became the primary language of global science and commerce for the empire. In addition to responding to perceived threats to the ethnic language, which were well founded despite the easing of censorship and regulation that came about through cultural policy, most attempts to form the Korean national language, such as the work of the Korean Language Research Group, nonetheless departed from the culturalist principle that national language is one requirement for belonging to modern humanity. Many of the colonized intellectuals who worked to develop a Korean national language were also involved in the discourses of culturalism and cultural science, and drew from the models provided by the German Reformation, Romanticism, and neo-Kantianism, as well as discourses in Japan proper such as the unification of speech and writing.

One unfortunate consequence of the culturalist view of national language in colonial Korea was that it granted the linguistic unity of Japanese, and therefore legitimated it in colonial assimilation, in order to provide a model for Korean national language and communicative translation. As in colonial social theories of personhood, however, this view of the Japanese language was often referenced vis-à-vis German intellectual history. For Yi Kwang-su, the spread of *han'gŭl* had a Christian basis, and Martin Luther's conscious creation of a vernacular German national language through the translation of the Bible became his model for the development of Korean.[56] In a series of essays in which he delineates the positive and negative aspects that Christianity had brought to Korea (1917), Yi lists the formation of a Korean national language as one of Christianity's significant contributions:

> The sixth benefit that Christianity has brought to Korea is the spread of *han'gŭl*. The Christian church is actually what has given to Koreans the idea that *han'gŭl* is also writing. The invaluable Old and New Testaments and the Psalms have been translated into *han'gŭl*, and since then the authority of *han'gŭl* has emerged and spread. In the past, there were colloquial interpretations of Chinese scriptures, but these were not widespread and were so unskillful that one could hardly call them translations. They were just spewed forth.
>
> However, we can say that even though it is not yet complete, the translation of the Bible is pure Korean language. If Korean writing and Korean language are to truly become dishes on which we can serve elevated thought, then the translation of the Bible is a good beginning.

> If in the future Korean literature is constructed, then on the first page of the history of this literature, the translation of the Old and the New Testaments will be recorded.⁵⁷

The idea of cosmopolitan individuality in the Japanese empire was often connected to some version of Christianity and Yi claims that the very foundations of the national language and national literature lay in the possibility of translating scripture. Missionaries and Christian nationalists saw the language created from a translation of the Bible to be a potential foundation for a national language community. For Yi, who sought more than anything to free the Korean language from what he saw as the premodern, imperial, and overly pictographic regime of literary Chinese, the nationalization of the individual depended upon the formation and spread of literary *han'gŭl,* which he imagined to be a pure signification of the orality of the Korean language as opposed to the imposition of the regime of writing that Chinese characters had placed on Korean national subjectivity.

As a critic of Confucianism and the stagnation of traditional Chinese literary culture, Yi also turned to Japan for a model of translation and speech suitable to modernity. In the following passage from a later essay, "On the Korean Nation" (1933), he reiterates the culturalist idea that culture is the totality of human historical activity, but turns to the universalizing capacity of language in stating that language is the foundation and the spirit of this encompassing culture. He also explains why translation is necessary for this cosmopolitan view of modern nationality:

> That which constructs the essential elements of the nation is culture. Politics, philosophy, literature, art, science, customs, interests, and so on are included in culture. However, needless to say, what lies at the foundation of all of these is language.
>
> Language is the spirit of a nation, because language alone conveys the thoughts and emotions of the nation, allowing for conversation between one another, and for transmission to the next generation. . . . If the Koreans had not read the Four Books and the Three Classics in Chinese characters, but rather translated them into Korean, then they would not have been Sinicized.
>
> Even when the Japanese nation read Chinese writing, they interpreted *(segida)* it precisely into Japanese; therefore, they were not Sinicized like the Korean upper classes and sustained the characteristics and spirit of the Japanese nation.⁵⁸

Yi Kwang-su attributes the modernity of Japanese thought to the history and tradition of speaking and transliterating Chinese characters into Japanese. Yi sees such a tradition of translation between image and oral national language as a prerequisite for cultural autonomy, going so far as to claim that the Korean intellectual class of the Chosŏn period could not nationalize, and therefore was colonized, because it did not establish the "regime of translation" necessary for belonging to modern humanity.⁵⁹ As in Rickert's and Sōda's understanding, national language is not simply the preexisting mode of communication belonging to an ethnic group, but a medium through which the modern cosmopolitan view of culture can poetically establish its universality within a particular context. As I will describe in the next chapter, nationalizing the language and speech of the Korean peninsula was, for Yi, one of many means of humanizing the life of the population, of drawing Koreans out of the state of nature and into the world of culture. Positing the cultural nation in colonial Korea was not a way to break with imperial humanist discourse. Rather the nation was a concept through which to introduce a wholly new space and time in which the self-determining, free human subject establishes its national borders as internal borders between communicative national languages, thereby attributing to language the universalizing capacity to bring cultural practices and cultural life under the sway of the transcendental.

JAPAN'S AREA STUDIES: KOREA AS CULTURAL AND LITERARY REGION

The figuration of national language and the communicative translation between national languages is related to culturalism's cosmopolitan geography, and therefore to the racialization and normalization of space and the discursive construction of areas. In twentieth-century Japan and Korea, as well as in US area studies after 1945, liberal cosmopolitanism often arrived at the delineation of the nation as an area precisely through such a movement from the metaphysics of morals to the pragmatism of anthropology, or rather through the reciprocal relation between them. What Charles Mills refers to as the norming of space, which is involved in the movement from morality to anthropology, was powerful from Japan's institution of cultural policy in 1919 through the early Cold War era, when US area studies disciplines like modernization theory and cultural anthropology reworked many of the same principles that the discourses of culturalism in the Japanese empire had already articulated.[60] Modernization theory proposed a US-centered model of universal history, but empirical disciplines like cultural anthropology were necessary supplements, because they showed how the universals of modernization could at once mark the local differences within humanity and also contribute to the pragmatic transformation of local national contexts. Similarly, under cultural policy, the Korean nation form was the anthropological means to give a space and time to the transcendental principles of culturalism for colonial officials, Korean cultural nationalists, and migrant Japanese alike.

The collaboration between Japan's cultural rule and Korean cultural nationalists was characterized by a push and pull between different modes of anthropologizing universal history. For example, Ch'oe Nam-sŏn's debate with Japanese archaeologists was not about whether or not national history could make universal history commensurable with particular histories, but rather about the specific origins, cultural makeup, and geography of ancient Korea.[61] Reversing the relation between the world and Korea, Ch'oe went so far as to claim that Korea is the cultural and linguistic origin of Asia and humankind at large, in articles with titles like "Korea and the Common Language of the World."[62] Likewise, migrant Japanese writers and intellectuals rarely questioned the cultural homogeneity of Korea or the continuity of its cultural history, although with a very different sense of how Korean particularity related to cosmopolitan universality. Just as Kuwaki and Sōda thought of culture as the aggregate of all human historical activity in its fundamental difference with nature, prominent colonial Japanese writers such as Arai Tetsu and Kitagawa Sukehito defined the "local color" of Korea through a comprehensive and encyclopedic cultural history that included art, literature, architecture, language, politics, myth, and any other object that could be interpreted through the human sciences. In this way, the culturalist framework of universal history inaugurated modern area studies in East Asia. By transforming empirical anthropology into the epistemological double of a priori universal history, culturalism did not simply construct Koreans as the primitive Other; it also constructed the area and the nation form called Korea as a local, spatiotemporal incarnation of the transcendental human as defined by the human sciences.

The area studies texts produced about Korea during the Japanese empire are innumerable, particularly if we include metropolitan political science, colonial government documents, and scholarly histories. However, the literature and scholarly work of Japanese migrants to Korea are perhaps the most revealing because they show the degree to which culturalist ideas informed the organization of knowledge and the mediation of cultural difference even for those living their everyday lives in colonial Korea. In the preface to *The Dictionary of the Intrinsic Colors of Korea*, a significant document of Japan's area studies, the editor Kitagawa Sukehito writes,

> In order to clearly exhibit the intrinsic color—the local color or regional color—of Korea, I decided to seek out and pick more than two thousand terms from the fields of custom, convention, religion, religious festivals, music, sport, astronomy, geography, governmental institutions, education, hygiene, commerce, finance, industrial arts, mining, farming, forestry, fishing, aquatic products, animals, plant life, and history.[63]

Printed in colonial Keijō, or present day Seoul, in 1932, this text can be characterized as a form of area studies knowledge because of the broad disciplinary orientations that are included in its lexicographic mode of organization. The only unity that could possibly hold together these various fields of knowledge in a single text is the area Korea, a hypothetical space in which the various objects of these various sciences connect with one another under the specificity of the anthropologically and linguistically defined territory. In terms of temporality, all of these very different objects are related to one another because they are part of the same cultural history and cultural history includes everything performed and constructed consciously by humans. However, the human is more than the transcendental subject of cultural history; it must take local, empirical forms. It is not just the definition of "Korea" as a territory that makes it an object of area studies in the Japanese empire, but also this interplay between transcendental ideas about human historical activity and the localization of these ideas through the nation form. "Local color" was the most prominent anthropologizing concept for colonial culturalists like Kitagawa.

Poetry was one field in which culturalist discourse confronted the limits to its knowledge without being able to return coherently to the transcendental determination of space, time, and the human. In its migratory forms of knowledge and literature, Japan's area studies opened up culturalism to the possibility of its disorientation. Probably the most important poet with a culturalist bent who wrote in colonial Korea is Arai Tetsu. Pushing against the unity of national language proposed by many culturalists, Arai became a kind of bilingual writer, titling his collection of haiku poems about Korea カチ (1930) (a katakana transliteration of the Korean word for "together"). While themes of assimilation and brotherhood between colonizer and colonized are undoubtedly a significant part of his poetry, it also tends to move outside, however occasionally and inadvertently, the typical play between Japanese national exceptionalism and the logic of cosmopolitan assimilation.

Compared to the philosophy of culturalism, Arai's poems often speak for the colonized in a more transcultured and translated voice. In the following poem, "The Magic of Architecture," Arai uses the Korean word for "the universe" or "the whole world" *(unae)*, marking textually the translation involved in positing the concept of the world. He marks the foreignness of the word with diacritic points, italicized in my translation, as if to at once cite, appropriate, and be transformed by the speech of the colonized. He does the same with the name for heated water pipes placed in the floors of buildings, or *ondol*, which were an object of fascination for many migrant architects and writers.

THE MAGIC OF ARCHITECTURE (1930)

Arai Tetsu

When I walked one day
The *whole world*
Was an expansive field
When I walked one day
The *whole world* was crushed
There were tens of trees set up there
When I walked one day
A magnificent *ondol* was built
Supported by earth and small stones

In fewer than five days
It was constructed
The magic of architecture

The architecture of the simple
And we could say free
Ondol
Thick earthen walls
Shut out the midsummer sun
And fill the air with coolness
The fire beneath the floor
Re-creates the joy of the southern countries
While the snow flies in the dead of winter
Making the indoors into heaven

With muddy walls
Low to the ground
Shabby silhouettes
Unsullied by ostentation
Standing there wild
Out of the surrounding nature
These houses formed themselves
Truly
There live the natural people wearing white clothes
Magic we should praise
Transported to the present world
From ancient origins
The mysterious architecture of the *ondol*[64]

Arai's mode of foreignizing and domesticizing in this poem is in many ways caught in the movement of supplementation involved in the philosophy of culturalism, whereby the whole world is reflected in Korea as anthropological object and Korea, in turn, becomes worldly as its "ancient origins" gain a "magical" connection to the general human capacity for architecture. He writes of the "natural people wearing white clothes," the traditional clothing of the Korean peasantry, and puts himself in the position of speaking the language of modern culture for them. On the other hand, the poem also imagines the limits to the world somewhat differently from the philosophy of culturalism's articulation of external borders as internal ones through the regime of translation and its transformation of the limits of knowledge into the very regulative principles of knowledge. There is a suggestion, at least, of a bilingual poetic language through which the human being might write not as a localized transcendental subject, but rather as a constantly translating and translated being. In the philosophy of culturalism, cultural value contributes to the architectonic of reason, to the extension of its constructive power to its fullest potential. Arai's poem inverts constructive reason into "the magic of architecture." On the one hand, he occludes the subjectivity of Koreans, who as "natural people" perform their architecture unconsciously. On the other hand, like Rousseau's noble savage, the architecture of the natural Koreans is idealized for its simplicity and freedom. He praises its lack of ostentation and the way it seems to emerge magically out of the landscape. This invocation of magic points to another kind of telos in culturalist anthropology, a discourse that otherwise sees the goal of a fully formed person as existing at the opposite pole from the lack of consciousness found in nature and natural humans.

In my reading of culturalism, there is not a stable binary between civilization and barbarism, but rather this sort of interplay between the signs of civilization and barbarism, and the eventual arrest of this play through the arbitrary distinction between the person and the natural people. Arai's poetry, like most migrant culturalist discourse, points at once to the instability of transcendental knowledge in a region of translation where self and other, transcendental and empirical, and civilization and barbarism threaten to blur permanently into each other. In this poem, however, we can also see how "magic" as the inversion of reason can function just as normatively. The cultivated spectator is still the subject who sees and reasons about what he sees. The poetic voice is alienated from the spontaneity of natural people and the divine, and therefore must speak for them in order to arrest the play of signs that exposes the properly human subject to the limits of the colonizing culture. The poetic voice speaks for the natural people by declaring, through a celebration of local color, the magic of its own thinking reflected back to it as an ideal otherness.

Despite this inversion of reason and magic in which each becomes the mirror of the other on each side of the binary of culture and nature, the virtue of Arai's poetry is that it points more clearly to the problem of the limit in the anthropology of culturalism. Whereas the philosophy of culturalism posited the pure form of general cultural value as the limit concept for knowledge, turning what is beyond the scope of concepts into the very ethical norms for concept formation, his poetry recognizes the limit of what he can know as the migrant colonial subject, particularly in the turn to bilingual writing and the disruption of the hypothetical unity of national language upon which the philosophy of culturalism established the localized transcendental subject. His use of the Korean word *unae* rather than *sekai* as the proper name for the world inserts the difference of translation precisely at the limit where the philosophy of culturalism hypothesizes the unity of the idea grounded in national language. It suggests that the proper name for the world is not an idea through which ethnic worlds and the cosmopolitan world can be unified, but only ever a translation or transliteration of its foreign name. Arai recognizes the convolution of languages, which remains largely hidden in the localization of the universal that we find in the communicative model of translation belonging to the philosophy of culturalism. The connection between the universal moral practice of the human subject and its particular origins only gains its coherency through the translation of a modern anthropological universal. Arai's poems suggest that we can only represent this translation as a direct communication between two ethnic worlds by shrouding the magic of poetics in the abstraction of the human will and its general culture. However unintended, this ability of the anthropological perspective of the area studies intellectual "in the field" to be disrupted in translation brings to the fore the semiotic limits of the idealism of the philosophy of culturalism, even if Arai does not directly confront the way that the inversion of reason into magic also means that the binaries of culture and nature, the person and the natural people, are themselves myths, part of a magical thinking invented to mediate his experience of social difference.

2

The Colony and the World
Nation, Poetics, and Biopolitics in Yi Kwang-su

What is the difference between a nation that has the life view that "the universe is a production of the ego" and "the essence of the ego is perpetual activity and conquest" (Fichte), and a nation that can only cry out, "Alas! There is nothing you can do about Fate"?

—YI KWANG-SU

In Yi Kwang-su's early stories, such as "Maybe Love" (1909) and "Yun Kwang-ho" (1918), he portrays the internal emptiness and coldness of his young protagonists.[1] The eponymous protagonist Kwang-ho receives a scholarship to study in Japan, but feels isolated, disconnected, and alone. Even as he is externally very successful as an economics student at K University (Keio), Yi compares his interiority to an icy cave, to a void deepening inside of him. His family and friends warn him not to work too hard, but he remains driven to exhaust himself in his studies. The gap between his external successes and his internal feeling of extreme lack reaches a crisis point when he feels that he can have no ideals concerning society because he has not felt and expressed romantic love. After his feelings for another young man, P, are unrequited, he commits suicide.

How do such stories of lack, isolation, and disappointment relate to Yi's other works, in which the nation and the enlightenment of the nation provide a political framework to rethink the relationship between desire, love, morality, and national community? What happens to Yi's ideas and his fiction in the passage from finitude, death, and the meaninglessness of individuality to the idea that a national community with a national literature and language can extend the life of the individual beyond his or her own mortality? Yi conceives of the Korean cultural nation and Korean national literature as a means of conquering finitude and finding a way into humanity and the world through the poetic formation of the national self. In order to understand how he does so, and how this project amounts to a biopolitical project of literature and philosophy, it is necessary to compare his work with that of his teacher, Kuwaki Gen'yoku, but to also situate them, despite all of their peculiarities, within the problem of the human in modernity. More specifically, I read Yi's works through the problem of the moral genus-being and the way that Yi turned to culture, aesthetics, and education at the point of uncertain connection between universal morality and the unformed external and internal landscapes of the colonial nation and the national self.[2] Yi began this biopolitical project of reforming individual life practices with the Korean nation as its purpose, but by 1941, in "The Relation between Life and Death," he was conceiving of this life-and-death relation between the individual and the totality vis-à-vis the Japanese nation-state and its world-historical mission: "That which most often demands death from a human life is the state. It is not an exaggeration to say that in the history of humanity war never ceases and that the majority of history is war or preparation for war. How many wars have there been throughout the world in the last fifty years?"[3] In examining the assimilatory effects of the philosophy of culturalism and life philosophy in colonial Korea, it is important to trace how the attempt to construct a moral Korean self in the 1920s was epistemologically and politically compatible with Yi's later advocacy of using individual Korean lives for the perpetuation of the Japanese nation-state. I argue that this compatibility was enabled principally through moral concepts of universality, the connections made between morality and aesthetic education, and a biopolitical relation between the individual and the totality expressed through an anthropological discourse.

As mentioned in the introduction, in order to confront the freedom of action in modernity, a whole network of discourses around practice developed in the Japanese empire of the 1920s. In culturalist discussions of practice, education was primary, and it was the means toward cultural development. Although it was no longer suitable for ethical action to be mechanical behavior, culture gave the subject a foundation for sound judgment and facilitated the internalization of moral maxims. It provided the human with a proper ethics without practice being reduced to the mechanistic adherence to principles of morality. Yi Kwang-su distinguished the cultural development of an autonomous, moral individual from the "natural" or "mechanical" education of Chosŏn period (1392–1897) Confucianism.[4] He circumvented the question of popular sovereignty and developed a cultural nationalization project that emerged out of distinctions between heteronomous, sovereign law and the internal, spiritual cultivation of modernity.

Therefore, beginning with "On the Reconstruction of the Nation" (henceforth "Reconstruction"), he emphasized that the reconstruction of Korean national character toward the telos of the person *(in'gyŏk)*, the exemplar of self-legislated and universal morality, was more urgent than national liberation in the sense of political sovereignty, and was indeed foundational preparation for it. Therefore, national reconstruction was to begin and end with morality as visible anthropologically and empirically in cultural practices: "In reconstructing a nation, we must begin from morality, which is the foundation of its nationality *(minjoksŏng)*."⁵ Furthermore, Yi tied the capacity for a specifically self-legislated and self-conscious morality to aesthetics and art, because for the human subject to act both autonomously and universally he or she had to arrive at moral freedom through aesthetic and cultural experience rather than by following a heteronomous law dictated by predetermined relations. One could certainly call this a displacement of the problem of colonialism and Korea's loss of sovereignty into a cultural and aesthetic problematic. However, this displacement is politically ambiguous and not "antinational" *(panminjok)*, because everything that culturalists argued concerning the formation of a Korean national self suggests a popular nation-building project mediated by journalism and literature, a project that asked the people of the Korean peninsula to make themselves into modern Koreans by committing to the moral and cultural practices of the ideal individual, the person. In connecting the Korean nation to the world through anthropology and moral universality, Korean cultural nationalists such as Yi imagined that the colonized nation could gain a cultural connection to humanity that transcended the mechanical workings of sovereignty and statecraft. However, just as culturalism differentiated humanity anthropologically in relation to the regulative idea of the person, Yi's project to cultivate individuals capable of moral practice also depended on anthropological and psychological concepts that could code the differences internal to the Korean nation—traits, behaviors, emotions, languages, and customs.

In 1922, Yi called the conscious transformation of human cultural life "reconstruction" *(kaejo)*, a term borrowed from the post–World War I Wilson Doctrine.⁶ However, in place of the doctrine's term for sovereignty, "self-determination," he used a term derived from Japanese translations of Kant, "self-consciousness" *(Selbstbewusstsein, chagak)*. Yi's political essays and fiction show how in the aftermath of the March First Movement, the culturalist idea of the self-conscious subject became integral to the cosmopolitan and liberal understanding of the individual, his or her education and formation, and his or her relation to the nation and the world. Yi's political essays and his fiction are all expressive of a philosophy of practice that states that the individual must transform himself or herself into a cosmopolitan person at the same time as the national spirit, the vernacular national language, and the technology of national literature promise to preserve the life of this individual beyond his or her death. In this sense, Yi's notion of reconstructing Koreans is a pragmatic political project of reforming human life so that it can belong to both general world culture and national culture as the local sphere of difference.

Yi's intellectual path led from an early engagement with neo-Kantianism, Lev Tolstoy, and the White Birch Group (Shirakaba), through an admiration of Adolph Hitler's patriotism and blood nationalism, to support for the ethnic unity of Japanese and Koreans in the 1940s. The overall trajectory of Yi's work from the 1910s to the 1940s shows that a culturalist cosmopolitanism centered on morality, with its teleological claim to be gradually forming a community of persons, could transmogrify into a mythopoeic and fascist discourse of blood, ideal leadership, and the nation as organic totality. For much of the scholarship on Yi, the difficult contradiction to understand is how Yi then came to give up altogether on the Korean nation in changing his name to Kayama Mitsurō and supporting the complete subsumption of Korea into Japan in the 1940s. I would certainly not argue that Yi's whole career is somehow continuous, or that the transformations in his thought are simply variations of his essential "pro-Japanese" character. However, in general epistemological terms, there are important continuities between the modes of enlightenment that he advocated in the early 1920s, the period of Korean blood nationalism, and his attempt to appropriate Japanese nationality and culture. These are the continuities with which I am interested.

The centrality of a moral cosmopolitanism in Yi's nationalist ideas cannot be overemphasized. In fact, one could say that the anthropological construct of a future moral world took precedence over the nation, but that the nation was vital to the survival of the cosmopolitan individual, because without it that individual would remain anonymous, internally empty, and without a community to preserve his or her life. The biopolitics of the individual and the nation we find in his work was a biopolitics of cultural cosmopolitanism, because making the nation adequate to the world meant first transforming the individual's everyday life to suit the requirements of modernity. In this sense, the path of Yi's thought presents us with a concrete case of how a cosmopolitan humanism that seeks the biopolitical transformation of life through the pragmatic application of anthropology is compatible with the imperial project. In the way that this mode of cosmopolitan humanism discusses the cultivation of the anthropologically defined natural substrate in order to form a world community and a national community guided by leaders, such humanism is also a prefiguration of the biopolitics of the late Japanese empire.

Assimilation in Korea has historically been discussed as a question of the national status of ethnic minorities in the Japanese empire. However, scholars such as Kim Hyŏn-ju and Hwang Chong-yŏn have looked in more detail at the epistemological and scientific underpinnings of Yi's and other intellectuals' gradualist nationalism and their support for Japanese empire.[7] Kim has shown that Yi's appropriation of ideas of culture and civilization led him to view the capacity for collective planning, particularly in the realm of spirit, as a necessary condition for the formation of a nation-state and a modern society. Hwang has explained how notions of civilizational, historical, and scientific progress informed Yi's naturalization of modern, secular subjectivity. This chapter departs from similar concerns, but it addresses more specifically Yi's reading of the empirico-transcendental doublet of modern humanism, and the ways that the very notion of the human being as the subject and object of knowledge in modernity contributed to the assimilation of colonial intellectuals. In order to do so, it emphasizes three central concerns of culturalist philosophy that Yi picked up from Kuwaki Gen'yoku and applied in each of his phases: life, morality, and art.

For a cosmopolitan intellectual like Yi, assimilation did not primarily mean becoming Japanese in the 1920s, but rather assimilating to the culturalist notion of the human being as a genus formed through the reconstruction of everyday cultural practice and the bios that enacted it. He thought of this reconstruction as a contribution to the unity of world culture. The discourse of assimilation meant more than the imposition of Japanese national identity; it asked Korean individuals to consciously transform the raw material of their natures into something worldly and culturally human. It meant liberating human life from nature while at the same time teaching it to obey the laws and duties of freedom. It meant reconstructing human life according to its genus-being, or self-legislated morality, and through modern aesthetic means, or art.

CULTURAL RECONSTRUCTION

Culturalism was most influential among those Korean liberals who were concerned with the enlightenment and modernization of individuals and the creation of a national culture through which individual cultural achievements could be preserved. At Waseda University in Tokyo, Yi Kwang-su studied in the philosophy department, where he was a student of Kuwaki Gen'yoku from 1915 to 1918. During this period, he began to formulate his theses for the reconstruction of the Korean nation. Because he started his project for national reconstruction before Japan's institution of cultural policy in 1919, his fiction and philosophy were by no means only a response to changes in colonial policy. However, after 1919 there was an increased emphasis on the cultivation and self-empowerment of the subject in discourses of Korean nationality, a kind of cultural nationalism that Sin Ch'ae-ho, in an essay from 1923, showed was quite compatible with Japanese colonial rule.[8]

In Yi's understanding of cultural history in the 1920s, appearing most famously in "Reconstruction" (1922), cultural reform and historical progress required the formation of the individual national self, but forming this national self was also a process of humanization, and therefore a cosmopolitan project.[9] Yi borrowed the term "reconstruction" from post–World War I discussions, but emphasized its spiritual and moral meaning more than its material and infrastructural one. For him, "reconstruction" in Korea referred to something more fundamental than the call for social reforms, democratization, and the liberation of women. It referred to the complete pragmatic reconstruction of the national character of Koreans, from their current entrapment in the fatalism of nature to a self-conscious and free national self formed through culture. In an earlier essay that questions the idea of fate and promotes self-strengthening as a practice of freedom, Yi writes, "What is the difference between a nation that has the life view that 'the universe is the property of the ego' and 'the essence of the ego is perpetual activity and conquest' (Fichte), and a nation that can only cry out, 'Alas! There is nothing you can do about Fate.'"[10] Yi's quotation of Fichte is apt, because the philosophical concerns of his essays and fiction are closely related to those of German idealism: how to overcome mechanism and create an organic relation between the individual and the national totality; how to engender self-consciousness in national individuals; how to manufacture a national self through language, culture, and literature; how to establish institutions of education that could nationalize students while promoting and guiding their use of freedom.

Yi begins "Reconstruction" by situating the problem of reform in Korean society within a global concern for reconstruction in the aftermath of World War I. He invokes a world mood for reconstruction in order to make his argument for nationalization, a mood that requires an emotive response on the part of Koreans. He states that the "thoughts of world citizens *(segyein)*" are commanded by the need to rebuild the world out of the ashes of war: "All of the voices of the contemporary world of thought are saying, 'reconstruct the world of imperialism into the world of democracy,' 'reconstruct the world of competition for survival into a world of mutual aid,' and 'reconstruct the world of respect for men and the denigration of women into a world of equal rights for men and women.'"[11] The call for the fundamental reconstruction of the Korean national character does not come from any local political situation, but rather from "the human heart."[12] The world's desire for reconstruction provides an emotive impetus for the movement for reconstruction in Korea and the pronoun "we" shifts rather effortlessly between a community of world citizens and Korean national subjectivity. The reader is drawn into a crucial moment in global politics, a moment of both crisis and potential. The nation and the historical individual are both spurred on by the collective mood of the world. To be interpellated by Yi's discussion of the nation was also to be hailed as a subject of a world human community, a community with sensibilities and emotions tied to the circumstances of a collective human history. A decade later, in 1932, he would discuss this ongoing crisis and opportunity as an "exceptional time," a time that required the spiritual dedication of "exceptional individuals."[13]

In "Reconstruction," Yi used two main anthropological criteria for the modernization of Korean national subjectivity: the neo-Kantian distinction between cultural and natural phenomena and Gustav Le Bon's differentiation between fundamental and attributed traits of national peoples.[14] Yi's mode of historical comparison references culturalism when he discusses the difference between natural change and purposive change. According to Yi, civilized individuals and nations are characterized by their capacity for planning historical transformations.

They participate in the creation of cultural phenomena because they are free and because they belong to a cosmopolitan nation that can preserve the worldly meaning of their actions. On the other hand, individuals and nations without self-consciousness experience only natural, incidental changes. This distinction between nature and culture was derived from neo-Kantianism's distinction between the epistemologies of natural science and cultural science, with all of the entailed contrasts between mechanism and organism, spontaneity and freedom, fate and purposive consciousness. Through the discussion of human culture as something metaphysical and entirely outside of nature, Yi was able to code every previous event in Korean history, even the very recent March First Uprising, as having occurred in nature, as merely incidental occurrences without the mark of human will.[15]

To give the distinction between natural and cultural phenomena an anthropologically observable content, Yi borrowed the conservative sociologist Gustav Le Bon's differentiation between fundamental national characteristics and attributed national characteristics.[16] He stated that leaders could not transform the fundamental anatomical and psychological traits of individual members of the nation, but that they could change attributed traits that had developed historically. If Koreans hoped to reconstruct their national characters, to educate their daily life to fit the conditions of modern humanity, these attributed national characteristics had to be located and worked on pragmatically through social science, literature, and aesthetic philosophy. The leaders who could change these characteristics and bring about a cultural transformation were those individuals who had the fewest negative attributed traits. The human genus as regulative principle returns to the problem of governmentality in Yi's colonial nationalization project.

Yi gives many examples of other national reconstruction efforts, but focuses in particular on Socrates.[17] Socrates attempted to reconstruct the "nation" of Athens by going to the agora and discussing matters with the youth. While Yi states that Socrates should serve as a model for the intellectual leaders of national reconstruction, he was wary of Socrates's failure and his execution by the state that he attempted to transform. According to Yi, Socrates failed because his efforts at reconstruction did not create a collectivity that could transcend the finite individual.[18] Without such a collectivity, the possibility that the gains made by a single individual would be lost to history threatened the longevity of the enterprise of reconstruction. The collectivity capable of transcending the finitude of the individual is, in broad terms, the nation and, in narrower terms, the group of intellectuals capable of guiding reconstruction. In this sense, Yi thought that the logos of the individual, his or her ability to think with conceptual categories and self-consciousness, could only be sustained by a group with a shared language, a shared historical purpose, and a shared sentiment toward the global situation. The term "nation" *(minjok)* in Korea, as in Japan, was not a simplistic expression of ethnic nationalism that negated the histories of other nations, or a natural-scientific term for race, or an idea of the nation directly bound to political sovereignty. For cultural nationalists, the nation mediated between the individual intellectual, an international system of nations referred to as the world, and the local population that the individual sought to govern.

Yi refers to many past cases of individuals driving reconstruction, including the leaders of Japan's Meiji Restoration, Socrates and his failed attempts to reform Athens, and Lenin leading the Russian Revolution.[19] Yi thought of these sorts of historical comparisons between national histories as an example of applying reason, of bringing together the general and the particular. This mode of comparison led to inapt statements, such as his equation of the historical significance of the American Revolution and Russian Revolution as national reconstruction efforts. However, through such comparisons he introduced a powerful form of historical consciousness into the public sphere of colonial Korea. For better or worse, in the 1920s and 1930s it became common for intellectuals to reflect on the Korean national situation through universal history, which did not necessarily entail cooperation with imperialism, but could facilitate such cooperation. Through the philosophy of culturalism, for which the free acts of individuals are valued primarily, Yi elaborated a model of cosmopolitan history in which the cultivation of individual subjects of judgment *(p'andan chugwan)*, acting in the interest of national and world culture, brings about the pragmatic reconstruction of the Korean national character.[20] As in the Japanese political scientist Yoshino Sakuzō's theory of *mimponshugi*, which he distinguished from popular democratic sovereignty, the sovereignty of the people was less important than the cultivation of leaders who were capable of leading in the interest of the people. Such a group of leaders would transform Koreans and Korean national culture through art, literature, and daily practice, in order to bring them in line with general world culture.

Yi's views on reconstruction were based on cosmopolitan ideas concerning the universal faculties and values of the human subject. He early on appropriated a version of the Kantian system in asserting that the subject's primary faculties are reason, morality, and emotion.[21] Reason allows the subject to reflect upon its knowledge and judgment, in order to understand particular experiences in relation to the general knowledge that has accrued in civilization. It also enables one to view the Korean national situation by way of comparison with universal human history.[22] Modulating the usual political definition of popular sovereignty, Yi wrote, "Even if human reason is incomplete, we have no more certain sovereign beyond reason, and nothing to believe in beyond reason."[23] Reason is sovereign because through it the human can become aware of itself as a legislator of the world and reflect on that belief and responsibility. More specifically, the subject that Yi refers to as the subject of judgment has the power to reason about the relation between the general and the particular, to see Korea's particular situation as reflective of general world trends.[24] Reason allows the subject to reflect upon the application of the general knowledge of civilization to a lived experience that often seems incommensurable with that knowledge. However, because the particular did not always appear immediately commensurable with the general, Yi's model for enlightenment was poetic—the application of the general to the particular required a reformation of the particular. He thought that human life as it should be did not exist empirically in colonial Korean society, but that reason should bring it about. In his writings, "self-consciousness" means more than the epistemological subject's passive reception of phenomena; it must actively transform phenomena. The relationship between the general and the particular is not solely theoretical, but also a pragmatic application of knowledge, because reason becomes biologically and organically involved in a poetic process of forming the particular so that it can be commensurable with human culture in its generality.

This poetic relation between the general and the particular and its biopolitical dimension are the primary concerns of the remainder of this chapter. In this regard, Yi's appropriation of Fichte's idea of the "national self" as an ego "whose essence is infinite activity and conquest" suggests complicity, rather than conflict, between the universalist ideas of imperialism and the particularist ideas of self-formation of colonized nationalism.[25] We should not dismiss Yi as someone who warped the modern and cosmopolitan Kant to fit a xenophobic and antimodern political platform; his ideas about national subjectivity are too endemic to modernity, and too intimately intertwined with Kant's transcendental philosophy and cosmopolitanism, to be considered merely an antimodern response to enlightenment. Cultural nationalists' attempts to bring the colonized nation in line with the world of humanity became an internal colonial project directed at the natural raw material of the colonized people. Just as Fichte argued that Germans needed to be sculpted and made self-conscious of their Germanness in order to become proper human beings, thereby translating the imperial Napoleonic Code into a nationalist framework, Yi's own project conflated humanization and nationalization, translating tenets of Japanese culturalism concerning the formation of the person into a model for the formation of a Korean national self. Yi discussed the national people variously as an artwork, as a group of students in need of education, and as the raw material to be given shape, but he always did so through the discourses of universalist humanism.

FORMING LIFE FOR HUMANITY

Comparatively less attention has been given to a text on aesthetics that Yi also published in 1922, "Art and Life: The New World and the Mission of the Korean

Nation."[26] In it, Yi discusses the relation between art and morality in the anthropological project of bringing the Korean nation into the world:

> I think that the path to a happy life is in the teaching of Jesus "to make one's life moral" and in the words of Tagore "to make one's life artful." For each individual to be happy, it is necessary to make one's life artful, and for each individual to participate in the life of society, it is necessary to make one's life moral. In general each of these sides is present in the life of the individual and cannot be divided; they are the same individual life and social life....
> How, then, does one make one's life artful and moral?
> There are two ways, but their basis is the same.
> The first is the bodily and subjective reconstruction of the individual. Here, too, of course there is the moral side and the artful side. Through the moral we discard falsehood, slander, anger, indignation, resentment, and jealousy; however, other than falsehood and slander, which are matters of knowledge, all of these others are emotions. Because the power of action is a function of feeling more than knowledge, the center of moral cultivation is in the restraint of the lower emotions. Secondly, falsehood, slander, and all of the inferior emotions listed earlier were necessary to ensure one's survival in the life of the animal world or the life of past humanity, which had inferior culture, but in human life's construction of a happy new world close to the divine, we must root them out of the soul of every individual.[27]

Yi goes on to argue that such a rooting out of inferior thoughts and emotions is admittedly subjective *(chugwanjŏk)*, but that without this educational process no change in the objective *(kaekkwanjŏk)* political and economic conditions will be able to create a "new world" worthy of humanity's higher moral purpose. In this passage, Yi brings together many of his most central assertions about the need to transform human cultural life to make it both moral (Jesus) and artful (Tagore). First of all, subjective matters of spirit, particularly the emotions that are felt at the intersection between moral action, art, and aesthetics, are more significant than social and economic structures, and the moral and aesthetic education of the individual is a necessary condition for social change. In addition to his application of the idealism and normativity of culturalist causality to the individual, Yi adds a more overtly biopolitical dimension to the philosophy of culturalism in stating that "reconstructing" the individual culturally is primarily a matter of training the body, particularly the emotions that govern the states and actions of the individual body. Forming human life in Korea through culture and education will bring it in line with an incipient cosmopolitan order, a "new world," but this program will be enacted at a micropolitical level of everyday behaviors and poetic creations. This telescoping of the cosmopolitan scale into the minute emotions and dispositions of the individual was a significant aspect of the colonial governmentality and biopolitics of the philosophy of culturalism.

According to Yi, in addition to their differing notions of time and causality, the natural sciences and the cultural sciences also adhere to different notions of life, and educating the human means distinguishing its life from that of natural phenomena.[28] Intellectuals, educators, and students should lead the way in embracing a new concept of the human bios as neither spontaneous activity (that is, unconscious and unfree activity) nor mechanical activity (that is, activity directed by external cause). Yi thought that life should rather be seen as a force of poetics.[29] The organicist metaphors for culture were appropriate, because they position freedom neither in the purely spontaneous activity of nature nor in the mechanism of natural laws, but rather at the point where the human being, through its conscious and vital use of life, forms life consciously and becomes conscious through life. Culture became biopolitical in colonial Korea through the idea that the human being's primary vocation is to transform its bios *(saengmul)*, to enter the poetic force of life and to guide it consciously, in order to make it suit the practical and theoretical requirements of modernity.[30]

Within the borders of the organismic nation, Yi imagined the formation of the national self as a pragmatic action directed both at one's inner life and at the lives of others. This subject-and-object relation was often a complexly gendered relation. For example, the English teacher Hyŏng-sik, the main character of Yi's first long novel, *The Heartless* (1917), tells of his desire to help "sculpt" his two love interests into proper human beings, or persons.[31] Of the wealthier but less talented young woman, Kim Sŏn-hyŏng, he thinks of her as raw material and an unconscious machine, not yet a cultured and civilized person:

> She was like a machine that had been in a storage shed and never actually been used. She was not yet a person....
>
> One could say she was "virginal" and "pure of heart," but she was certainly not a human being. She was only potential material for a human being. She was like marble that was to become a sculpture. Marble became a sculpture with eyes and a nose only after it had been worked with a chisel. Similarly, someone like Sŏn-hyŏng would become a true human being only after she had received the fiery baptism of life and the "person" within her had awakened.[32]

If Sŏn-hyŏng is moral and pure, but lacks consciousness and artfulness, the other female protagonist, Yŏng-ch'ae, is artistic and talented, but at first lacks an independent sense of morality. She has a traditional education and traditional talents, but little independence, and is forced to become a courtesan *(kisaeng)*. A group of immoral, hypocritical men, including the dean of Hyŏng-sik's school, rapes her. She believes that it is her fault and decides to commit suicide, only to be saved by a modern woman named Pyŏng-uk. Hyŏng-sik sees both Sŏn-hyŏng and Yŏng-ch'ae as examples of human beings in their natural state, incapable of becoming proper independent individuals, or persons, through the fusion of art and morality discussed in "Art and Life." The milieu within which the protagonists will gradually become capable of both art and morality is cultural life and the cultural nation.

Although critical of the fatalism of his female counterparts, Hyŏng-sik does not assume that his own artistic and moral formation is complete. He takes on the role of pedagogue and patriarch simultaneously as he himself struggles with the formation of his own inner self. In its most effusive passages, the novel employs romantic metaphors of organic life to describe the formation and revelation of the inner self:

> The inner self within Hyŏng-sik had opened its eyes. He could now see the inner meaning of all existence with his inner eyes. The inner self within Hyŏng-sik had been liberated. A pine seedling hides within its shell, and is confined there, for a long time until, under the warmth of spring, it bursts with great strength through its shell and sprouts outward into the pitilessly wide world. Then it becomes tendrils, branches, leaves, and flowers. The inner self within Hyŏng-sik similarly constituted the seed of the person named Hyŏng-sik. This inner self had broken through its shell, sprouted into the wide world, and started to grow endlessly in the sunshine and dew.[33]

In passages like these, the blossoming of the self appears like the kind of infinite expanse of the ego that Yi contrasts to Confucianism in his quotation of Fichte. In other passages, particularly those critical of Elder Kim's superficial appropriation of "civilization" and the self-interestedness of the men who rape Yŏng-ch'ae, Hyŏng-sik denounces the lack of internal spiritual culture and emotion in Korean society.[34] He also laments the incompleteness of his own humanity. He struggles to apply the metaphors and technologies of self-formation to himself at the same time as he directs this artistry toward Sŏn-hyŏng and Yŏng-ch'ae, whom he perceives both as love interests and as artworks. A great deal of the drama in Yi's fiction emerges through such allegories, in which characters struggle to form their own bodies and minds while educating and forming others. It is a struggle to radically transform life through an internal spiritual revolution.

However, in *The Heartless,* it is not Hyŏng-sik who is able to save Yŏng-ch'ae from suicide and to encourage her to become educated. Another female character, a modern woman Pyŏng-uk, convinces her to take her talents and develop them. This assignation of personhood to women is ambiguous; at the end of the novel, this female-female friendship is subsumed into the national narrative when all of the young people see their personal growth in light of national reconstruction. Yi advocated vigorously for the education of women, but only insofar as it contributed to the reconstruction of the nation and the creation of persons. By 1935, he had distilled his reason for advocating the education of women to the nation's need for the biological reproduction and household training of persons:

> We must reconstruct the Korean nation, but those who have the most responsibility in that regard are Korean women, the wives and mothers. . . . "Person" refers to the unity of various emotional customs established on foundational beliefs and the various

sensibilities, manners, customs, and so on that emerge in the house and become the foundation of a person, as in the saying "habits at three years old cannot be corrected at nine." But women are the saints who carry the duty of household training.³⁵

Yi's advocacy of women's education did ask that "women's issues" be considered equally, but this value was assigned according to a culturalist idea of subjectivity and personhood whose teleology was the national reconstruction of customs and sensibilities rather than political equality. Therefore, despite the seemingly progressive ideas about female-female friendship and independent female personhood that appear in his works, one should understand them within the larger biopolitical project of reconstructing the cultural life of the nation, through which Yi was able to see the value of women's education primarily in the production of good "persons" in the youngest stages of life in the household.

What, then, of the larger project of forming and reconstructing cultural life? The philosophy of culturalism articulated by Sōda Kiichirō and Yi's teacher Kuwaki Gen'yoku provided Yi with a model for the individual human's development toward general consciousness (for example, cosmopolitan, transcendental subjectivity). He transformed this model for development into a more overtly biopolitical concept by emphasizing the cultural reformation of "life," by which he meant both biological life and everyday life, in his discussions of subject formation. Yi took up the idea that education is primary for moral training, but he was particularly concerned that education be suitable to life as temporal activity, which he opposed to the idea that life belongs to static, inorganic nature. In "On the New Life," he describes the difference between conscious and unconscious historical transformations by contrasting the differing temporalities of inorganic and organic nature.³⁶ He argues that the lives of Koreans are becoming temporal, in other words, that Koreans are entering both the temporal multiplicity of modernity and the temporal homogeneity of history. In an organicist manner, he argues that this change is tantamount to passing from inorganic to organic nature, a passage indicated by the modern character compound for "life": "As the two characters in the word 'life' indicate (生活), life is not something that takes the shape of a stone, but rather something that flows and transforms like an animal."³⁷ Yi goes on to argue that the new education and the new culture must be adequate to the new life of the modern era, when life has begun to transform and flow at the speed of organic nature rather than the inorganic geological time of the stone. However, this new education and culture must also master life consciously, so that the transformations and flows of the organism will not be left to chance, but rather will be the effect of a human will and a human history guided by what Yi repeatedly refers to as "purpose" *(mokjŏk).*³⁸

This biopolitical application of culturalism was explicit in Kuwaki's discussions of the need to govern life by the universality of the moral law and in Sōda's model for subject formation. Taking up the culturalist mission to reform physiological being toward the limit concept of general consciousness, Yi Kwang-su wrote frequently on the need to completely revolutionize the individual's life for both the individual and the nation to enter the modern era. In distinguishing between natural humans and cultural humans, and between natural education and cultural education, he translated the culturalist discourse of subject formation into colonial Korea, making colonial discourses concerning the necessity for culture to transform physiological being into the dominant idea of modernization. The universalism and biopolitics of culturalist ideas about subject formation allowed Yi, in the name of cosmopolitan community, to begin another colonial project internal to the colonial population. Nationalization in the name of cosmopolitan humanity can be considered an internal colonial project, and not only because Yi's culturalist rhetoric was consonant with the Japanese colonial state's appropriation of culturalism for cultural policy a few years later. *The Heartless* uses metaphors of organic life to figure the blossoming of the national self in the colonized country as a means of humanizing its population, of bringing the supposedly unconscious subjects of Korean society into the modern world, which requires self-consciousness and moral purpose.

This biopolitical perspective on modernity was in many ways a logical outcome of the philosophy of culturalism's discussions of cultural-historical time, cultural-historical causality, and education. Culturalism introduced new notions of each of these into colonial Korea. For the philosophy of culturalism, cultural-historical time is the time of human freedom and history is a record of free actions undertaken by individuals. Individual causality is the type of causality proper to cultural history and is opposed to the mechanical causality of nature. While nature functions according to mechanical cause and effect, cultural history is created by moral actions that have no determining cause other than the will of the acting person.[39] Education is necessary for this philosophy precisely because if human beings create history out of their own free will and their own free manipulation of life, then the will also has to be properly educated, so that it can form itself and form life according to some sort of self-administered law. In other words, without education, the teleology of cosmopolitan history could easily be jeopardized by the misuse of freedom, and the individual causality of human history could easily be the impetus for anarchy in history, historical knowledge, and the life to which they give shape.

Although Yi remained critical of many of the effects of Japanese colonialism, he appreciated the advancements in education made by Japan, particularly the way it had adapted educational methods to actual life *(silsaenghwal)*. In an early essay addressed to educators in 1916, Yi argued that among the countries of the East, Japan had "destroyed the old dreams" and "sought a new education based on actual life," and had therefore "become a powerful country in world civilization."[40] In more concrete terms, Yi supported basic Japanese national education as a foundation for equality in work, between classes, and for society as a whole. This education would instill fundamental ideas that students would carry with them as they progressed to higher levels of education (at specialty schools and the like).[41] However, upon this basic foundation, Yi also sought the more dynamic life of the cosmopolitan individual, in which he or she participated actively in the formulation of ideas that could transform the bios of the nation and the world. This education would be an improvement upon and refinement of the mere repetition of principles that Kim Kyŏng-mi described as the primary goal of early Japanese normal school education in Korea.[42]

In his statements concerning the need for a new education, Yi echoes J. G. Fichte's and Matthew Arnold's criticisms of mechanism in education, referring to the old education as natural education and the new education as "manmade."[43] Yi used the idea of new education, or "cultural education," most forcefully in his many criticisms of Confucianism and Confucian schools *(sŏdang)*, which he derided as forms of "natural education." In a criticism of Confucianism, he wrote, "A fourteen or fifteen year old who has received a manmade education is superior and stronger intellectually than an eighty-year-old man who received a natural education. Being human means being cultured."[44] Under natural education, the student is expected to gain practical knowledge through the repetition of prescribed behaviors and ethical principles (she or he becomes spontaneous in the bad sense). Conversely, the new manmade, cultural education would create the capacity for self-conscious spontaneity, judgment, and reason, which were all necessary for a sustained and reflective engagement with the cultural life of the nation and the world.

In "The Reform of the Individual's Daily Life Is the Basis for National Power" (1926), Yi discusses the kinds of ethical principles that culture should locate and cultivate in the individual life.[45] In this essay, Yi appeals to the seeds of good in the human and asks which older traits of the human should be developed through culture and education. Despite differences between individuals, he argues that there are certain customs that the national community can agree upon to be foundational. These customs are largely based on Christian ethics, but he nonetheless presents them as age-old rules for the behavior of the national community.

> These four are the custom and spirit that have become the basis for a healthy person.
> Among readers there may be some who think that number 5 [Do not hate, do not be jealous, do not get angry. Love. Live for men. Forgive. Make men happy and beneficent] is not a custom. Of course, psychologists discuss these factors as lasting tendencies of emotion and refer to them as "temperament." Shall we refer to them as "disposition"? However, "disposition" also results, after all, from the conventionalization of the operation of the emotions. A child who has grown up and learned manners under a wicked stepmother will develop, to a degree, the emotional tendencies of enmity, mistrust, and jealousy. Just the same, "disposition" is, after all, a custom of emotion, and in one's daily efforts one can nurture good dispositions and one can

nurture bad dispositions. Furthermore, what ethicists call "sentiment" comes almost entirely from education and cultivation.⁴⁶ The honor to love the truth and hate falsehood, to love good and hate wickedness, and to love beauty and hate ugliness, or, to put it more conventionally, the sentiment for truth, justice, and beauty—all of these come, finally, from the cultivation of customs; we call cultivation the "training of character" for the same reason. If an individual or a race does not have these noble virtues it is because it lacks cultivation, and if it did not have these virtues, would it be capable of acting nobly for a state or humanity? Certainly not.

However, all of these customs are formed in everyday life. They are actualized each time we do something in everyday life; each time we use a word more often, each time we clean a room a little more, each time we encounter another person, each time we grow and mature. There are counterexamples of degradation, like when children who work in a cigarette factory become addicted to nicotine little by little, and after two or three years their skin becomes very yellow. Therefore, I say to all my readers, "Before carrying out any revolution, you must revolutionize yourself. The way to revolutionize yourself is to revolutionize your everyday life."⁴⁷

It is revealing that Yi presents most of these rules as maxims that everyone should immediately agree are important, while the inclusion of emotions such as love, hate, jealousy, and happiness (#5) in a tract on ethics requires further elaboration. He asserts that dispositions have a natural element, but are also cultural, because patterns of emotion are cultivated over time. Sentiments, or generally held moral emotions like sympathy, are entirely the product of cultivation. He again expresses the importance of emotions for the "training of character."⁴⁸ This moral training cannot occur suddenly, but is rather a matter of transforming the daily life of the nation by gradually reorganizing the daily practices and emotional states of the individual. As suggested by the earlier discussion of Jesus and Tagore, of the moral and the artful, this cultural project is also a project of bringing the nation into the world and world culture.

At the end of this passage, Yi argues that the individual must first transform himself or herself before any dramatic collective change can occur. The reference to industrial labor is significant in this regard, because Yi focused on the damage that factory labor causes to the individual person and ignored any class dimension of labor exploitation. The theme that social classes could be overcome through proper individual cultivation appears frequently in his writings, particularly in his critiques of proletarian literature.⁴⁹ He argued often that social classes would disappear through the collective organization of the nation through national culture. In this passage, Yi pays particular attention to those individual practices that have collective significance, such as work ethic (the production of value), hygiene (the prevention of communicable disease), and consideration for others (an ethics of responsibility). The biopolitical regulation of the individual was simultaneously for the individual's own good and necessary for the overcoming of collective suffering caused by underdevelopment and disease.

Yi connects culture and cultivation to biopolitics; culture gives life to the individual and lack of culture amounts to letting oneself and one's nation die.[50] This life-giving capacity of culture is in its ability to perpetuate the life of an individual life beyond its own finite existence, to create a nation and a world that could preserve the works of the individual. Foucault's analysis of governmentality is concerned not with developing a theory of the state, but rather more with this individuating dimension of political thought and political technologies in their liberal, neoliberal, and fascist modes. Foucault pointed out that along with figuring the population and the people, discourses of modern government have dictated the terms of the governance of one's individual self. Governmentality implies an individual ethics that cultural nationalists like Yi Kwang-su assumed was underdeveloped during the Chosŏn period (1392–1895) and the Korean empire (1894–1910), which became an explanation for Korea's colonization by Japan. For these nationalists, Korea became a site where the national population had to be given form through individual morality, precisely in order to also preserve the individual and his or her cultural work.

In 1936, a few years before casting off his Korean identity altogether and attempting to "become Japanese," Yi again used the language of a secularized Christian humanism, an idealist language of self-abnegation and sacrifice, to describe how some select Korean individuals could transform themselves into valuable historical subjects and the Korean nation into a "world cultural nation":

> A life without ideas is a brutish life. The saying "in an intoxicated life, dreams die" expresses this fact. When people do not have ideas, they have already become slaves to the senses. When there is no task with greater meaning to which one strives and dedicates one's body, the animal instinct for food, color, and so on governs the spirit. Therefore, such a life is "brutish."
>
> Those people who value nothing other than the body are no different from beasts. Jesus valued human love more than the body, and all the martyrs of religion, science, and patriotism valued righteousness and truth above it. They all began from the idea that the value of a life lies in something more important.
>
> "Greater meaning" refers to this kind of idea. We call those who embrace this greater meaning "people of purpose" (chisa), and those who sacrifice their bodies for this greater meaning "righteous people" (ŭiin). The culture, freedom, and prosperity of a society are the flower that blooms from the blood of those people of purpose and righteous people who embrace the greater meaning that lies in these ideas. A society without people—both men and women—who embrace this greater meaning cannot but fall into ruin.
>
> The majority of people cannot hope to embrace a greater meaning and become people of purpose or righteous people. Still, in Korea those who have graduated from college or the university cannot be distinguished from among the ordinary people. In Korea, those who have graduated from college or the university receive a unique societal blessing and are a great force for reviving the whole of the Korean people.
>
> If these graduates considered adequately the duty to accept the expectations of the people, and of themselves, they would be greatly inspired, and would burn with the desire to serve. Aren't they the ones who will resolve the spiritual and material

poverty of Korea? Who else will educate the Korean people and lift them up to the highest levels of a world cultural nation?[51]

Through education, people of purpose become dedicated to a greater meaning by valuing more than their animal senses and their bodies, by valuing the ideas of freedom and culture that can only belong to human beings. Those who are capable of transforming their lives into something valuable become young leaders who will guide the Korean people, forming them into a cultural nation belonging to the world. Yi's appeal to the moral genus-being of the human as cosmopolitan subject is embedded in a series of Christian oppositions between bodies and ideas, brutishness and a valuable and meaningful life, and, ultimately, the purposelessness of nature and purposefulness of humanity. Despite this division between nature and culture, Yi states that the flowers of culture and freedom bloom from the blood of righteous people, incorporating nature metaphorically when discussing the teleological form of cultural life. Blood not only differentiates Koreans from other nations, but the righteous people and the people of purpose from the "majority of people" who "cannot hope to embrace a greater meaning."[52]

Already in 1933, in "On the Korean Nation," Yi made it clear that such patriotic invocations of the blood of righteous people were not only projective toward what Balibar calls the "ideal nation," but also projective toward the past, toward a "fictive ethnicity" of shared Korean origin:[53]

> What are the essential components of a nation? First, blood lineage is one of the primary components. Although we can presume looking at past history that the blood of the Han race, the blood of the Mongol race, and the blood of [the Japanese race] have flowed in the Korean people in some proportion, within the limits that the record of our nation can trace, we are not any other nation. We are a nation that has received the particular blood lineage of the Korean race.[54]

Although Yi's earlier enlightenment project for national reconstruction might seem at odds with this later discourse of blood lineage, these phases were in most respects continuous. The anthropological distinction in "Reconstruction" between fundamental and attributed traits brought to the fore the importance of distilling the positive natural and historical traits and developing them as aspects of modern life, consciously over time. Likewise, in "On the Korean Nation," Yi follows this claim for a substratum of blood lineage with discussions of what the national subject can actively do in the passage from nature to culture, with sections on national character (constituted by culture and language), as well as religion. Blood is a mythic symbol of a substantive yet malleable cohesion that was already implied by the poetic confluence of the transcendental subject and anthropological determination we find in Yi's earlier articulations of "Korean."

Both the moral-artistic articulation and the blood lineage articulation of the cosmopolitan-national individual reflect much more than an internalization of colonial racism. Although Yi's denigration of the current state of Koreans does suggest such internalization, the more powerfully operative regime was the anthropocentrism centered on ideas of human generality. In order to norm the space of Korea according to a universalist anthropological model, Yi transformed the external borders of the nation—for example, borders as they would appear on a map—into internal borders that could differentiate proper national subjects from the blood lineages of Japan and China and from the unconscious and premodern forms of "natural" life that had held back the Korean people in history. It is further on in "On the Korean Nation" where Yi discusses language as the universalizing medium that brings all historical activity under the sign of cultural history, and the litterateurs as the "technicians" who mold this language (see chapter 1).[55] In turning to literature as a technique for creating the national language, he was not simply inspiring civic spirit through art. He was attempting through the artwork to create an aesthetic experience of linguistic unity, cultural unity, and (by the 1930s) sanguine unity. This aesthetic experience was to serve as a foundation for the transcendental moral subject of modernity within the local sphere of the world cultural nation. This was an act of poetics performed to instill the greater meaning of a life governed by ideas within the vernacular sphere of communicative language and communicable sentiments, or common and general emotions that can direct proper practice.

In this respect, blood was simply the most naturalistic metaphor for the regulative distinction between the national population and its outside, and between the instincts of beasts and the sentiments of the proper human. In order to actively and poetically overcome the taint of the beast and the lasting effects of "other" blood lineages, the aesthetic project of national literature had to create, actively and poetically, a Korean national community made up of cosmopolitan-national individuals. After becoming a Japanese imperial subject, Yi again brought together a model of developmental cultural history and a poetic notion of bios in essays such as "Faces Change," which argues that the physical features of Koreans will gradually transform as they commit themselves to becoming Japanese.[56] His early romantic portrayals of the biological formation of the national self were primarily metaphorical, but they already pointed toward the more concrete penetration and technological transformation of the bios that he imagined to be the primary task of his later thought and fiction.

COSMOPOLITAN SENTIMENT AND THE ROLE OF LITERATURE

One primary consistency in Yi's conception of the bios, and in the mission to make life adhere to self-legislated moral laws, is his theories concerning emotions and their representation in literature. In the quotation from "The Reform of the Individual's Daily Life Is the Basis for National Power," Yi feels obliged to explain the new relation between emotions and ethics in modernity, because it is ultimately through emotions, particularly a love of others felt through love for the nation, that Koreans will also gain the capacity for universal moral practice necessary for modern subjectivity. For the life of the individual and the nation to belong to the culture of the modern world, subjects must not only revolutionize their behaviors and customs, but also cultivate their emotions over time, so that these emotions can properly guide their use of practical reason in history. For Yi, Confucian morality is based on principles of action entirely determined by one's familial or social relations to others. When action is determined by a dictate in this manner, there is no free will, and there is therefore no need for a nonconceptual source for moral judgment. Questions of beauty or artistry have no bearing on action, because in morality there is no need for a source of judgment besides the principle of action dictated by the type of relation. However, Yi argues that for free human individuals coming together to form a nation that supersedes social classes and the Confucian hierarchies, emotions must be freed from external determination while also coming to inform ethical decisions. For example, in "What Is Literature?" (1916) Yi argues that the writer must abandon given social norms and not fall into didacticism, because emotions are autonomous from the will and the mind. However, he also states that the beauty that one discovers in literature should also contribute to the civilization and acculturation of the national subject.[57] Emotions must be freed to pursue beauty but also must be an aspect of daily moral training and objects of cultivation throughout the lifetime of an individual and the history of a nation. Reforming the bios of the nation was not solely about behavior and custom, but also a matter of restructuring sensations, of providing an aesthetic and artistic education, so that emotions could become intentionally and consciously connected to practice.[58]

In various places Yi discusses this common emotion, created through literature, as a cure for the feudal class relations of the Chosŏn period and for the emerging class relations of colonial modernity. For example, in "Literature and 'Bourgeois'/'Proletariat'" (1926), he criticizes proletarian literature for dividing thoughts and emotions only according to social class.[59] He states that thoughts and emotions are different both for every individual member of humanity and also according to different social classes.[60] At the end of the essay, he asks how these differences of thought and feeling between individuals and classes relate to "general culture," including politics, religion, art, and philosophy.[61] Therefore, despite differences of thought and emotion, general culture is the historical horizon within which all individuals and classes think and feel. The assumption is that there should exist a cosmopolitan and national collectivity beyond social classes. However, this collectivity was not a race in the sense of a group sharing phenotypical traits. Yi rather defined the commonality of this collectivity in terms of common emotion through a logical distinction between the general human and its various species. Common emotion allowed for subjects belonging to various species to come together toward a common, general purpose: "In Korea there has been a proliferation of 'ethnicities' *(chongjok)*. They observe and confront one another and they do not have any common emotion. The self should be able to cast off the class to which it was born and form a new class through its positing of a common purpose."[62] In such statements, Korean nationality is multiethnic and multiclass, because various regional and local affiliations—or what he calls "tribes" or "ethnicities" *(chongjok)*—are to be overcome by cultivating purposeful emotions common to both humanity and the nation. The process of humanization is at the same time a process of nationalization, a process of forming the national self out of the various other existing modes of identification. It is more specifically the common emotions created through national literature and the formation of the national language that will transform Koreans from natural humans immersed in their shortsighted class and tribal conflicts into cultural humans with a common historical purpose.[63]

How could the global mood that Yi references in "Reconstruction" be transformed into a common emotion with a specific purpose? In other words, how could the feeling that he gave his readers of belonging to the world be actively transformed into a cosmopolitan sentiment, a love of mankind with a bearing on moral and political action? In order to square cosmopolitan and national history through moral universality, he had to frame "common emotion" as both a cosmopolitan and a nationalist emotion, one belonging to humanity as a whole and to the Korean nation in particular. This attention to world sentiment and its subset of national sentiment comes across in both his theory of literature and his political essays. Yi charged literature with the task of creating this new connection between emotion and morality necessary for modernity and for participation in world culture. In his early essays "What Is Literature?" and "The Value of Literature" (1917), Yi appropriated Kant's division of the faculties of the transcendental subject into the understanding (知), the will (志), and emotion (情).[64] Although Kant's aesthetic philosophy and his concept of *sensus communis* are more concerned with taste, and were slightly different from Yi's romantic theory of emotion and sentiment, Yi clearly had Kant's three critiques in mind when he proposed these three faculties of the subject. Yi argued that there was a strong tradition of knowledge and will in Korean thought, particularly in Confucianism, but that emotion, as well as emotion's bearing on ethical decisions, was in need of development. The purpose of literature was to cultivate the emotions of readers, to transform emotions into shared sentiments that could serve the moral culture of the national collectivity. It is no accident that his first long novel, *The Heartless* (1917), is an allegory about individuals gradually overcoming the mechanical performance of inherited moral dictates and cultivating an emotional interiority that will guide their actions. The novel discusses this as the process of becoming a human being, and the ending unveils the modern nation as the most important object of sentimental identification.

In other words, for Yi Kwang-su, writing novels was a matter of poetics, of forming the national language and a national community out of the raw material of the Korean population. I have already discussed how culturalism assumed the communicative translatability of the cultural concept of the human across national boundaries, which was the linguistic basis for its cosmopolitanism. At the same time, it required the idea of distinct and internally whole national languages between which the concepts of humanism could be transmitted. However, as one of the first vernacular novelists in Korea, Yi knew that the languages of the Korean peninsula were far from unified, particularly if one took into account all of the variations in spoken dialects and the hybridity of the writing systems. In "On the Korean Nation," he describes the role of men of letters as that of a "technician" who forms a national language where none existed previously: "Literature is the music that establishes the spirit of the nation and depicts its movement. Language is the fragments of the life of the nation, and literature is the sustained effort of life to gather these fragments and form something whole. And the technicians *(kisulja)* who do this work are the poets and the men of letters."[65]

The national language is the foundation that could give life, spirit, and historical purpose to culture, and therefore its poetic formation is central to the cultural reformation of the national bios. National language is both universalizing, because it brings its speakers and readers into the human community, and a medium for the expression of the particular, because it is connected to the spirit and life of the national people. National language can represent the temporal experiences that are nonidentical to the field of available concepts in the human sciences; however, language can also bring such experiences under the sway of a priori concepts, giving the particular experiences of Koreans a universal import. In imagining that language could bring experiences under the regulation of the transcendental, the transhistorical, and the purely translatable, he posited a communicative translation between the nation and the world. He also imputed to literary language the capacity to give shape, in a "technical" manner, to those cosmopolitan and national sentiments required of the reader if his or her moral action were to be guided not by natural impulse, but rather by "common emotion." Achieving general culture and the capacity for self-legislated morality was a matter of aesthetic experience, of transforming one's sensorium, primarily through language, so that it could properly guide the freedom of will held by all civilized and modern people. This enlightenment connection between emotion and action makes Yi's works quintessentially modern, but the collapse of morality and politics into art and aesthetics also opened up his philosophy and literature to the possibility of fascism.

FINITUDE AND THE ALLEGORICAL NOVEL

The effort to represent the previously unrepresented through the formation of national language and national literature is a response to Yi's philosophical problem of how to construct a nation out of nothing. Heidegger discussed poetics as a "bringing-forth" *(Hervorbringen)* and Yi refers to the poets and the men of letters as "technicians" who give shape to the national language and the national community.[66] Each thinker opposes his idea of technology and technique to any utilitarian or mechanical concept. Literature is a technique and its practitioners are technicians because they give wholeness to the language through their literary production, and in the process they form the people who come to speak the language. National literature, particularly fiction, is reflexive and allegorical, because the writer transforms himself into a national subject through his poetics but also represents this poetic process in his fictional characterizations. Nationalists imagine poetics as part of an internal civilizing mission, as a historical process of making human beings and national subjects out of the prenational, and indeed prelingual, masses. Literature "brings forth" a national people.

Both Paul de Man and Walter Benjamin, in their critiques of Romantic literary criticism, point to the temporal, fragmentary, and material qualities of allegory, which they contrast to the Romantic definition of the symbol as the organic integration of the idea and the material, the signifier and the signified, the divine and the natural, and the general and the particular.[67] Yi's national allegories represent ideas from his philosophies of history through typological characters that are affected by sociological concepts, but they also allegorize the temporal movement of these concepts as they intersect with the everyday experiences and historical past of Korea. Yi's narratives are not symbolic in the Romantic sense, but rather allegorical, because they are immersed in time and the very modern, historical, and temporal *problem* of how to make visible in an anthropological representation a model of history based on an abstract concept of the genus-being of the human—for example, its developing capacity for self-legislated reason and morality. The human as empirico-transcendental doublet becomes a problem of allegory because, as Benjamin shows in his reading of the German Baroque sorrow-play, allegory is a response to a persistent and irreconcilable gap between the transhistorical and the historical. In the Japanese empire, modern allegorists, including national and Marxist literary allegorists, tried to reconcile their transcendental definitions of the human genus-being, derived from anthropology, with fragmented, finite, and spatiotemporal experiences. In his attempt to reconcile the transhistorical and the historical, the allegorist Yi turned to particular kinds of chronotopes in his novels.[68]

Yi's particular turn to humanism had very much to do with an experience of alienation specific to the elite colonial intellectual, and it is the passage from descriptions of nothingness to the committed nationalist novel that most clearly marks this turn. Yi's descriptions of alienated life as an exchange student in Japan occasionally resembled Japanese intellectuals' discussions of their experiences in Europe during the same period. Yi's cosmopolitanism was, like Kuwaki's, a universalist method of critiquing how external representations objectified the minority's selfhood. Kuwaki's citation of his viewing of *Madame Butterfly* in Berlin is one cultural experience that convinced him of the need to reimagine Japanese culture as a world-historical development guided by a priori values, rather than a hodgepodge of fragmented clichés cobbled together by European and American Orientalists. Before his first long novel, *The Heartless* (1917), and his essays on the reformation of national cultural life, Yi described, in his short fiction, a similar feeling of misrecognition, although his narratives focus more on the difficulty of minority assimilation than on combating Orientalist misrepresentation.

Yi's first published short story, "Maybe Love" (1909), written in Japanese when he was seventeen years old, depicts a Korean exchange student in Japan.[69] This story describes the alienation of the male student Mun-gil and his unrequited desire for a Japanese boy, Misao. His disappointed desire contributes to his thoughts of suicide as he crosses the train tracks in Shibuya. This story is easily read as a depiction of Mun-gil's colonial desire to become Japanese, expressed through his attraction to Misao, and as an autobiographical reflection of Yi Kwang-su's own experiences as an orphan and scholarship student in Tokyo. However, the description in the story of Mun-gil is not just a symptom of Yi's colonial desire to become Japanese, and the story is not only a preamble to Yi's later discovery of his Korean nationalism. In comparing "Maybe Love" to a similar story written eight years later in Korean, "Yun Kwang-ho," and keeping in mind his later novels and political theory, one of the most striking aspects of Yi's early short fiction is its nihilism and its obsession with suicide and death. In both stories, this concern with the finitude of the individual is entangled with a perceived inaccessibility of love and the inadequacy of the mundane accolades and expectations that came with being one of a few students given the opportunity to leave colonial Korea to study in Japan. More generally, however, the stories describe the detachment of the modern subject, the fearful nihility that accompanies the act of writing the modern self, as much as they are concerned with the alienation of the immigrant, the desire for assimilation, and the negativity that leads to an assertion of colonial nationalism.

In order to understand the literary forms, devices of national self-formation, and humanist rhetoric that Yi came to use in his narratives of cultivation, it is important to recognize the diversity in his early portrayals of lack. The protagonist's lack of a sovereign nation, his inability to be recognized as fully Japanese, and his unsatisfied same-sex desires are certainly present in Yi's early works, but the nation and national culture would eventually enter his discourse at a more basic ontological and political level as well. Without the nation or the national self, the work of the individual, written as he confronts his own finitude, would be forgotten to history and culture; hence the focus, taken from Kuwaki's personalism, on the need for "groups" of persons and not mere individuals.⁷⁰ His later anxiety in the 1920s that the individual subject will have no reason to write himself into the modern world if he cannot belong to a national community with the language, spirit, and culture to sustain him emerged out of an early confrontation with death, the possibility that the finitude of modern secular humans means that their lives are without reason or purpose. His humanism and his view of national literature as a poetic enterprise of subject formation both intervened, from *The Heartless* until his embrace of Japanese identity and Japanese national literature, to fend off finitude and the nihility of modernity, so wrenchingly explored in his early fiction.

In "Yun Kwang-ho," the eponymous protagonist feels great joy upon receiving a special invitation to study economics at K University in Japan. He studies so hard late into the evenings and during school breaks that his friends warn him that he is endangering his health. Even though he seems happy with his success, during his second year in Japan, at the age of twenty-four, he is overcome with melancholy: "However, there was a weakness in Kwang-ho's heart. There was a large, deep void that was difficult to fill."⁷¹ He is attracted to P, who, we find out in the last line of the story, is also a young man, but, like Mun-gil, he is rejected. Unlike Mun-gil, he commits suicide, which we discover in the final section, when his friend of ten years, Chun-wŏn, and the contrite P see an article about the incident in the newspaper. Chun-wŏn writes on his tombstone, "The grave of Yun Kwang-ho, who was born in a world of ice, lived in a world of ice, and died in a world of ice."⁷² Because P's gender is revealed in the final line, Yi accentuates the same-sex attraction and the tragic consequence of it not being consummated, owing to Kwang-ho's misreading of P's desire or, perhaps, the ethnic difference between the metropolitan student and the colonial exchange student. However, the void in Kwang-ho's heart and the iciness of the world around him are not solely the result of unfulfilled sexual desires. He feels detachment and lack toward the young women he sees on the train and toward P, but other uses of the term "love" *(sarang)* show that Kwang-ho's desires, as well as his death-drive, are tied to other objects: "His love for humanity, his love for his brethren, his love for his friends, and his longing for his own honor and success could no longer satisfy him. He needed to embrace someone and be embraced by someone. He was not satisfied with tepid and abstract love and needed a burning and concrete love."⁷³ Lines like these seem to place romantic love above all other affections, but from Yi's subsequent political writings it is clear that the problem is not simply that Kwang-ho needs a partner, but rather that his public forms of love feel abstract and disconnected from his libido.

Fictionally narrating the struggle to cultivate one's inner self became Yi's poetic endeavor to reform desire, to create new objects of affection, like the nation, toward which the individual could feel a concrete libidinal bond. From *The Heartless* onward, romantic desires become intertwined with love of nation and love of humanity, so that the former does not become entirely personal and the latter is not just an abstract idea detached from desire. In Yi Kwang-su's writings in defense of free love as opposed to arranged marriage, practicing the freedom to desire the person whom one consciously chooses to desire and freely directing one's libidinal energy toward the nation together promise to give form to the formless void that plagues the interior life of Yi's early characters. This confluence of themes points to the intersection of romantic literature, melodrama, and biopolitics in Yi's fiction and political philosophy, and in Korea in the 1920s more generally.[74] In "Yun Kwang-ho," the finitude of the individual human is both personal and perilous, because in pursuing romantic love Kwang-ho turns away from social relations and achievements that cannot fill his internal void. Because Kwang-ho's self-affection is at odds with his external attachments, he cannot imagine that his life or his death could be meaningful to others.

Yi worked out his ideas of the nation, the political group, and the language community precisely around this problem. If a nation can be formed, then the individual life of the colonial subject can be sustained by the emotional attachment the individual has for the nation and the nation can extend the meaning of the individual life beyond personal finitude by preserving his or her works through its spirit, history, and language. Both "Maybe Love" and "Yun Kwang-ho" show that being an outsider and a colonial subject without a sovereign country contributed to the young elite students' feelings that personal success is meaningless. Yi's political response in the 1920s was not anticolonial revolt, but rather to build a cultural nation through the creation of commonly held emotions in the readership of serial fiction, the construction of an imagined community beyond family, brethren, or friends. The life world, or bios, of this community would be held together by a sentiment analogous to romantic love.[75]

In this model of cultural enlightenment, artists, writers, musicians, and scientists are favored strongly against entrepreneurs, bankers, and capitalists, because they are concerned with the refinement of the spirit rather than with material gain. Therefore, another early long novel, *Pioneers* (1918), picks up thematically from the ending of *The Heartless*, in which the characters collectively dedicate themselves to the cultural progress of Korea. *Pioneers* portrays a young scientist, Sŏng-jae, whom other characters call "Tokyo big brother" because he has studied in Japan, and his sister, Sŏng-sun, who struggles to have her love of Min, a painter, recognized by the still largely Confucian society. Rather than taking up a financially solvent vocation, Sŏng-jae spends seven years upon his return to Korea on a single scientific experiment, tirelessly working toward an adequate result. Even though an evil creditor, Ham Sag-wa, seizes the family home, the novel presents Sŏng-jae as a noble and humble person who credits the world with his successes and himself with his failures.[76] He remains dedicated to science, despite the economic failures it brings to him and his family, because the nation requires him to seek enlightenment and to eventually contribute his knowledge. Interestingly, the novel values the fact that Sŏng-jae works in his laboratory every day, that he has mastered the practice necessary to produce knowledge, even though his practice has yet to produce results. Similarly, Min is the object of Sŏng-sun's affections because he eschews the careers of lawyer and banker and instead dedicates himself to "introducing artistry to the artless Koreans."[77] Such melodramatic contrasts between spirit and material interests, between moral authenticity and deceptive self-interest, and between national culture and capitalism create a mode of enlightenment in Yi's text that differs significantly from the rationalization process associated with capitalist modernization. This enlightenment is not antimodern per se, but rather emphasizes the modernization of emotions, morality, and the spirit as conditions for material or infrastructural development. As Sin Ch'ae-ho pointed out in immediate response, such a spiritual and cultural view of modernization was nonetheless a tacit justification of continued material exploitation.[78]

Although most of Yi's novels could be described as "novels of ideas," in that they allegorize his philosophy of life and philosophy of history, a number of ambiguities arise in the fictional representation of his ideas. On the one hand, Yi's advocacy of the liberation of women from feudal relations, and the liberation of male-female relationships from arranged marriages and Confucian dictates, presented progressive possibilities for the colonial bourgeoisie. On the other hand, he still tended to apply his concern that life be governed by self-legislated morality differentially according to gender and class positions. As socialism entered colonial Korea and became a powerful counterdiscourse to culturalism, Yi applied this feminization of questions of cultivation and morality to the political difference between culturalism and socialism, particularly through the figure of the "new woman." In "Wife of a Revolutionary" (1930), Pang Chŏng-hŭi marries a socialist with whom she shares political ideals, but he dies when she does not care for him faithfully.[79] She begins a relationship with a medical student who was treating her husband and carries his child. However, he deceives her, the baby is stillborn, and she dies of the effects of the labor. Yi approaches themes of life, illness, and death through a female focalizer, making the trials and failures of the cultivation of life a female matter. The failure to properly regulate life culturally, under the rule of the moral universal, becomes a failure of political ideology as much as of the personal limitations of female characters. Yi expresses an anxiety concerning whether or not culturalism and bourgeois cosmopolitanism can compete ideologically with socialism in a place with Korea's dire material conditions, but he does so through a morality tale in which the personal choice of free love fails, melodramatically, when it becomes intertwined with macropolitcal concerns of capitalism and social class.

Yi's historical novels reveal how his idea for the anthropological reform of the nation into a world cultural nation greatly affected how he saw the distant historical past of Korea. Two of his major historical novels, *The Hemp-Clad Prince*

(1926–27) and *The Sad History of Tanjong* (1929), focus on a moment of acute political crisis in the history of Korea.[80] He highlights the individual's incapacity or lack of opportunity to affect the political situation for the benefit of the unification and prosperity of the nation. *The Hemp-Clad Prince* is set during the Later Three Kingdoms period (892–936 AD). This period was one of the most turbulent politically in the ancient history of the peninsula. Two short-lived kingdoms, Hubaekje and Taebong, were at war with the quickly fading Silla kingdom (668–935 AD), until Koryŏ, led by Wanggŏn, was able to unify the peninsula under a single government. Rather than presenting Wanggŏn as a national hero, however, Yi Kwang-su makes the defeated leader of Taebong, Kung'ye, the protagonist of the novel. Meanwhile, the titular hemp-clad prince withdraws to the mountains early in the story and becomes an ascetic. A favorite among the readership of colonial Korea, *The Hemp-Clad Prince* provides few prescriptions for modern nation building. Yi's turn to the national past is more in the style of a "sorrow-play" *(Trauerspiel)* in which the depiction of the despair over national history never arrives at the catharsis of a tragedy.[81] The implication is that ancient Korean history does not provide material for the renewal of modern Korean subjectivities. Without a Korean state in the present, Yi could not present the history of dynastic rulers as a prehistory to the nation-state. As a national allegory, *The Hemp-Clad Prince* conveys the problem of a past in which the dynastic state existed, but not a modern national self that could provide cultural unity during a tumultuous time of political division. *The Sad History of Tanjong* recounts events in the history of fifteenth-century Chosŏn, but rather than focusing on the cultural and political successes of King Sejong, it rather takes up the history of Sejong's grandson Tanjong, whose power was usurped by his uncle Suyang and who was exiled and eventually executed at the age of sixteen. The melodramatic and mournful themes and style of these historical novels certainly contributed to a popular sense of shared suffering and injustice among the colonial Korean readership, but the primary political lesson is that treachery and selfish ambition accompanied each moment of progress in Korean history, and that these intrusions had limited the possibility for the kind of fundamental reconstruction of national character necessary for modernity.

This long view of Korean history had a significant influence on the ways that Yi represented the contemporary political and social moment of colonial Korea, because his turn to quasi-mythical ideas for the origins of Korean national identity in the countryside and in blood emerged in part out of the difficulty he had in finding a cultural and moral national identity in the overly Sinocentric dynastic history of Korea. Some of the internal problems with Yi's notion of cultural and spiritual enlightenment come through in his back-to-the-land novels, which echoed the Russian Narodnik movement of the nineteenth century. In the 1930s, Yi's enlightenment narrative returned to the countryside, to the rural villages where most of his characters, and most of his readers, originated. Yi's *Soil* (1933) inaugurated a series of other back-to-the-land novels with varying political perspectives, including Yi Ki-yŏng's treatment of class conflict, *Home Village* (1933–34), and Sim Hun's melodrama of idealist self-sacrifice, *Evergreen* (1936). The Marxist An Hamgwang criticized Yi's kind of approach to the countryside as overly "metaphysical," and associated it rightly with the European fascist aesthetic of blood and soil.[82] In the back-to-the-land novels, the connections between enlightenment and life that Yi formulated in his abstract political philosophy are expressed in concrete images of the human body in its physical metabolism with organic nature. The protagonist, Sung, has given up his life as a lawyer in order to return to his home village and help to enlighten the farmers, who have been resisting the Japanese. His wife, Chŏng-sŏn, remains in Seoul, eventually having an affair. His boyhood love, Sun, contrasts to his modern and licentious wife, and he comes to idealize her. Although a great deal of its action takes place in the city, the novel presents the urban petit-bourgeoisie's return to the land of their ancestors as a solution to the problems of modernity and a pragmatic mode of cultural enlightenment in an increasingly stifling colonial situation.

The following passage describing Sung's connection with Sun is "metaphysical," in An's sense, because it states that the soil has mixed the blood of the two main characters' ancestors, allowing them to blossom in those fields like flowers:

> Sung's ancestors had cultivated these fields, probably along with Sun's ancestors. They had cut down all the trees and dug up all their roots, made a reservoir to provide water to Sayŏul, and mixed their blood and sweat to plow the fields. Sung's ancestors and Sun's ancestors ate the rice grown in this field and lived and enjoyed life generation after generation. Weren't the bone, flesh, and blood of Sun and Sung flowers that sprouted, grew, and blossomed in this soil where the blood and sweat of their ancestors mixed?
>
> However, these fields for the most part no longer belonged to the houses of Sung and Sun. They had all become part of some company, bank, union, or plantation. These days those living in the village Sayŏul, Sung's home village, had become like grass whose roots were cut. The sounds of the birds, dogs, beasts, horses, and oxen, which had risen peacefully and leisurely in the valley's morning mist, had also diminished greatly this year. It wasn't just that the number of animals had decreased, but that the peacefulness and leisureliness had left their voices. They were painful, weary, and resentful.[83]

The passage is critical of imperialism, on the one hand, because it contrasts the connection that Sung, Sun, and their ancestors once had with the land to the current enclosure of those lands by finance capitalists, imperial companies, and the local landowners that they support. On the other hand, the use of images of organic nature in their dynamic metabolism with the laboring body idealizes the internal physiology that the families externalized into the land, figuring a natural substrate for the collective subjectivity of the nation. The ancestors of the village stand in for a larger national community that was once tied to the land but has been displaced from this organic connection by the outside forces of capitalist modernity.

Considering that Yi Kwang-su was writing admiring essays about Adolph Hitler around the same time that he wrote *Soil*, the fascist aesthetic in passages like these should not be ignored.[84] There was a significant temporal compression in Yi's intellectual path that can make this shift to blood nationalism seem like a sudden turn away from his earlier enlightenment discourse, and perhaps a sign of his inconsistency and confusion. However, Yi's beginnings in the biopolitics of neo-Kantian thought are continuous in many ways with his blood nationalism. Whereas the romantic inner self grew out into the world like an infinitely expansive plant in *The Heartless*, the young student who returns to the countryside to rediscover the soil nurtured by his ancestors' bodies sees a more immediate but all the more metaphysical connection between the reproduction of humanity and the reproduction of organic life. This metaphor is consistent with Yi's earlier version of enlightenment, although much more nostalgic, because Sung and Sun understand their moral purpose only when they witness and "return to" a state when consciousness was integrated fully with organic life. In the 1920s, Yi saw this integration as a project directed toward the future—Koreans had to be reconstructed anthropologically to suit the new life of modernity. By 1933, this temporality was reversed, both in the back-to-the-land novels and the historical novels; modernity did not re-create life, but rather threatened it. This threat was not complete, however, and the fascist response to capitalist modernity would look at once toward the future technologization of life and toward the past as a mythical time when the community and the land had not yet been separated from each other.

Yi's explicit support for Koreans becoming Japanese national subjects began in 1940. He soon changed his name to Kayama Mitsurō and called for the unification and expansion of East Asia under the Japanese nation-state. "You Can Become a Soldier" (1943) is an exemplary story supporting the implementation of the volunteer soldier system in Korea.[85] A father's first son dies of illness because he cannot join the Japanese military, but the second survives to become a Japanese soldier. Yi's Japanese patriotism has been the object of a great deal of controversy, not just in the immediate aftermath of World War II, or within the national traditions created in South Korea and North Korea respectively, but even in present-day national canonization efforts. One primary question is what kinds of continuities and discontinuities can be drawn between his nationalist work in the 1920s and his Japanese patriotism. A continuity that has not been emphasized in statements that depend on a dichotomy between Korean and Japanese national identity is the generally modern problem of how human life comes to be governed under the regulation of the transcendental, and the connection between this conceptualization and the regulation of life with political power. "You Can Become a

Soldier" and so many other literary and cinematic texts of the late Japanese empire celebrate the capacity to control the life and death of oneself and of others. In Yi's belief that every young Korean man who died fighting for Japan would give meaning to his life and contribute to the preservation of the national totality, there was an iteration of his previous celebration of modernity as the capacity to control life and death and to preserve life beyond death through the collective spirit and language of the nation. In "You Can Become a Soldier" the father/narrator feels pride when his son can join the military, and the son's volunteering saves him from the illnesses of his older brother. This kind of mastering of life and death through the sacrifice of the individual for the extension of the life of the nation-state was a very common and paradoxical logic in the biopolitical regime described in detail by Takashi Fujitani.[86] Just as cultural policy was in many respects a preparation for this regime, because it transformed "culture" into the mediation between the life and death of the cosmopolitan-national individual and the life and death of the nation or nation-state, Yi's life philosophy of the Korean nation, which situated the finitude of the individual in direct relation to the potential infinity of the nation, had its own significant analogies with the work he wrote in explicit support of Japan.

Yi's turn to the formation of the national self through literature was a response to the alienation and confrontations with finitude that appear in his early fiction on the experience of exchange students in Japan. The novels he wrote in an attempt to form this national self became allegorical in a specific sense. By connecting the lives of individual characters to the life of the nation, these two levels, of the individual and the totality, were linked through a model of universal history. Individual experiences became connected to collective experiences through depictions that emphasized the emotional bonds of sympathy and ideological dedication that would enable the perpetual transformation of the Korean people into a nation belonging to the world. The allegorical novel for Yi was always a means of making individual life and death matters of the larger national community of sympathy, and this is one thing that did not change when he began writing for the Japanese state.

CRITIQUES OF CULTURAL PERSONHOOD

There are multiple ways to criticize culturalism's idea of moral personhood and to take a more materialist approach to humanism. One can contrast the universalism of the idea of moral propriety with the historical circumstances under which morality is practiced. For example, in colonial Korea, where property relations elevated a few male landowners and industrialists to positions of power, the replacement of a natural law theory of equality with culturalism's regulative notion of individual cultivation and the moral progress of humanity was clearly an ideological justification for gender and class exploitation. Nonetheless, culturalism's universal claims about the human transformed the terms of debate, even for those who were skeptical of its abstractly cosmopolitan perspective. Early criticisms of culturalism and cultural personhood show that rarely was culturalism confronted without asserting another problematic term for human subjectivity, another claim to the universal with a different set of parameters and limitations. Sin Ch'ae-ho opposed the Korean ethnos *(chongjok)* to culturalism and Im Chŏng-jae wrote of the popular masses. Eventually, in both Japan proper and colonial Korea, intellectuals posited the proletariat as a subject of history and subject of culture opposed to the individualism of the bourgeoisie. Even if the problems in culturalism were clear, the responses to it were not transparently subversive, particularly when it came to addressing the humanist desire to establish the unity of subjectivity.

The concern on the part of culturalists that their cosmopolitan ideas of culture and history would be criticized on political grounds was well founded. For example, as Sōda's essays on cultural value, Kuwaki's work on cultural reconstruction, and Yi Kwang-su's "Reconstruction" were being published around 1922, the nationalist historian Sin Ch'ae-ho was dismissing the idea of culture at the foundations of cultural policy. He continued to insist on the need for violent anticolonial revolution. In his earlier writings on historiography (1908), Sin argued that the formation of nations and national histories comes about through the dichotomy of self and other, the differentiation of the I from the non-I.[87] In his later criticisms of cultural policy and studies of ancient history (1920–25), he developed a concept of the Korean nation that was tied to world history not through the concept of culture, but rather through a shared ethnic origin, on the one hand, and colonial war, on the other. For the former, he turned to the Tan'gun origin myth of the Korean people. For the latter, he insisted that under conditions of colonialism, the mutually constitutive relation of the I to the non-I is transformed into a belligerent struggle between friend and enemy.

In "Manifesto for Korean Revolution" (1923), Sin attacks the idea of culture at the foundations of the cultural policy:

> Who is calling for a cultural movement under the rule of the thief Japan? "Culture" is a term that refers to the developed accumulation of industry and cultural products, but if the very "preservation of the ethnos" is in doubt for a nation that has been deprived of its right to survival under a system of economic plunder, is there any possibility for cultural development? . . .
>
> For this reason, we should declare to be our enemy all those who seek to compromise with the enemy of our survival, the thief Japan (advocates of domestic independence, self-rule, and the right to political participation), as well as those who adhere to ideologies that parasitize under the rule of the thief (for example, advocates of cultural movements).[88]

Yi Kwang-su had argued that national survival could be secured through cultural development and cosmopolitan subjectivity. For Sin, on the other hand, national survival is an existential matter of life and death and the ethnos is in danger of perishing as long as it is threatened by a foreign power. Colonization and imperialism are not means toward modernization and cultural development; rather, they have brought about a war between the powerful and the weak. For Sin, any view of history or culture that obscures this state of war between Japan and Korea is ideological and serves the enemy. Sin points out that the liberal attempt to develop civil society out of a cultural idea of politics tied the colonized bourgeoisie to a notion of history that masked the perpetuation of colonial exploitation.

Like his contemporary Carl Schmitt, Sin attacked the depoliticizing tendencies of liberal cultural politics and thought of the political through the categories of self/other and friend/enemy.[89] Prefiguring Korean nationalism after 1945 in both the South and the North, he attempted to reestablish and purify the connection between ethnos and political sovereignty, against the imposition of Japanese imperialism. Unlike later Marxian intellectuals, Sin did not develop a sophisticated political economy or realist narrative form that could describe the various social relations and social institutions that perpetuated this exploitation. However, he did recognize that the effort to depoliticize the cultural basis for civic life was also an expression of political authority. It was this skepticism toward political authority that later led him to an anarchist position.[90] Despite his deduction of some of the ideological aspects of culturalism, there were significant problems in Sin's view of the Korean nation and Korean national history, in addition to its obviously mythical dimension. At the turn of the century, Sin had written a historical defense for the expansion of the geographical territory of Korea into Manchuria, which ironically came about through the surrogate of Japanese imperialism in the 1930s.[91]

Criticisms of culturalism did not come strictly from intellectuals whose primary unit of political thought was the colonized ethnic nation. The New Tendency Group in colonial Korea was a precursor to KAPF (Korea Artista Proleta Federacio), a proletarian arts organization. Its members were the first in Korea to politicize the individualist view of culture from a class perspective. In 1923, in the journal *The Opening*, Im Chŏng-jae published "Advice to the Litterateurs," in which he articulates a mass view of culture that was in opposition to culturalism's focus on individual cultivation and expression. In a critique of the culturalist view of personhood, Im wrote,

> Therefore, in art too [in addition to politics], acts of class consciousness, as forms of humanity, are expressed in the manner of a person *(in'gyŏk-jŏk)*. The personal action of expressing the class "I"' occurs in art, and it becomes, for the practical human, an action that is directed toward the unity of a world idea.
>
> In any class, self-perfection is gained through human expressive action. Therefore, if art fails because it is pure self-expression or expresses only singular individuality, this means stagnation in the perfection of the self as well.
>
> In bourgeois art, the activity of the individual self crumbles into a fragmentary and imperfect deformation. Furthermore, as a partial object of pleasure, bourgeois

art produces further dissatisfaction with the unequal human rights and lack of freedom in human life. Because it lacks class content, bourgeois art becomes incapable of avoiding the creation of merely playful, vulgar, and pleasurable objects. The bourgeois class has survived without having the space to develop historically; therefore, its artistic movements have been exclusive to a separate class (a class with special rights)....

If exclusive art is to be liberated from specialization and enter mass consciousness, if it is to contribute to the progress of humanity and the perfection of society, then it is reasonable that it should be established upon a movement that seeks the liberation of the popular masses *(minjung).*[92]

Im Chŏng-jae formulates a humanism that would not rely on the culturalist ideal of the individual person as the teleology of cultural development. However, he also appropriated some culturalist terminology and resituated it within a theory for a popular art of the masses. He refers to "the person," the teleological principle in Yi Kwang-su's philosophy, as a class subject whose self-consciousness and cultural activity are acts of class consciousness. He argues that an idea of culture that primarily seeks the cultivation of the individual cannot produce the desired effect of personal self-perfection. Individual expression is never entirely individual; it is also an act of class consciousness that requires some sort of basis in a collective class history. Because bourgeois art seeks this collective basis in an idea of humanity severed from historical conditions and is exclusive to a separate class with special rights, it can never achieve the moral and cultural perfection that is its ideal. The teleological principle of the completed person is in contradiction with the historical reality of class relationships in bourgeois society. Only by connecting art and culture to movements that seek the liberation of the whole of the popular masses could culturalism's goal of the self-perfection of the individual also be accomplished.

Im's assertion that bourgeois art is incapable of perfecting the self is partially a reflection of the colonial situation, in which attempts at an indigenous *Bildungsroman,* such as Yŏm Sang-sŏp's *Mansejŏn* (1922), had revealed the instability of the naturalist literary perspective for colonial intellectuals who had returned from their studies in Japan proper.[93] Such novels highlighted the sense of fragmentation felt by writers who had tried to translate the narrative forms of "bourgeois literature" into the colonial context. From the articles in *White Tide* until Im Hwa's socialist realist study from 1937 of the history of Korean literature, the popular masses, and later the proletariat, were invested with the power to potentially overcome this problem of what Im Hwa called the "transplantation *(isik)* of Western literary forms" into a Korean context that had yet to establish an autonomous and native "new literature."[94] The popular mass subject was a way to politicize culturalism's notion of disinterested individual cultivation and beauty, both of which met with a kind of crisis when they were "transplanted" into the political and economic atmosphere of colonial modernity.

In Japan proper as well, confrontations with culturalism emerged from the left, as intellectuals questioned the aesthetic and cultural ideologies that had converged in a new manner with doctrines of political rule. Earlier in the century, Kōtoku Shusui had imported Lenin's theory of imperialism and monopoly capitalism, and by the early 1920s Marxist social scientists were beginning to develop theories of economic development that accounted for the historical particularities of Japanese capitalism and imperialism.[95] However, as culturalism became significant as a mode of governmentality in the metropole and the colony, cultural critics added theories of culture to the political economic critique of capitalism. As with the New Tendency Group in Korea, early writers and critics of proletarian literature in Japan proper based their criticism of culturalism on class politics and on a criticism of the culture of individualism. By 1924, the opposition between the culture and cultivation of the proletariat and the culture and cultivation of the bourgeoisie had established itself as the primary opposition in cultural politics. That year the proletarian arts critic Aono Suekichi wrote,

> Proletarian class consciousness is in no sense compatible with bourgeois individualism. If we think of proletarian class consciousness as opposed to bourgeois individualism, then it is really illuminated by the spirit of anti-individualism. People are often troubled by the relationship between socialism and individualism, and engage in arguments with concerns such as "if the world becomes socialist, then won't the individual be annihilated?" However, if the content of the individual that is referred to in this question has a different meaning from what bourgeois individualism holds in high esteem, then the "individual" of bourgeois individualism should naturally die off in the future, when class society has disappeared under the rule of the proletariat. This is clearer than pointing to the sun. The individualist spirit is only a moral principle that modern bourgeois society has perfected. As a product of ideas, this historical spirit assumes the place of eternity; it is something enshrined as a transtemporal, eternal ideal. The whole path of bourgeois cultivation has proceeded accordingly, and bourgeois rule, under the name of "cultivation," gave rise to the illusion of eternity. However, from below, revolutionary proletarian consciousness grew, and a mood with a new content spread, following its necessary advance.[96]

Similarly to Im Chŏng-jae, Aono argues that the bourgeois individual is an abstract ideal, and that culturalism's ideology of individual cultivation creates the illusion that the bourgeois class would govern in perpetuity. Aono was one of the first critics to oppose the ideals of bourgeois individualism and cultivation to the proletariat as historical subject. As the proletarian literature and culture movements expanded, the proletariat as universal historical subject became the primary position from which culturalism could be challenged. From the early 1920s, two versions of universal history, two concepts of the subject, and, in a word, two humanisms—culturalism and the proletarian arts—were in persistent political and theoretical conflict in Korea as well. Yi Puk-man, Kim Ki-jin, and Pak Yŏng-hŭi, in particular, translated Aono's theory of purposive consciousness and used it to articulate the "proletarian nation" as a conscious subject of history. In the late 1930s, this divide would come under critical scrutiny by fascist and other state-centered philosophies and literatures that sought a higher unity of culture that would be concerned neither with individual cultivation nor with class consciousness, but rather with the overcoming of this modern division through the practice of nation-state subjects.

Marxism and proletarian literature elaborated on these criticisms of bourgeois culture and were committed to their own reading of the human genus as the laboring and productive subject. In its modernizing mode, this turn to the figure of the human as producer eventually facilitated compromises with imperialism, but it also opened up possibilities for alternative narratives that exposed the disunity of humanity, or the disunity between laboring and producing, particularly within the actual lived spaces of production where the human's labor to produce the world takes place under conditions of rural primitive accumulation and nascent industrial capitalism.

3

Labor and *Bildung* in Marxism and the Proletarian Arts

> *We trust in the growth of the culture of the proletariat. However, what makes us committed to proletarian culture is the anti-individualist spirit that is truly oppositional to the individualist spirit, the basic origin of bourgeois culture.*
>
> —AONO SUEKICHI

In criticizing the "illusion of eternity" in the bourgeois idea of subject formation, or *Bildung,* Aono Suekichi drew a line in the sand between the individualistic, transtemporal view of arts and literature and a politically and historically engaged arts and literature. However, like so many proletarian arts critics, he did not reject the terms of bourgeois humanism, but rather appropriated themes of culture, spirit, and humanity to give a foundation to an oppositional and collective subject in world history, the proletariat. Culturalism spoke of culture in terms of moral progress, individual achievement, and each nation's place in universal history. Aono's assertion of the "anti-individualist spirit" of proletarian culture seems to provide an alternative understanding of the human genus and its cultural historical forms. It would seem to follow Marx's critique of Feuerbach's abstract essentializing of the genus without concern for sensuous activity and practice. However, taking up the proletariat as the subject of history, Aono subsumed sensuous activity and practice into the idea of culture. In this respect, culture remained at the center of the historical development of the human being, only now it gained new analogies with productive labor, rather than self-legislated morality, as the genus-being. The teleology of culturalism was a global society governed by individuals who had attained superior moral cultivation. Aono addresses the class difference that this view of the teleology of history both implies and masks, a difference between the culture of the elite individual and the culture of the proletarian masses.

Aono's cosmology of a world divided into two classes suggests that the identities of the bourgeois subject and the proletarian subject have a material basis in the global capitalist system. In discussing the genus-being of the human not as morality, but rather as productive labor and productive relations, Marxists and the proletarian arts movement posited the unity of the international proletariat in the industrial stage of the genus-being. Aono also discusses the culture and spirit of these two class subjects, their distinct worldviews, cultural practices, and political positions in his narrative of universal history. However, if the economic system of capitalist modernity creates these two class subjects historically, then why must the proletariat have a culture and a spirit, that is, a subjectivity that exceeds mere economic conditions and is formed through culture? If the economic determinism of the stage theory of history guarantees a proletarian revolution and the transition to socialism, then why would history require a subject with its own knowledge, culture, and spirit? How much do the notions of anti-individualism and the masses change the ideas of culture and spirit themselves?

As the problem of the role of culture and spirit in history suggests, Marxism and the proletarian arts of the Japanese empire were not the political or rhetorical obverses to neo-Kantian thought, or culturalism more broadly, but rather belonged to the same field of discourse; likewise, they confronted many similar problems of the modern metaphysical and anthropocentric epistemologies. This intertextuality between culturalism and Marxism is apparent in the shared search for the genus-being of the human. Despite their critiques of culturalism's transhistorical and moral concept of the genus-being, Marxists and proletarian arts critics often took Marx's concept of the human's genus-being, or productive relations, and Georg Lukács's figuration of the proletariat as the subject/object of history, as universals in world history, rather than as ideas with their own history of translation. In the language of Giorgio Agamben's reading of Marx, they defined the human being as the being that "produces universally," articulating the human's essential practice as productive labor.[1] They grappled with how to locate this transcendental essence in particular, identifiable, empirical traits within specific historical contexts. They imagined that the human as the object of knowledge progresses toward a regulative norm for modern subjectivity, the industrial worker. As I will show, the application of the idea of the genus-being as productive labor, represented in the world by productive laborers, led to a break from sensuous activity and revolutionary practice (as articulated by Marx in his original critique of Feuerbach) and to an anthropological, social-scientific discourse of modernity that coded history, culture, and aesthetics according to developmental models.

Repeating the structure of the empirico-transcendental doublet that characterized neo-Kantianism, Marxism and the proletarian arts employed general anthropological categories—including nation, race, gender, and social-class types—in order to make sense of the differences that persisted despite the general historical transition to industrial capitalism, when the proletariat takes on its role as the primary subject of world history. Despite their universalist concept of productive labor as the substance of the human's genus-being, they required anthropological categories and a theory of culture to articulate the historical process of the global proletariat overcoming its internal differences and eventually bringing about world communism. Furthermore, just as culturalism discussed cultivation and culture as the pragmatic processes through which difference could be actively subsumed into the universal, proletarian arts critics discussed proletarian culture, arts, and literature as aesthetic projects that could form the oppressed social classes into a single proletariat. The proletariat was the exemplar of the human's genus-being—productive labor—in the capitalist stage. However, only through culture would the proletariat overcome its historical determination through its historical freedom, becoming the identical subject-object of world history that Lukács proclaimed it to be.[2]

Although critical of the reification of the human being in bourgeois ideology, theories that pose the proletariat as the identical subject-object of history maintain a similar relation between transcendental and empirical to the one with which Kant inaugurated modern anthropocentric thought. As a symptom of this problematic of the empirico-transcendental doublet in Marxism, Nakano Shigeharu thought of proletarian culture as an integrative culture that would unify the colonizer and the colonized in their shared revolt against imperial sovereignty, which defined the colonized peoples anthropologically while asserting their eventual sublation into the national proletariat and the national subject. His interlocutor in Korea, Im Hwa, considered proletarian culture to be a means to humanize and modernize Koreans so that they could overcome the transplantation of Western literature and establish a subjective autonomy over culture.[3] In each case, classes, genders, and ethnic minorities were united under the signs of the proletariat and proletarian culture, understood as the ideal type of the genus-being in the capitalist stage.

The idea that the proletariat is the most essentially human of social classes in world history was central to the proletarian arts of the Japanese empire from the mid-1920s, when the proletarian arts organizations NAPF (Nippona Artista Proleta Federacio) and KAPF (Korea Artista Proleta Federacio) were both founded. Writers and intellectuals often contrasted the proletarian subject's full immersion in capitalism to other, premodern, precapitalist exploited classes, such as the peasantry. The primary political and cultural problem that emerged in asserting a clear division between properly willful humanity, embodied in the proletariat, and the passive, represented classes of peasants, colonial subalterns, and ethnic minorities is that in the violent transition from feudal relations to capitalism, no individual subject belongs self-identically and a priori to the national proletariat. In colonial Korea, for example, there was no tradition, no longstanding forms of consciousness, and no cultural precedent at all for those large numbers of people who were expelled from their lands through primitive accumulation and found themselves working in the dreary factories of Kyŏngsŏng (Seoul), Inch'ŏn, or Tokyo, the harbor of Pusan, or the mines of Tōhoku. Therefore, the proletarian arts movements could not seek to represent an existing social class with an existing class consciousness, but rather had to manufacture a class through culture in order to make social reality fit into the universal history that was defined by the most advanced social science of the time. It is this project—the production of a new social class through culture—that I refer to as proletarian *Bildung*. The proletarian arts were an aesthetic and cultural project that served as a solution to the problem of the human subject as it emerged in Marxist philosophy and social science.

Opening up the knowledge of Marxism to literary and other artistic representation also revealed certain limits to its capacity to represent the temporal and spatial complexity through its human scientific categories and its notions of universal history. Many discussions about the proletariat and the peasantry within proletarian literary theory, as well as the more complex leftist novels of the 1930s, became increasingly suspicious of the use of stable class categories like the proletariat and the peasantry, particularly when they were understood to belong, respectively, to the capitalist and precapitalist stages in universal or national history. Realist fiction became particularly adept at depicting social conflict while also revealing the multiple temporalities and multiple spaces that people inhabited in everyday life. Through what I call "other chronotopes," the more complex anthropological knowledge and literary narratives showed how the reduction of the time of human life to the time of human history was a questionable abstraction of modern philosophy and modern social science. To trace the development of proletarian literature in colonial Korea, and the Japanese empire generally, from the simple early assertions of a unifying "proletarian culture" to expansive and highly intricate realist novels is to see Marxism in motion, not stilted by platitudes about human history, but rather in constant need of refinement to fit the context into which it is translated. On the other hand, to read the philosophers of modernization of the same period, who utilized Marxist analysis in their support of the Japanese empire, is to see how the humanism in Marxism can also lead to a defense of imperialism as a temporary political process leading to a better economic and social condition in the future. As the concept of "culture" did for cosmopolitans who saw history as a gradual development toward a more perfected moral society, concepts of economic and cultural modernization allowed Marxists of the late Japanese empire to see imperialism as a necessary project for liberation from the past. This chapter and the next are concerned with these two tendencies in Marxist humanism, their relation to each other, and their eventual and necessary political opposition.

AN UNCERTAIN INTERNATIONAL: NAKANO SHIGEHARU AND IM HWA

In "Shinagawa Station in the Rain" (1929), a poem dedicated to two Korean socialist critics who had been studying in Tokyo (Yi Puk-man and Kim Ho-yong), Nakano Shigeharu calls on the Korean proletariat to take the lead in the international revolution against the feudal emperor system, calling for the colonized working class and their vanguard to raid the halls of the Imperial Palace and to cut the throat of the sovereign. However, no one in Japan proper, except perhaps Nakano's close confidantes, knew the precise content of his poem, because it appeared heavily censored in its Japanese version. Nakano also rewrote the poem after the war, rethinking his interwar statements on colonialism and proletarian revolution and introducing into his work a complex layering of political sensibilities concerning the problem of Japanese imperial rule. This censorship and rewriting are symptomatic of the difficult questions that Japanese colonialism posed to the metropolitan intellectual who viewed universal history through the lens of national proletarian revolution, particularly as national circumstances changed rapidly through war and defeat.

Although no readers in Japan proper at the time would have known its exact content due to censorship, Nakano's poem was translated into Korean in 1929 and published with little censorship in *Musanja*. It is possible to fully reconstruct the original version only by way of these Korean translations, a task first undertaken by Mizuno Naoki and then Chŏng Sŭng-un in his book on Nakano and Korea.[4] Chŏng points out that Mizuno's translation of the poem back into Japanese in 1975 had some infelicities that suggested it was calling for Korean revolutionaries to stab the emperor in the throat and to "bathe in his blood."[5] Chŏng improves the translation and questions how Mizuno's translation has Nakano calling for Koreans to commit an act of terrorism. However, it is still clear from Chŏng's translation that in the final lines Nakano calls on his Korean comrades to commit violence against the emperor, even if the graphic images of assassination in Mizuno's translation were not true to the original:

> Pass through Kobe and Nagoya and enter Tokyo
> Approach his body
> Appear before his face
> Grab him
> Push his throat and hold him
> Press the blade against the nape of his neck
> Blood surging through your whole body
> Cry out in the delight of warm revenge[6]

Nakano's metaphorical treatment of history figured Koreans' act of messianic violence against the sovereign as a means to liberate themselves from the lifeless, frozen, and shameless state of colonial society, to "go and break apart that hard thick ice" of colonial society and enliven a subjectivity that had been negated and stagnated by colonization.[7] Although the poem is perhaps more metaphorical than propagandistic, it still uses a voluntarist rhetoric that should be analyzed critically. Nakano did not consider the political consequences of such a representation of violence, particularly the type of retaliation Koreans could expect from the Japanese state, were they to follow Nakano's version of revolution (particularly following the popular and state backlash against resident Koreans and Chinese in the aftermath of the Kanto earthquake of 1923). Perhaps recognizing the foolhardiness of suggesting such an act of violence, Im Hwa, in his Korean-language poem "Opening an Umbrella on Yokohama Pier" (1929), responded very ambiguously to Nakano's call for Korean anticolonial revolution to lead the way for the proletarian revolution (see the appendix for my translation).[8] As others have pointed out, Im's poem is noticeably more personal in tone and is addressed to "the woman of Yokohama," with whom the male Korean voice of the poem has become a comrade and friend.[9] While the voice refers to the imprisonment of Korean communists in Japan proper and his own banishment and return to Korea, the poem reads the colonial relationship through mundane and melodramatic images of suffering and struggle, in contrast to Nakano's images of absolute, subject-forming revolt against sovereignty. The voice entreats the woman of Yokohama to forget "this man of the colonies" and to care for the suffering, colonial workers who remain in Japan proper.

The missing pieces of this important moment in modern Japanese and Korean literature, when Marxists tried to make good on the internationalist promise of Marxism, can only be retrospectively restored with an attention to the vicissitudes of translation. As with so much culture in an imperial context, however, the translation of Marxism and the proletarian arts at the time was for the most part a unidirectional transmission. Im's poem was not translated into Japanese and what could have become an exchange confronted a barrier in the hierarchy of the two languages. This barrier and hierarchy of languages are unfortunate, because they mean that despite Nakano's sympathy for the conditions in Japan's colonies and Im's critical reflections on the view of universal history expounded in the metropolitan proletarian arts, a certain insurmountable divide remained within the international, drawn along the same colonial lines that determined so many attempts to articulate oppositional political positions at the time.

As Miriam Silverberg mentions, Nakano later rethought the way that "Shinagawa Station in the Rain" sought to mobilize Koreans to lead the charge against the emperor system, protecting and defending the "Japan proletariat" as its "front and rear shield."[10] Nakano's casting of Koreans in the role of "shock troops"—as Silverberg put it—is a slippage, frequent in twentieth-century Marxism, between figures of anti-imperial nationalism and an ideal of proletarian subjectivity. This slippage is a matter not simply of poetic language, but also of the social-scientific theories at the foundations of the Marxist view of universal history. Nakano's manifesto is informed by Soviet theories concerning the role of colonized peoples and peasants within proletarian revolution. These theories have their origins in discourses of developmental history in the Soviet Union, which was undergoing its own dramatic processes of primitive accumulation and industrialization (and eventually the imperialist expansion of socialism in one country and Russification). For Marxists who understood the proletariat in terms of national historical development, the colonized and the peasants occupied positions at the peripheries of the historical time of the proletariat proper. The aesthetics of this view of history entailed that the colonized and the peasantry be represented entering the universal historical process and its primary opposition between bourgeoisie and proletariat. In other words, the colonized and the peasantry, as supplements to the national proletarian revolution, could achieve their political and historical goals by subordinating their interests to proletarian revolution. Nakano clearly had this developmental and Hegelian model of proletarian subjectivity in mind when he called on Koreans to lead and protect the Japan proletariat in an attack at the perceived center of political power. Nakano thought that such a proletarian revolution would also achieve the end of Japanese imperialism in Korea. And yet, paradoxically, and in a kind of reversal of the spatiotemporality of Hegelian world history, the original context of his manifesto can only be read in translation, preserved as it was in the colonial periphery. At the time of its composition, it remained unknown to the metropolitan proletariat that he perceived as the primary agent of radical political change, despite his attempts to appropriate the political resentment of the colonized subaltern.[11]

With the knowledge that his poem would be translated into Korean, Nakano relied upon a model of universal history in order to figure his addressee. As I will show in a reading of "What Is Proletarian Art?" (1931), this figuring of the colonized was derived from Soviet versions of multiculturalism that saw the ethnic cultures of the colonized and the peasantry (somehow conflated) as internal differences to be subsumed within the culture of the national proletariat. In "Shinagawa Station in the Rain," the colonized has a determined place in national proletarian culture and that position provided Nakano with an optic for his manifesto. As the superexploited, the colonized are the most primed for revolutionary action against the sovereign, but as minorities within the national proletariat, the interests of the various classes of Korea were the same with one another and the same as the metropolitan proletariat. In viewing the colonized of Japan through the Soviet multiculturalism that emerged during the Soviet Union's nation-building period, Nakano ignored the complex issue of national liberation within the political left in colonial Korea. He also assumed the internal unity of the Korean proletariat and the Japanese proletariat in their respective political spheres, as if the problem of the divide between the countryside and the city could be overcome in each place through the imagination of an international. The possibility of this unity of the international was created through social science and was based on the assumption of the cultural and economic unity of the genus-being of the human (productive labor) in the capitalist stage of development (exemplified by the figure of the "proletariat"). The absolute negation of sovereignty proposed in the poem could occur because Japan and Korea were united in universal history, although the sign of "Korea" continued to reference the colonial difference in exploitation, as well as the persistent question of the relation between proletarian revolution and national liberation. Nakano views the colonized as the negated element of the process of world history, but also as history's potential redeemer. His sublation of Korean nationality into Japanese proletarian revolution is one instance of mimesis between the Hegelian logic of the negation of the negation as a representation of colonial revolt and a class-based version of the same logic. The unity of the Japanese and Korean proletariats is premised on the inclusion of Koreans within the dialectical and progressive history of Japan, a country supposedly divided primarily into two—bourgeoisie and proletariat—because it has uniformly entered the capitalist stage of development.

The many amendments he made to the poem, even years later, suggest a lingering uncertainty about this figuration. Nakano confronted the "unevenness" of capitalist development (that is, the fallacy of reducing historical time to a stage theory) in attempting to position the colonized within universal historical time. However, as Brett de Bary points out in her introduction to a translation of Nakano's novella from 1939, *The House in the Village,* Nakano was also deeply aware that despite capitalist development, older social relationships continued in Japan proper as well, particularly in the countryside.[12] Upon returning to his home village—following his imprisonment, statement of conversion, and release—he wrote about rural daily life, and confronted the nonlinearity of historical time in a domestic setting. His observations of rural life suggested that political-economic development is not as uniform as many of the Marxists of his day, and some of his own theories of the proletarian arts, had proclaimed.

Despite the mobilization of the colonized for national revolt at the end of the poem, Nakano's public expression of regret for his Korean comrades leaving Tokyo and his support of their desire for national liberation were certainly bold steps to take in the context of imperial Japan. In the historical context, it is remarkable that Nakano thought about the colonies in other than a governmental manner, and he is recalcitrant in his insistence that anticolonial revolution is a justified and necessary response to imperialism. Neither of these positions was easy to take, as evidenced by the illegibility of much of the poem following state censorship. It is possible that the state backlash against proletarian literature was greatly influenced by the fear of such metropolitan support for anticolonial revolution.

The nationalization effort of enforced conversion was as much an attempt to crush the sprouts of a multinational affront to imperialist rule as it was a product of the fear of the Japan proletariat. There was something immediately threatening in intellectuals' willingness to place the collective struggle of a (vaguely defined) proletarian class over the national interests of imperialism. Therefore, even if Nakano's poem simplified the position of the colonized in history a great deal, his idea of an international proletarian subject was also an assertion of universality quite threatening to the kind of moralistic governmentality we find in culturalism.

In reading the poem Im Hwa wrote in response to Nakano's, we confront a very different sense of history, and a different sense of the possibility for international solidarity. Im's lamentations to the "woman of Yokohama" are a stark contrast to the violent political agitation of Nakano's poem. Im's poem weaves together and contrasts the emotions of romantic love, and its loss, with the feeling of solidarity between the working classes of different countries. The impossibility of a romantic reconciliation between the woman of Yokohama and the poet is rendered analogous to the impossible reconciliation between Japan and its colonized. The fate of the "woman from another country" and the fate of the poet are at odds, because his temporary banishment from Japan proper and the imprisonment of his fellow agitators mean that "they have not lived in the embrace of your country's love / Nor have they lived in your beautiful heart."[13] The poet compares the failed embrace of Japan with the failed love between a "man of the colonies" and the woman of the metropole.

Despite his melodramatic proclamations of love, the poet maintains a certain stoic distance from the personal loss. Most of the overt expressions of personal loss and sadness are imputed to the feminine addressee. The poem entreats the woman to recognize the impossibility of their romantic love overcoming the macropolitical conflict between her country and its colonies. Rather than dwelling on his banishment to Korea, the poet insists that the woman should care for those comrades from the continent who remain in Japan, and who have been spurned and oppressed by her country. By taking care of those foreign workers and activists who remain in Japan, the woman of Yokohama can make amends for the cruelty of imperialism. The poet's appeal for the woman to be hospitable toward the imprisoned men is a way to deflect the individuality of colonial desire, and to transform the gendered relationship into one of national debt and repayment. In the gendered aspects of the poem, therefore, the woman is figured as an unambiguous representative of her country. However, from the details of her life that we can gather from the poem, she is not a desirable national subject. She is a factory worker participating in dangerous labor demonstrations alongside foreign workers, and her future seems to be as tenuous as that of the colonial intellectual who is forced to return home. In this sense, the stability of her nationality is a fiction that allows the poet to introduce the problem of the colonial relationship.

In his ostensible rejection of romantic nostalgia, the poet claims that the love between them is a result of their shared experience of daily life, work, and political struggle. The meaning of that daily life, and of their political ideals, will persist, despite individual fates and their intractable connection to nationality. The resistance to romantic nostalgia is at once an assertion of masculine toughness in the face of personal loss and political repression and an affirmation of a higher ideal of love that is seemingly more political than individual. At the same time, the feeling of solidarity between working men would also lose its emotional content without the figure of the woman as addressee. The poet struggles to overcome the feeling of lost love in order to reassert the collective political struggle, but romantic desire also provides an emotional charge to the poem's expression of solidarity. The cadence and imagery of the poem follow this movement between romantic desire and an idea of love founded in labor and struggle. Because of the way that the poet perceives the problem of colonial rule through a gendered optic, the woman of Yokohama at once belongs to the colonizing nation unambiguously, and is also capable of a kindness and hospitality toward men that are necessary for international solidarity. The literary quality of Im's poem lies in its capturing of the complexity of these various desires—colonial, romantic, political—as they conflict with one another in a situation of great existential uncertainty.

Unlike in Nakano's poem, it is impossible for the "man of the colonies" to belong to Japan, or the Japan proletariat, much less perform something as world-historical as an attack of the emperor. The exclusion and banishment of the "man of the colonies" are a matter not only of class revolt, but also of colonialism. In response to Nakano's poem, Im seems rather indifferent to the call for the colonized to struggle against empire by attacking its center. This indifference toward Nakano's historical model is accompanied by a feminization of Japan. The model for masculinity is the foreign worker and activist who is at once victimized by capitalism and the imperial state, and owed a debt that the woman of the metropole can repay with her kindness to his countrymen. The unfortunate limitation of Im's poem is that in order to assert the internationalism of proletarian struggle, he nationalizes the feminine. This nationalization of the feminine is present in his representations of other women characters, including, most famously, Suni, except that in the case of the woman of Yokohama, she is a figure for the colonizing nation.[14] The subjectivity of men is at once national and international, whereas women are innately bound to national identity. In this sense, the nationalization of the feminine is a question not only of male national subjectivity, but, in this case, of the universality of the category of man in the internationalism of the period. Much as Yi Kwang-su used female characters as models for the cultivation of artistic and national subjectivity, Im suggests that the possibility for internationalism depends upon the awakening of the woman of Yokohama to her political duty. But like the character of Yŏng-ch'ae in *The Heartless,* whose personal development is likened to the enlightenment of the Korean nation, the woman of Yokohama can be a model for humanity only insofar as she remains unambiguously Japanese.

In the literary exchange between Nakano Shigeharu and Im Hwa, various symptoms and problems of anthropocentrism take literary form. The exchange is symptomatic of how stage theory, the aesthetic and cultural philosophy of the proletarian arts, and the gendering of the proletarian subject all greatly affected how male intellectuals in the proletarian arts movements addressed one another, particularly in translation, across the divide between imperial and colonized subjectivities. If Marxism and the proletarian arts required the illusion of communicative and transparent communication between national contexts for the formation of the international, the exchange between Nakano and Im shows that translation does not perform such a metaphysical function, but is instead profoundly historical. Our ability to read Nakano in Korean retrospectively does not provide a resolution to the question of the author's politics; it rather forces us to understand how his views of history took shape, and the ways that the history of his poem's translation and interlocution goes against the grain of his own human scientific understanding of history. In particular, the ways that Nakano and Im articulated theories of what I call proletarian *Bildung* reveal the degree to which the existing Marxist social science and Marxist aesthetics of the time were inadequate for understanding Japanese imperialism, the relations between metropolitan and colonial intellectuals, and the divide between city and countryside.

SOVIET DEBATES: UNEVENNESS, ANTHROPOLOGY, AND CULTURE

The questions about universal history and proletarian culture that emerged in the poetic exchange between Nakano and Im were greatly affected by each writer's perspective on history, humanity, and proletarian culture. These perspectives, which become clearer in Nakano's and Im's literary criticism discussed in the next section, were very much translations of particular anthropocentric epistemologies that developed in pre-revolutionary Russia and in the Soviet Union. One blind spot in work on East Asian proletarian arts has been the formative debates around the concept of proletarian arts, culture, and literature in these contexts and a related conflation of the East Asian proletarian arts movements with Marxism-Leninism. In my view, it is necessary to determine why intellectuals turned to the proletarian arts as a specifically cultural, artistic, and aesthetic modernization project and, simultaneously, to show how their discourse was intertextual with both culturalism and the humanist language of empire. Furthermore, it is necessary to trace how intellectuals and writers dealt with or failed to deal with the emergence of Stalinism, as well as the ideas through which intellectuals were able to reconcile their Stalinist theories of culture, politics, and economy with the dominant cultural policies of the late Japanese empire, including the East Asian Community and the Greater East Asian Co-Prosperity Sphere.

Lost in the tendency to conflate Marxism-Leninism and the proletarian arts movements is the early debate between V. I. Lenin and Alexander Bogdanov—one of the primary initiators of the Proletkult movement—as well as the ongoing conflict between Lenin and the various proletarian arts organizations in the post-revolutionary Soviet Union.[15] Despite the widespread view that East Asian proletarian arts are a direct legacy of the Russian Revolution, Lenin repeatedly denounced the establishment of proletarian culture organizations prior to the October Revolution. His only extended philosophical text, *Materialism and Empirio-Criticism* (1908), was largely directed at the "reactionary" empirical philosophy of Bogdanov, which according to Lenin failed to overcome the apolitical humanist ideology of the bourgeois class, defined primarily by the confusion of immediate experience and divine intentionality.[16] Only after the revolution, in a response to Lunacharsky in 1920, "On Proletarian Culture," did Lenin make his first positive statements about Proletkult, but this was an explicitly political attempt to guarantee their lack of autonomy and their subordination to the educational work of the party and the commissar of education.[17] In contrast to many who took up his legacy in East Asia, Lenin attributed little value to the idea of a cultural or artistic proletarian subject.

In *Literature and Revolution* (1924), Leon Trotsky echoed Lenin's earlier criticisms of Proletkult, directing his attack more specifically to the idea of proletarian culture:

> The formless talk about proletarian culture, in antithesis to bourgeois culture, feeds on the extremely uncritical identification of the historic destinies of the proletariat with those of the bourgeoisie. A shallow and purely liberal method of making analogies of historic forms has nothing in common with Marxism. There is no real analogy between the historic development of the bourgeoisie and of the working class.[18]

According to Trotsky, dominant classes require hundreds of years to create their cultures. Because the modern industrial proletariat was only some decades old and had had a state that represents its interests for only seven years, it was foolish to expect that it had already created its own culture, or that it could do so in a matter of a few years. Furthermore, following Marx, Trotsky argued that the proletariat is not a class like any other dominant class, but rather the class that brings about the end of social classes. Therefore, to speak of a proletarian culture was to simply mimic the bourgeois idea of culture and apply it mechanically to a different class, ignoring the universal historical purpose of the proletariat to seek the abolition of classes and the transition to socialism. Trotsky wrote of the possibility of a socialist art that could develop in the wake of revolution, and that would be built upon a critical engagement with the aesthetic legacies of classical, bourgeois, and modern art and literature. However, he argued against the idea that proletarian culture already existed in a hypostatized state, and that it could be quickly created by opening up the practice of writing and artistic creation to workers.

Despite their use of Leninist terminology like "purposive consciousness," the critical discourse of the proletarian arts in East Asia did not derive from Leninism, but rather echoed the most influential advocate of the cultural substantiality of proletarian consciousness in Russian and Soviet criticism, Lenin's adversary and the Proletkult leader Alexander Bogdanov. It also took up the discussions that took place after 1932 of the socialist realist aesthetic system, which accorded to culture the capacity to form socialist subjectivities in post-revolutionary societies and revolutionary proletarian subjectivity in pre-revolutionary societies. In East Asia, therefore, Marxist-Leninist concepts like "purposive consciousness" took on a particularly cultural valence.

With his concern with systemic and organic integration, Bogdanov became influential not primarily in Marxism-Leninism, but in strands of modernization theory and systems theory.[19] He argued that workers, or the "executants" of modern economic systems, are historically and anthropologically superior to the "managers." By virtue of their class position and their practical activity as laborers, the executants more perfectly embody the human's genus-being of laborer. First in his *Empirio-Monism* (1904–06), and later in his three-volume work *Tektologia* (1912–20), Bogdanov attempted to produce a general science of organization that could explain how the human being comes to conquer nature through the organization of working collectives. He derived "tektology" from the Greek word *tekton*, or "builder," and argued that nature, technology, and the human being are all organized into systems through a constant process of differentiation and unification, or what he referred to as "the formulating principle of ingression and the regulating principle of selection."[20] Bogdanov criticized Kant for locating organizing principles solely in the thinking subject, and sought the basis for organization in the empirical world. However, as Lenin pointed out, the force of organization in Bogdanov's science resembles Hegel's Absolute Spirit and Kant's God, supplements through which the rationality of the world could be seen as a materialization of an ideal organism.[21] Lenin was correct in pointing out that Bogdanov was masking his idealism in an empirical study of "man," particularly through his designation of the historical role of the proletariat, proletarian perspective, and proletarian culture for a humanist epistemology.

Bogdanov sought an intersection of social organization and cultural formation similar to that of cultural science, but connected it to the perspective and historical purpose of the proletariat. He thought proletarian social existence was historically final, because it would create a collective subject of organization through the overcoming of specialization and the capitalist division of labor. He connected tektology to the primacy of the proletarian subject in world history:

"Mankind needed a point of view on a universal scale; in other words, a new mode of thought. But historical changes in thought occur only when a new organization of the entire society develops, or when there appears a new social class. In the 19th century exactly such a class came into being—the industrial proletariat." For him, the proletariat is not a mode of becoming, but rather a state of being, a substantial subject whose perceptions, practices, and social organization are a necessary result of the industrial mode of production. Although his idea of the proletariat had some analogy with Lukács's view of this class as the "identical subject-object of history," it is comparatively ahistorical and static.[22] He writes that the proletariat is capable of unifying the world into an organized system because of its identity as a subject that had already overcome, through its interactivity with machines, the division of labor between the organizers (or managers) and the executants (or workers). Like the person in the philosophy of culturalism, the proletariat is a teleological figure that regulates the epistemological organization of human social life. The human being's domination of nature through collective work and collective cultural activity is what provides order to the universe, an order regulated by principles of organization that originate in the ideal human form of the executant.

Once the proletariat is transformed into a "point of view on a universal scale" and executants are hypostasized as the ideal, historical embodiment of labor as the genus-being of the human, a duality between practical universality and empirical anthropological difference very similar to culturalism begins to emerge. If only the "industrial proletariat" in the abstract can serve as the point of view on a universal scale, through what categories and concepts do we account for failures to obtain this perspective, whether or not the subject in question is engaged in industrial labor? In the first half of the twentieth century, the theoretical dispute in Marxism that tried to resolve, but was also the most symptomatic of, this problem of the anthropological difference implied by the unity of the proletariat was the debate between stage theory and "combined and uneven development."[23] The problems of anthropology and anthropological difference are embedded in even the most nuanced versions of theories of uneven development, suggesting that the concept of unevenness may not liberate Marxist thought from its traditional intersection with the categories of bourgeois anthropology: the nation, race, character, and types.

Rather than being solely an issue of historical modeling, what is called "unevenness" is a problem of the human sciences and how they affect the modes of translation and modes of address within the supposed unity of the Marxist international. Reading Trotsky's critique of Stalin's stage theory and situating it within the discursive contexts of the 1920s and 1930s, we can see a very similar sociological and anthropological problem in his reading of national social types. While he incisively deduces how the project of "socialism in one country" leads to Stalin's use of "uneven development" as an empty abstraction in phrases such as "socialist in content, national in form," he nevertheless does not critique the notion of a national social type:

> Stalin's characterization of national peculiarities as a simple "supplement" to the general type is in crying and therewith not accidental contradiction to Stalin's understanding (that is, his lack of understanding) of the law of uneven development of capitalism. With the help of the law of uneven development, which he has converted into an empty abstraction, Stalin tries to solve all the riddles of existence. But the astonishing thing is that he does not notice that *national peculiarity is nothing else but the most general product of the unevenness of historical development, its summary result, so to say*. . . . The peculiarity of national social type is the crystallization of the unevenness of its formation.[24]

Trotsky rightly questions Stalin's reduction of (national) particularity to a supplement to the universality of the general types of socialism and the proletariat. However, Trotsky does not completely undermine the human scientific concept of the "national social type," a concept that allows the history of capitalism to be read through national history and national character. For Trotsky, the national social type is still a coherent anthropological category; he only questions Stalin's reading of the particular type as a supplement rather than as an expression or crystallization of the unevenness of development within a single nation. The problem is that the nation is assumed to be an integrated cultural and economic region, despite the recognition of temporal and geographic diversity within it.

Communists in the Japanese empire did not follow either Stalinist stage theory or Trotsky's ideas about uneven development directly, but rather worked through them in both the social sciences and the arts. Many intellectuals involved in the proletarian arts recognized unevenness and the possibility of skipping stages of development when politically necessary, but they also tended to repeat the logic of supplementation in both Stalin's theory of economic development and Trotsky's critique. It is precisely this version of unevenness—the one that thinks through the existence of multiple modes of production and temporalities within a single milieu as ultimately expressed in a national social type—that the developed realist novels of the early 1930s, including some of Nakano's own work, questioned further. These novels, by breaking decisively with allegory and its consistency of the identity of the type, showed that economic development was neither even nor uneven, but rather itself a fiction that required the reduction of the space and time of human life to the space and time of universal history. Through their representation of other chronotopes, they did not find a space outside of capitalism or modernity, but rather revealed the properly temporal, rather than human scientific, quality of the lived spaces of a peripheral modernity that belonged to capitalism proper in a way distinct from the anthropological view of temporal difference in both stage theory and the theory of uneven development.

PROLETARIAN *BILDUNG* IN EAST ASIA: THE CULTURAL FORMATION OF A NATIONAL PROLETARIAT

Why, then, did the proletarian culture and arts become the primary medium for the translation of Marxism-Leninism into the Japanese empire? Part of the answer is in the intertextuality between the cultural modernization project of culturalism and that of the proletarian arts organizations. Proletarian *Bildung* refers to this conflicted place of culture, art, spirit, and literature in many Marxian perspectives in the Japanese empire. One distinct feature of discussions of proletarian literature and culture in the Japanese empire was the way that critics tended to combine the Bogdanov position on culture with the Marxism-Leninism view of history and consciousness. Therefore, when Aono Suekichi, Kurahara Korehito, Hirabayashi Hatsunosuke, Kim Ki-jin, and Pak Yŏng-hŭi differentiated between the spontaneous consciousness of premodern political subjectivity and the purposive consciousness of the modern proletariat, they did so through the binary of nature and culture. They read culture as the necessary mediation for the unity of the proletarian class in a historical situation characterized by uneven development, ethnic difference, and gendered forms of exploitation. Somewhat adumbrating the socialist realist project of displacing political and economic conflict into the realm of the aesthetic, these critics tended to see culture as central to the formation of a class subject, a humanist claim for proletarian culture that differed from the political strategizing of Lenin's or Trotsky's mostly consistent separation of political questions from cultural ones. The specifically cultural formation of a unified class subject became central precisely because the political unity of this class, particularly between metropolitan Japan and its colonies, was only incipient and was very early on undermined and defeated by the state.

Aono argues that the human being in general and the proletariat in particular are conditioned by social relations but also culturally and spiritually exceed them. His references to the culture and spirit of the proletariat point mainly not to a real class conflict in history, but to an intellectual struggle over the foundations of humanity and human subjectivity. Both culturalism and his theory of proletarian culture delink the human from a reified Nature in order to isolate it as the subject and object of knowledge, culture, and spirit. His concern with the culture and spirit of the proletariat emerges out of his recognition that the proletariat does not come about spontaneously from the conditions of capitalist modernity, but has to be formed through culture, particularly in social contexts in which a very small percentage of the population is engaged in industrial labor. Employing an enlightenment distinction, similar to culturalism's, between humans who are tied mechanically to spontaneous nature and humans who have both culture and free will, Aono and the other critics whom I will discuss examined proletarian class consciousness through the divide of nature and culture, and through a pragmatic humanism that isolated human consciousness as the only proper object of the historical arts and sciences.

After reading Lenin's "What Is to Be Done?" Aono argued that proletarian consciousness does not come about naturally and spontaneously through capitalist development, but that the true historical purpose of this class could only be achieved when the class obtained purposive consciousness. In passages surprisingly similar to Yi Kwang-su's neo-Kantian discussions of subjectivity in "Reconstruction," Aono writes,

> The proletarian class grows naturally. Along with it growing naturally, its desire for expression also grows naturally. One of its concrete expressions is proletarian literature. An intelligentsia that stood in the position of the proletariat emerged. Workers who wrote poetry emerged. Plays are produced from inside the factory. The hand of the peasant writes novels. This literature grew naturally.
>
> However, even though these literatures emerge naturally, they are not a movement. They became a proletarian literature movement because, in addition to natural growth, purposive consciousness arose. Where there is no purposive consciousness, there will be no movement.
>
> What is purposive consciousness?
>
> By themselves, descriptions of the life of the proletariat, or the proletariat's search for expression, provide individual satisfaction; they are not whole class actions with the self-consciousness of the purpose of proletarian class struggle. Only when art is self-conscious of the purpose of proletarian class struggle can it become class art. In other words, only when it is guided by class consciousness does art become class art. The proletarian literature movement emerges, and has emerged, only under these circumstances.[35]

Aono's discussion of purposive consciousness was enabled by a binary, very similar to the divide of culture and nature in cultural science, between the spontaneity of nature exemplified by the naturalist representation of the individual lives of workers and a purposive consciousness that represents the workers as a collective class subject. The theory of purposive consciousness is ostensibly derived from a Leninist political platform; however, it is here expressed primarily as a matter of aesthetic form and literary subjectivity, as part of a political program for art, or proletarian *Bildung*.

The theory of purposive consciousness worked against the natural and mechanistic notion of causality that assumed that particular historical conditions necessarily produce the effect of revolution, and the anthropocentric binary between culture and nature repeated itself. The theme of cultural and aesthetic education of consciousness became central, as it did in culturalism and cultural nationalism. On the one hand, it was a matter of how to properly guide freedom, so that freedom would not become mere spontaneity or impulse (for example, anarchy and anarchism); on the other hand, it was a matter of creating, through culture, a subject that would be adequate to its objective position in world history. The proletariat is the subject of world history that brings about total freedom from social classes, but if this subject can only be formed through the will and not by nature, then it must be constructed through the pragmatic intervention of culture. The idea of purposive consciousness echoes Japanese neo-Kantianism's emphasis on Kant's teleology and its concern for making transcendental knowledge pragmatic, for unifying humanity and nature through the mediation of culture. This analogous use of the term "purpose" reflects the intertextuality between two discourses that were otherwise politically opposed to each other throughout the 1920s and early 1930s.

This intertextuality of culturalism and proletarian literature is expressed most clearly in their shared understanding of the human being as both a conditioned, historical species and the only genus whose consciousness and activity supersede its natural conditions. Theories of proletarian arts and culture were in this way tied epistemologically to the search for the general qualities of the human. Another early critic, Hirabayashi Hatsunosuke, drew from the neo-Kantian differentiation between the causal laws of nature and those of culture in order to explain how human relations and human consciousness exceed the determinism of nature. At the same time, he redefined the cultural and historical conditions that shaped the human being in order to challenge the moral universality upon which culturalism based its regulatory knowledge of cultural history. In "Literary Methodology" (1927), Hirabayashi explains the difference between the human activity of literature and the workings of nature by referencing the problem of causality. Echoing Yi Kwang-su's distinction between the speed of the organic life of human culture and the speed of geological time, Hirabayashi states that causality in the history of literature occurs at a much greater speed than anything imaginable in nature. However, he goes on to state that the general characteristic that separates the human from natural time and natural causality is not moral reason, but rather economic relations that precede the birth of any individual:

> If we take natural conditions to be the single cause determining the vicissitudes of literature, then the cause will hardly change at all while the effects will change at a bewildering pace, and the principle of causality must be annulled. The human subjugates nature and its conditions do not remain simply compelled by it. This is something that the astounding progress of modern science and industry has demonstrated. For the various transformations caused in a society's ideology, and thereby in its literature, there must be a condition outside of nature, one that is more direct and that operates in a much shorter time frame....
>
> We are born into a natural environment and the imposition of the natural conditions that are independent of our will is as stated above. However, natural conditions are not the only things that exist independently of our will before we are born. In addition there are definite economic conditions. Whether we like it or not, when we are born we enter into definite economic conditions according to which we must live, rightly or wrongly.[26]

Drawing from Marx's "Theses on Feuerbach," Hirabayashi defines the genus-being of the human not as a transcendental essence, such as the capacity to apply a universal moral law to itself, but rather by the totality of economic relations through which humans dynamically transform nature, or the economic relations that precede the birth of individuals.[27] Nonetheless, it was necessary to both borrow from and critique neo-Kantianism's separation of nature and culture so that proletarian culture could be opposed to bourgeois culture within a framework of universal history that continued to assume a fundamental separation between the human being and nature. More specifically, in the discourses of proletarian literature, the neo-Kantian epistemological divide between natural science and cultural science allowed critics to categorize all bourgeois realism of the nineteenth century as a kind of naturalism, an empirical or positivist mode of representation concerned only with facts, and to argue instead for a literature that revealed the dynamic social and ideological conflicts teeming beneath the surface of these facts, in the economic conditions that constitute the genus-being in a given period. The opposition between nature and naturalism, on the one hand, and the dynamic life of the human genus, on the other, led critics to discuss the struggle between the bourgeoisie and the proletariat as a conflict between the static spirit of bourgeois individualism and a more dynamic proletarian subjectivity that Aono references with terms like "culture" and "spirit."

In this sense, the kind of dialectical critique of bourgeois humanism espoused by proletarian literature and culture critics (and in a different way by Marxist social scientists) required an appropriation and rearticulation of anthropological universals, not a more basic questioning of the epistemological premise of the human's supersession of nature and natural laws. In addition to the two main anthropological categories introduced by Marxism and proletarian literature—the genus-being as productive relations and the proletariat as social class—they also borrowed other anthropological categories directly from the traditions of liberal thought, including, most prominently, the nation. As in culturalism, these anthropological categories were conceptual means to address the problems of historical causality, subject formation, and freedom from necessity. In interpreting genus-being in terms of productive relations in their totality, read through the modes and relations of production, they contested the idea of a transcendental human essence that inhered in each properly human individual and his or her cultural works. At the same time, because reading the genus-being in terms of productive relations meant seeing the human being as the being that produces universally in all periods, there was another strain in the discourse that defined the genus-being of the human more abstractly, as the producer of the world, a being whose actions were a constant process of willful poetic creation more or less detached from nonhuman factors.[28] In the proletarian arts movements, such a conceptualization of production as the poetics of the human being is not simply a claim about economic relations, but also a claim about culture and literature. Therefore Hirabayashi characterizes the producer of literature, the proletarian artist, as the subject whose capacity for literary language allows for the supersession of nature and an active entrance into history. In the analogies they drew between labor and culture, proletarian literature critics gave literature and culture the same capacity to contribute to human subject formation.

A statement from Kurahara Korehito in "The Content and Form of Proletarian Art" (1929) provides just one of many examples of how this translatability of labor and culture required anthropological categories as mediators, in this case the "nation" *(minzoku)*:

> Nations with different relations of production have different artistic forms. For example, the music of those nations engaged in hunting and the music of those nations engaged in agriculture have different rhythms, and so on. However, this is not just something to be said about completely external forms like rhythm. The same can be said of the subject matter of art. For example, as Ernst Grosse has already indicated in his *The Beginnings of Art,* nations engaged in agriculture mainly make grass and trees the subject matter of their drawings, whereas nations engaged in hunting mainly make animals the subject matter of their drawings.
>
> In other words, we can say that forms of art are determined in the last by the development of the means of production (technology) that determines the form of labor of a given period and a given society.[29]

Kurahara is able to conflate culture, art, and labor and to present their activity as unified in an organic way only through the idea of the nation, an anthropological universal referring to a community with a shared origin and a shared destiny. In the background of his discussion of art's relation to labor is the stage theory of history that was gaining prominence in the Soviet Union at the time, which states that all nations are collectively at a single stage of development in the modes and relations of production. Kurahara assumes that the human being's art and culture transform in direct correlation with such changes in the mode of production, and the underlying concern is to define the present as the stage of capitalism and to assert that the proletariat is the proper artistic and cultural subject of this stage.

Kurahara must borrow the concept of the nation from liberalism in order to manufacture a sense of economic homogeneity for a particular people at a particular stage. His discourse nationalizes the economy in order to assert the universality of proletarian culture and proletarian art, a move that appears, in my reading of Nakano Shigeharu, as a way of accounting for colonial difference. The project for the cultural formation of a class subject was therefore dependent on a conceptual confusion between labor and culture, and on the idea that both labor and culture are determining and liberating, conditioning and without condition. Within nations that had entered the stage of capitalism, with its primary conflict between the bourgeoisie and the proletariat, mass proletarian culture arose spontaneously out of historical conditions, but intellectuals had to step in to unify the exploited into a subject adequate to their objective conditions through culture's active and pragmatic dimension. The analogies between proletarian *Bildung* and the model of individual cultivation in culturalism lay in this understanding of the political purpose of cultural, literary, and artistic activity both as conditioned by the economic stages and as an active and conscious force in history.

The universalism of this theory of both the objective and the subjective conditions required for modernization was highly translatable into the colonial territories. The antinomic idea that nations were integrated communities passing through economic and cultural stages in universal history but that the exploited classes of the nation required culture to become a collective subject adequate to that image was extremely powerful in the proletarian literature, culture, and arts movements in colonial Korea. The first literary criticism that problematized the relationship between aesthetics and class appeared in the journal *The Opening* (1920–25), where Im Chŏng-jae published his critical essay on the culturalist notion of personhood discussed in the last chapter. In his essay, he used the term "popular masses" *(minjung)*, rather than "the proletariat." With the founding of KAPF in 1925, the first chairman, Pak Yŏng-hŭi, coined the term "New Tendency Group" to refer to earlier attempts to write a literature of and for the popular masses. In the same year, Pak edited a publication of the New Tendency Group literature, gathering ten stories and one poem.[30] The New Tendency Group had provided, for the first time, a developed forum in the public arena for discussing the conditions of colonial modernity in terms of class exploitation. It was an attempt to develop an aesthetic, and an idea of culture, that would turn the critical eye of the writer to everyday social conditions. This view of life contrasted with Yi Kwang-su's early novels, in which "society" was more or less conflated with the nation and the improvement of social conditions was allegorized into a matter of individual-national cultivation. Pak and other members of KAPF took the New Tendency Group's interest in the lives of the popular masses and provided it with a more dramatic narrative of universal history. While Im Chŏng-jae formulated a general criticism of culturalist elitism, Pak criticized Yi Kwang-su's literature directly on class grounds, injecting the concept of class consciousness into the critique of bourgeois literature.[31]

Yi Puk-man, later the addressee of Nakano Shigeharu's poem "Shinagawa Station in the Rain," imported the content of Aono's essays on purposive consciousness into colonial Korea from Japan proper; they had a significant effect on theoretical discussions in the KAPF organization. In an essay that compares the New Tendency Group to an emergent proletarian literature, Pak argues that proletarian literary forms would elaborate on the accomplishments of the New Tendency Group, but with a more purposeful political program. Even though Pak sought to shift the focus of the depiction of everyday struggle from the individual life to a collective class subject, he nationalized this class subject in referring to Korea as a "proletarian nation." As proletarian culture was considered through theories of purposeful historical consciousness, national subject formation was often conflated with class subjectivity. At the same time, because the proletariat was a substantial state of being, however unformed and incipient, Pak had to criticize Trotsky's argument that proletarian culture did not exist and would not soon arise:

> There is the argument that proletarian culture and art will embark toward becoming a perfected culture only after this class has [had its revolution]. Also, Trotsky insisted that a culture of the propertyless classes cannot arise. He thought that there is no opportunity to construct such a culture in the time of class conflict, and that after [the revolution] a classless culture for all of humankind would be constructed. However, Trotsky's argument is very close to idealism.[32]

Pak's accusation that Trotsky's argument is "idealist" is revealing. Trotsky argued that if the historical purpose of the proletariat is to abolish social classes, then there is no reason to seek a culture proper to this specific class. However, in a situation in which revolution is practically impossible, what good is there for an art of the working classes to wait for revolution? Pak's accusation of "idealism" is a criticism of Trotsky's historical model and a way to assert the substantial existence of a collective class culture and collective national subject in colonial Korea.

This criticism opened up a space for new modes of representation, because it questioned the desultory narratives of individuals living under oppressive conditions and asked the writer to delve into and represent the collective dimension of political and social struggle. However, Pak did not critique nationalism as a bourgeois ideology, but rather maintained that Korea is a "propertyless nation" *(musan minjok)*.[33] This understanding of representation homogenized the class stratifications, various modes of production, and different temporalities that overlapped in Korea, reducing the whole of society to a synchronically unified subject of oppression. For Pak, Trotsky is idealist because he does not recognize this coherency of the capitalist stage and the national proletariat's unified culture within it. Pak assigned to culture and literature the capacity to intervene to give purpose to consciousness, to enact the organization of class and national consciousness in colonial Korea.

The other prominent proletarian literature critic and founding member of KAPF, Kim Ki-jin, engaged in a number of debates with Pak Yŏng-hŭi in both *The Opening* and a later journal, *Criticism*. Having studied in Japan until the early 1920s, he was present for the inaugural publications by Komaki Oki on Henri Barbusse and the Clarté movement.[34] At around the same time as Komaki and Sasaki Takamaru were publishing their translation of *Clarté* and looking to Russia as a model, Kim wrote in *The Opening*, "What kind of literature is necessary in Korea (and in Japan and China, too)? Prolekult is necessary. A pedagogical literature for the masses is necessary. . . . Thought that contributes to actual revolution, determined by the changing of the times, the misery of life, and the brutality of the established class, must become a single bundle and engulf the world like a ball of fire."[35] Kim's basic concern in his essays of this period is to criticize art for art's sake and to advocate the pedagogical function of literature for the impoverished and largely peasant majority of Korea and East Asia. Similarly to Im Chŏng-jae's statement that art could not fulfill its goal of perfecting the human being until a popular mass movement was created, Kim argued that the theory of "value" in culturalism and art for art's sake was mistaken: "the literature after the revolution will exist for its own sake; literature before the revolution exists for a secondary purpose, which is the revolution."[36] Kim transformed the language of a movement of the popular masses into the language of proletarian revolution. In his work, the word "proletariat" does not refer to the industrial worker per se, but to the propertyless masses organized into a unified class through art, culture, and literature. Until proletarian revolution occurs in East Asia, literature must organize the masses into a revolutionary subject. The proletariat is more of an idea of the subject to be formed than anything that exists objectively in the historical present. Kim's foundational essays on proletarian culture represented another kind of cultural modernization project in colonial Korea, one based on an idealist theory of proletarian consciousness and cultural identity more than on political economy. As Kim Ki-jin and Pak Yŏng-hŭi had their debates on form and content, which I discuss in more detail in the next chapter, they began to question how literature should properly represent the spatiotemporal process of the proletarian subject becoming aware of its collective historical purpose.

In this way, critics in both Japan proper and colonial Korea called upon the project of proletarian culture to create a unity of proletarian subjectivity based on an aesthetic ideology where it did not yet exist as a unified political or historical subject. Just as culture, the arts, and literature in culturalism were the mediations that allowed for the human in its raw form to accede to its proper genus-being as moral subject, proletarian arts critics thought that the germs of class consciousness existing within the highly differentiated masses had to gain a collective sense of purpose and accede to their own genus-being as an ideal laboring and revolutionary class through these same mediations. Along the way, social differences were coded as deviations from the norm, as the supplementary cultures of minority nations, women, the colonized, peasants, and other types. What this view of proletarian culture as a poetics of the subject occluded most was the fact that most exploited people continued to live in multiple temporalities, multiple modes of production, and between multiple class, ethnic, and gender identities.

This coding of culture according to the norm of the proletariat comes through in Nakano's theories of proletarian arts, in addition to his exchanges with Korean communists. In the article "What Is Proletarian Art?" from 1931, Nakano Shigeharu condenses many of his reflections on proletarian art. This essay is revealing as a document of proletarian *Bildung*; it combines the stage theory of history, an assertion of the primacy of the proletarian subject in world history, and an aesthetic theory of class consciousness in order to delineate the unity of the capitalist stage and the unity of the proletariat as the subject of transition to the next form of society. It is also a very anthropological text that uses the categories of the nation and the peasantry in order to explain the internal differences within this unified subject. Nakano begins his essay with a reading of *Historical Materialism* (1921), in which Nikolai Bukharin defines science as the systematization of thought, and art—including literature, music, dance, and architecture—as "a method for socializing the emotions."[37] Nakano echoes Bukharin and defines art as a method of organizing the emotions, but also states that in the performance of an artwork, ideas and thoughts are communicated as well. He writes that in singing a song like "The Internationale," art organizes both thoughts and emotions. Interwoven in this song are "the idea of the internationality of proletarian struggle and the thought of international solidarity."[38] In much the same way as Im Chŏng-jae had tried to redefine personhood in terms of the popular masses, Nakano uses collective performances as examples of how art is not merely reflective of a personal emotion, the way that bourgeois literature had imagined it, but rather a mode of socializing emotions and thoughts. Bukharin had relied on a dichotomy between reason as the organization of thought and art as the organization of emotions, but Nakano points out that it is not always so simple to separate scientific thought from art. A song can communicate a concept like internationality as much as it provides social meaning and organization to the desire to participate in a collective struggle.

Nakano then defines this organization of emotions more specifically as a class phenomenon. He writes, "Art is primarily a method of organizing the emotions, but thoughts and emotions are not the same for everyone. They are different for each person. But are they different only for individual people? No. They are different for the classes to which people belong."[39] In other words, thoughts and emotions are reflective of the historical positions of classes and the art and culture of classes organize those thoughts and emotions into a form. The object of proletarian art and literature is the life of the proletariat, and the content of proletarian art is the thoughts and emotions of this historical subject. However, the form that proletarian art takes depends upon its mode of organizing emotion and thought. Nakano relates the history of art to what I referred to in the previous chapter as the poetics of the subject, or the giving of form to the formless. History and the history of art are what give form to proletarian art, because proletarian art appropriates the languages and ideas of all of the other classes to create something that is historically unprecedented.[40] He argues that proletarian art is not simply the left wing of a homogeneous art world, a label that suggests that bourgeois cosmopolitan art and proletarian art are compatible opposites within a singular aesthetic field. Rather, proletarian art is the historical sublation of previous forms into the most historically advanced stage of art: "proletarian art is the historical development of earlier art, an art that creates the history of art."[41] Proletarian art is not the art of one class in a multiclass global society, but rather the historically necessary art for the historical present. It is superior and more historically advanced than all of the previous arts upon which it draws: "the movement of proletarian art is the concretization of the historical superiority of proletarian art."[42] It is the final historical stage of art in the period of transition from capitalism to socialism.

For Nakano, proletarian art is the aesthetic basis for the production and reproduction of a proletarian subject that exists but has not been organized into a complete form. Proletarian culture is a mode of cultivation that organizes the various thoughts and emotions of the proletarian classes into a unified political and historical subjectivity. This unified subject is international. Forms of art might maintain a national character, but they have to be created and interpreted from an international position: "even when we treat Japanese proletarian art, we must depart from an international position."[43] By 1931, this international position was defined in Stalinist terms of "socialism in one country" and Nakano also argued that socialist art should be "national in form" and "socialist in content." Bukharin and Stalin had asserted the theory of "socialism in one country" between 1924 and 1926, and the movements in Japan and Korea, as long as they derived their theoretical basis from Comintern doctrine, tended to maintain this view of the relationship between the national and the international.[44] Stalin recognized that nations without states were still national communities and defended the linguistic and cultural autonomy of national minorities within the Soviet Union. Nakano applied this formula to the peasantry and to the colonized nations within the Japanese empire, stating that their arts would also be national in form and socialist in content.

The way that Nakano imagined the Korean proletariat as his addressee was very much influenced by such a conflation of the metropolitan Japan proletariat with Moscow and colonial Korea with national minorities in the Soviet Union. Such a translation was only possible by way of the universality of Soviet human sciences, including Stalin's various influential discussions of the nation.[45] With the rather mechanical delineation of national form and socialist content, it was possible for Nakano to imagine the colonized as a homogeneous national subject and therefore attempt to mobilize them as a unified subject in "Shinagawa Station in the Rain." With this view of the relationship between the national and the international, the metropolitan Marxist comes to imagine that metropolitan acts of violence are the only possibility for the social revolution of the colonized and a necessary means of subsuming the ethnic minority into the metropolitan party. Art is elevated to a method of socializing and organizing emotions toward such a national and socialist solidarity between colonizer and colonized. Nakano's dependence on the idea of "art in the period of transition from capitalism to socialism" shows the extent to which the historical determinism of stage theory came to serve as the foundation of the idea of proletarian art and culture. Along with this historical determinism, the nation form became the ideal cultural form through which the socialist content of art could be expressed, which allowed for a number of political and economic issues related to imperialism, the state, and colonialism to be sublated into an aesthetic theory.

Nakano goes on to argue that organization is ideology considered as something social. Art is what organizes both thought and emotion, so he reduces all of ideology to an ideology of the aesthetic. This aestheticization of socialism reflects the shift to socialist realism occurring in the Soviet Union in the early 1930s. The idea that socialization occurs through the aesthetic is related to another prominent phrase in proletarian arts discourse, that existence determines consciousness. Art is the way that perception is organized into a consciousness of existence, but existence also precedes this organization and is its very foundation. The proletarian artistic subject is a universal, organizing aesthetic faculty with a foundation in the substance of class consciousness. Rather than referring specifically to the industrial working class, "proletariat" means this historical subject that is organized ideologically through the arts; it can therefore include all of the multiple class and ethnic origins within it. Barbara Foley has discussed the US Communist Party's assertion that the colonial regime in the American South would be overcome through the inclusion of African American struggles within the proletarian struggle.[46] A similar sublation occurred in the aesthetic theories of proletarian literature in East Asia, as colonial subjects and peasants (somehow conflated) were to have their interests represented only as they were included within representations of metropolitan proletarian struggle. Therefore, Nakano called on Koreans to enter history by leading the charge against the emperor system in "Shinagawa Station in the Rain."

The cultural formation of the proletarian class subject entailed two primary models of historical development concerning the human genus-being—on the one hand, productive relations of a given period determined the cultural forms of a nation and its classes; on the other hand, within the period of capitalism and the communist international, the transition to socialism could be accomplished through a cultural organization of humanity and its class representative, the proletariat. This model of a modernization puts the development of productive relations at the foundation, but cultural and other superstructural processes are the key to the unity of ideology and subjectivity, to the organization of that which exceeds nature and society—human labor and human freedom. Although a communist revolution had of course not occurred in East Asia, intellectuals in the Japanese empire nonetheless appropriated the project of socialist realism and the transition to socialism, which, as Evgeny Dobrenko has analyzed, was primarily a project of discourse, representation, and the consumption of aestheticized images of socialism, rather than a revolutionary leveling of class relations and the end of exploitation.[47] In addition to their severe suppression by the police, this discourse of cultural modernization became one of the primary languages through which Korean proletarian literary critics and writers came to reconcile themselves with Japanese empire, imperial subjectivity, and the gradual masking of capitalist crisis in humanist aesthetic forms.

The career of the poet and critic Im Hwa, who became the leader of KAPF in the 1930s, shows how the concept of a universal history of productive relations leading to the formation of the proletarian subject intersected with both humanism and empire in the context of colonial Korea. Im's best-known statement on the "new Korean literature," or Korean literature written after the late nineteenth century, is that this literature is a "transplanted literature" *(isik munhak)*.[48] According to Im, a history of the first new literature in Korea, such as the works of Yi In-jik, should be approached as a combination of the history of Korean vernacular literature and the history of Korean literary Chinese. However, this combination only occurred through modernity and the transplantation of Western forms into Korea by way of the colonizer Japan. Therefore, there is nothing indigenous about the new Korean literature.[49] According to "Method of the History of New Literature" (1940), which represents Im's fully developed and schematized theory, the history of the new, transplanted literature must take into account six primary factors: objects, social base, environment, tradition, form, and spirit.[50] As Kim Yun-sik argues, these categories of Im's theory of literature refer to both the universal qualities of modern literature and the regional, national, and local differences within these qualities; the theory is an attempt to find a method to study the mediation between modernity and universality, between the proliferation of differences entailed by modernity and the tendency toward a convergence of world literary culture. In this sense, Im did not suppose that a return to purely indigenous forms was possible after the influx of transplanted literature, but rather that the dialectic between transplantation and indigenization had to be explored through each of these six primary factors, with modernity being the shared condition for world history and world literature. Im turned to a theory of the anthropological conditions of culture in order to create a logical coherency between the universality of productive labor, embodied in the propertyless classes, and the social and cultural issues particular to colonial modernity.

Im's theory of transplanted literature, with its juxtaposition of concepts of both translation and organic rootedness, offers a more complex picture of the history of modern Korean literature than either the foreign literature group (for example, Yi Ha-yun and Chŏng Chin-sŏp) or the national literature group (for example, Yi Kwang-su and Ch'oe Nam-sŏn), which engaged in debates throughout the 1930s and whom Im Hwa criticized as advocates of petit-bourgeois ideologies.[51] As the chairman of KAPF in the 1930s, Im asserted the historical, culture, and political superiority of the propertyless class and their vanguard representatives. He also identified a colonial problem of time lag between Western literature and Korean literature, a time lag that potentially put into question whether or not the universal history of class struggle was truly as singular as the historical model of stage theory and the proletarian arts movements had assumed. However, what has been often ignored in Im's work is how his universalist and culturally focused Marxist humanism offered him a way out of the problem of transplantation and the colonial time lag, because by superimposing the universal history of culture upon a history of national culture, in much the same way as Nakano Shigeharu, Im could imagine that the history of new literature in Korea progressed in Hegelian fashion, through the gradual sublation of artistic forms.

Writing in the aftermath of the RAPP meetings in the Soviet Union in 1932, and the First Soviet Writers' Congress in 1934, both of which mark the beginnings of the formation of the socialist realist aesthetic system, Im imputed to socialist realism, or "critical realism and revolutionary romanticism," the capacity to overcome the underdevelopment of a native bourgeois literature.[52] He made this argument regardless of the fact that nothing resembling a socialist revolution had occurred or was likely to occur in the late Japanese empire. Just as Stalinism gradually made culture and art the realm and the means for the "transition to socialism," Im's history of new Korean literature narrates the progressive sublation of literary forms toward the end point of socialist realism.[53] He marked earlier attempts at a nonbourgeois literature as inadequate precursors, calling Ch'oe Sŏ-hae's New Tendency works "naturalist" and Pak Yŏng-hŭi's poetry and fiction "romantic."[54] Like Nakano, Im found in socialist realism what he thought to be the most historically advanced cultural and literary form, one that was realist, but also mythical, romantic, and expressive of a historically grounded yet universal human spirit. That Im's theory of literature participated in the problem of the empirico-transcendental doublet is apparent in that, on the one hand, he insisted that literature overcome, through engagement with universal history and the class consciousness of the proletariat, the kind of empirical and physiological determinism that he found in short stories such as Kim Nam-ch'ŏn's "Water" and Yi Ki-yŏng's "Rat Fire," while, on the other hand, he came to ground this transcendental subject of history and revolution in the geographic context of the Korean nation and, eventually, the East Asian community.[55]

Im Hwa appropriated and rearticulated the precepts of socialist realism and historical materialism in order to deal with the perceived lack of a native modern literature, using the new ideas of Soviet humanism in order to challenge bourgeois literature, overcome the colonial time lag, and maintain an international proletarian position.[56] He only turned to socialist realism—with its emphasis on everyday heroes, a new romanticism, and presentations of socialist man—after two major police crackdowns on KAPF (in 1931 and 1935), the latter of which led to his dissolution of the organization. Beginning in 1935, the central issue debated among the colonial Korea literati was the meaning of the "new humanism" and the European antifascist movements. Following the International Writers' Conference in Defense of Culture (in Paris in 1935), Paek Chŏl and Kim O-sŏng connected their notions of humanism to the European Renaissance and to the ideas of European antifascist writers like André Gide and George Orwell, eventually criticizing proletarian literature on these grounds.[57] Im Hwa criticized the neohumanists' discussions of the human as overly psychological and transhistorical, stating that in both life and literature the human should not be transformed into an "-ism" through mere symbolism, but that a worthy "-ism" must rather express the truth of the human and problematize all of previous human history.[58] Along with Kim Tu-yong and An Ham-gwang, Im maintained a Bolshevik position on the human and human culture, which by this time had taken the form of socialist realism.[59]

Considering that the Japanese empire was entering a period of rule that has been described as fascist and the proletarian arts movements had been suppressed by the growing police state, these debates concerning humanism in Europe seem to be strangely disengaged from the historical present. However, in Im Hwa's critique of the new humanism and in his appropriation of socialist realism to critique ahistorical ideas about the Renaissance, modernity, and the human, the problems of proletarian culture, genus-being, and imperial subjectivity intersect. He criticized the bourgeois and decadent quality of Paek Chŏl's new humanism, which treated the human as an abstract generality rather than as a social human; Im followed earlier proletarian arts criticisms of bourgeois culture in insisting that society and its productive relations condition the human being in its various historical moments.[60] However, in *The Logic of Literature* (1939), he differentiated his approach from historical determinism, stating that the human being's metabolism with and transformation of nature brings it into social relations, but that the human being also always exceeds both nature and social conditions.[61] He discussed this excessive human element in various ways—as the capacity to dream, as the capacity to labor consciously, and as the capacity to act freely in creating culture and history.[62] He argued that naturalism and the old nineteenth-century realist aesthetics were inadequate to this human subjectivity that transgresses nature and thereby comes to constitute and be constituted by objective, historical actuality. Again borrowing from Gorky and Soviet socialist realism, he states that in order to capture this subjectivity in representation, revolutionary literature needs romanticism, which is not perspectival or epistemological, but practical, active, and expressive of the pathos of the subject's historical experience: "Revolutionary romanticism is not essentially one side, aspect, or element of the new realism; it refers to our noble pathos, which emerges not in the thoughts of an epistemological subject (*chugwan*), but rather where our practical subjectivity *(chuch'e)* intersects with objective actuality."[63] Translating and utilizing the philosophical distinction in Japanese between epistemological and practical subjectivity, and also adumbrating theories of socialist realism that would later come to dominate literature and film in the DPRK, Im conflates the subject's metabolism with nature—in other words, its labor—with the free activity of producing and witnessing, through romantic representation, the pathos and suffering of objective, historical actuality.

Just as critics formerly endowed the proletarian arts with the task of creating through culture and the aesthetic a world-historical class subject, Im's class subject, his national subject, and ultimately his human subject intersect with objective history not through economy or politics, but rather through the mediation of the revolutionary romanticism of socialist realist representation. In essays such as "The Reconstruction of the Subject and the World of Literature" (1937), written in the aftermath of the disbanding of KAPF and at the beginning of Im's turn to Japanese imperial nationalism, the subject refers to both the national subject and the human as social and historical subject.[64]

As in Paek Nam-un's later theories of national economy, the generality of this subject was no longer precisely the genus-being of productive labor, but rather a universal culture, a state communist culture through which social class could disappear. Proletarian *Bildung* and its eventual iteration as a socialist realist version of cultural modernization required a certain conflation of the activities of labor and culture, an assumption of translatability between the idea that labor is the substance of human subjectivity and the German idealist notion of culture from which Marx's critique of transcendental humanism departed. Through anthropological categories like the nation and national culture, proletarian arts criticism was able to unify the proletariat theoretically as a collective subject of cultural production. This conflation of labor and culture allowed them to see the unity of the human genus-being, its labor, where in actuality there were differences of gender, class, and ethnicity. The aesthetic theories of proletarian literature and culture were perhaps the most effective in the colonies, because they made it possible to connect socialist revolution with a nationalization project. If the past of the colonized nation is disregarded and deliberately obscured by the colonizer, then proletarian literary and cultural criticism is one way to cull this past for the signs of socialist content, while at the same time giving it a progressively more national form. However, it was just as possible for Im Hwa to argue in the early 1940s, through the same logic and the same intersection of texts, that Japan's new peasant literature would come to represent the universal home and origin of all East Asian state subjects.[65] After reading proletarian literature as a national literature with both an origin and a telos, Im could later apply this structure of the nation form to a Japan-centered East Asia, finding in representations of the rural hometown in Japanese peasant literature a universal East Asian origin that also pointed to an alternative modern future. Im transformed the idea of a realist and secular peasant literature that was to unify the proletariat and the peasantry in the capitalist stage, as proposed by An Ham-gwang, into an imperial literature that could bring together various ethnicities and social classes under a Japanese and East Asian state.[66] Genus-being transformed from productive relations to nation-state subjectivity, and state art became the means for the dialectical and aesthetic overcoming of both imported culture and the alienation of the East Asian proletariat from its origin and its social essence.

ECONOMIC STAGES OF GENUS-BEING: PAEK NAM-UN

One result of reading the national economy and universal history in tandem was that Marxist political economists grappled with economic questions in terms of national history. The primary issues in the debates on Japanese capitalism were stated in the language of national history: How could one explain the persistence of feudal relations? And was the Meiji Restoration a bourgeois revolution? The famous debates on Japanese capitalism in the 1930s between the Lectures School and the Labor-Peasant School concerning the possibility of revolution in Japan, as well as the various discussions of the "Asiatic Mode of Production" (AMP), attempted to understand Japan's position within the progress of the global history of capitalism. The Lectures School argued that a bourgeois revolution was required before proletarian revolution could occur, while the Labor-Peasant School argued that stages could be skipped. Among the Korean intelligentsia as well, Marxist political economists such as Paek Nam-un applied the stage theory of development to Korean economic history, and theorized the effects of Japanese imperialism on Korean economic development.[67]

Paek Nam-un's writing of Korean national history as a history of stages, both during the colonial period and as Minister of Culture during the founding of the DPRK, is one significant example of how the return to humanist metaphysics can occur, even when one would expect that the concrete social conditions of Korea would have led social science to different conclusions.[68] As in Im Chŏng-jae's theory that personhood would be actualized through popular struggle, or in Aono Suekichi's theory of the proletariat as an anti-individual subjectivity, the stage theory of history also had its critical edge and its critical usefulness. Paek Nam-un began by critiquing the neo-Kantian concept of cultural value through "social science" *(sahoe kwahak).*[69] He wrote that society is formed through social relations between humans, and more specifically relations of production, not through the ethnic, national, and cosmopolitan identities discussed by culturalists. As he presented in his most famous work, *The Economic History of Korean Society* (1933), Paek thought of history as a series of modes of production transitioning from primitive communism, to feudalism, to capitalism, socialism, and finally communism, mechanically matching these stages to periods in the dynastic history of Korea, asserting the primitive communism of Tan'gun's ancient kingdom, the slave state of Unified Silla, the feudalism of the Chosŏn period, and contemporary capitalism.[70] He opposed this theory of history and its basis in the relations of production to the dubious geographic determinism of culturalists, whose area studies made a region of Korea. Drawing from the work of his Japanese mentor, Hani Gorō, he insightfully pointed out that the return to geography in the work of culturalists like Watsuji Tetsurō, or Ch'oe Nam-sŏn in the Korean context, was a last-ditch effort for moral philosophers to give a sense of spatial location to their metaphysical claims. This return to geography in Kantian cosmopolitan framework is apparent in Kant's attempts to delineate the boundaries of Europe or in Watsuji's search for a geographic determination of national culture. For Paek, the stage theory of history at least took social relations out of the abstract spatial normativity of cosmopolitan geography and assumed that social relations are what determine the genus-being of humanity at a given time in history. Despite his cogent critique of geographic determinism, however, he did not intervene significantly in the spatiotemporality of national historical narrative, and remained tied to a kind of humanist metaphysics in his assumption that the space of the Korean population transformed uniformly from one economic stage to the next.

In addition to showing that the neo-Kantian theory of cultural value was too disconnected from social relations, and connecting this abstraction to the problematic culturalist geographies that accompanied culturalist colonial discourse, through his introduction of Marxist social science into colonial Korea Paek also tried to formulate a different way of connecting the universal and the particular, one quite distinct from the cultural nationalist tendency to see national culture as the particular means toward the internalization of modern moral universals. He was especially critical of what he called the "particularistic view of history," by which he meant ethnic national histories that assumed the uniqueness and particularity of Korea. He wrote,

> In looking at the history of a cultural nation, the historical facts of that country are not something seen only in that country. The feudal system is not something that existed only in England or Japan; it existed throughout the world; looking at the history of the development of culture, we can see that in ancient times there was primitive communism throughout the world and after that there were slave states.
>
> From the above it is clear that the particularistic view of history is very dangerous and illogical.[71]

Paek refers to culturalists like Ch'oe Nam-sŏn and ethnic nationalists like Sin Ch'ae-ho in his criticisms of the particularistic view. While he was aware that culturalists and ethnic nationalists had their own notions about universal history, he was mainly concerned with the way that cultural history eventually returned to an essentialist idea about the particular character of the nation. He thought that stage theory provided a more accurate way to connect the generality of humanity to the particularity of national history: "Finally, I would like to say that we cannot complete a history of Korea through the particularistic view of history that thinks in a particular or singular way through fragmentary facts, and that we can only complete this history through a universalist view of history."[72] This universalist view of history is the history of the stages of economic development. Paek appropriated this universalist history in order to write a more complete and accurate national history. He did not entirely replace a particularistic view of history with a universalist one, as he himself claimed, but rather articulated a different relation of translation between national history and the human, defined generically as a producer whose form of labor is determined by the economic stage. For Paek, the general model is the stages of productive relations, the particular is Korean national history, and labor, as the practical activity that defines the genus-being of the human, is the generality that connects the nation to world history. In this respect, both culturalism and Marxist social science worked within the logic of anthropocentric thought, the universality of which allowed for translation and cooperation between empire and colony.

Despite his critique of culturalism, however, Paek eventually returned to a moral idea of practice when he began to write and speak in favor of the Japanese state as the agent of social reformation, from a society that values profit above all else to a society that satisfies the needs of humanity as a whole. In his discussion of the state control of the economy in the Greater East Asian Co-Prosperity Sphere, he began to write of the ethics of the economy, and how the state could step in as the "subject" *(chuch'e)* guiding the economy in a more ethical fashion than the drive for personal profit.[73] Paek's humanism of stage theory returned to a subjective ethical theory in which the Japanese empire could fulfill the ultimate purpose of human history, for the human being to return to its essence as laborer by producing only what is socially necessary, with an anthropomorphized state regulating production and consumption according to universal ethical laws. The communist Sŏ In-sik argued similarly that the appearance of the "socialized human" in communist society would mean the overcoming of the human's alienation from its essence as laborer, and saw the Japanese empire, or East Asian Community, as the historical subject that would bring about this socialization.[74] This type of "conversion" was only possible because two different transcendental definitions of the genus-being of the human—laborer and moral personhood—became translatable. The translatability between the proletariat and the state allowed the state as the moral and sovereign actor to reorder production and consumption in order to solve the problem of crisis through what Paek imagined as a culturally and ethically superior form of Keynesian intervention. In the conflict over the meaning of the genus-being, the productivist ethic and the state as the embodiment of human will became the dominant social-scientific concepts.

In order to mark his sociological break from German idealism, Marx wrote of stages of development in the mode of production and property relations (tribal, ancient communal, feudal, capitalist), particularly early on in "The German Ideology."[75] However, based on such sketches, the Comintern developed a simplistic doctrine on the modes and relations of production, which greatly affected historiography in later imperialist countries like Japan, as well as in their colonial territories. Stage theory became a political problem in Korea, which was marked by obvious uneven development (or underdevelopment) and, under the Comintern's "one country, one party" policy (1928), was unable to maintain communist parties that were autonomous from those of their imperial rulers (which made it difficult to theorize the economics of imperialism and colonialism within the context of the international).[76] In the case of Paek, this political problem is a matter that touches on the more general question of humanism, as well as the coherency between Paek's support for the Japanese empire and his previous understanding of universal history and the genus-being of the human. A planned economy, run by a strong central state, was, according to Paek in the 1940s, a historical necessity. He recognized this tendency in world history equally in the New Deal of the United States and the fascist states of Europe, but sought a better form of state regulation of the economy in the Co-Prosperity Sphere, enacted by the morally superior pragmatics of the Japanese state.

In Paek's stage theory, the subject of social relations is the entirety of humanity, and the genus-being is determined by the relations of production. However, when it came to advocating the state in the arena of world history, the state stood in place of the proletariat, but more importantly came to represent humanity as a whole. This is an example of how the practice of the proletarian subject, understood in humanist terms as the exemplar of universal production in the capitalist period, can become imperialist. Once we take up an abstract social science and imagine that the proletariat is unified within the capitalist stage of history, the intervention of the imperial state on behalf of humanity seems rational, and the universalism of imperialism asserts itself. By intervening ethically on behalf of the needs of people, the state replaces the working class as the subject guiding history toward its final, utopian end. The state overcomes division in a manner analogous to Lukács's notion of the proletariat as the historical subject that will dissolve alienation. Through the ethical action of the state, the human being also regains its essence, but only through the same kind of humanist reading of the genus-being that Marx gradually left behind. For the major philosophers and economists in Korea, the role of the state in world history and the degree to which the state could act in the interests of humanity as a whole became the primary questions. In literature and the arts as well, critics on the left grappled with the humanism of the socialist realist aesthetic and whether or not this humanism could be distinguished from the kind produced in support of the Japanese imperial state. Only through the figure of the human and the positing of the possibility for a new ethical humanism could the Japanese state replace the proletariat's position in world history. Paek's humanism began with economic stages of the genus-being and a conflation of national economic development and universal history; it passed through a support for the Japanese imperial state's intervention, as an ethical subject, in the crisis of the national and world economy; it ended in a nation-building project for the postcolonial DPRK, one in which a "democratic ethic," a "democratic culture," and a "democratic economy," all instituted by the "subjectivity" of the state, would unite nationalism (and its goal of national liberation) with communism (the science of universal history).[77]

PROLETARIAN CULTURE AND THE EAST ASIAN COMMUNITY

One unfortunate consequence of the figuration of productive labor as the human's genus-being is that it allowed intellectuals to eventually see the Japanese imperial state as a historically necessary subject of world history and as a redeemer of the humanist aspirations of colonizing and colonized subjects alike. In the late 1930s, many Marxists began to argue that the East Asian Community, with the Japanese state at its center and a regional East Asian *culture* as its mediation, would create a new human being and a new human society. In his earlier Marxist-Leninist works on the "culture of communism," and its superiority to both liberal and fascist cultures, Sŏ In-sik called this new human being the "socialized human."[78] In his later speculations about an East Asian culture that would be multiethnic, imperial, state-centered, and historically unprecedented, he made a similar formulation in his discussion of "heroism," keeping human culture at the center: "The human as the substratum of history is the oppositional unity of subjective action and objective being."[79] Thus for those Marxists and proletarian literature critics who came to support the Japanese empire, it was the idea of culture, and more specifically proletarian or communist culture, that allowed them to rethink the class subject as an imperial subject and the genus-being of the human (that is, the totality of its social relations) as rather a new form of universal cultural practice. The metaphorical and real relations between the concept of culture and the concept of labor, a relation deeply ensconced in nineteenth-century European epistemologies and the rise of the human sciences, allowed for a translation of human genus-being and the class consciousness of the propertyless into the cultural subject of empire. Analyzing Marxist and proletarian arts interpretations of the human as the being that "produces universally" is to also reflect on the imperial humanisms of the late Japanese empire and their theories of culture. In the case of Im Hwa, the fungibility between the concepts of culture and labor allowed him to propose in the 1940s a literature of the laboring countryside as a national literature for the whole empire (thereby ignoring, like Paek Nam-un, the ongoing problem of primitive accumulation in the countryside, which was the focus of radical feminist writers such as Kang Kyŏng-ae, who were able to connect the class problems of the countryside and the city without relying on a state-centered culturalist model).[80]

Only through such an articulation of the genus-being could philosophies in the Soviet Union, as well as some versions of the East Asian Community, arrive at the idea that a particular nation-state can represent all of humanity in more authentically representing the proletariat, the most essentially human social class. Such humanist ideals concerning history and subjectivity contributed to some colonial Korean intellectuals' capitulations to the Japanese empire and the hegemonic versions of world history. This capitulation required the structure of the empirico-transcendental doublet and an illusion of its universal translatability, as well as the concomitant practice of locating in one historical and particular national identity a representative of the human's essential social practice. Therefore, despite the continuation of exploitation and the reproduction of hierarchical class relations in the late Japanese empire, certain modes of Marxist humanism allowed intellectuals to see the Japanese imperial state as a representative of the East Asian proletariat, and humanity at large, in world history.

4

Other Chronotopes in Realist Literature

The image of man is always intrinsically chronotopic.
—MIKHAIL BAKHTIN

"So, all you, is name proletariat. Understand?"
—A CHINESE WORKER IN KOBAYASHI TAKIJI'S *THE CRAB CANNERY SHIP*

CHRONOTOPE AND HUMANISM

In 1924, a year after the Kanto earthquake and the subsequent racist attacks against Korean and Chinese minorities in Japan proper, Yoshino Sakuzō began publishing the works of the Meiji Culture Research Group, celebrating the cultural legacy of Meiji and bemoaning the new complexities of ethnic and class politics.[1] Cultural policy was in full swing in Korea, and Sōda Kiichirō was continuing to formalize the philosophy of culturalism. In the same year, Etsuzandō published *The View of Life of Death Row Inmates* by Nakanishi Inosuke, a leftist writer from Japan who spent a good deal of time in Korea and was critical of Japanese colonial racism against Koreans.[2] This text is remarkable in many ways, but particularly in how it uses the chronotope of the prison to test the coherency of the empirico-transcendental doublet of culturalist humanism.

Nakanishi himself was incarcerated in Tokyo's Ichigaya and Nakano prisons as well as in Korea. The final chapter of *The View of Life of Death Row Inmates*, "Life in a Korean Prison," compares the prisons in Japan proper with colonial prisons, testifying to the more horrific conditions inside the latter. The text is not solely a work of social criticism, however; it is also a work of philosophical anthropology with many insights into the history of humanist thinking. In contrast to much more abstract and academic works on human life later written in the mode of philosophical anthropology, such as Miki Kiyoshi's *Notes on Human Life* (1941) or Watsuji Tetsurō's *Ethics as the Study of the Human* (1934), Nakanishi's text resists the attempt to find some sort of regulative solution to the antinomy between the transcendental and empirical aspects of humanism.³ Rather than figuring the nation and the world as hypothetical unities that could give the metaphysics of morals some kind of ideal space in which to be actualized, he instead argues that experiences of life are too manifold and complex in their social and institutional contexts to belong so easily to the organic wholes imagined by anthropocentric epistemologies. Human life could never come under complete regulation of the concept, the way that the philosophy of culturalism asserted through the limit concept. More interesting, however, is the way that Nakanishi arrived at this insight by situating his philosophical anthropology in another general chronotope of modernity: the prison.

Nakanishi's contextualized anthropology of the prison included direct rebuttals to the neo-Kantian philosophy of culturalism espoused by Kuwaki, Sōda, and the administrators of cultural policy:

> If the life view belonging to this person were what Kant calls "a priori," and if it adhered to his twelve categories, then it would have to be knowledge; however, the life view belonging to each person or individual does not adhere to Kant's a priori synthetic judgment. Therefore, life views are not the same as what Kant calls knowledge.
>
> Shall we say that while knowledge can mean understanding a thing, such as a table, it cannot mean understanding human life? What causes this contradiction?
>
> The material given to our understanding causes this failure. Certain materials for understanding—such as a table, a teacup, a dog, a cat, or a cow—can easily be transformed into knowledge. However, as the materials for understanding become more complex, understanding becomes more difficult. For material as confounding as human life, even if sensation can produce the concept of one life, understanding and reason are perplexed to find any organized unity, and therefore cannot find an a priori synthetic judgment that has universal necessity. For an object like human life, art can emerge through the movement of sensation, but what Kant calls knowledge cannot emerge. Therefore, we can propose this idea: views of human life are actually not knowledge, but rather a kind of art.⁴

Nakanishi states that human life cannot be an object of knowledge, because it is too complex to be organized into a unity that corresponds to the a priori categories of the transcendental subject. The underlying argument of Nakanishi's text is that the transcendental subject cannot entirely account for the individual's existence and intuitions, because the everyday practices and perspectives of the individual occur in a political and social context constituted by institutional power relations that are dispersed within a complex field, represented in this work by the chronotope of the prison. Anticipating Nishida Kitarō's critique of Sōda three years later, Nakanishi questions the identity of the knowledge of the transcendental subject with the active intuitions of the individual.⁵ The material of human life and views of human life are too complex as objects to be considered knowledge in the Kantian sense. Kant also recognized the artistry involved in the empirical philosophy of the *Anthropology,* but the ultimate point of doing anthropology for him was to define empirically the essence of that being (the human) that makes all knowledge possible, to arrive at knowledge of the totality of the world through knowledge of its most important part, the human. Nakanishi questions humanism's attempts to come to a total knowledge of the world through the human by refusing to bracket the human from the political, social, and institutional context, a bracketing enacted through the philosophical chronotopes of the nation, the world, and their histories. In taking up the chronotope of the life of prisoners awaiting execution, he introduced another sense of space and time, one in which life and death, beauty and ugliness, sentiment and thought are not metaphysical abstractions pertaining to the developing genus-being of the human, but rather modes of existing as an individual within a regulated, political space and time. Nakanishi uses the chronotope of the prison not only to expose some of the real social conditions at the foundations of the Japanese empire and its cosmopolitan cultural policy, but to show that the very division in anthropocentric knowledge between the empirical and the transcendental originates in or is consubstantial with modern institutions like the prison.

The intervention is remarkable because it shows how anthropocentric thought—with its regulative concepts of the genus-being and its positing of the limit as the very unifying principle of knowledge about the human—must work politically and socially against other senses of space and time. This is the case even for seemingly counterhegemonic discourses. For example, the appropriation of stage theory by Marxist social scientists and proletarian literature critics is indicative of the force that abstract humanist models of space, time, and history had even for those discourses that critiqued the philosophy of culturalism. Nakanishi's point was not merely to question bourgeois morality as the genus-being of the human by posing another idea of the human's historical essence (for example, productive labor). He rather questioned humanism by pointing to another experience of space and time—that of the death row prisoner—while at the same time insisting that human life is too complex to be unified under transcendental ideas, transhistorical substances, or the empty time that they imply. Like many writers of realist works who confronted the hegemony of culturalism and cultural policy, Nakanishi questioned transcendental humanist thinking effectively by challenging the chronotope of world history, which in both its culturalist and its Marxist versions sought the unity of humanity in the confluence of the world and the nation. The chronotope of the prisoner awaiting execution allowed him to explore the finitude of life and the subject without redeeming death under the transcendental laws of cosmopolitanism or nationalism. The death row inmate cannot posit a view of human life transcendentally, because he or she confronts the finitude of his or her existence at every moment, unable to see one's own death from a transcendental perspective. Furthermore, Nakanishi generalized this confrontation with death, rather than arguing, like culturalists, that the purpose of cultural generality and national particularity is to preserve the individual's life after his or her death: "Human life is one large ward of death row inmates. How many among them have received a verdict from God, 'you will not die, eternally'? Isn't the human being nothing other than a death row inmate with an indefinite time limit, one who has been given the verdict 'you must die.'"[6]

The theme of death is common in philosophy and literature in the 1920s, the most iconic example being Martin Heidegger's *Being and Time* (1927), in which he explores the limits of the transcendental subject through the ontology of finite Being. However, Nakanishi's text develops another kind of anthropology out of this philosophical problem of finitude, with sections on the psychology of death row inmates, the morality of the death penalty, the problem of false prosecutions, and the like. Heidegger would articulate a broken metaphysics of being-in-the-world precisely within this problematic, whereas Nakanishi instead develops an allegorical and taxonomical discussion of being-on-death-row. This anthropology makes observations within a field of power relations governing human lives differentially and individually. If modernity is considered a matter of giving form to the raw material of the human body, then time is reduced to the unfolding of human history within individual and collective consciousness and space is reduced to national space as the container in which the individual lives out the progress and travail of universal history. The colonial prison is another time and space—another chronotope—through which Nakanishi exposes the institutional and governmental techniques at the heart of the regulation of life by anthropocentric knowledge.

Nakanishi's analysis and critique of the prison show how culturalism was not simply a form of knowledge, but a form of knowledge embedded in concrete practices and techniques of government—the prison, the colonial school, the metropolitan university. Nakanishi's turn to the chronotope of the prison is explicitly directed toward culturalism as a colonial discourse, but it presents a challenge to colonized cultural nationalism as well. Yi Kwang-su's fiction shows how in colonized nationalism, national allegory and melodrama were used to overcome temporal and spatial differences within the national territory through the allegorical representation of the cultural nation, which redeems the finitude and meaninglessness of the individual life by situating it within the time of cosmopolitan history and the spaces of the nation and the world. In order to redeem the loss of the nation and to unify what has been broken into multiple, local spaces and times, Yi's national allegorical novels seek the transcendental unity of cosmopolitan history through the national community's emergence into world culture and the transcendental unity of national consciousness through the creation of a unified interiority. Nakanishi discusses how such an imaginary unity of human life is materially dependent on institutional methods of representation and control.

Later colonial Korean novels, such as Kang Kyŏng-ae's *From Wonso Pond* (1934)—or, with its original cosmopolitan title, *Human Problems*—also critiqued the enlightenment nationalist version of the countryside precisely by situating the discourse and rhetoric of enlightenment within a fuller chronotope of the rural village Yongyŏn, the growing port city of Inchŏn, and the roads in between.[7] While the complexity of Kang's chronotope suggests the advances made in realism by the mid-1930s, proletarian literature novels in the Japanese empire often tended toward national allegory, figuring the problem of spatial and temporal difference within the homogeneous empty time of the nation and the world. The exchange between Nakano Shigeharu and Im Hwa shows that proletarian literature had its own idealist allegories of politics and history, particularly when it sought to conform to the paradigm of universal history and its situating of nations and populations within a spectrum of possibilities defined by what Paek Nam-un called "social science." The types of Marxist social science easily became the types of historical allegory, whether of the cultural nationalist or proletarian arts variety. Imagining lived time and space otherwise than through an allegorical narrative of history required a great deal of critique and experimentation. The chronotopes of humanism were primary and set precedents, but critical debates and writing practices gradually came to reveal the complexity and overdetermination of social life, particularly through the creation of more detailed descriptions and narratives that took into account both the radical transformation of time and space in modernity and the differences within this transformation—the nonconvergence, the incommensurable elements, and the ignored places.

In his analysis of the chronotopes of the novel form, Bakhtin pointed to this kind of frictional relation between modern anthropological thought and the chronotope of the novel. He was very much indebted to the way that Kant gave primacy to space and time as indispensable forms of intuition, but he explained how his work on the novel broke from the image of the human as empirico-transcendental doublet, and therefore with national and world culture in the modern sense. In a footnote to his statement "the image of man is intrinsically chronotopic," Bakhtin echoes his contemporary Nakanishi in thinking the chronotope against the grain of Kantian thought and, more generally, against the abstraction of space and time that is an aspect of humanist epistemologies:

> In his "Transcendental Aesthetic" (one of the main sections of his *Critique of Pure Reason*) Kant defines space and time as indispensable forms of any cognition, beginning with elementary perceptions and representations. Here we employ the Kantian evaluation of the importance of these forms in the cognitive process, but differ from Kant in taking them not as "transcendental" but as forms of the most immediate reality. We shall attempt to show the role these forms play in the process of concrete artistic cognition (artistic visualization) under conditions obtaining in the genre of the novel.[8]

The empirico-transcendental doublet is the image of man that belongs to the Kantian system in which space and time are a priori intuitions. While Bakhtin and Nakanishi begin with the premise that images of the human and human life are intrinsically chronotopic, they explain that when the a priori forms of space and time are understood instead as forms of immediate reality, representation transforms. Representation becomes a matter of an intuition about life that exceeds any complete determination by concepts and knowledge. As a novelist who came to write extensively about Korea and Manchuria, in novels such as *Manchuria* (1929), Nakanishi understood the great potential in the genre of the novel for exploring this complexity of lived space and time in the colonial context.[9] Nakanishi's text on the life of prisoners also shows how arriving at a novel form with a fuller chronotopic imaginary may also require another mode of anthropology and social science. This was certainly the case for realist novels of proletarian literature, the forms of which, as I showed in the last chapter, were intimately related to social-scientific discourse. The literary texts of the period show that the relationships between peasant and landlord, uneven processes of industrialization and proletarianization, and the collective experience of primitive accumulation were comparable problems in the metropole and the colony. Although in practical terms political solidarity between Japanese migrants like Nakanishi and colonial writers like Kang Kyŏng-ae or Yi Ki-yŏng was not easy to create or maintain, they shared a concern with formulating other modes of representing the politics of space and time.

ALLEGORY AND REALISM IN FICTION AND CRITICISM

The intermixture of spaces, times, languages, and perspectives belongs to the novel form in general. However, I differentiate and compare two modes of Bakhtin's "heteroglossia," connecting them to his other concept of the "chronotope." These modes are allegory and realism. As I stated in relation to Yi Kwang-su's fiction, modern allegory is immersed in historical time and the historical and temporal problem of how to make visible in an anthropological representation a model of history based on an abstract concept of the genus-being. Allegory seeks to unify time through a historical model, and unify heteroglossia into national language, while at the same time apportioning spatial differences within this unity of time. This apportioning of spatial differences within the unity of time inevitably accords to different spaces a position within the unity of time. Spaces are thereby normed through the spatialization of time, and time is, paradoxically, differentiated again according to a teleology or norm. We only need to think of the place of "The Oriental World" in Hegel's universal world history or the "Asiatic mode of production" in Marxism to see how the unity of time called History leads to the imagination of spaces existing at different points in that unity, according a different historical time to these different spaces.[10] The relation between anthropological concepts and allegorical narrative is apparent in the works of both Yi Kwang-su and Nakano Shigeharu, even though they lived in the colony and the metropole respectively and were also on disparate ends of the political spectrum.[11]

Realist narrative, on the other hand, tarries more consistently with the spatial and temporal problems of progress and memory. There are clear differences between Im Hwa's notion of socialist realism as the dialectical fusion of romanticism and realism and the gradual transformation of allegorical representation in an attempt to expose the multiple temporalities, economies, and subject positions within the proletariat as subject of history. However, the turn to this other mode of realism did not emerge in any immediate way, as the strong influence of Yi Kwang-su on leftist writers in colonial Korea attests.[12] Although debates about bourgeois and proletarian literature in the Japanese empire often took shape around the question of whether to pursue art for art's sake, the cultural movements, or engaged art, this division cannot account for the intertextuality between the works of writers with varying political positions, particularly as they engaged in allegorizing history. Critical or social realism in the Japanese empire was not, from its inauguration, a complete turn to "reality" and turn away from the merely symbolic. Allegory was the mediating form, and realism often remained allegorical, particularly as Marxist models of history proliferated and were incorporated into politically engaged literature. In the criticisms of mere naturalism that we find in theories of critical realist art, we see that the difference between the national allegories of Yi Kwang-su and realist novels of the time was in the different political ideas around which representation took shape, and therefore different chronotopic images of the intersection between ideas and the material, the signifier and the signified, and the general and the particular.[13] Realism did not mean a rejection of symbols and allegory, but rather a transformation of the chronotope of allegory, a deepening of its temporal dimension. Realism was a chronotopic transformation of allegory, not a direct turn to reality.

This chronotopic transformation of allegory into critical realism was gradual. In order to understand how it occurred, it is necessary to trace debates in literary criticism in addition to analyzing fiction and poetry from the early 1920s into the 1930s. Modern literary criticism began in colonial Korea in the early 1920s, when Kim Tong-in and Yŏm Sang-sŏp, in the journals *Creation* and *Ruins*, discussed the role of the critic and the criteria that should be applied in the interpretation of literature. The first discussions concerned Kim Hwan's short story "Consciousness of Nature."[14] Kim Tong-in argued, in the journal *Creation*, that Hwan's story failed to describe the psychology of the protagonist P in any depth and that it lacked any philosophical principle or life view that could unify its elements. Yŏm also argued, in another journal, *Modernity*, that the story lacked both adequate description and personhood, adding that it read like blatant self-promotion on the part of the author. Therefore, the first literary criticism in Korea centered on how writers should depict lifelike characters in a natural style, giving them psychological depth and ideological motivations beyond the writer's desire to self-fashion. Although they basically agreed about why Kim Hwan's story was not good fiction, Kim Tong-in and Yŏm Sang-sŏp continued to debate the issue of authorship. Kim made a "formalist" argument that only the work should be considered in criticism, whereas Yŏm insisted that facts about the writer's life and personhood were relevant and applicable to an evaluation of literary texts. Despite this disagreement, both writers continued to refer obliquely to the personal conflicts within the small group of literary journal writers and editors in Korea at the time.

Significant in these discussions of the purpose of literary criticism is the attempt to articulate how space, time, characters, and action should be represented in modern fiction, a set of questions that would continue to be debated in the following decades. Although Kim Tong-in is often referred to as a "naturalist," his call to unify description through a life view or a philosophy points to his concern with morality, the primary motivation behind his use of melodramatic scenarios. In criticizing the didacticism in Yi Kwang-su's national allegories, Kim Tong-in advocated the inherent value of literature beyond politics and history. However, as with most of Kim's criticism, this argument was not always reflected in his own literary texts. His most famous story, "Potatoes" (1925), certainly lives up to the naturalist demand for lifelike psychologies and settings, but it is also a morality tale about the dangers of idleness, infidelity, and subordination to Chinese hegemony (all familiar themes in modern Korean film and literature). Pong-nyŏ, a young woman whose family was formerly of the scholar class but became farmers, gets sold by her father to a man twenty years older. This man sells his family's last bit of land for the purchase. Pong-nyŏ's husband is too lazy to properly farm the fields he rents as a tenant famer and shirks his work after they move to Pyongyang to become laborers. They end up living as beggars near Seven Star Gate and she eventually becomes a prostitute. Her "moral attitude" transforms and she and her husband see no shame in her selling her body, eventually to a wealthy Chinese man named Wang. She becomes jealous when Wang is about to marry another young woman and she follows him to his home and kicks the bride in the head. Wang retaliates, killing Pong-nyŏ.

However critical Kim Tong-in was of Yi Kwang-su's political and moral didacticism, "Potatoes" is a melodramatic moral allegory about the dangers of being idle, licentious, and jealous. It is a story that is in many ways about primitive accumulation, the process of a Confucian social order collapsing, and the precariousness of those who have lost out in the transition to private ownership of rural lands and the formation of an urban proletariat. However, all of these social processes are represented naturalistically, as circumstances that befall individual characters because of their psychological attitudes and their behaviors. The melodramatic aspect of the story is that the sacrifice of Pong-nyŏ is a tragic fate brought about by her own moral decay, one that serves to articulate a universe in which the failure to become properly modern leads to internal corruption and to external exploitation by ethnic Chinese. The space of this allegory moves from the countryside to the city, but only insofar as this transition highlights changes in the individual character. Likewise, its time is that of a gradual four-year fall from precarious social standing to untimely death. Therefore, while the subject matter refers obliquely to the massive social transformations occurring in colonial Korea at the time, its chronotope stays limited to two iconic spaces (the countryside and Seven Star Gate) and the life of a single individual. The story does not have a purely symbolic meaning, but rather it addresses the temporal and material problems of primitive accumulation, urbanization, and poverty through a moral, allegorical, and ultimately melodramatic mode of description and narrative. In literature the relations between humanist morality, historical change, and modern temporality are often represented through such an allegorical mode of mimesis.

The chronotope of Kim Tong-in's moral allegory can be usefully compared and contrasted to allegorical short stories of KAPF, such as Pak Yŏng-hŭi's "The Hound" (1925) and Kim Ki-jin's "The Red Mouse" (1924).[15] When KAPF was first established, a critical realist aesthetic did not emerge suddenly out of the importation of the Marxist view of history. Pak and Kim rather wrote in an allegorical style similar to Kim Tong-in, but instead of representing historical transformations as individual moral conflicts, they rather represented the Marxist-Leninist view of universal history. Working independently in Korea and Japan proper, these writers and writers such as Kobayashi Takiji developed a genre that I will refer to as "proletarian allegory."

As discussed in the previous chapter, Pak, along with Yi Puk-man, introduced the concepts of proletarian culture, purposive consciousness, and the propertyless nation into colonial Korea. However, like his colleagues Kim Ki-jin and Im Hwa, he was also a fiction writer. In his early works he tended toward aestheticism, and he published mostly poetry in the journal *White Tide (Paekjo)*. He would eventually return to this aestheticism, and to assertions of the autonomy of art, following his conversion to Japanese nationalism in 1934. In 1925, he moved from poetry to short stories, which was followed by another turn, in 1927, to writing solely criticism.[16] In 1927, Pak appropriated the demand for collective purpose in Aono's aesthetic and political philosophy, and applied it to literary and cultural production. In his collation and interpretive readings of New Tendency Group literature, he was favorable to its depiction of the struggles of the popular masses, but thought that the kind of psychological description that appeared in Ch'oe Sŏ-hae and other writers' texts did not sufficiently connect the representation of individual experiences of destitution and oppression to the historical purpose of a class subject, the proletariat.¹⁷ The rearticulation of the "popular masses" *(minjung)* as proletariat involved redefining literary narrative as a mode of storytelling that drew particular individual and national experiences of oppression into relation with the purposeful time of universal history.

The first attempts to transform individual psychology into an expression of class consciousness were not expansively realist, but rather more localized and allegorical. Before his introduction of a theory of proletarian culture into Korea, Pak had already been using a more allegorical narrative approach in his New Tendency Group writings. Pak's most famous story, "The Hound" (1925), marks his turn to Marxism-Leninism. It recounts the demise of a paranoid landowner who attempts to protect his money and property by buying a dog, but who is then killed by the dog. The dog has usually been interpreted as a direct symbol for the proletariat, even though the story has more to do with the greed of rural landowners than with capitalists. Pak represents an idea of the social whole through a localized individual conflict; in distinction from Yi Kwang-su's allegory, however, individual characters stand in for social classes, rather than present or future national leaders. Pak's allegory gives similar attention to the individual psychological effects of economic relationships. However, instead of focusing on the tragedy or moral corruption of individual characters living in poverty, Pak depicts class conflict within a moral allegory about the greed of the wealthy. In his attempts to protect and hoard his money, the landowner brings the dog into his isolated world—a symbol for the confrontation of social classes in modernity—only to suffer the ironic effect of his desire for security and protection.

Although Pak wrote "The Hound" two years before publishing on "purposive consciousness," the story is exemplary of the transition toward connecting dispersed depictions of poverty and hardship—or what Aono and Pak later called "spontaneous consciousness"—to the macropolitical and historical opposition between oppressors and oppressed, propertied and proletariat. In an allegorical narrative of history, the individual character is more than an object of description or subject of thought; he or she is a social type situated in history understood as a history of class struggle. The idea that narrative should more forcefully assert a historical subject led to the perception that New Tendency writings were contiguous with nature and naturalism, and lacked both culture and historical purpose. Pak's early allegorical narratives show that he was developing his own allegory of universal history, one that was more suited to a "propertyless nation" in which a few wealthy landowners, in collusion with Japanese imperial rule, had taken over large swathes of land and subjected the majority of the population to very precarious tenant farming. In "The Hound," political commitment does not lead to collective class conflict, but he did begin to use social types in his characterization of economic and social conflict, while situating types, actions, psychology, and morality within an allegorized political and historical context. Along with the theorization of spontaneous and purposive consciousness, the genre of proletarian allegory developed as a mode of narration that allowed isolated confrontations to be represented as part of a grander movement of history. The moral condemnation of the landlord's greed encapsulates the social failures of his class and his death is an allegory for revolution and the dialectical laws of human history that dictate the necessity of revolution.

Kim Ki-jin's early works are similarly concerned with representing the history of capitalism through the mirror of an individual's psychology. "The Red Mouse" (1924) is one of the first stories of proletarian literature written in Korea. The intellectual Hyŏng-jun has become nihilistic and impoverished in the aftermath of the March First Movement and comes to question the "contradictions" in the "civilization of capitalism" and in Japan's colonial rule: "What is the cause of undernourishment? It is a particular quality of the civilization of capitalism. It is solely a result of the curse of commercialism and collectivism. Who would say that mass production and colonial policies do not all originate in capitalism? The world has been disgraced by it."[18] He has become nihilistic about the ideals of humanity by comparing the material conditions in Korea with the rhetoric of cultural policy: "At present, in his head, there were no lofty ideals, no superior aspirations, none of the happiness of humanity, no relief measures for Korea, no procedure for engagement, and no theory of edification."[19] Stopping his walk through the city and lying down on a bench, Hyŏng-jun sees a bloody red mouse on the ground and "the corpse of this nameless animal" leads him to reflect on how it managed to get there despite being attacked.[20] He determines that human beings are no different from mice, and in a play on the "life philosophy" of Yi Kwang-su's culturalism, he thinks, "For the sake of life *(saengmyŏng)*, which we cannot throw away even though we try, we cannot but act until we have exhausted it—this is the 'life philosophy' of the mouse."[21] Feeling hunger pangs, he brandishes a pistol and steals a watch, a ring, some bread, and some fruit. While being chased by the Japanese colonial police, he gets hit by a fire truck and dies bloody on the side of the road. The police arrest three other youths in connection with the pistol, but the newspaper in Seoul carries a "false report on the incident."[22] Similarly to Nakanishi's anthropology of the death row inmate's relation to death, Kim's story politicizes the concept of life that was at the foundations of culturalism by introducing hunger and undernourishment, rather than moral values, as the true limits to the economic system of "the civilization of capitalism." Like Kim Sa-ryang twenty years later, he also introduces the figure of the animal as a being that exists both inside and outside of the cultural system, and prefers the struggle of this nameless creature to survive the negation of life to the concept of the human's mastering and overcoming of its historical conditions through the power of its practical will.

The year before, in 1923, Sin Ch'ae-ho had criticized Yi Kwang-su, the cultural movements, and self-rule on similarly materialist grounds, stating that cultural and spiritual development was impossible under the impoverished conditions caused by colonialism. The term "capitalism" began to circulate in Korea as Kim and others translated Marx's theory of the extraction of surplus value and other basics of *Capital* in the early 1920s. This introduction of the term "capitalism" shifted the language from Sin's ethnic national struggle to one that saw Japan's colonial policies and the creation of the system of mass production as emerging out of an integrated and global economic system. At the same time, Hyŏng-jun's thought retains and critiques the term "civilization," which was at the center of the debate between Yi Kwang-su and Sin Ch'ae-ho, connecting the ideology of technological-spiritual progress in Yi's culturalist discussions of civilization to imperialism as an expansion of a nation-state's capital beyond its national borders. Like Pak's "The Hound," Kim Ki-jin's early works represent capitalism and the continuation of agrarian class conflict through the depiction of a single character's coming into class consciousness. However, in both "The Red Mouse" and "Death of a Young Idealist" (1924), in which a protagonist similar to Hyŏng-jun commits suicide due to his loss of ideals, an awareness of the economic and ontological limits to accumulation and the fallacies of culturalism as a resolution to the crisis do not lead to any possibility for a collective confrontation with power.[23] Most importantly in the context, however, the endings of these stories do not presuppose, like the Yi Kwang-su of *The Heartless,* that the cultural nation can resolve the historical and economic effects of colonial modernity.

There were two main approaches that leftist writers and critics took to this problem of how to relate the life-and-death struggle of individuals living under colonial capitalism to a collective political project. The first I have discussed at length, which was to imagine that the "proletariat" and the "proletarian nation" were subjects unified by the capitalist system, but in need of an aesthetically manufactured "purposive consciousness" in order to organize their spontaneous revolts into world-historical subjectivity. The other approach was to reimagine the subject of literature and the subject of revolt not as a group of individuals united into a class or a nation, but rather as a dispersed and fragmented subject made up of displaced peasants, idealist intellectuals, an emerging industrial working class, domestic laborers (particularly women), and a number of other positions overlapping in time and space. The transformation of allegory into realism entailed the creation of a literary form less unified in time and space than Kim Tong-in's melodramatic naturalism, less concentrated through the prism of an individual type than the works of Pak Yŏng-hŭi and Kim Ki-jin, and more expansive in their attention to the intersection of multiple temporalities and multiples spaces within the singular system of capitalist modernity. The transformation of allegory into realism required another way of imagining the human within a chronotope, one that recognized that there is only one modernity, but that did not then assume that this unity was a cultural unity in which the national subject and world culture were reconciled through morality, productive labor, nation-state subjectivity, or other iterations of the generally human.

In the late 1920s, debates on form and content emerged in both Japan proper and colonial Korea in order to address the question of how to make NAPF and KAPF texts not simply political statements, but also more elaborate literary constructions. In the debate on form and content in Korea, Kim Ki-jin questioned the extent to which the depiction of class conflict through the allegorization of the psychological conflicts of individual subjects achieved an acceptable literary form. Even if these allegories represented the way that proletarian purposive consciousness could come about, their spatial and temporal fields were limited and lacking the kind of architectonic form that Yi Kwang-su had developed for the representation of cosmopolitan history in his national allegories. The debate concerning form and content began when Kim Ki-jin suggested that proletarian literature should not function solely as propaganda for revolution, or present a symbolic model for action, but should also develop an advanced literary sensibility and a literary form of its own.[24] In other words, proletarian literature should not be the pure expression or description of mentalities (content), but should develop a structure proper to realist literature (form). His analogy was with architecture; he argued that just as a building cannot stand without pillars, literature does not have political or aesthetic value without foundational structural elements. Pak Yŏng-hŭi responded that Kim Ki-jin was returning to bourgeois aestheticism, and sided with Proletkult's criticism of Trotsky and his defense of bourgeois culture. Kim eventually recanted his criticism, and the issue gradually dissipated into other debates, including those on anarchism, on the purpose of peasant literature, on Bolshevik vs. popularized literature, on class vs. national literature, and eventually on fascism and the new humanism of the late 1930s. Nonetheless, the debate on form and content in many respects established the ground for these other debates, because it pointed to the problem of how realist literature could at once convey an abstract idea about history and have the formal complexity of a lifelike imitation of social relations and the multiplicity of spaces, times, and ideologies in colonial Korea.

The debate on form and content was one impetus for the creation of an allegorical type of realism that expanded the chronotope of historical allegory beyond individual consciousness and represented the coevalness of rural primitive accumulation with urban industrialization, the syncreticity between the feudal ideology of landlords and their modern practices of land accumulation and tenancy, and contradictions in the communist and socialist movements themselves (such as the need to modernize but to also overcome capitalism, or the need to educate the population without reestablishing the hegemony of a dominant class). Works written after the debates on form and content, such as Yi Ki-yŏng's *Home Village* (1933) and Kang Kyŏng-ae's *From Wonso Pond* (1934), have more complex formal structures and chronotopic imaginaries that allow for the exploration of all of these spatial, temporal, and ideological differences within the collective everyday experience of colonial modernity.[25] Kang in particular, by moving from the rural village, to the landlord's house, to the factories of Inchŏn, focuses in on the different experiences of colonial modernity had by men and women, as well as by the urban proletariat, migratory displaced peasants, and rural domestic workers. The necessary dispersion and fragmentation of proletarian subjectivity that emerge out of such a complex tapestry of social types constantly on the move mean that her realist allegory of history is never reflected through a single universal point of action. Therefore, at the end of the novel, when Sŏnbi has died from tuberculosis and the intellectual Sin-chŏl has converted to Japanese nationalism, the tenant farmer who is now a worker and activist, Chŏtch'ae, thinks: "These human problems! More than anything we need to find a solution to them. People have fought for hundreds and thousands of years in an effort to solve them. But still no one has come up with a solution! And if that's the case, just which human beings will actually solve these problems in the future? Just who?"[26] Just as Im Hwa was beginning to imagine a new synthesis of realism and revolutionary romanticism, created by the practical human subject of history *(chuch'e)*, Kang posed the identity of the collective subject of action to her readers as an unanswered question. By situating the human being as a set of "human problems" to which the "human being" itself cannot be an adequate answer, she also politicized the notion of what it means to invoke "personhood" or the "subject" in a male-dominated society founded on and reproduced through the physical, mental, economic, and political exploitation of the subaltern female worker.

Before returning to these novels by Yi Ki-yŏng and Kang Kyŏng-ae in order to see how they relate the countryside to the city, I would like to discuss in the context of Japan proper this kind of poignant image of the proletariat as an empty space rather than a substance, but relate it more directly to the question of translation as it appears in Kobayashi Takiji's *The Crab Cannery Ship*.[27] Although contemporary scholars of the proletarian arts movements of Japan proper have discussed how ethnically Japanese writers viewed colonialism and imperialism, there have been few comparisons of the shared literary debates and literary forms developed in Japan proper and the colonies around the Marxist-Leninist view of history. By introducing the term "proletarian allegory," I would like to call attention to the fact that in both Korea and Japan, transforming the naturalist or, in Japan, I-novel description of individual psychology into a fictional and allegorical representation of universal history and class consciousness required both criticism and experimentation. Likewise, further criticism and experimentation were required to transform proletarian allegory into a more detailed realism that combined a model for universal history with more expansive and detailed chronotopes representing the complex intersections of social classes.

In this regard, writers in Japan proper confronted many of the same questions concerning the relation between literary form and the content of universal history. Early works of proletarian literature appearing in *Bungei sensen,* such as Hayashi Fusao's "Apple" or Sata Ineko's "From the Caramel Factory," tended to focus on the everyday lives and psychology of individual workers.[28] However, in the works of Kobayashi Takiji we find allegories of universal history that expand spatially and temporally to include not just a representation of psychological states as an expression of class consciousness, but also an attention to dialogism and the multiple languages and historical relations that contribute to the constitution of class consciousness and the instigation of revolution in an international context. Kobayashi's attempt to allegorize proletarian revolution as the next logical step in history and to create a unity of differences by symbolizing proletarian subjectivity still presents class consciousness as a unity; however, the expansion of the chronotope of his novels also serves to bring to light the spatial and temporal multiplicity within the proletariat and the overdetermination of each situation of capitalism.

Kobayashi's *The Crab Cannery Ship* is one of the most elaborate and memorable proletarian allegories written during the time of the Japanese empire, and has experienced a somewhat anachronistic resurgence in popularity in the last ten years in Japan. Kobayashi sought to do away with the description of individual thoughts and actions, and to describe how classes became opposed to one another in the capitalist system. At the same time, his later work "Life of a Party Member" and his diaries suggest that he was also concerned with literary persona, and with depicting the everyday consciousness of a vanguard intellectual.[29] The attempt to limit character development in the stories that dealt directly with class conflict and his use of a more personal style in his autobiographical works show a certain dualism in the role of the party cadre as part of the intellectual vanguard. He depicted his own life in terms of personal mission and purpose, and the real political dangers to which this exposed him, while describing the "social totality" as the interaction of political and economic groups and social types. As Foley shows, the genre of the intellectual *Bildungsroman*—to which Kobayashi's autobiographical writings were similar—was widespread globally in communist writings of this period.[30] The genre difference between the political as personal commitment and the political as social movement in Kobayashi's work is indicative of his attempt to, on the one hand, create a literary narrative that could represent the historical evolution of proletarian subjectivity and, on the other hand, describe the heroic life of the vanguard intellectual who conveyed the necessity for revolution to the working class.

Many passages in *The Crab Cannery Ship* show that among the novelists and poets of his day, he had developed one of the clearest images of the economic and political order of the Japanese empire. Like his counterparts in Marxist political economy, such as Yamada Moritarō, he understood many of the complexities of capitalism in its imperialist phase, including the various interrelationships between primitive accumulation, the cooperation of monopoly corporations, overproduction, the role of the state, colonial projects as a salve for domestic class conflict, relationships between the city and countryside, imperial nationalism, nonregular workers, the use of scabs, interworker colonial racism, and so on.[31] In reading his works solely as "literature," and judging them only according to their aesthetic value, one misses his reading of Marxist political economy as a discourse not of modernization, but rather of the various overdetermined situations of imperial capitalism.

In contrast to Pak's "The Hound," in *The Crab Cannery Ship,* individual characters are immersed in the action of the narrative and their internal sensibilities are less intricate, but situated more fully in a social context. At the same time, the novel maintains an allegorical dimension in the way it imagines the progress of universal history moving from the Soviet Union to the factories and ships of Japan. It is set on a crabbing ship, the *Hakkōmaru,* which is fishing in the waters north of Hokkaido, near Sakhalin Island. The plot focuses on the conflicts between the workers on the ship and the agents of the company (particularly the superintendent, who is a brutish and oppressive manager). The main characters among the workers are "Big Talk," the student, Shibaura, and the stutterer. The ship, particularly the workers' quarters, is depicted as a dirty, hellish place, worse than a prison. Telling lewd stories and circulating pornographic photos take up the workers' moments of reprieve. The workers' understanding of the hopelessness of the situation opens the story, when one tells another, "Buddy, we're off to hell!"[32]

The allegorical form of the narrative is partially a function of its setting, the *Hakkōmaru.* Kobayashi based the story on information he had gathered from newspapers concerning strikes occurring on fishing vessels. The isolated context of a ship moving along the border with Communist Russia provided a situation in which the workers' strike—a collective effort to slow production—could be distilled into a very localized conflict (even more so than if he had described an urban factory). At the same time, the setting allows for the influence of Russian workers on the fishermen, which occurs by way of a Chinese translator when one of the trawlers runs ashore on Kamchatka. The impetus for the strike occurs through the fishermen on this boat recounting this experience ashore. The theoretical distinction between "spontaneous consciousness" and "purposive consciousness" is apparent in the inspiration to strike that the workers gain from the encounter with the Russian and Chinese communists. The suggestion is that the degrading economic conditions of the proletariat will encourage revolt against capitalism and imperial Japan, but that the history of the Russian Revolution is what will make workers conscious that historical change is possible. The chronotope of the narrative is greatly affected by Kobayashi's view of universal history, and its advancement from Russia to East Asia. As Kobayashi's tragic death at the hands of the police in 1933 suggests, these counternarratives of universal human history were threatening for officials of the imperial state.

One advantage of Kobayashi's choice of scene was that it allowed him to give an image of capitalism's constant expansion into new territories, including imperialism, and also to criticize the political imaginary that supported this expansion. In the story, Kobayashi discusses the constant pushing of the border of the nation-state outward as a result of domestic class conflict. He claims that new territories had to be assimilated into Japan because the available workers in Tokyo and the other metropolitan centers of Japan proper had become unruly:

> When workers on the mainland grew "arrogant" and could no longer be forced to overwork, and when markets reached an impasse and refused to expand any further, then capitalists stretched out their claws, "To Hokkaido! To Karafuto!" There they could mistreat people to their hearts' content, ride them as brutally as they did in their colonies of Korea and Taiwan. The capitalists understood quite clearly that there would be no one to complain.[33]

Kobayashi states that the colonized suffers most from this imperialist expansion, not primarily because of the loss of national sovereignty, but because they are treated most cruelly by both the managers and the nationalized domestic workers.[34] He does reify the "colonized" into a stable category; however, he also describes the colonial projects in Hokkaido and other outlying regions as inspiring displaced mainland Japanese to pursue the utopian possibilities of settler colonialism, only to fall further into poverty. In this story, imperial expansion is a process that draws workers into potential combative relationships between one another, but it also allows them to gain consciousness of world history and the oppositional forces within it.

As the workers on the ship become politicized through their contact with Russian and Chinese workers, another picture of the international begins to emerge, one in which the translation of proletarian politics across borders is no longer a transparent communication of the principles of universal history through discrete nationalized proletariats, but rather a message delivered in the pidgin language of peripheral encounters. In the middle of the story, one of the fishing boats goes missing, but eventually returns to the *Hakkōmaru* with the crew alive and well. The narrative recounts how they had been washed up on the shores of Kamchatka and saved by a Russian family. At first the Japanese workers find the different appearance and language of this family to be "eerie"; "However, it soon dawned on them: 'Hey, they're human beings, same as us!'"[35] The crew plans to return to the *Hakkōmaru*, but the night before they leave one of the Russians has a message for them that a Chinese man is asked to translate:

> At a word from the Russian, the Chinese who had been watching him began to speak in Japanese. It was a jumbled sort of Japanese, with words out of sequence, scattering and staggering about as if drunk.
> "All you, sure thing, have no money."

"That's right."
"All you, is poor."
"That's right."
"So, all you, is name *proletariat*. Understand?"
"Sure."
The Russian, laughing, began to pace about. Sometimes he stopped and looked at them.
"Rich mans do this all you." (He grabbed himself by the neck, as if in a chokehold). "Rich mans get more, more big." (He indicated an expanded stomach.) "All you, no good, get more, more poor. Understand? Japan, no good. Working people, this." (He frowned, making a face as though he were ill.) "Rich man boss, this. Ahem. Ahem." (He strutted about.)[36]

The Chinese man continues, telling the stranded fishermen that in Russia there are no capitalists or exploited workers and to not believe the lies told to them about the evilness of "turning Red." The scene highlights the problem of translation within the international and gives a different narrative of the emergence of class consciousness. Whereas the theories of purposive consciousness insist that the vanguard intellectual must step in to transmit his knowledge of history to the exploited but unformed masses (giving them a unified identity as the proletariat), in this passage proletarian identity is delivered in a pidgin Japanese at the periphery of the empire, in a simple but accurate combination of stuttered words and pantomime. This difference in the translation of proletarian identity is important, particularly if we compare this encounter to the idea of modernity and class consciousness present in proletarian arts criticism, which tended to assume, following the social science, that certain modes and relations of production create certain cultural forms, and that the national proletariat emerges out of the nation's stage of economic development. In *The Crab Cannery Ship*, the Japan proletariat only comes to recognize itself as such through an encounter at the periphery, where integration and inclusion within the national economy and the ethos of imperialism come into question. This chronotope maintains a sense of a Hegelian spatialized history, as historical time moves from Russia to imperial Japan, but it also disrupts the emanationist model, because it is at the peripheries of Japan proper where the site of exploitation has moved and where the possibility for revolutionary opposition, transmitted in a pidgin language, has begun to emerge.

This recounting of the fishermen's experiences of landing in Kamchatka and encountering Russian and Chinese communists becomes significant, because it is through this geographic proximity to Russia that the fishermen of the *Hakkōmaru* begin to organize against the bosses. When another ship has to land on the shores of Kamchatka for a repair, the fishermen bring back "Red propaganda" translated into Japanese that describes the injustices of Japanese capitalism and imperialism. The fishermen begin to see their exploitation as unjust and to agitate and make demands to the bosses. In the novel's allegory of universal history, Russia is Japan's ideal future, and the fishing vessels' chronotopic proximity to that future, as well as its sheer isolation, allows for a class conflict to arise. By putting historical allegory to work for critical realism, Kobayashi shifted its focus from the representation of singular experiences of individuals to the mass experiences of industrial labor, political movements, and geopolitics, as well as newspapers and propaganda as the media that report these events. In this expanded chronotope in which the national proletariat is both inside and outside the space of the nation, the meaning of the Japanese fishermens' recognition of the humanity of the Russian family that saves them has a very different semantics from the invocation of the human in Marxist discourses that claimed that national culture is an expression of a nation-state's stage in human history.

As communist, socialist, and proletarian literature writers came under increasing repression by the police, the place of national culture within the international became more and more significant. Many early proponents of the proletarian arts such as Hayashi Fusao and Sata Ineko began to apply the techniques of realism for the purposes of documenting and supporting Japanese imperialism and the war effort, rather than proletarian internationalism. Sata, who had written about the daily life of female workers, including Korean women, traveled to Korea and Manchuria and wrote positively about the new gender and class relations enabled by the imperial project. In a chapter of *The Words of Women* (1941) titled "From Peace Industry to a Wartime System," Sata remarks how reading Hayashi's *Continent Bride* (1939) in the newspaper helped to convince her that Japanese women should emulate the dedication to war of European and American women by immigrating to Manchuria as brides or taking jobs in the factories.[37] She writes about receiving an inspiring letter from a woman who had given up her position at a bank in order to work in a large factory.[38] In both Hayashi's and Sata's wartime fictions and essays, the figure of the industrial worker has transformed from an ideally modern type into an ethnicized nation-state subject that expends its life for the total war effort. In many ways this turn from proletarian identity to national identity was prepared for by the concept of the national proletariat that existed from the outset of the proletarian arts movements, no matter how much the violence of police interrogation was the ultimate motivation for many instances of political "conversion."

Colonial proletarian writers were just as prone to translating their former proletarian politics into Japanese patriotism, despite the harsh conditions and coercion under which the workers and peasants of the empire labored. Pak Yŏng-hŭi's recantation of proletarian literature, very similar to Hayashi's, marked a similar return to art for art's sake, a disavowal of political art, and eventually patriotic support for Japan's war effort.[39] In the patriotism of the former political left in both Japan proper and Korea, Japanese national literature—sometimes articulated as monoethnic and sometimes as multiethnic—was no longer imagined as a porous culture that bordered sites of justified political revolt against capitalism and empire. Such imperial literature and culture developed new chronotopes that included continental experiences, but it also territorialized culture, language, and politics under the power of the state. As the communist In Chŏng-sik's essays on the need for cultural and linguistic unity in the late 1930s show, the pidgin language of the international found in Kobayashi's novel had to be supplanted by Japanese national language and culture for both the imperial project and the mainstream of Marxism to transition to the era of Japanese-Korean unification *(naisen-ittai)*.[40]

CH'OE SŎ-HAE: MIGRATION, LETTERS, AND DEATH

Although one might imagine, like Kobayashi did, that the colonies would be the site of superexploitation and uniform proletarianization, and therefore that these spaces constituted a pure periphery of empire, in actuality a very similar question of center and periphery existed within both cultural nationalism and the proletarian arts in Korea. This question was also responded to with similar humanist discourses that could norm the historical space and time of the colony while also accounting for temporal and spatial difference through anthropological categories. Therefore, for Yi Kwang-su, the Korean countryside became the place where "races" and "tribes" that needed to be nationalized still existed, but it was also the object of nostalgia and an origin that could be tapped into in imagining Korea's future. This anthropological view of Korea was very influenced by Yi's proximity to the centers of imperial knowledge through his elite educational experiences in Japan, and was an expression of the chronotopic imaginary of the colonial-cosmopolitan intellectual. For KAPF writers and critics as well, the political and historical meaning of the countryside became more and more important in urban writers' attempts to represent national class politics and the modernization project. How could the Marxist-Leninist narrative of history, with its focus on the national urban proletariat, account for the vast rural areas of Korea without falling into nationalist nostalgia? This was the concern of theorists of peasant literature such as An Ham-gwang.[41]

Within this dynamic of center and periphery, coded as it was by a variety of humanist discourses, areas beyond the border of Korea, particularly the Kando region to the north, became increasingly important as a colonial frontier. Like Hokkaido in Kobayashi's stories, Kando was not the rural origin (or "home village") to which the urban writer returned; it rather offered a future to those who were expelled from their lands or otherwise excluded from the national economy. It was a place to which the displaced tenant farmers of Korea could migrate and settle, and a semicolonial environment that promised to offer an escape from the harsh conditions in the Korean countryside. At the same time, because it offered a place for excess population to migrate, Kando also became a site of imperial governance, particularly as the Japanese empire expanded into Manchuria and China. Writers who wrote about the experience of Kando migration, particularly Kang Kyŏng-ae and Ch'oe Sŏ-hae, developed a very different chronotopic sense of Korea, including its internal spatial and temporal differences, compared to both the enlightenment perspective of Yi Kwang-su and the Marxist-Leninists who saw Korea as a unified proletarian nation.

At the age of eighteen, most aspiring intellectuals and writers in colonial Korea were likely to try to study abroad in Japan, if their families could afford it or they could obtain a scholarship. In 1918, the eighteen-year-old Ch'oe Sŏ-hae, born into a poor farming family, instead decided to divorce his wife and migrate to the Kando region, or the present-day Yanbian Korean autonomous prefecture of the PRC.[42] Before going to Kando, Ch'oe was greatly inspired by Yi Kwang-su's *The Heartless,* but he must have taken notice of a large gap between his own life and those of the main characters, who upon devoting themselves to improving the Korean nation choose to study abroad in Japan and the United States and mainly concern themselves with individual cultural improvement and the national education of the people.[43] Upon returning to Korea in 1923 and gradually establishing himself as a writer, Ch'oe had some contact with Yi. However, his stories of migration and return do not follow the familiar trope of a Korean man who has returned from Japan a modernized intellectual and is alternately nostalgic and dismayed in observing the present conditions in Korea. Ch'oe's stories of migration and return are concerned instead with the loss of spatial proximity and emotional intimacy between family members and friends caused by attempts to escape grinding rural poverty. Ch'oe effectively uses the epistolary form, diaries, framed stories, and other modes of personal address to highlight the sense of distance, loss, and social fragmentation in colonial modernity. Rather than representing a failed *Bildungsroman* for the vanguard intellectual that we find in Kim Ki-jin's "The Red Mouse," Ch'oe's stories rather represent the failed attempt of displaced tenant farmers to construct a life within the social and economic crisis of colonial Korea, particularly the massive displacement of rural peoples to both the growing cities and the expanding frontier of Kando.

Ch'oe was a writer of the New Tendency Group, and an early member of KAPF, but he tended to maintain some distance from the organization and did not get directly involved in the debates between the main theorists. Unlike those theorists, he worked a number of proletarian jobs. He also died at the age of thirty-two of stomach illness likely brought about by extended periods of hunger. As the critic Kwak Kŭn has written,

> Of course, other writers of the time, such as Na To-hyang, Hyŏn Chin-gŏn, and Yŏm Sang-sŏp, lamented and were heartbroken about the reality of extreme poverty; it is also true that others, such as Kim Ki-jin and Pak Yŏng-hŭi, did not disregard it. However, the former recognized it from the standpoint of an observer or thinker and

the latter grasped it too conceptually and schematically. Compared to these writers, Ch'oe Sŏ-hae, who himself experienced acutely the realities of extreme poverty, was more able than anyone to give form to it objectively and factually. Therefore, Ch'oe's fiction, which exposed the truth of that time, was definitely remarkable, and garnered the sympathy and response of the literati.[44]

For an intellectual class made up largely of nationalists and Marxists, Ch'oe brought to literature an "authentic" national and class experience of exploitation that they had also tried to represent in their own works.

On the other hand, Ch'oe's stories also left very little hope for individual or collective redemption, and critics wondered whether they were too tied to tragic personal experiences to contribute to a political project based on the principles of human history. Therefore, Pak Yŏng-hŭi questioned whether or not the characters in New Tendency Group fiction lacked purposive consciousness.[45] The gradual deepening of proletarian allegory into a structured portrayal of class conflict constituted the main Marxist-Leninist thread of literary experimentation and criticism in proletarian literature of the Japanese empire. However, the drive for class unity and purposive consciousness often led to the facile dismissal of earlier works that did not narrate universal history in a local context, but were still works of social criticism that brought to light important aspects of the political and economic system. In his dialectical and progressive history of modern Korean literature, which eventually culminated in a defense of socialist realism, Im Hwa argued that Ch'oe Sŏ-hae's stories are examples of "naturalism."[46] He stated that they portray the spontaneous and misguided revolt of individuals against their conditions, but lack any unity of political consciousness or dedication to collective emancipation. Although Im presented his critique on political grounds, what was really at stake was that the chronotopes of Ch'oe's stories did not fit the narrative of national literary progress, in which various forms were sublated through the development of the modern subject, ending in a proper synthesis of realism and romanticism. In this sense, Ch'oe's stories provide various ways of reading the space and time of colonial modernity against the grain of the cultural modernization projects of both cultural nationalism and the proletarian arts.

The anthology *The Reillumination of Ch'oe Sŏ-hae's Literature* and Kwŏn Bodŭrae's *The Era of Love* have attempted to explain in which ways Ch'oe's works are modern and to defend their form, content, and aesthetic against the kind of historical claim made by Im Hwa (that his works are overly fragmentary and lacking in characters with modern consciousness).[47] There are two main consequences for politics that we can retrospectively recognize in Ch'oe's works: (1) that his foci on primitive accumulation, rural poverty, migration, broken families, and partisan struggle are more representative of the prevalent social conflicts of colonial Korea, compared to the romantic, urban Marxism-Leninism of Pak Yŏng-hŭi or Kim Kijin, who abstractly and allegorically declared Korea a proletarian nation; (2) that his use of the epistolary form, as well as diaries and other private genres, made his works appear more fragmentary compared to what I am calling proletarian allegory, but that the mediated fragmentariness of letters addressed between characters disrupted notions of a unified human, national, or class subject, revealing the relationality involved in self-expression, confession, and other modern speech. In addition to these observations already made by Kwŏn, I argue additionally that Ch'oe's texts present another chronotope of colonial Korean society. In Ch'oe's chronotopes, time is the time of migration from the countryside to the frontier region (Kando) or to Seoul, as well as the time of the delays created by sending, receiving, and missing news about one's family and friends. The space of Korea is neither the underdeveloped home country to which the elite intellectual returns, nor an anthropologically defined space of the ethnic nation or national proletariat, but rather a porous territory with dramatic internal spatial and temporal differences as well as its own frontiers that promise a better, decolonized future, but whose realities are as grim as the troubled situations that the displaced farmer attempts to escape. Through these other chronotopes, his stories effectively emphasize relationality rather than subjectivity, borders rather than nations, and the intractability of rural poverty rather than the unity of the urban proletariat.

Some of Ch'oe Sŏ-hae's stories focus on urban migration, such as "Paekkŭm" (which is a semi-autobiographical account of a father who moves to Seoul to work as a laborer, becoming estranged from his family and learning only secondhand of the death of his young daughter, Paekkŭm) or "Farewell" (an epistolary fiction, written in 1926, that Ch'oe imagined as a letter from a younger brother, who has migrated to Seoul and become a shoeshine, to his older brother).[48] However, he is associated more with rural migration to Northeast Manchuria, because many of his stories of migration are drawn from his own experience of moving to Kando as a young man. Hyun-ok Park has written a thorough modern history of the Kando region, detailing the history of sovereignty disputes, colonial government, land-ownership laws, flows of labor, and the burgeoning of the North Korean revolution.[49] Japan had attempted to colonize Kando between 1907 and 1909, but during the Kando Convention of 1909 it agreed to cede the territory to Qing China in exchange for railroad rights. Afterward, and particularly with the establishment of the Manchurian puppet state in 1931, Japan actively encouraged Korean migration to Kando, because Koreans were imperial Japanese subjects and increasing their already large presence in the region helped to provide legitimacy to Japan's rule of Manchuria.[50] In 1918, when Ch'oe moved there, Kando was still an ambiguous territory to which Japan, China, and Korean nationalists such as Sin Ch'ae-ho all laid claimed. For thousands of rural Koreans who were displaced through the enclosures of Japan's cadastral surveys, who were exploited by tenant farming practices, and who suffered under intense and growing rural poverty, Kando was a frontier that offered the possibility for better economic and social conditions. In the Korean literary and cultural imaginary of the 1920s and 1930s, Kando was the site of both hope and despair. It represented the possibility of escaping the imperialist economic conditions in Korea and was a centerpiece of nationalist ideology and the guerrilla movements for national liberation. It was also a place where Koreans were an ethnic minority and where migrants encountered similar economic uncertainties and discrimination (for example, from native Chinese ethnic groups).

Ch'oe's five years in the Kando region working as a dockworker, a cook, a messenger, and a Korean-language teacher were formative for both the themes and the forms of his fiction. In Ch'oe's second published story, "Native Land" (1924), Na Un-sim has just returned to the city of Hoeryŏng from Western Kando: "It was the middle of March 1923, when the shadow of Un-sim, who had left his native land with great aspirations, appeared again on Korean soil."[51] He tells how immediately after the March First Movement he went to Kando and found a place where various Koreans escaping from the crimes or failures of their past gathered to hunt, farm, or steal: "Therefore, there were no ethics, morality, or education."[52] As for the local Chinese, "the policemen arrest opium dealers and beat them, while themselves eating opium."[53] Such depictions by a writer returned from Kando were certainly cast as adventure stories, of a sort, for the Seoul literati. At the same time, they revealed the seriousness of the economic and political crisis brought about by Japanese colonial expansion, which appeared very differently when approached from the peripheries of the empire compared to metropolitan Tokyo or the colonial capital of Seoul.

"Record of Escape" (1924) is typical of Ch'oe's stories set in Kando.[54] Like other of Ch'oe's stories, it is an epistolary fiction, narrated by Mr. Pak and addressed to Mr. Kim. The story begins with Pak thanking Kim for his letter, which he seems to have received quite some time ago. In this letter, Kim had implored Pak to return to his family and his role as household provider. Pak's response comprises the entirety of the text. He is partly embarrassed and partly defensive about having abandoned his mother and wife, and insists repeatedly that he is also a human with emotions. He writes that he wants to explain to Kim why he left his family, so his friend will better understand his circumstances. Pak begins by describing how he left his home village for Kando five years previously. He had heard that it was very easy to farm there and that there was plenty of wood to be had from the mountain forests. With great hopes and high ideals, he set out with his mother and wife. However, when he arrived in Kando, he could not find any land to farm and his family lived on the edge of starvation. He tried to establish a bean curd business, but it was unsuccessful. He resorted to salvaging wood from the mountaintops, but was caught by a landowner and taken in by the police. Out of his frustration and embarrassment at not being able to feed his family, he decided to leave. In the only censored portion of the text, he writes that he entered the XX group (the censored part probably states "Liberation Army," as in other of his stories).

Kwŏn Bodŭrae has written extensively about the significance of the epistolary novel in Korea in the 1920s, and reads stories like "Record of Escape" as part of a broader tendency in Korean fiction in the early 1920s.[55] In this story, Ch'oe uses letters to great effect, as the reader's glimpse into the scene of writing and the performativity of the narrative provides an added stylistic complexity. Kwŏn states that scholars tend to view the epistolary form in terms of the expression of subjectivity and the self-fashioning of confession. However, she argues that epistolary literature is not merely about subjectification *(chuch'ehwa),* but also relationality. She interprets this aspect most poignantly in her readings of the new ideas of romance that emerged along with the postal system and the practice of letter writing.[56] Because of the letter form of Ch'oe's story, the reader is figured as a second addressee, and feels the ethical conundrum of the plot more strongly. The hints of embarrassment and regret that appear in the narrator's letter increase the sense of tragedy, because the position of the reader as addressee is that of a sympathetic friend, rather than an anonymous observer. The relation between narrative voice and reader is more vital and demanding, because the reader is drawn not only into the expressive world of an author, but also into the relationship between author and addressee.

Kwŏn argues that as proletarian literature became the dominant mode of representing the popular experience of colonial modernity, the epistolary novel unfortunately lost its prominence.[57] She situates Ch'oe Sŏ-hae's fiction in between the "era of love" and the ascendency of socialist literature in the mid-1920s. Like other recent readings of Ch'oe, she sees his work as committed to representing the economic hardships of the popular masses, but in literary forms that better capture the new possibilities for social life that emerged in the 1920s. Later proletarian literature and literary theory, emblematized in Im Hwa's synthesis of the humanism of socialist realism with the humanism of the late Japanese empire, were weighed down by the dogmatic claims of dialectical historical development. Ch'oe's works provide one model for a politically committed literature that did not subject the lives of its characters to the abstractions of dialectical logic and the imaginary unity of the proletarian subject.

Ch'oe's stories tend to treat economic and social problems through a depiction of their psychological and emotional effects on individual subjects, and he did not attune his stories to the possibility of a collective subject of political struggle. Many of Ch'oe's stories portray the progressive destitution of a struggling family man who is eventually led, by way of his *ressentiment,* to commit acts of murder or arson. In "Bloody Flames" (1926), a migrant tenant farmer who has lost his land in Kyŏnggi-do moves to Western Kando, only to become indebted to a Chinese landlord, In-ga.[58] He is forced to give his daughter Yong-nye to In-ga as payment for overdue rent, but then kills In-ga with a hatchet in order to rescue his daughter. In "Starvation and Slaughter" (1925), Kyŏng-su's family is barely surviving in Kando.

He has no work and is forced to steal and sell trees. His wife is sick with palsy, but the doctor will not treat her because he has no money. His mother is bit by a rabid dog belonging to a Chinese man. Experiencing dislocation, unemployment, and starvation, as well as racism on the part of the native Chinese, he kills his family, stabs others, and is eventually shot and killed at the police station.[59]

How to view such depictions of violent criminal acts is an important question in an evaluation of Ch'oe's works. Some see this violence as an expression of the inability of the colonized intellectual to escape the logic of imperial rule, and the reduction of political revolt to barbaric crime as a reproduction of imperial enlightenment ideology. Others have related this violence to the relatively unmodern character of Ch'oe's works, and their dispersive, rather than integrative, aesthetic. Because his impoverished and desperate characters have no context in which to organize into a proletarian subject, they remain psychological individuals who can only respond to oppression through spontaneous acts of violence, rather than with purposive consciousness (to use the binary that KAPF eventually applied to such New Tendency Literature). However, there is nothing unmodern about Ch'oe's depictions of the violent psychological effects of alienating and impoverishing economic and social conditions. The moral question of whether or not crime is a proper or improper response to economic inequity or familial conflict is at the basis of many modern stories, Fyodor Dostoevsky's *Crime and Punishment* and *Brothers Karamazov* being just two famous examples. Furthermore, the acts of violence are always contextualized, particularly within the realistic economic and social struggles of Korean migrants to Kando. Rather than poverty and violence being depicted as primarily questions of morality, as they are in Kim Tong-in's naturalism, the violence of Ch'oe's male protagonists is not judged in ethical terms, but rather as images of the failure to survive conditions that in many ways are unlivable.

In this respect, Yi Kwang-su's development of a modern vernacular certainly inspired Ch'oe's emergence as a writer, but in choosing Kando as his frontier, rather than Japan, which remained out of reach, he represented both a different chronotope for modernity and a different sense of the relationship between writing and questions of life and death. For the cultural nationalist Yi, writing in the Korean national language, and then in Japanese, was a matter of surviving death, because nations, as organic and preservative communities, allowed for the continuation of the individual beyond his or her mortal existence. In stories like "Starvation and Slaughter," as well as "The Death of Pak Dol," in which Pak dies because he cannot afford medicine, death is not a fact to be overcome through a higher meaning, but rather a real material limit that gains its clearest image at the borders, where the stateless and nationless individual, even when he embraces the hopes of the frontier and a new life, confronts the impossibility of "escape." Such stories were popular and interesting to the literati of Seoul in part because they offered another image of the colony proper, where the overcoming of death was politicized by culturalism and cultural policy, but remained an abstraction for the majority of Koreans whom Yi saw as the raw material for modernization and cultural development. In this sense, despite being critiqued for his depictions of "spontaneous consciousness," Ch'oe's stories are in many ways the most reflective of the crisis of a rapidly expanding Japanese capitalism, in which massive numbers of people were displaced from rural areas and left to try, and in Ch'oe's stories always fail in, various preindustrial economic ventures at the edges of the economic system. Ch'oe stories were critiqued by KAPF because their chronotope challenged the developmental image of Marxism preferred by the Marxist-Leninists who preferred to think of capitalism not as a system of crisis and the maintenance of crisis, but rather as a stage within which the emergence of the national proletariat could be assumed as a historical eventuality and a completion of the allegory of history. The maintenance of crisis was political, and the Japanese state eventually intervened to try to remake Kando and the rest of Manchuria, and in this sense Ch'oe's image of Kando was also a kind of political and ethical warning against seeing the imperial frontier as the place of opportunity it would eventually be presented as to displaced rural Koreans.

Rather than seeking ever further levels of integration into national history, Ch'oe Sŏ-hae's chronotopes direct our spatial consciousness to the frontier, where historical progress dissipates or is channeled into rural partisan struggle; they direct our sense of time to the tremendous and irrecuperable loss brought about by colonial modernity and rural poverty, and to the melodrama of arriving too late to a destination or missing an important letter from a long-lost family member or friend. His focus on the irredeemable death of the migrant as the limit to both the imperial economic system and nationalist politics questions the crisis and crisis management of Japanese imperial capitalism, with the understanding that the primacy of historical necessity in metropolitan and colonial Marxisms could come to legitimate imperialism. In this respect, his stories are an important counterdiscourse to the abstract assertions of the dialectics of cultural development through which Im Hwa asserted the human being as the subject of history.

COUNTRYSIDE, CITY, PRIMITIVE ACCUMULATION

Ch'oe Sŏ-hae's stories depict an experience of rural displacement and poverty that was not specific to Korea, even though Kando was the particular destination and hope for resolution to the incredible gaps between the growth of the colonial capital and the underdevelopment of the countryside. Japan proper gradually became a place where not only the intellectual elite but also displaced tenant farmers migrated to find jobs in industrial labor, eventually by force beginning in the late 1930s. In proletarian literature, there was a gradual attempt to make sense of these kinds of migrations in the context of the expansion of the empire. In Kobayashi's Takiji's *The Absentee Landlord*, he explores the process of primitive accumulation in the context of Hokkaido, where displaced farmers travel from Honshū as part of a government settlement project, only to find themselves subordinated to landowners, managers, and soldiers. Kobayashi compares the situation of the Hokkaido farmer with Koreans living on the outskirts of the city:

> It was more than likely that the peasant, who got up earlier than any city laborer and who stooped for hours at his work, led a more miserable life than any Korean living in squalor in a hovel on the outskirts of a city. Did the young men on the farm really deserve to be called frivolous and undisciplined? Was more to be expected of them, in addition to their labor? Enough of your hypocrisy, thought Ken.[60]

The comparison between the Japanese peasant and the urban Korean worker and the recognition of a differential exploitation not easily mapped onto a model of national development were a significant reversal of the anthropological concepts informing Nakano's theory of proletarian art. Nakano divided class cultures between the metropolitan national proletariat and its various others, particularly the cultures of the colonial nations and the peasantry. In Kobayashi's description, again formulated through a chronotope of frontier expansion, the Japanese peasant is shown to work within an ordering of time more ruthless than even that of the ethnic migrant worker.

The character Ken's parsing of the degrees of exploitation is less interesting than the attention to paradoxical class relations that emerge within a capitalist regime reproduced through the management of populations. Kobayashi's comparison between the Japanese peasant and the migrant Korean worker reflects the increasing attention of Marxism and the proletarian arts concerning how to represent the countryside, present in both the debates between the Lectures School and the Labor-Farmer School on Japanese capitalism and the debates on the peasant novel in proletarian literature. In colonial Korea, Paek Nam-un sided with an even more stagist theory of history than the more complex positions in the Lectures School itself, reading capitalism as a story of a nation's uniform passage between synchronically integrated systems that would eventually become influential, through Paek's notion of "national communism," in the founding of the DPRK. Paek's perspective was consistent, in spatiotemporal terms, with his later position that the Japanese state is a subject that intervenes to unify the economic system under a more ethical governing of production and consumption. In the language of Louis Althusser, Paek's position as a colonial stage theorist shows that the history of the economic base is not determinant of the superstructure, but that the translation of (humanist) intellectual and literary discourse has a "relative autonomy" in relation to the economy, even if the economic system is "determinant in the last instance."[61] Furthermore, as Paek's national history shows, the idea of the base is itself relatively autonomous from the economic base, if ideas of the stages of the productive relations (or genus-being) can be translated and applied to new contexts with the sole mediation and difference in the translation being the particular content of the nation form. In this respect, breaking with the chronotope of stages of national history, particularly in the vein of the Lectures School or Paek Nam-un, was a matter of the politics of representation, through which a paradoxical comparison like Kobayashi's, between the Japanese peasant and the Korean migrant worker, could unmoor Marxism from its anthropological reductions. This is significant, because in Paek's case, it was precisely this anthropological reduction that underlay "conversion" to support for the East Asian Community and other state projects of crisis management in the late Japanese empire.[62] Likewise, Im Hwa could propose that a socialist realist peasant literature could become the foundational canon for the whole of the East Asian Community only by assuming that social classes were unified under anthropological categories such as the nation or regional community.[63]

In place of the parsing of relative degrees of exploitation between the various positions of peasants and workers, Marx's concept of primitive accumulation provides a more useful way of connecting the forced and coerced movements of populations with the general logic of the accumulation of capital. Marx theorized primitive accumulation as the separation of the peasant from his means of subsistence through the cordoning off of rural lands and villages into private property.[64] Rosa Luxemburg expanded Marx's concept of accumulation to discuss imperialist expansion as an effect of capitalism's inability to make the circuit of production and consumption an even cyclical process.[65] In order to continue to accumulate, the monopoly form of capitalism had to expand in order to incorporate new, "external" territories by transforming them into new consumer markets, new sources of commodifiable variable capital (workers), and, we can add, new areas for natural resource extraction. More recently Marxists have expanded the notion of primitive accumulation so that it no longer represents a singular moment in time, such as sixteenth-century England, but rather a basic principle of accumulation itself—the constant need for capitalism to separate the "commons" from their autonomous means of subsistence.

In literature and social science this historical process can of course be represented in multiple ways, with important political differences resulting. In his works on the stages of the genus-being and the "ethicality of the command economy," Paek Nam-un symptomatically did not theorize primitive accumulation, because this would have introduced the very political problem of how the state will resolve, ethically, the need for capitalism's circuits of production and consumption to incorporate new territories and new populations. Paek could only imagine the Japanese state as the anthropomorphized agent for the passage to the next stage of development by ignoring the "ethical," or rather political, dimension of Japanese capital and military expansion in Manchuria and China. Yi Kwang-su, on the other hand, focused intently on primitive accumulation, but through a metaphysical and romantic nationalism connected, in 1933, to fascist notions of the moral authenticity of the petit-bourgeois intellectual in his identification with rural farmers. In the version of nationalist rural enlightenment that Yi Kwang-su presents in *Soil,* which is equally nostalgic and modernizing, he imagines the process of primitive accumulation both as a transhistorical and as a historical process, both as a singular moment in mythical time when the organic nation was separated from its essential connection to the land and as an ongoing imperialist negation of the potential for artistry and self-formation in both urbanites returning to the countryside and rural people imagined as (potential) Koreans. Using metaphors of blood, soil, and the rural toil of ancestors, he saw primitive accumulation as a loss of national origin to be overcome through modern technologies of national self-formation (for example, the serial, vernacular novel).

If we return now to Yi Ki-yŏng and Kang Kyŏng-ae, it is apparent how the representation of primitive accumulation became significant in leftist literature as well. The representation of multiple contradictions between various classes emerged with the portrayal of characters living in between feudal peasant relations and the life of the industrial proletariat. Yi Ki-yŏng's *Home Village* (1933) draws together concerns of history, subjectivity, and political economy into a well-told narrative structure. Like *Soil, Home Village* deals with the position of a colonial intellectual (Kim Hŭi-jun, just returned from studying in Japan), the conditions and struggles of farmers, the emergence of an industrial workplace, the divisions between city and countryside, and the maintenance of feudal land relations by Japanese colonial rule. A realist attention to detail is brought to bear on most of the important debates within KAPF, and the true complexity of class relations and class ideologies within everyday life is exposed. In this narrative, we see that the abstract category of the "proletariat" was somewhat naïve in its historicism, not only because of the persistence of rural peasant life, but also because industrialization was creating workers who often lived between peasant existence and industrial wage labor. Although the entrance into factory labor represents a certain crossing of a threshold for younger characters in the novel, particularly Kapsugi and Kyŏng-ho, characters continue to move between their jobs in textiles and other factory labor and the peasant farming life of their families.

The main class conflict in *Home Village* does not occur in the factory, but rather between the farm supervisor An Sŭng-hak and the tenant farmers who work the land. What Yi reveals through the juxtaposition of different modes of production operating simultaneously in a single economic system is that the deduction of the urban proletariat as the revolutionary subject of history and certainly the conflation of national liberation with proletarian revolution were based upon an idealist conception of time that smoothed over the movements between rural life and the linear temporality of abstract labor. In this regard, Yi does insert a vanguard intellectual in his narrative, but unlike Kim Ki-jin he does not turn to the allegorical representation of his subjective experience of the injustice of capitalist civilization as the primary source for the narrative structure. This realist move away from works like "The Red Mouse" was a significant change in proletarian literature in Korea and owed some of its sophistication to the aesthetic debates on form and content and on the peasant novel within KAPF.

From Wonso Pond also presents a more developed picture of class relations in colonial Korea, but Kang's inclusion of a more nuanced reading of colonial-period gender politics gives the novel a different perspective on the problem of primitive accumulation. As in *Home Village,* the fullness and diversity of workers' temporal experiences come to the fore as the novel moves from sites of peasant labor to sites of industrialized labor. In this sense, the novel is a story of primitive accumulation, but the narrative is much more linear in the sense that the enlightenment project of the engaged and nostalgic intellectual is a much less significant element. The male intellectual, Sin-ch'ŏl, first has a romantic interest in the countryside and then unsuccessfully tries his hand at factory labor. However, the majority of the novel focuses on the passage from countryside to city as experienced by the female subaltern Sŏn-bi, not the male intellectual, and eventual Japanese imperialist, Sin-ch'ŏl.

With its focus on subaltern female subjects, *From Wonso Pond* is unique in its treatment of gender issues within the context of proletarian literature, and critics have discussed the gendered forms of violence and the seduction narratives that appear in the work, as well as the reading of Kang's writing as "masculine" by her male counterparts.⁶⁶ Like Ch'oe Sŏ-hae, Kang wrote on the periphery of KAPF and lived in the Kando region in Manchuria between 1932 and 1942. *From Wonso Pond* can be usefully read alongside *Home Village* because in each novel we are presented with the problem of primitive accumulation and representations of women's experiences with factory labor and with romantic, Platonic, and violent gender relations. However, Yi Ki-yŏng uses the love-triangle trope between the supervisor An's daughter Kapsugi, the illegitimate son of an aristocrat, Kyŏng-ho, and the intellectual Kim Hŭi-jun. Yi presents the new public presence of women coming about through their entrance into industrial labor in somewhat more ideal terms. The subaltern woman does not have a strong presence and Kapsugi enters the textile factory only because her parents disapprove of her relationship with Kyŏng-ho. Her admiration for Hŭi-jun leads her to enlightenment about her father's position in the village and the plight of the workers and peasants of the region, and her Platonic friendship with him at the end of the story becomes a symbol for solidarity in struggle. The story is inspiring in its depiction of the possibility of political solidarity across gender lines, but it relies on a certain occlusion of the subaltern female subject position through which the entirety of *From Wonso Pond* and most of Kang's other stories are focalized.

From Wonso Pond depicts the particularly repressive relations that women were forced into through primitive accumulation in the process of industrialization, and therefore provides an important counterpoint to Yi's treatment of gender difference as a matter of romantic love. This difference in the treatment of gender is related to the chronotope of each novel. In both novels, the process of primitive accumulation takes precedence, as peasants who formerly practiced subsistence farming, or participated in the village organization of agriculture, are forced into tenant farming and eventually industrial labor. The separation of the farmer from his means of subsistence through the tenancy system is the fundamental problem and each novel presents it as a problem of class rather than of the nation. However, *From Wonso Pond* breaks completely with the back-to-the-land storyline of both *Soil* and *Home Village*. At the beginning of the novel, the female protagonist, Sŏn-bi, is taken in as a domestic servant by the landlord, Tŏk-ho, who has killed her father, his former tax collector. Tŏk-ho hides that he killed her father, takes her in as a "daughter," and rapes her repeatedly. The male farmer Chŏtchae is displaced from his land when he and a friend revolt against the unfair taxation and tenant debt in the village. Both Chŏtchae and Sŏn-bi flee the village and the second half of the novel takes place in Inch'ŏn, where both become involved in the urban labor movement as a dockworker and a textile factory worker, respectively. The novel completely elides any possibility of returning to the land in order to reintegrate with nature or to reform the practices of farm supervisors and landlords. The intellectual Sin-ch'ŏl momentarily feels nostalgia in the countryside through his attraction to Sŏn-bi, and joins the labor movement briefly in Inch'ŏn, but by the end of the story he has become a Japanese patriot and has left for Manchuria. There is no reason that Sŏn-bi or Chŏtchae would return to the village, because they would undoubtedly be punished severely by Tŏk-ho. Sŏn-bi is forced to work for her father's murderer, who promises to be her father and to educate her, but instead subjects her to sexual violence. She becomes a "free laborer" by leaving the village, but ends up in a factory where the sexual abuse continues and where she eventually dies of tuberculosis.

In *Patriarchy and Accumulation on a World Scale,* Maria Mies discusses primitive accumulation not as an originary moment in the past or as the time before wage labor and capital, but rather as an ongoing and violent process.[67] This process is gendered, not only because the desire to dominate "nature," to cordon it off as property, is a desire of patriarchy, but also because "subsistence labor" is often feminized labor, from childbirth to household labor to, we could add, affective and sexual labor. The separation of peasants and workers from their means of self-reproduction is therefore, necessarily, a gendered form of violence. Kang takes as her protagonist a subaltern domestic servant whose labor is not valued, in the traditional sense of wage labor and capital, until the final chapters, when she works in the textile factory. Yet this novel about the passage from the countryside to the city provides us with the most intricate realist depiction of capitalism in colonial Korea, its maintenance of the landlord system, its dependence on gendered violence, its displacements and forced migrations, and the incapacity of the male intelligentsia to respond without repeating the mentality of patriarchy.

Although returning to the countryside and rural enlightenment are impossible in the novel, primitive accumulation is present at every moment, both as the general condition of the passage to wage labor and as a literary metaphorics. The first scene of *From Wonso Pond* describes the pond in the village as a life-giving force and tells the story of how it was formed by the tears of suffering peasants who starved while the warehouse of the landowner was filled with their harvest. This opening registers the sense of loss and the dramatic feeling of displacement from the commons that accompany industrialization and the commodification of land, but it does not fall into nostalgia about the precapitalist past; the image presents both the feudalism of the past and the tenancy system as a means for appropriating life and the means of subsistence. The pond of tears sets the stage for Kang's exploration of the "human problems" of her time, in which the lot of the peasantry and the workers, particularly women, has not improved through cadastral surveys and industrialization. This sort of image of the lost past can be usefully distinguished from national allegory, because there is no illusion that what has been lost can somehow be regained in its full form. The image lingers melancholically without becoming a presence such as the blood and sweat of ancestors, which Yi Kwang-su imagined could be regained through a new practice and new poetics of the national subject.

Kang saw the danger in the attempt to recuperate the lost past, and to close its gap with the historical present. Her writings show that there is neither an ideal past to which one can return nor a desirable future without a radical transformation of the gendered economic and political system. Her descriptions of the inescapable flux experienced by those who lived between the countryside and the city were one mode of narrative that allowed literary representation to break away from its ideal wholes and to capture the lived spaces of modernity as spaces of differentiation, rather than of historical convergence. Arriving at such realist representations was more difficult than one might expect, as chronotopes that homogenized historical time, ignoring its inconsistencies and its relation to the unvalued and "unproductive" labor of the subaltern subjects, carried a universalist appeal to the national proletariat, the embodiment of genus-being, that was not easy to resist. If Nakanishi approached his critique of the subject of governmentality through the chronotope of the prison, Kang did so by rearticulating the "human problem" of proletarian literature as in part a question of how to represent gendered labor and the alienation of life and labor in production through a chronotope proper to colonial capitalism. This is a position that distinguishes her work from both culturalism and the mainstream of proletarian literature.

5

World History and Minor Literature

A fundamental quality of subjective culture lies in breaking from anthropocentrism, even as one returns to anthropocentrism.
—KŌYAMA IWAO

THE WORLD-HISTORICAL STATE

In an essay from 1943, "On the Characteristics and Direction of Korean Literature," An Ham-kwang, a Korean proletarian literature critic who became a supporter of imperial Japan and then a prominent South Korean critic, wrote, "History is not something established by nature or the human, nor by reason or through a consciousness of the forces of production; it is, in actuality, something created and preserved by the state."[1] In 1931, An was critical of "metaphysical" representations of the countryside, particularly in fascist literature.[2] However, in promoting the Japanese state's intervention into capitalist crisis, he ended up advocating a politics that was not ethnic nationalist, but did imagine the Japanese state's mobilization of rural Koreans for the war effort as marking Korea's entrance into world history. At the height of the Pacific War, An defended state-centered culture and literature in a manner typical of *People's Literature*, a mostly Japanese-language journal published in colonial Seoul (1941–44). He also criticized the formerly dominant perspectives on history—that of culturalism, which considered the human in general to be the subject of history, and Marxism, which considered the forces of production to be the motor of history. In positing Japan as a world-historical state, he followed many of his contemporaries in arguing that the generality of humanity was in crisis and could only be salvaged if a specific imperial state made up of nation-state subjects intervened concretely into world history in order to represent the generality of the genus *homo*. Genus-being, or that category that mediated between the transcendental ideas of cosmopolitan humanity and its empirical manifestations, became nation-state subjectivity, and Koreans were obliged by history to become state subjects of Japan, now explicitly cast as an inclusive and multiethnic national community.

Like many other colonial and metropolitan subjects whose Japanese patriotism led them to proclaim a complete break from the ideologies of the past, An criticizes the ideas of history in the epistemologies of the past: natural science, culturalism, and Marxism. He argues that the general characteristics of the human being—its nature, its moral reason, and its labor—do not directly and immediately affect its primary determination, History. As in Hegel's philosophy of history, only the state and the spirit of the state can be truly historical, because it is the subject that gradually and dialectically actualizes the political and moral destiny of mankind. An states that the human does not make history, but by this ahistorical human he means the general, abstract human, the cosmopolitan and merely formal human that is not necessarily or not yet a state subject. For imperial nationalists, the cosmopolitan individual of culturalism had become what Hegel called derisively the "sheer *empty unit* of the person."[3] Despite such critiques of cosmopolitanism and defenses of the historical primacy of state subjectivity, An and other imperial nationalists did not break from humanism. They critiqued culturalism and its cosmopolitan rhetoric and appropriated cosmopolitan claims to the universal in defense of the role of the Japanese state in world history. This discourse of world history assumes that empires, states, and nations gradually overcome others through war and cultural conflict for the eventual betterment of general humanity. It still posits the human's return to its essential identity as the telos of historical development. This discourse also performs what I refer to as the "anthropomorphizing of the state," the figuration of state power as an individual and collective acting-out of human will.

In the case of the Japanese empire, arguments for the world-historical state should not be conflated with European fascist ideology and its symptomatic relation to enlightenment. While European fascist ideology naturalized race and nation through the assumption of an essential relation between morality and origin, imperial nationalists in Japan often broke from such a simplistic expression of the empirico-transcendental doublet. An's critique of any natural, cultural, or generally human foundation for history is an idea of the state distinct from the natural view of race in National Socialism and the ethnonationalist Hegelian philosophies of Italian fascists such as Giovanni Gentile (both strongly criticized in imperial Japan).[4] For imperial nationalists, the state is the earthly representative of general humanist principles and of the progress of world history, and therefore should not be ethnocentric, culturally specific, or based on racial science. Unlike culturalists, who often returned to some kind of substantial connection between national or racial origin and the faculty of practical reason, imperial nationalists delinked moral practice from origin and emphasized the futurity of the Japanese state, which would be inclusive of those ethnic minorities who sacrificed their lives to belong to it. Because they required a theory of the state that would allow for Korean individuals to be included in the national political community, Korean intellectuals were particularly drawn to deethnicized ideas of the state that would supposedly allow colonizer and colonized to overcome the ethnocentrism of National Socialism, Italian Fascism, and Japanese ethnic nationalism.

For former Marxists in Korea like An Ham-kwang, Sŏ In-sik, Im Hwa, and others, such a notion of an inclusive Japanese nation-state was in many ways an extension of their previous works criticizing fascism. An had previously written on the problem of peasant literature within the proletarian literature movement, where he established himself as an advocate of Marxist universalism. He made important critical insights into the metaphysical representation of the countryside, relating the romantic and lyrical depictions of rural life and nature in colonial Korean literature to the false organicist ideology of fascism, and calling for a realist and secular peasant literature that would contribute to its unification with the proletarian class.[5] Sŏ made a more complex dialectical critique of fascism, stating that it was the most dangerous expression of the enlightenment subject's need for identity and that the way its "intellect" subjected thought to the national totality could not solve the economic and cultural problems of capitalism.[6] Both remained skeptical of ethnocentrism and religiosity in their later works extolling the virtues of the multiethnic Japanese state. When they argued in the late 1930s and early 1940s that the state creates and preserves history, they were referring not to the emperor as the monarch or religious figurehead of a monoethnic society, or to the leader-centered and ethnocentric state of European fascism. Yet through a secular and humanist model of world history still loosely connected to the history of capitalism, An nonetheless anthropomorphized the state by elevating it to the status of a being: "The expansion of capitalism happens along with the establishment of the state. The state is at the center of this expansion. Today we must grasp the state as the highest being in world history."[7]

As in Paek Nam-un's argument for a Japanese state that could govern the economy ethically in order to overcome the global economic depression, An and Sŏ impute universal historical agency and historical subjectivity to the state. The economy is something generally human that the state should intervene into in order to regulate it in a universally valid manner. In referring to the state as a "being," An anthropomorphizes it in a similar manner as Paek, not precisely through the figure of the morally perfected person, but as a subject formed through the ethical actions of the individuals that it governs. Just as it is not entirely possible to conflate the culturalist concept of the "person" with the Japanese emperor, anthropomorphizing the state entails something more than representing the state by a single figurehead, particularly for an ex-Marxist like An. The universality of subjective action is at once collective and totalizing, because autonomous individual humans are free only when their free actions contribute to the nation-state's spiritual mission in world history. For Korean intellectuals such as An and Sŏ, this mission was to liberate East Asia from European imperialism, European racism, and even the economic and cultural crises of capitalism, all of which were most symptomatically expressed in the European fascist social formation.

In order to discuss the state as the earthly representative of ideal mankind and as a deethnicized political body, imperial nationalist philosophers, particularly Tanabe Hajime, reorganized the Kantian taxonomy of races. They discussed the species *(shu, chong)* not as one racial or ethnic variation within the genus human, but rather as the historical and self-determining nation-state that could mediate between individuals and world history. The species was no longer a specific racial or ethnic variation belonging to the genus *homo,* as in the Linnaean system inherited by Kant in his *Anthropology.* Tanabe Hajime and Sŏ In-sik considered such a notion of a unified human genus divided into species to be an illusion of the past.[8] They considered the substantial racial, national, or geographic connection between the individual and the world to be broken and the species of the multiethnic state had to intervene for individuals to again become worldly. To connect the individual human again to universality, the state, as the necessarily particular, historical, and concrete embodiment of general humanist principles, had to shed its racial, national, and ethnic particularity.[9]

Sŏ In-sik, who began as a Marxist-Leninist but eventually supported the idea of the East Asia Community, explained the role of the category of species within the logic of a Japan-centered East Asian regional body, drawing from various interlocutors, but particularly Tanabe. Sŏ differentiated his idea of the East Asian Community from European fascism, while also critiquing the kind of liberal cosmopolitan perspective that assumes a direct connection can be sustained between the individual and the world despite the crises and contradictions of capitalism. For him, the contemporary cultural crisis made it impossible for the individual, the nation, and the world to be integrated in the simplistic way imagined by neo-Kantian liberals, but ethnocentric fascism—referred to as "totalism"—was also an inadequate and atavistic response to the crisis of modern liberal culture and its "modern intellect." In writing about what the species (that is, Japan or East Asia) can do for the individual and humanity at large, Sŏ considers how the political community of the nation can live up to universal humanist principles while also having a concrete historical subjectivity:

> Is not contemporary "totalism" an intellect that cannot have the principle of universalization in individuality, in opposition to the modern intellect that fails to have the principle of individualization within the universal? Looking at the basic trends in contemporary culture's central structure, the path that leads directly from genetic origin to the world appears broken. And in this sense the nation and the

world appear as absolutely contradictory concepts in the current stage of historical progress. If so, is not a middle term that can mediate humanity's passage from the nation to the world necessary? The concept of species is always required to mediate the individual and the general. Therefore, only the standpoint that establishes the concept of the species as the subject again can sublate the nation and world, which cannot be reconciled from the standpoint of contemporary culture.[10]

As Naoki Sakai has explained in his reading of Tanabe, philosophies of the multi-ethnic state require that state subjectivity be delinked from ethnicity and origin, that its theories, in Sŏ's terms, "seek the principle of universalization in individuality." For Sŏ, the breaking of any direct line between genetic origin and the world is a product of the cultural crisis of global capitalism, which both enables the possibility for a cosmopolitan community and makes such a community impossible, because it deterritorializes the human from any natural and originary cosmopolitan order while also encouraging the ethnicization of bourgeois society. For any ethnicity, or genetic origin, to become worldly within the cultural crisis of capitalism, it must have a historical state, or a species, that can mediate between the individual and the universal and sublate the relation between the nation and the world—this species must seek to deethnicize in order to act as a universal in world history. Sŏ asserts an insurmountable distance between the species and any natural origin, which highlights the historical constructedness of the mediating term of the species, as well as its national culture. The species that sublates the nation and the world does not refer to a natural race or ethnicity, but rather to the imperial state in its dynamic historical, social, and political relation with its internal and external others.

Although philosophers at the time often presented the Japanese empire as an ideal dialectical synthesis, or the One that could incorporate the Many, it is not physically possible to actualize a completely universal state detached from all particular experiences. Dealing with the seeming detachment of the world-historical state from any particular identity, figure, or tangible expression remained a problem of anthropology, despite philosophers' best efforts to evacuate the universal of any particularity. Another Kyoto School philosopher, Kōsaka Masaaki, in his *Philosophy of the Nation* (1942), clarifies how the universalist perspective on the state remains anthropological in the attempt to define how it is that actual living people might assimilate themselves to the ideal picture of dialectical synthesis that we find in many metropolitan and colonial writings that advocated imperial Japan. In Kōsaka's work we find that what An Ham-kwang calls the "being" of the state cannot be completely evacuated of anthropological content. In the following statement, as throughout the text, nation, or *minzoku*, is a sign of this difficulty. When he adds "nation" and arrives at the term "nation-state" *(kokka-teki minzoku)* to refer to the chief actor in world history, he simultaneously makes an anthropological differentiation between natural nations, cultural nations, and nation-states, using the language of nationalism to rearticulate earlier culturalist claims about the cultivation and development of the individual human:

> I will differentiate three stages for the nation. These are natural nation, cultural nation, and the nation-state. Among the six aspects stated above, the natural nation is a nation that is defined mainly according to blood and soil. A cultural nation is a nation that is defined mainly according to religion and language. What is called the "nation-state" is a nation that has become a single historical subject through the formation of the state. However, I do not intend to think of the differences between these three nations in a superficial manner. I intend to consider these three nations practically, actively, and in stages, setting up the natural nation in the way of a substratum, the nation-state in the way of a subject, and the cultural nation as the *mediation* of these. The nation is not simply natural, but subjective, self-determining and powerful, with culture as the mediation of these actions. In being self-determining, and, moreover, something in the world, the nation must be ethical.[11]

In Kōsaka's argument in *The Philosophy of Nation*, culture and the cultural nation mediate between nature and self-determination, specifically between the substratum of the natural nation and the subjectivity and self-determination of the nation-state.[12] Whereas Kuwaki divided humanity into cultural and natural nations, Kōsaka adds the third level of self-determination and the modifier "static" (*kokka-teki*) to the requirements for generality. Culture cannot itself be the motor of historical development; however, the state as subject of history requires culture—religion and language—in order to mediate the various natural nations (or ethnicities) that participate in its formation. In other words, Japanese national culture is to mediate between the given Korean or Taiwanese ethnic difference and the subjectivity of the nation-state. The notion of national culture and national languages as the mediations between the state and given ethnicities brings the anthropological back into the universality of the world-historical state. If the multiethnic state is not to remain an empty universal, the mediation of national culture—including national language, national literature, and national custom—must construct and rearticulate the nation of the nation-state. For Sōda Kiichirō, individuals develop from physiological beings, to psychological beings, to owners of transindividual general consciousness. Kōsaka sets up a similar arc of historical development from nature to self-determination, but the anthropological knowledge of consciousness has become more explicitly centered on the state and state formation has replaced the development of the cosmopolitan person as the telos of human development. As a being that is self-determining and worldly, the state must be ethical, creating an anthropological analogy between the Kantian cosmopolitan individual who self-legislates his morality and the state that is the unity of individual ethical actions.

Therefore, even as Tanabe was criticizing the conservative cosmopolitan version of culturalism in essays such as "The Limits of Culture," and arguing instead that students should give their lives to the state rather than dedicating it solely to culture, and as many were arguing for the universality of the specific imperial state, anthropological thought and the idea of culture both remained central to the project of empire.[13] The leading literary critic in Korea, Ch'oe Chae-sŏ, changed the name of the most important general humanities journal, *Humanities Critique (Inmun pyŏngnon)*, to *People's Literature (Kokumin bungaku)*, advocating national literature and the national language *(kokugo)* rather than world culture; however, the journal maintained its concern with formulating a humanist response to modern cultural crisis. Despite his background in the modernizing project of Marxism-Leninism, Sŏ began to discuss the need for a dynamic engagement with the shared cultural tradition of the East Asian Community (one that would not be a feudal mythology).[14] In 1941, Miki Kiyoshi published his philosophical anthropology, *Notes on Life*, and Kōyama Iwao synthesized a number of ideas on the cultures of the East and the West, national geography and culture, and world history in his *Research on the Typology of Culture*.[15] In colonial Korea, these new codifications of anthropological knowledge were collectively discussed as the "new humanism," which incorporated both antifascist European humanism and ideas about a superior East Asian modernity.[16] Both bourgeois humanists like Paek Chŏl and former Marxist-Leninists like Sŏ In-sik came to identify with versions of the utopian idea of a new "East Asian humanism," and even Im Hwa, who was critical of the "liberal ideology" of the new humanism, sought the most advanced human culture in a rurally based socialist realism, which he thought could become a proper mediation between Korea and the progress of world history represented in the Japanese state.[17] In other words, the world-historical state remained a world-historical *nation*-state, one that required new artistic and cultural practices that were adequate to a state that included differences, but was also a cultural, linguistic, and political unity.

Kōyama's text is perhaps the most expressive of a contradiction in the philosophical projects that advocated the East Asian Community and a multiethnic Japanese nation-state: he appropriated distinctions between the West and the East first discussed in the anthropocentric epistemologies of European Orientalism, particularly by Hegel in his *Philosophy of History*, and used them to claim that Western culture is anthropocentric *(ningenchushinshugi-teki)* and that Eastern culture is anti-anthropocentric *(hanningenchushinshugi-teki)*.[18] Referring to the Kantian worldviews, including that of the philosophy of culturalism, as "objective" *(kyakkan-teki)* and the Eastern worldview as "subjective" *(shutai-teki)*, he claimed that Western culture separated the human from both the divine and nature whereas anti-anthropocentric Eastern culture integrated them:

> I think we can say that the communal thought that unifies the three elements of the divine, the human, and nature is something that has run through Eastern thinking for a long time, and actually constitutes its fundamental character, whereas it is a quality we cannot find in the objective culture of the West. Therefore, as we find

ourselves in these communal relations, or rather because we find ourselves in these subjective, communal relations, I think the point that the ideal of the human being is not anthropocentric will be important and requires serious reflection. A fundamental quality of subjective culture lies in breaking from anthropocentrism, even as one returns to anthropocentrism.[19]

The Copernican turn of enlightenment humanism distinguished the human from both the divine and nature and made it the constituting and constituted agent of knowledge. In opposition to this objective culture of modern Western science, as well as the uncritical translators of Kantian anthropocentrism in Japan in the 1920s, the (practical) subjective culture of the East integrates the divine and nature with the human, through an ethical community centered on the "home" (*uchi*) and brought about by an acting, transindividual subject (*shutai*).[20] Like many intellectuals in East Asia at the time, Kōyama diagnosed a crisis in European humanism, but used this humanism's very cultural categories in order to posit the Japanese nation-state as a world-historical community that would unify the East according to its shared cultural principles, at the same time reintegrating the acting human subject with nature and the divine. Most importantly for colonial subjects and colonial intellectuals, this discourse stated that overcoming Western modernity was a universal matter for humanity at large. The Japanese nation-state, with its particular culture, space, and history, not only represented the other nations of East Asia, but was also responsible for solving the problems of Western metaphysics for the world at large. Kōyama expresses this problematic confluence of universal and particular quite self-consciously, but nonetheless in a politically coercive and contradictory way, when he states that the new "subjective culture" of East Asia entails "breaking from anthropocentrism, even as one returns to anthropocentrism."

Leo Ching has discussed the shift to the policies of *kōminka* (imperial subjectification) and its meaning for colonial subjects in Taiwan. In debates about the policy of Japan-Korea Unity in the late 1930s and early 1940s, the issue of imperial subjectification was central. Therefore, Ching's analysis of imperial subjectification is relevant, despite the different colonial contexts. Ching writes,

> Unlike *dōka*, which remained an unrealizable ideal of colonial integration, what *kōminka* entailed for the colonized, then, as exemplified in the construction of a "good and loyal Japanese" and the so-called *kōmin* literature, is the "interiorization" of an objective colonial and class antagonism into a subjective struggle within, not between, colonial identities. In other words, cultural representations under *kōminka* displaced the concrete problematic of the social and replaced it with the ontology of the personal.[21]

According to Ching's clarifying reading, a displacement occurred from the concrete problematic of the social—which includes the interrelated hierarchies of metropole and periphery, Japanese and non-Japanese, man and woman, bourgeois/

proletariat/peasant, and so on—into the ontology of the personal. The burden of overcoming the colonial relationship was put on the colonized, whose ascension to the position and ethical practice of a loyal nation-state subject would allow for the transcendence of the concrete situation of colonialism. As Ching points out, the focus on the internal struggle between ethnic identity and Japanese imperial subjectivity is still prominent in many readings of minority texts from the period. However, this internal struggle is not natural, but historically conditioned by the colonial ideologies of imperial subjectification and Japan-Korea unification. As I will show, the fact that the most prominent Korean advocate for a multiethnic Japanese national literature, Choe Chae-sŏ, framed the problem of people's literature in terms of personal ontology—in his view, as the overcoming of the modern humanist division between the level of consciousness and the level of existence—reflects these larger historical tendencies in colonial discourse.

The remainder of this chapter is primarily concerned with theories of national literature and culture as mediation for the universalist and multiethnic state subject, as well as the way that the minor literature of writers such as Kim Sa-ryang and Kim Nam-chŏn intervened into the dialectical, concentric circle that was the dominant image for this new cultural-national subjectivity and its world. One primary approach taken by minor literature was to contextualize the philosophical idealism of national literature within the mundane urban spaces occupied by imperial subjects and within the modern institutions through which the imperial state actually asserted its power and its laws of history (for example, the courts and the prisons). Another approach was to highlight a gap between the ideal notions of practice demanded by the state—speaking the language, sacrificing one's life, and acting as a state subject in the name of general humanity—and the performative aspect of this practice, which was always situated and contingent. In taking up characters like a former communist brought to court to perform the role of convert, a proletarian stage actor whose proclamations of his humanity are nothing but a psychotic delusion, and a colonial writer who begs divinity to transform him into a proper Japanese *(naichijin)*, their texts of minor literature show that individual action does not concretize the ethical substance of the imperial state, in the manner of Ching's "ontology of the personal," but is rather only a performance that is always fragile and tenuous, or, even beyond the absolute sacrifice of dying for the Japanese state, completely impossible. In his most radical stories of the early 1940s, Kim Sa-ryang creates a relay with Franz Kafka and prefigures Gilles Deleuze and Félix Guattari in suggesting "becoming-animal" as an alternative ontology to that of the national subject's cultivation.[22] By reversing the process of cultivation, literary characters who turn to the animal as the teleological figure for individual development at the onset of total war question the ontology of imperial subjectification, which continued to rely on tropes of the human's self-mastery, its overcoming of its fear of death, and its capacity to willfully define the conditions for its future.

OSMOTIC EXPRESSION

In her history of Manchuria and Korean migration, Hyun Ok Park refers to the form of colonial assimilation in the late Japanese empire as a kind of "osmosis."[23] In *Difference and Repetition,* Gilles Deleuze writes of the concentric circles of dialectical thought and the way that Hegel's philosophy, through "Orgiastic representation," incorporates difference through the expansion and contraction of the subject and the constant internalization of externalized, negative difference.[24] Drawing from Louis Althusser, Frederic Jameson, in *The Political Unconscious,* critiques the "expressive causality" of the Hegelian dialectic, which improves upon the mechanistic causality of eighteenth-century Enlightenment thought, but still masks the overdetermination (or multiple causes) of any situation of capitalism.[25] Each of these readings of the assimilation of difference through dialectics addresses itself to the subject as osmotic being and expression as the causality of the dialectical totality. In the period of the discourses of the world-historical nation-state in the late Japanese empire, expression, which was also anthropologically defined in terms of national language and national culture, was understood as the cultural mediation through which identity and nonidentity, the positive and the negative, the present and the past, and space and time could be united. Expression became central to the practice of the imperial subject, and therefore speech and action were often conflated. To speak in support of the empire was at the same time to act in its interests. The idea that the nation-state as expressive totality is the subject of the world and world history requires such a conflation between speech and action. The projects of Japanese national literature and national language took on a renewed urgency in colonial Korea, while at the same time critical minor literature addressed the contingency of the performance of imperial subjectivity, of speaking in the language of empire.

Philosophies of the world-historical nation-state in the Japanese empire imagined that culture could mediate and facilitate the process of osmosis and dialectical incorporation. Read in sociological terms, Hegel argued that the moral action of the state synthesizes the idea of the nation and this idea's externalized elements.[26] In the *Science of Logic,* Hegel defined the absolute as the "identity of identity and nonidentity."[27] In terms of nation-state building, the subject that acts and thinks in history synthesizes the positive idea of the nation-state with what is negated, nonidentical, or internally external to this idea (the feminized, the minoritized, the colonized, the proletarianized, and so on). The nation-state subject is formed when the nonidentical is again contained in identity through a shared sense of absolute historical purpose and the collective action of the members of an inclusive nation-state. Diverse thinkers in the Japanese empire agreed that it was through practice that those who were Japanese in a given sense and those who were somehow excluded or negated by this identity could come to form a single, self-determining national subject. This practice was the practice of national literature, the practice of national language, and ultimately the practice of committing oneself to the cause of the war.

One of the earliest and most complex philosophical discussions of the osmotic movement of the Japanese imperial subject is Tanabe Hajime's "From the Schema of 'Time' to the Schema of 'World'" (1932).[28] This essay was the first essay in his series "The Logic of Species," and a detailed discussion of the aesthetic and spatiotemporal dimension of his model for imperial subjectivity.[29] For Tanabe, an international state representing the entirety of the human genus *(rui)* was impossible, or an absolutely negative possibility; however, the species, which was a possible and actual world-historical state, could mediate between the genus and the individual.[30] In his earliest aesthetic articulation of the subjectivity of this imperial nation-state, Tanabe begins with the term "schematism." For Kant schematism is that inexplicable capacity of the human to give form to an idea. For example, one might know what a rectangle is a priori, before any experience of objects, but in order to build a table, it is necessary to be able to draw a rectangle, at least in the mind's eye. This ability to draw the rectangle, to give it an image, is the work of schematism. Therefore, schemas mediate between the ideal and the material world and allow us to imagine that our ideas may be adequate to the objects that present themselves to our intuition. Arguing against Heidegger, who Tanabe states prioritized time over space and interpreted Kant's schematism only in relation to the temporality of *Dasein,* Tanabe asserts that without the external intuition of space, there could be no schematism. In particular, without the external intuition of Otherness, of something that approaches us from outside of our own internal sense of time, we would remain only in a state of autoaffection, sensing only our internal time. Space, as an external sense, allows us to externalize our own internal sense; it allows us to give figures and schemas to our ideas. In this sense, space and time do not simply oppose each other, but rather space and time are both opposed and unified through dialectics.

Tanabe deduced that while space is determined by time, time is also determined by space, and stated that schemas are neither strictly spatial nor temporal, but are rather the oppositional (or dialectical) unity of space and time. He calls the dialectical unity of space and time the "world." Therefore, being-in-the-world is not strictly a matter of the internal time sense of the individual *Dasein.* Through the faculty of schematism, our internal intuition of time is externalized and the external intuition of space is internalized. However, space and time are not immediately unified through this activity of creating and applying schemas. The world is not a stable and given external object. Space and time, and other and self, come into constant opposition with one another. The unification of space and time, of the internal time sense and the spatial sense of an outside, does not take the form of a seamless organism. The world is a schema, and not a thing-in-itself, because it is provisional, and subject to both constant change and constant imagination. Nonetheless, the world is also an ideal future toward which the subject of history projects itself. The theme of unity through change that marks the world of Hegelian world history is apparent.

Following Park's reference to osmosis, I term Tanabe's schema of the world as a kind of "osmotic space" whose spatial boundary is not a limit beyond which the world becomes foreign, but rather an active site of communion between identity and negativity, where there occurs a constant confrontation with and sublation of the otherness of space and the otherness of the historical past. In osmosis, the organism's boundary, which limits it as an organism, is also its means of internalizing the outside and externalizing its inside. The border of an osmotic organism is what allows it to constitute and reconstitute itself, to transform at the same time as it survives. The difference between osmotic space and the spatiotemporality of culturalism is clear. Despite the neo-Kantian foundations of his scientific distinctions and his teleology, Tanabe's world is not that realm of general cultural value through which a cultural artifact, as an expression of an individual creator and his national particularity, can become part of the larger cosmopolitan community. That world was a formal construction that allowed for a communicative translation between general, particular, and individual. It lacked the dynamism of space and time we see in the world imagined as an osmotic space-time.

In the same essay, Tanabe becomes concerned about the relation between the past and the present, and uses the term "expression" to discuss how it is that the past can become alienated from the present, but also recaptured by it:

> Expression is both an expression of the ego and an existence that opposes the ego; that it carries the significance of being proper to another ego that opposes the ego of the present is because it contains the principle of the nonego that negates the ego, and yet expression is unified with the ego of the present, and I am aware that the expression is my manifestation because expression is something formed by the absolutely negative unity of the ego.[31]

If we consider expression to be the externalization of the ego in space, as in a written text, photograph, or oral statement, this externalization necessarily drifts into the past and becomes separated from the subject by time. Again, an externalization of the ego in space can never be entirely spatial, because the world is both temporal and spatial, so the expression immediately enters time and the subject becomes temporally alienated from its former self. However, what allows the ego of the past to again be present is that expression in the present is formed by the absolute negative unity of the ego. The ego is only identical to itself insofar as it is not itself; the fact that the subject is not the same as it once was is what allows it to be a subject.

He refers to an absolute negative unity because it is a unity only recognized through nonbeing, through the recognition of the difference between the ego of the present and the ego of the past:

> As the past becomes conscious as something that opposes the present, its content is at once extinguished from the interior and preserved in the exterior. However,

because consciousness is the unity of internal and external, in which the external becomes the internal again, this past must be synthesized with the present in a projected manner. This structure that is both external and internal is nothing other than expression.[32]

Expression holds together the continuity of past and present, space and time, in their actuality. Further on, he writes,

> Expression is the manifestation of worldly existence, but is, at the same time, the manifestation of human existence. In expression, the exterior existence of space is unified with the past of time. . . . The world's unified structure of space and time is concretized in expression. We understand that the schema of the world as the unity of space and time has the character of expression. Schema as world is a principle of expression, and is an a priori expression.[33]

It is expression that holds together the space-time continuum of Tanabe's world in its actuality, and it is deeply connected to the collective and personal ontology of the human, or what Tanabe calls "social existence."[34] The schema of the world is the a priori schema that has no relation to experience, whereas expression is the actual being of this ideal unity of the world. This giving of ontological form to the schema of the world is what alienates the subject from itself, because this expression necessarily drifts into the past. However, this past can always be recuperated back into the present through dialectical logic and the dialectic process of history, which is also expressive. The boundary of the osmotic space of Tanabe's world is not only between the subject and its others, but between the present and the past; however, this past can always be reinvigorated and drawn back into the present by way of the movement, formed through expression, between externalization and internalization. Expression is what allows for this actual, historical aspect of the world to be reconciled with its a priori, natural unification of space and time. This entails a constant reintegration of the past into the present, an integration that does not resemble the immediacy of tradition and modernity that I discussed in relation to culturalism. This integration does not really occur between two discrete languages, or between the particular and the general, but rather between two simultaneous but disjunctive moments that negate each other, but can nevertheless be unified through expression—expression being that mode of externalization that, in its absolute negativity, can unify the past and the present, space and time, in their concrete actuality.

Not surprisingly, considering this linkage between external and internal sense through concrete expression, Tanabe's discussion eventually moves on to the problem of aesthetic judgment and its purposiveness, drawing from Kant's *Critique of Judgment*.[35] Tanabe states,

> [The present] enacts the absolute negative actualization of intuitive understanding that is the unified principle of the "world." The place of the practical subject who acts

with absolute purposiveness, in obeyance with "purposiveness without a purpose," is none other than the present. Because expression is such an action, it has the character of the unity of the epistemological subject *(shukan)* and the object.[36]

For Kant, the epitome of this purposiveness without a purpose was the aesthetic object, toward which the subject of judgment maintains a disinterested pleasure, and in which it comes to recognize the possibility of its own form in the form of a beautiful external object (particularly in nature, but also, perhaps, in an artwork).

This move to aesthetic judgment in Tanabe's understanding of expression is significant because it is where a link can be made between his imperial philosophical project, centered on the practice of the state subject, and art. How did Tanabe's ideas concerning reflexive judgment relate to the schema of the world? I argue that Tanabe's discussion of culture and aesthetics here is implicitly monolingual, and explicitly logocentric, not only because expression, or what we would now think of as writing or text, remains a supplement to the a priori ideality of the world as schema, but also because the translation that occurs in the ecstatic temporality that forms the world occurs only through the absolute negative unity of expression. In other words, this concrete form of expression is nothing but the materialization of logos. Expression is subsumed into the osmosis of the imperial subject, with its dynamic incorporation of the outside through the externalization of its inside. At the same time as expression materializes at this boundary between ego and nonego, it draws the nonego into the subject.

CH'OE CHAE-SŎ AND *PEOPLE'S LITERATURE:* THE CRISIS OF MODERN HUMANISM

Echoing the German idealist and late Kyoto School philosophical assertion that the human subject is the free and active center of such a dialectical process, the Korean critic Ch'oe Chae-sŏ referred to this osmotic subject of the world-historical state with the term "people's standpoint" *(kokumin-teki tachiba)*.[37] He did not characterize this subject with given racial or ethnic characteristics; the term rather indicated a dynamic mode of consciousness, practice, and expression similar to Tanabe's image of a concentric dialectical circle as the spatiotemporal, human subject that gives form to the world. Just as "expression" was the absolute mediation that for Tanabe could unify space with time, as well as the a priori world with concrete human existence, Ch'oe discussed a poetic and expressive national language as the form-giving mediation for a multiethnic national culture. However universalistic the notion of the world-historical state became, it was impossible to avoid such a turn to the anthropological, to a philosophical understanding of the language and culture through which the seemingly deethnicized idea of the world could take on a concrete form inclusive and exclusive of its internal others. Ch'oe identified how the detachment of the human subject from any natural origin was a symptom of a crisis in cosmopolitan humanism, one to which the world-historical state, the multiethnic empire, and his own project of Japanese national literature must respond. In the essays he published in the journal *People's Literature* (*Kokumin bungaku*, 1941–45), of which he was editor, Ch'oe demanded that colonial writers write from the people's standpoint, meaning through the cultural, linguistic, and political practices of a Japanese national subject situated in world history. Yi Kwang-su's Japanese-language writings during the war are exemplary of people's literature in that they depict the reformation of the colonial subject's practice as the means for colonial subjects to become Japanese national subjects. In addition to going to war for Japan, writing in the national language and mediating one's consciousness entirely through national culture were the primary conditions for Korean writers to become Japanese.

Ch'oe was a literary critic with a background in English literature, a famous interpreter of the modernist poet Yi Sang in the 1930s, and a translator of Shakespeare into Korean in the 1950s and 1960s.[38] In the 1940s, he drew from his readings of I. A. Richards, European Romanticism, and T. S. Eliot's idea of tradition in order to formulate a theory of a politically unified, monolingual Japanese national literary culture in which colonial writers from all over the empire would participate. Ch'oe approached assimilation in terms of the inheritance of and elaboration upon the Japanese national tradition.

In *Korean Literature in a Time of Transition*, published in 1943, Ch'oe discusses the cultural crisis of modernity and modern individualism and asserts that people's literature will constitute the cultural overcoming of this crisis. Just as philosophers reconsidered the logical and political relations between nations, states, and the world in the late 1930s, a number of literary scholars formulated new theories of people's literature, world literature, and their connections. Niizeki Ryōzō's *People's Literature and World Literature*, which appeared two years before Ch'oe's book, undoubtedly influenced some of his formulations.[39] Niizeki argues that literature is both specific to nations and peoples and has a general humanity (*ningensei*), and that the current task of criticism is to understand this connection anew. He claims that literature that is only world literature, in the sense that it only addresses universal themes in a dislocated, individual way, cannot achieve true universality, or be effective in a global time of war and national strife. This notion of world literature's universality is "as naïve a dream as the idea of world peace."[40] On the other hand, people's literature, which is "born of the people and exists for the people" without devolving into either mere intellectual play or trivial mass culture, can become true world literature precisely by being immersed in the concerns and experiences of its particular national community.[41] Ch'oe articulated a similar skepticism toward any concept of cosmopolitanism unmediated by the nation-state, and defended people's literature as the overcoming of both detached intellectual individualism and mass culture, but he did so from the position of a colonial subject. The idea that belonging to a state and a national community was necessary in order to participate in the general theater of human history was both a rhetorical means of addressing a perceived crisis in colonial modernity and itself a technology of colonial governmentality.

Writing from the people's standpoint required giving political support to Japan's war in Asia. It also meant returning to a more organic and primordial poetics that was a particularly romantic variation on ideas for a multiethnic national language community put forward by linguists such as Tokieda Motoki, then a professor at Keijō Imperial University in Seoul.[42] In asserting the subject position of the people's standpoint, Ch'oe sought a more egalitarian and more inclusive Japanese national literature founded on a flexible notion of Japanese national tradition. According to Ch'oe, for Korean writers to become true national subjects and to write from the people's standpoint, they not only would have to write exclusively in the national language, but would also have to appropriate the national traditions, ways of thinking, and dispositions of the Japanese people: "As for the truth in literature, the idea of merging with the traditions and disposition of the Japanese people will be adopted and the symbols and inferences of the arts will appear with a new meaning."[43] His appropriation of tradition was ambiguous insofar as Japanese national culture, on the one hand, would be unprecedented and future-oriented in its overcoming of modern individualism and its transformation through the inclusion of Korean literature, and, on the other hand, would be based upon the traditions, morality, and ways of thinking of Japan. The appropriation of Japanese tradition and Japanese spirit amounted to more than performing Japanese ethnicity, especially in its concern with transforming Japanese national culture internally. Tradition designated a continuous cultural sphere that opened out onto both the future and the frontier—Korea and the rest of the Asian continent—while it masked or repressed any relationality or border between the imperial nation-state and its alterity. In relation to Christian cultural reunion, Eliot had written, "The ideal reunion of all Christians does not, of course, imply an eventual *uniform* culture the world over: it implies simply a 'Christian culture' of which all local cultures should be variants."[44] In effect, Ch'oe replaced Christian with Japanese and, also drawing from Eliot, Scottish and Irish with Korean in order to articulate a Japanese national culture no longer troubled by ethnic and sectarian divisions, a multiethnic culture politically unified and linguistically homogeneous.

The first thing one notices in reading *Korean Literature in a Time of Transition* is that Korean literature is not mentioned until the seventh chapter of the book and is, despite the title, a somewhat minor topic compared to the discussion of modernity in general. The main theoretical argument of the first chapters addresses the importance of *People's Literature* in relation to the cultural and moral crisis of modern individualism. Being a scholar of English literature interested in the history of world literature, Ch'oe periodizes the break that gave rise to modern individuality with reference to the Renaissance. For him, Renaissance humanism posited the modern individual in its criticism of medieval feudalism and the medieval view of the world. Though Italian Renaissance humanism was the beginning of modern individualism, the humanist individual remained connected to the nation through the adoption of Roman texts and a dedication to moral and aesthetic cultivation. Beginning with nineteenth-century Romanticism, however, the individual became totally disconnected from the nation and cosmopolitanism was born. Using the poems of Shelley and Byron as examples of this denationalized cosmopolitanism, he states that the Romantic expression of, on the one hand, great genius and heroism and, on the other, lowly cowardice shows how the modern individual fell into progressively more exaggerated states of illness and weakness. Ch'oe argued that the illness of the modern individual had reached its greatest proportions with Freudian psychoanalysis and modernist literature, which accentuate the pathologies of individual psyches and reflect a total disconnection of the individual from national culture.[45] In order to show that such literature was quickly coming to an end, he quotes an article from the *New York Times* by the Austrian exile Stefan Zweig, which states that the kind of literature that told the story of a boy meeting a girl and falling in love can no longer be meaningful under the present historical circumstances.

Ch'oe's reading of Romanticism is a misreading, because it ignores its obvious connections to nationalism and highlights only the illness of its cosmopolitanism. However, Ch'oe is reading the situation of Korean colonial modernity through the lens of European intellectual and literary history, and we can intuit that his statement about Romanticism has more to do with the failure to establish a cultural nation. By reading Romanticism as an early cosmopolitan literature, Ch'oe is able to criticize the native bourgeois literature that failed to become a national literature in colonial Korea while simultaneously calling for a new nationalization effort that would solve the illness of colonial modernity and its failed forms of individuality. Ch'oe recasts the crisis of Japan's colonization of Korea as a moral and cultural crisis internal to the past individualism of Japanese national culture. By articulating the crisis in this way, he could lay claim to a minority Japanese national subjectivity and offer what he saw as an adequate solution to the crisis of modern humanism.

Ch'oe's emphasis on the cultural and moral nature of crisis is clear in his discussion of capitalism, or "profit society." For him, capitalism was not primarily an economic problem, but rather a cultural one. He states that "culture for culture's sake" and "profit for profit's sake" are two sides of the same crisis of modern individualism because both are abstract in relation to the daily life of the nation.[46] The modern individual does cultural, economic, intellectual, and scholarly work and becomes dedicated to an abstract internationalism that lacks any connection to the national masses. Scholars are especially prone to this individualism, which is the result of the autonomy of the international economy from the nation-state:

> The autonomization of the economy, as I already stated above, removes the national base and must establish international, traversing combinations. However, if scholarship is sought for the sake of scholarship, then it is easy to employ oneself for an abstract internationalism rather than for the daily life of the people *(kokumin)*.[47]

In this way, Ch'oe connected a modern individualism that seeks culture or scholarship to "abstract internationalism," using modernist literature (for example, James Joyce) as an example of the worst form of this cosmopolitan individualism. The crisis of modernity was for him economic only in a subjective or cultural sense, which allowed him to argue that capitalism could be overcome along with the subjective overcoming of internationalism and individualism. Against Marxists who argued that internationalism arose through the unification of the world by a crisis-ridden capitalist system, he argued that the basis of the crisis of internationalism lies solely in a subjective problem of the modern individual. In his analysis of fascism, Nicolas Poulantzas described this sort of petit-bourgeois critique of capitalism as "status quo"—an anticapitalism that complains about economic corruption but more in terms of culture or morality than in terms of class struggle.[48]

In his criticism of the crisis of culture in modern individualism and its groundless internationalism, Ch'oe pointed to two states of division in which this crisis had been expressed. He stated one division, referring to existentialist philosophy, as a division between the level of existence and the level of consciousness. Quoting Oswald Spengler, he argued that this division gives rise to spiritual uneasiness and is indicative of a crisis of morality and tradition that occurred along with urbanization and industrialization. This division between consciousness and existence leads to the notion that literature is an expression that reflects consciousness. For people's literature, according to Ch'oe, the level of consciousness should reflect the level of existence correctly or else it will devolve into simple word play or a literature of self-consolation.[49]

The second division that Ch'oe identified lay within the nation between the culture of daily life and culturalism. The culture of daily life refers to daily habits, including wearing Western clothes, watching films, drinking black tea, owning a radio and a record player, and other activities that were superficial imitations of daily life in Euro-America. For him, all of these activities lack belief and spirit. In opposition to these habits, the intellectual proponents of culturalism had separated themselves from those wrapped up in the culture of daily life and attempted to wrest culture away from their frivolous activities. Ch'oe was confident that in the period of transition into *People's Literature,* the masses, because their contact with Euro-American culture was superficial, would easily accept the new conditions (which, of course, meant that they would have no choice in the matter).

Ch'oe, then, addressed himself to the culturalists who were more deeply involved in Euro-American culture and were therefore more susceptible to continuing their cosmopolitan individualism.[50]

In positing these two states of division as parallel problems in the crisis of culture, Ch'oe was able to argue for a single solution: the formation of a new people's literature through the reimmersion of cultural elites back into the daily life of the masses. Because both states of division supposedly result from the same separation between the individual and the masses, he could assert that in the culturalists' return to the nation through the creation of *People's Literature,* the level of existence would come to be reflected by the level of consciousness and literature would no longer be mere individual expression. Using this future-oriented logic that articulated something yet to be formed, he could criticize leftist and class literature on the same grounds as he did the "literature of individual consciousness." In his logic, the depiction of class division reflected the same crisis of division in the individual as novels that dealt with psychological or family problems. Ch'oe asserts that leftist literature tries to depict objective divisions within society but it does not realize that this objectification of society is made possible and perpetuated by a division within the subject. For example, leftist literature took workers and peasants as its object, but failed to recognize that these classes have their own spirit, that they are subjects who can be objectified only if the writer divides himself through the assertion of a metaphysical position in relation to his object. Conversely, literature of individual consciousness dealt with psychological, aesthetic, and family problems in a very subjective manner without the writer realizing he is objectively separated from the national masses. In the case of Japan, the I-novel was for Ch'oe one example of this tendency toward the personalization of narrative and aesthetic form. *People's Literature* was to establish a new harmony between mass literature and the artistic literature of individuals. The agent that would mediate this harmony was the state; however, the state was not to dictate the content of literature to the passive masses. Rather, in order to unify the nation through national culture, this culture had to be believed in, supported by, and actively produced by the entire nation. The entirety of this nation was to be measured not in terms of sheer numbers, but rather in terms of classes. In other words, it was not necessary for every individual to believe in and support the state; rather, it was necessary for people from every class—in terms of both social class and social types—to participate in the production of national culture.

If the crisis of modern culture was tangible in the divisions within the individual that were to be overcome in the process of the creation of *People's Literature,* some idea of the agent of this creation was required. Although Ch'oe rarely if ever used terms like *shutai, shugo,* or *shukan,* which are some of the Japanese translations, all with different nuances, for the word "subject," he was theorizing the formation of a national subject insofar as overcoming the crisis of modern culture demanded a different kind of perception, a different language, and a different kind of participation of the writer in the life of the masses. The term in Ch'oe's argument that most directly suggests a subjective position is *kokumin-teki tachiba* (the people's standpoint), which refers to more than siding with the nation in a debate or to seeing oneself objectively as a national subject. As with national culture, this standpoint is something to be developed through certain forms of practice, including writing in the national language, treating national themes in literature, and concerning oneself with and addressing oneself to the national masses. The people's standpoint was also meant to mark a distinction between collaborating with the state and resisting the state through Korean nationalism (the elimination of antistate nationalism being one of his main requirements for *People's Literature*). Some of the other requirements for the people's standpoint were to stimulate the martial spirit of the nation, to collaborate with national policies, and to work toward the inclusion of Korean literature within the national culture of Japan. He argued from an antimodernist position that the general crisis of modernity required a nationalization of culture, and in so doing made very strict demands about what could and could not be said in literature. However, he distinguished the role of the state from the role it had taken under National Socialism by stating that requirements for literary critics to enroll as journalists, such as Josef Goebbels had instituted, were not tenable for Japan, and that any sort of criticism or publication should be allowed as long as it was not directed at the state. Literature was not to become mere propaganda or policy, but rather convey national policies, or what would now be termed "national interests," through cultural products legible to the masses.

According to Ch'oe's principles, the people's standpoint was to ensure the national quality of literature mainly through its treatment of subjects *(shudai)* related to the nation *(shudai* generally referring to a topic of writing or contemplation). However, Ch'oe's discussions of *shudai* returned to problems of *shutai*, or the practical subject—that is, the actions and behaviors that would allow writers to write from the people's standpoint.[51] These forms of practice were differentiated in a strict way from the consideration of conflicts generally thought productive for literature: subjective antinomies, class struggles, family or generational disputes, and so on. This intense emphasis on the practice of the subject, rather than on the object of his representation, is already implicit in his criticism of modern individualism. In order to overcome the states of divisions within the modern individual, he argued, it was necessary for writers to internalize national consciousness completely. Eventually, what they wrote about would not matter so much as the source, or, rather, the position from which they enunciated. Therefore, one of the most important practices was acting as a discursive subject of the national language.

In this way, the burden of occupying the people's standpoint was put on the writer and became an ontological imperative to be obeyed actively. To occupy the people's standpoint, the writer himself had to make sure that he had suppressed any other language that could disrupt the identity of the discursive subject. This made *People's Literature* an arena in which minority subjects could prove their loyalty to the Japanese nation. The popularity of confessions by colonized subjects that attested to the difficulty of learning the language and to the great effort they were putting forth to do so suggests that the desire of the colonized to become a Japanese national subject was, in the realm of *People's Literature,* made into a kind of spectacle in which being a discursive subject of the national language was grounds for inclusion within the nation-state. In this sense, the national language was not imagined in the same way as area studies has traditionally imagined the Japanese language because it was not superimposed with a Japanese ethnic identity or even a group of native speakers.

For Ch'oe, this is where the use of a unified and communicative national language emerged in a powerful way as the mediation that would allow for Koreans to appropriate Japanese traditions. That this appropriation and re-creation of Japanese cultural nationality was to occur through the formation of an imperial national subject is clear in his favorable readings of the German writer Hans Grimm, whom Kim Sa-ryang criticized contemporaneously as an ultranationalist who had given up on the Enlightenment ideals of the age of Goethe.[52] The disagreement between Ch'oe and Kim concerning Japanese nationalism occurred by way of their differing readings of German literary history and cosmopolitanism (Kim defending the German Enlightenment and the Jewish writer Heinrich Heine and Ch'oe appropriating National Socialist discourse for a multiethnic context). On Ch'oe's part, he wrote that Hans Grimm's *People without Land* is powerful because it takes the German nation's need for land as its subject *(shudai).*[53] In his reading of Grimm, Ch'oe approaches a "blood and soil" defense of Japanese nationality, whereas in other places he focuses on the flexible ideas of spirit and tradition. However, it is important to note that Ch'oe emphasizes soil and that he was using this reference to criticize Hayashi Fusao for stating that even if Koreans committed conversion *(tenkō)* they had no homeland to which to return. In other words, National Socialism and its idea of *Lebensraum* (living space) were a means for Ch'oe to argue that in becoming Japanese national subjects Koreans would also gain a homeland. The project of constructing national culture was to be predicated on the traditions and origins of a nation that could oppose itself to an international and cosmopolitan modernity, and therefore the empire had to be a single nation; however, at the same time, the creation of a homeland for Koreans required that the spirit and traditions of Japan shed the ethnocentric orientation they had gained in Japanism *(nihon-shugi).* The very idea of a single culture and language as the primary mediation for an imperial nation-state is, despite any claim to a future egalitarianism, necessarily a way to ignore colonial hierarchies. As Ch'oe's discourse shows, however, such an idea can also be very attractive for colonial subjects who have been subjected to inequality and oppression and who see an alternative in becoming an imperial subject. In the process of becoming a national minority, and no longer being a colonial subject, Ch'oe imagines that the nation he or she seems to have left behind is actually gained territorially through assimilation.

Ch'oe distinguishes his assertion of an inclusive and mediatory national culture from a claim for political citizenship. He criticizes citizenship *(kokuseki)* as the other side of a bad cosmopolitan internationalism, which is consonant with his overall distaste for modern individuality.[54] He claims that it was due to the very fact that the modern individual was a citizen of the nation-state that he was able to criticize the nation from a cosmopolitan perspective. Ch'oe's politics were more overtly fascist than T. S. Eliot's particular brand of monarchism and the poetics of the people's standpoint was also a poetics of death for which the dissolution of the individual into the warring masses became a means of inclusion within the nation-state. The stories that were written in line with Ch'oe's program were fascinated with the solemnity of war. For example, Yi Kwang-su's short story "You Can Become a Soldier" (1943) portrays war as the resolution to the psychological and social problems of colonial modernity. In this story, the Korean father of two young boys is elated when the governor-general establishes the volunteer soldier system in Korea. While the first son dies because of his despair over not being able to become a soldier, his second son is given a new life because he can join the Japanese military. To die fighting for Japan was to belong to Japan, to have one's death gain a social significance. In *Being and Time*, Martin Heidegger wrote that one's "anticipatory resoluteness toward death" enabled the authentic temporality of *Dasein*.[55] This authentic temporality was not only that of the individual, but ultimately that of a political community. The philosophical project of fundamental ontology did not escape Ch'oe. In his terms, the willful collapsing of the "level of consciousness" into the "level of existence" was one way to think of the becoming-national of Korean writers. Going to war offers the most concrete way to imagine what Ch'oe meant by the individual's complete incorporation into a poetic totality with no alterity.

Ch'oe imagines this aesthetics of immersing oneself into the imperial nation as a poetic act. In "What Is Poetic?" Ch'oe writes:

> It is possible for beauty to be perceived in the actions or poses of individual children, but we feel something truly beautiful when we see all the children of a national school marching in file. There is a cooperative beauty there that cannot be explained thoroughly with formalist aesthetic concepts like the beauty of order or the beauty of groups. Individual humans are demonstrating their own power to the greatest limit; however, they are by no means desirous. Because they are being conducted by one absolute idea, they show a majesty that has no individual plan and in this a sublime beauty is produced. This also differs from a formalist rhythmic beauty that arises from a wooden doll or machine that is only moving mechanically. There is a condition of strain between extreme repression and the demonstration

of extreme life and there shines forth an austere beauty that seeks only to scatter sparks. For that matter, one can say that modern warfare demonstrates the pinnacle of cooperative beauty.[56]

Through Ch'oe's notion of "cooperative beauty" he suggests what the cooperation of the East Asian Cooperative Community often meant in aesthetic terms (aesthetic in the narrow meaning of sense perception). There are two aesthetic experiences here: (a) witnessing the spectacle of cooperation and recognizing its beauty and (b) the experience of the children themselves in their state of "extreme repression" and "demonstration of extreme life." Ideally, it seems, these two experiences would be part of a single poetics; the adult onlooker feels the same strain visible in the children. This is what allows him to assert that the observation of this spectacle is not formalist (or a kind of disinterested pleasure in Kant's terms). The sublimity and austerity of the spectacle call upon the viewer to become part of the scene, to disappear into its beauty. Total participation in the poetics occurs through the renunciation of individual desires and casting the absolute idea as the sole object. While this absolute idea represses the child soldiers in taming their individual desires, it also allows them to demonstrate extreme life because they no longer suffer from the illness and divisions of modern individual subjectivity. This rebirth through the totality is beautiful in that the point of tension between the exertion of individual power through the totality and the repression of individual consciousness gives off a fiery energy. Warfare is the ultimate example of cooperative beauty, as it requires this tension to be its most acute. Because this aesthetics denies any formalism or any outside position, it engulfs the viewer and the dissolution of his separation becomes the sublime aesthetic experience.

Ch'oe developed this idea of poetics, as well as its relation to the crisis of modern culture, through his study of English literature, especially the critic I. A. Richards. While Richards's Romantic claims about the loss of organic poetics in modernity were perhaps not as extreme as this highly aestheticized poetics of war, the connection suggests that ideas of "cultural crisis" and the loss of a pure poetic production are not tropes to be taken lightly when considering their political effects. One wonders if Ch'oe would have taken a different position if an intense focus on cultural crisis had not been instilled through his studies at the university. This "crisis" is the most consistent theme in his writings and shows how modernist angst transformed into something very grave in the context of imperial war. To put it too crudely, his antimodernism was an elaboration of his modernism and eventually returned, by way of capitalist modernity, to a fascist politics and fascist aesthetics.

While Ch'oe claims that *People's Literature* would overcome the division between the proletarian arts and culturalism through a new mode of practice and writing, Korea hardly disappears as an anthropological object. The difference is that the anthropological objectification of Korea requires at the same time the Korean intellectual's complete immersion in the poetic totality of the Japanese empire.

The Japanese state is now the representative of humanity at large, the subject of world history. In a roundtable discussion that appeared in *People's Literature,* Paek Chŏl provides an interesting metaphor for the new situation of Korean literature, which shows that the problem of the anthropologization of Korea did not get resolved in *People's Literature*'s attempt to articulate a minority Japanese national subjectivity. If anything, the way Korea was made into an object and into a remnant carried by Korean-Japanese subjects became more banal. During a roundtable discussion in the inaugural issue of *People's Literature,* Paek offers an apt metaphor for the relationship between imperial space and the "area" as anthropological territory:

> I think what Mr. Ch'oe (Chae-sŏ) says is right, that there is no meaning in Korean literature setting forth as one wing of Japanese culture unless it can add something and enrich Japanese literature. However, there is the problem that Mr. Terada stated. In other words, there is one atmosphere in Korean literature, and if this atmosphere is not broken then there will be no attempt to get outside. For example, if there is a river running here and the natural landscape in this region is beautiful, then the flow of the river itself will also be extremely beautiful and writers must of course go along depicting the uniqueness of this river. However, the problem is that the flow of this river does not pass a single large sea or mountain range. Thus, what I want to insist is that before depicting this river, we first view the flow of this river from the sea. Now, the next time, when we look again, from the position of understanding the sea, at what we saw and felt in the atmosphere of the river, I think we will grasp a real uniqueness. I think that the uniqueness of Korean literature must be asserted in this way.[57]

Paek's assertion is that for the identity of Korean literature to make a contribution to Japanese literature, writers must break out of the confines of the territory of colonial Korea. Although there was dissent in the discussion about the kind of approach that would emphasize the uniqueness of Korean literature only in relation to the vantage point that the Japanese nation-state could provide, Paek's metaphor of breaking out, territorially and perceptually, from the confines of the Korean situation in order to better depict what was experienced there is an apt description of the way that the major figures of *People's Literature* perceived the direction of Korean culture at the time. An anthropological structure was at work. Koreans could view Korea from an outside position and thus construct their ethnicity as an object of their perception and creation. While this seems counter to Ch'oe's criticism of viewing nations from a metaphysical position, there was a double standard whereby Japan had no border that would allow it to be objectified (a boundless sea) and Korea was an object for contemplation (a river viewed from the sea). Such an intuition of the space of the empire reflects the pressure for the colonized to objectify his own ethnicity while actively producing national culture. This anthropological situation played itself out in *People's Literature,* where Ch'oe and others often served as native informants about Korea in roundtable discussions with Japanese intellectuals.[58]

Ch'oe discussed culture as a realm of value that could overcome class contradictions and colonial hierarchies. He grounded this realm of value in a traditional past that, while originally foreign, could nonetheless be appropriated to negate the antinomies of modernity and the divisions within the individual caused by the situation of colonial modernity. The aesthetics that emerged from this negation of the present was also an anaesthetic, in the sense that the horizon of death promised a teleological end to the crisis of humanism and the attendant crisis of vision and ontology.[59] The action of war and the anticipation of an identity achieved in death were ways of overcoming the perceptual and physical violence of colonial modernity. The perceptual violence of modernity that led to divisions within the individual was to be resolved further by language becoming metaphysical again, not in the sense of a transcendental concept, but through the invocation of a spirit in language, internally undivided and expressive of an untranslatable and territorial real, the nation. Ch'oe's discourse negated worldly perception, which he deemed metaphysical, and asserted the metaphysical within language as the central locus of culture. This reinscription of the metaphysical was not political solely because Ch'oe was a minority. However, as minority discourse, his writings show that only through extreme violence, and the aesthetics of violence, can a national language become a replacement for translation and a sign for indivisible community.

TRANSLATION AS TACTIC

Thus within the Korean intelligentsia of the metropole and the colonial capital Seoul, national language was linked to military mobilization, through the kind of confluence of romantic metaphors and militarist metaphors of poesis that we find in Ch'oe Chae-sŏ's writings on people's literature. Within this context, theories that reintroduced differences between and within national languages were not simply nostalgic appeals to the kind of liberal cosmopolitan world of communicative translation imagined by culturalists of the 1920s. For theorists of translation and writers of minor literature such as Kim Sa-ryang, the difference between Japanese national literature and Japanophone literature, as well as the difference between national language as the spirit of the totality and national languages as limited and differentiated spheres of discourse, amounted to the difference between imagining the survival of a global sense of the generally human and capitulating to a state-centered art that presented nation-state subjectivity as the only possible position in world history.

Kim Sa-ryang, in addition to being the most interesting, respected, and decorated Japanophone writer from Korea, studied German literature at Tokyo Imperial University, producing a master's thesis in German on the Jewish litterateur and Parisian expatriate Heinrich Heine.[60] Meanwhile, he remained active in the Korean literary and theater scene in Japan proper, including being nominated for the Akutagawa Prize, before returning to Korea in the early 1940s. While writing in Japan proper, he drew from German Classicism and Romanticism in his very different formulations about the cultural and vehicular status of "the language of Japan proper" during a period when colonial policy was demanding patriotism, monolingualism, and the political and cultural unity of Japan proper and Korea.

Kim Sa-ryang and Chang Hyŏk-ju are the two most significant Korean writers of Japanophone literature, understanding this term in the following sense: Japanophone literature describes a context in which a variety of languages, literatures, and intellectual traditions came into contact by way of Japanese as the major *vehicular* language, particularly in the more long-standing colonies of Okinawa, Taiwan, and Korea.[61] While many members of the intellectual classes in the colonies were adept at multiple languages, they often used Japanese translations of English, French, German, Russian, Sanskrit, and other literatures. They also wrote a great deal of fiction and criticism in Japanese, which allowed their works to be read by writers and intellectuals in other parts of the empire. At the same time as Japanese served this vehicular function, in the late 1930s it was increasingly cast as the national language of the whole empire. Therefore, the spiritual, cultural, and metaphysical status of Japanese as a national language was increasingly at the center of issues of national subjectivity and the preservation of local traditions, languages, and identities.

Kim Sa-ryang's ideas for Japanophone literature differed significantly from those of *People's Literature*. In Kim Sa-ryang's narrative of Korean modernity, the possibility for autonomy and self-determination is also mediated by culture, and he repeats a discourse similar to Kōsaka's philosophy of the multiethnic nation. However, whereas both Kōsaka and Ch'oe displaced the violence of colonialism into national war (the act of self-assertion and self-determination) and incorporated language and culture within a metaphysics and dialectics of the nation, Kim complicated the idea of national culture by revealing its dependence upon a relationship with alterity determined by translation. While one of Kim's figurations of translation inadvertently reproduced colonial hierarchies, his ideas and practice of bilingual writing did not attempt to arrest the proliferation of difference that occurs through translation. This writing appears as a challenge to the metaphor and metaphysics of nationhood and as an exploration into the allegorization of concrete problems of colonial domination.

Looking to local ideas, practices, and refusals of translation defamiliarizes the very notion of a single Japanese language, as when we find that among the Korean intellectual class of the 1930s and 1940s there were multiple names for this language. Ch'oe Chae-sŏ referred to it as the national language *(kokugo)* and Kim Sa-ryang referred to it as the language of Japan proper *(naichigo)*, a distinction that carried significant political and cultural stakes. Comparing Ch'oe's ideas for a monolingual Japanese national literature with Kim's plan to simultaneously preserve Korean literature through translation and transform the imperial language and imperial politics through a practice of bilingual writing shows how the questions of Japanophone studies are very pertinent to contemporary issues of canon formation, imperial histories, and minoritarian politics in the context of Asian studies.

Kim Sa-ryang's narrative of modernity differed from Ch'oe's in that he offered no criticism of the modern individual or political internationalism and he was careful not to invoke a cultural crisis in either Korean or Japanese national cultures. While he did maintain that the present was a period of transition for problems of language and culture, and that Korean culture would unify with Japanese national culture in some manner, this unification was not a matter of overcoming the alienations of colonial modernity through Japanese national subjectivity. According to Kim, the modern development of Korean culture occurred through a process of imitation and differentiation whereby outside literary and cultural forms were imported, worked upon, and eventually developed into something autonomous from other national cultures.

In 1939, Kim's ideas about transmitting Korean national culture relied upon a communicative notion of translation between ancient and modern Korean and between modern Korean and modern Japanese. Korean literature, once it had been written by a Korean national subject, and under the protection of the nation's cultural autonomy, could nonetheless be translated transparently into the language of Japan proper, thereby becoming part of Japanese and world culture. In his discussion of the role of translation in this historical process, he wrote:

> Considering the current situation in which Korean writers simply cannot write in the language of Japan proper, the demand to do so is certainly unreasonable. Instead we must create an organization that can translate Korean literature and announce that Korean literature must be written in Korean. For the moment, it would be fine if the governor-general of Korea took the lead and established a translation bureau, embarking on a profitable cultural enterprise. If not, there should be a desire among graduates of the Department of Korean Literature at Keijō Imperial University to translate and introduce ancient literature. The translation of contemporary literature, and, of course, of the literature of the Koryŏ and Chosŏn periods, must in large part be borne by the strength of students like these. This would broaden the respect for Korean literature at home and abroad and would also be one means to reward and encourage the labor of Korean writers themselves. . . . I think that in translation we must conceive of a way to keep alive as much as possible the nuances, maxims, and linguistic feelings of Korean.[62]

The idea of a nation-within-a-nation requires transmission as a metaphor for cultural translation and cultural translation as a metaphor for transmission. In this passage, Kim hopes that the "nuances, maxims, and linguistic feeling of Korean" can be revivified and preserved through the translation of ancient texts into modern Korean and the translation of both ancient and contemporary texts into the language of Japan proper.

At a time when the elimination of Korean writing was a legitimate fear and the demand for Korean writers to write in the language of Japan proper was both unreasonable and politically authoritarian, the preservative role of translation gained a heightened historical connotation. The task of preserving Korean culture through translation echoes the significance of afterlives in a text written contemporaneously, Walter Benjamin's "The Translator's Task."[63] Benjamin proposed that translation contributes to the survival of texts by reintroducing them into a later historical period and into a new linguistic and cultural context. For Kim, it was the danger that the language would be written out of history that required that the Korean intelligentsia engage in translation as a preservative act.

Kim Sa-ryang's discussion of cultural translation as a practice of unifying and modernizing the history of Korean literature through the communicative and preservative function of Japanese can be read alongside the structuralist view of translation put forward by Roman Jakobson in his essay "On Linguistic Aspects of Translation."[64] Jakobson distinguished between interlingual, intralingual, and intersemiotic translation: translation between two languages, translation within one language, and translation between linguistic and nonlinguistic signs. In his discussion of interlingual translation, or what he called "translation proper," he recognized the differences between languages, particularly at the level of the code-unit, but nonetheless asserted that two discrete languages have the capacity to communicate the same whole message. Kim's notion of transmitting Korean national culture also assumes the type of equivalence-in-difference that Jakobson discusses in relation to interlingual translation, or translation proper. This model establishes a mimetic relationship between the ethnic language and the imperial language and allowed Kim to imagine continuity between ethnic identity, imperial subjectivity, and world culture.

Jakobson's strict distinction between intralingual and interlingual translation falsely assumes that an interlingual translation will not also require an intralingual translation, and that equivalence-in-difference can be guaranteed by the hypothetical unity of two national languages. As Jacques Derrida points out in his reading of Jakobson, if one considers how "translation proper" relates to intralingual and intersemiotic translation, then "one starts down a road that quickly reveals how this reassuring tripartition can be problematic."[65] Kim was similarly aware of this problematic and his ideas concerning translation were more complicated than the communicative idea of translation that appears in his narrative of literary modernization and in his project for cultural preservation. Particularly in relation to bilingual writing, he understood the difficulty of translating transparently, especially within the imperial public sphere, where miscommunication and misapprehension were augmented. He was aware of the necessity for a different notion of translation that did not assume an immediate communicability between national culture, imperial culture, and world culture:

> Secondly, let us assume that one is filled with enthusiasm and motivation in the society or environment of Korea and would like to give shape to the contents that one grasps there. If one tries to write in the language of Japan proper rather than in Korean, the work will definitely be troubled by Japanese feelings and sensations. Sensations, feelings, and contents are connected to words when they first arise in the gut. To state it in an extreme manner, we not only know happiness and remember sadness with Korean sensations and feelings, but the expression of these will not come across unless it is through the Korean words that are inextricably connected to them. For example, if one tries to transmit either sadness or curse words into the language of Japan proper, one must translate intuitions or feelings in a very circuitous fashion. If this cannot be done, one will switch to purely Japanese sensations in composing the work.[66]

In bilingual writing, the intention toward perceptions is not determinable from a transcendental position where one could find equivalences in different languages for the same perception. Rather, sensations, feelings, and contents are already connected to words when they "arise in the gut." Language is not instanced in messages that have conceptual contents separable from sensation, but is itself a physical sensation with a metonymic relationship to other "nonlinguistic" perceptions (a relationship between language and the physical that puts into question the abstraction of the concept of interlingual translation as translation proper). These word-sensations are not completely untranslatable, but writing them in the language of Japan proper requires roundabout or circuitous *(mawari kudoi)* translations. If writers ignore the detours that change the target language internally, then they will reproduce Japanese literary expressions formalistically and language will lose its necessary connection to the materiality of signs. The attention here to disparities between an original word related to sensation and its translation into the language of Japan proper problematizes the idea of transmission between two distinct and stable languages and cultures.

In his study on the relationship between modern Japanese and Korean literatures, Kim Yun-sik referred to the formalistic Japanese used by some Korean writers, such as Yi Hyo-sŏk, as an "artificial language" *(in'gongŏ)*.[67] In Kim Sa-ryang's view, the artificiality of Japanese was not inevitable for Korean writers, but rather occurred from their inability to convey their most ontologically primary thoughts and perceptions adequately. Counterintuitively, "adequately" meant without adequation between original and translation, without a notion of equivalence-in-difference. The practice of translation in bilingual writing had a different historicity than the modernization and transmission of Korean national culture. Two contemporaneous presents, asymmetrical in their power, confronted, mixed, and folded into each other. Translation did not serve solely the preservation of national tradition, but was also productive, and the text produced was the afterlife of a submerged and nonidentical original belonging to the ethnic language. This sort of creation through translation is one aspect of minor literature, whose authorship can be usefully distinguished from the social-scientific definition of minority.[68] Minor literature arises where origins, community, and culture are the territory of the dominant and where the literature of the translated and translating minority deterritorializes culture. The metaphors of organicity prominent in both culturalism and the anthropological turn in theories of the world-historical state are disintegrated by the metonymies of sound, hallucination, and irony. This second mode of translation, which is not necessarily a translation between national languages, but could also be a translation between discursive regimes, returns the language of literature to the physical and the material, exploring an ontology that can perhaps confound that of imperial subjectification.

There are multiple links between Kim's ideas concerning translation and his fictional works, because the idea of *being* a minority and *becoming* a Japanese subject is dependent on the possibility of direct translation between the ethnic language and the imperial language; breaking away from this particular structure of ontology required an indirect translation and the consciousness that one was changing the imperial language "intralingually." This change of the imperial language did not necessarily occur at the level of syntax or phonetics, but rather in the figurative quality of the literary language. This literary language shifts the language of personal ontology and identity into an allegory of the social. This allegory of the social draws language away from its national-cultural territorialization, toward a differential and relational perspective on the identity of the subject. In so doing, it also rearticulates the meaning of acting human.

ACTING HUMAN: THE MINOR LITERATURE OF KIM SA-RYANG AND KIM NAM-CH'ŎN

In comparing the Japanese-language works of Kim Sa-ryang with the Korean language works of Kim Nam-chŏn, I will show how the difference introduced by minor literature is visible not solely at the interface between the ethnic and imperial language, but also in the way that the social practice of the imperial subject is represented. The language of imperial subjectification and the language of minor literature are not at odds solely within "Japanese," but also at the point where what Leo Ching calls the "ontology of the personal" is at odds with the intersection of speech and practice imagined in Tanabe's philosophy of expression or Ch'oe's theory of the people's standpoint.[69] In other words, the breakdown of the tripartite schema of interlingual, intralingual, and intersemiotic means that the interface between the language of empire and the language of a critical minor literature can occur in multiple "national languages," in Kim Nam-ch'ŏn's Korean-language stories that reflect on the prisoner's translation of the laws of world history as much as in Kim Sa-ryang's Japanese-language stories that question the plausibility of imperial subjectification for destitute and marginal colonial subjects.

In the contrast between Ch'oe's theory of multiethnic Japanese national literature and Kim Sa-ryang's concern with the practice of translation, we can see that the cultural territorialization entailed by the anthropological and anthropomorphizing theory of the world-historical state came to necessitate a theory of national language with the literary imperial subject, as the subject of the national language, at its center, while Kim's understanding of the practice of translation kept the relation between the imperial language and the ethnic language in play as an irresolvable problem. While we might then conclude that the contrast between the ontology of an imperial national literature and the ontology of minor literature is a contrast between a subject attempting to live in a single national language and a subject still living between languages, it is reductive to assume that "minor literature" refers solely to a cultural difference between monolingual and multilingual societies. There is another equally significant social difference that minor literature introduces into the sphere of imperial national culture, one that indexes the problem of personalization that Ching points to in his reading of imperial subjectification.

This difference is between representations of practice and representations of performance. In culturalism, practice is conflated with morality. In proletarian literary discourse, practice is conflated with productive labor. In theories of the world-historical state, practice is conflated with the ethicality of the nation-state. Kim Sa-ryang introduces another view of practice with the attention he gives to the (im)possibility of translation. However, minor literature's intervention into the sphere of discourses on practice is not simply to keep the ethnic language in play, but also to intervene into the way that speech acts are represented in literature, to show that speaking the language of imperial subjectification is not a matter of enunciating from the metaphysical position of Ch'oe's "people's standpoint," with its conflation of speech and political practice, but rather of speaking and acting within a context. This context cannot be reduced to the ideal context of the imperial nation-state, where speech and action can somehow coincide through the ontology of the personal and its metaphors; the contexts of minor literature are rather striated with social conflict, hierarchies of speech and position, and metonymic relations of power. The language of imperial subjectification assumes that performative language can correspond seamlessly with imperial practice, that to speak and write in the language of nation and empire is at the same time to act in its political interests. Taking as my examples the late stories of Kim Sa-ryang (written in Japanese) and Kim Nam-ch'ŏn (written in Korean), I will show how minor literature is not merely a disruption of the territory of cultural languages through a practice of translation; it also represents action within a contingent context for performance, thereby relativizing the ethicality of the nation-state, which rests on individual interiority as the site where speech and action can come to coincide. Insofar as morality, labor, and the ethicality of the nation-state are all anthropologically conceived perspectives on practice, minor literature also questions humanism and its basic assertion that the entirety of the world is the creation and product of human will.

Kim Sa-ryang's and Kim Nam-chŏn's literary texts are very conscious of both the concrete realities that the ideology of imperial subjectification tended to ignore and the necessity for a different ontology of the personal, one that was connected to a collectivity but irreducible to either a minority identity or an imperial subjectivity. By "concrete realities," I mean the racial hierarchies, gendered forms of violence, class antagonisms, and cultural hegemony that persisted despite the new forms of equality that imperial subjectification was supposed to entail. By a "different ontology," I mean a kind of becoming that could break away from the duality of Korean identity as "being" and Japanese subjectivity as "becoming."

It was in the ambiguous space between the crisis of humanism and the fundamentalist attempt to reconstitute cosmopolitan humanity through the nation-state and the practices of a new national subject where critical colonial writers like Kim Sa-ryang and Kim Nam-chŏn wrote deconstructive fictions exposing the limits to the new humanism of world-historical Japan. Their stories of the late 1930s are not concerned with a simple individual and national choice to be pro- or anti-Japanese, which has been the typical way of analyzing the cultural politics of late colonial Korea in the aftermath of Japanese empire.[70] They rather suggest a more complex issue, which is the cleft between abstract ideas about the cultural and moral practices of "the human" and the remaining narrow space for more contingent cultural performances. These writers were conscious of the operation, in imperial ideology, of the definition of the proper human (that is, person) in terms of moral cultivation and the capacity for practical reason. They were also leery of the new complicities between these ideas of the moral human and fascism's anti-intellectual, action-centered philosophy. Against the humanist call for moral regeneration, and its somewhat distorted version in fascism, they described the ideological aspect of moral humanism by contrasting colonial subjects' performances of prescribed social roles with the everyday impoverishment of society, culture, and the body. They illustrated that ideas of cultural practice derived from humanist philosophies were, in their conception of the moral society as an ideal, systemic whole, at odds with the fractious police and military violence that governed the everyday spaces of the war economy, as well as the economic destitution caused by the continuation of capitalist social relations beneath the propagandistic images of imperial unity and the formation of a new social order. The need to represent this gap between the ideology of systemic unity and the precariousness of everyday life became the difficult task for engaged literature, particularly after the demise of the proletarian realist arts and the rise of state-centered theories of art and society between 1935 and 1945.

In "The Snake" (1940), a Japanese-language work, Kim Sa-ryang successfully surrealizes and estranges the human-centered fictions of proletarian literature in order to critique some of its uncomfortable similarities to the melodramatic realism that characterized the moralistic humanism of the new fascist aesthetics.[71] He depicts a junkman and former amateur actor of the Korean proletarian theater group of Tokyo. Historically, Kim had written for such a theater group, but the Japanese government suppressed it as part of the crackdown against communists and colonial activists in the mid-1930s.[72] The actor in Kim's story is itinerant and delusional, left without the public stage that once provided a context for performance and for the left avant-garde's attempts to synthesize realist art and political life. Typage, or the participation of amateur actors, was one method of the proletarian theater. The story states that before the junkman's theater group was suppressed it was made up entirely of migrants from the colonies—cobblers, cleaning ladies, and newspaper delivery boys. Out of nostalgia, the junkman actor visits the small playhouse where the theater group had performed and imagines that he spends the night watching a rehearsal:

> A moment ago, this large man had left the nearby playhouse. A rehearsal of Gorky's *The Lower Depths* had been going on in that small theater. Since last night he had been crammed in there, watching the rehearsal. More than anything, he disliked the role of Satine. When he and his cohort had their own theater group in the past, he always performed the part of Satine when they did *The Lower Depths*.
>
> The large man raised his shoulders involuntarily and tried yelling out Satine's lines with the appropriate gestures.
>
> "Huumaan beeing! How's that? Doesn't it sound terrific?"
>
> He entered a dream, shaking both arms in the air, bending his body and yelling as though he were drunk.
>
> "Huumaan beeing! We must respect the human being! We should empathize with it!"[73]
>
> Just then, taking in a final breath, he gasped, "shouldn't we?" and then stopped. His stomach, empty since yesterday, responded to his question and he staggered.[74]

The abandoned playhouse may or may not exist in the diegesis and the rehearsal he watches is certainly a dream or hallucination. The junkman actor recites Satine's humanist proclamations, but the theater group and the theatrical audience are both absent. He ceases his recitation because he is weakened by hunger, wandering to a vacant lot where he encounters a giant snake. He goes to a snake store, where the owner has a large aquarium sitting on his desk "like a human figure from Greek ruins."[75] He tells the owner about the snake and the owner captures it and keeps it in the aquarium. After the junkman finally receives a meal at the house of a "foster parent" to the poor, he visits the snake store again. Similarly to Julio Cortázar's narrator in "Axolotl," without actually metamorphosing through the mirror of the aquarium, the junkman peers through the glass and the snake stares back at him.[76] The snake becomes the new object of the junkman's identification in an economic and social context where Satine's proclamations of his humanity cannot hide his physical and mental dehumanization.

In the darkness of the late 1930s, Gorky's classic humanist play can only be performed in the destitute and hallucinatory world of the junkman. Social life is akin more to animal captivity than to the noble suffering and quest for redemption portrayed in social realism. In Gorky's play, philosophical dialogue speaks of the natural equality of human beings of all social classes, but in "The Snake," the amateur actor's proclamations of his humanity are entirely invisible to society. Stanislavskian acting techniques and the fourth wall of the theatrical stage normally lend psychological realism to *The Lower Depths,* but the actor in "The Snake" performs the part of Satine in a waking dream, at the edge of death. The realism of his psychology is conveyed in the way he is forced or compelled to perform the hallucination of his humanity, not through the reality of his social type. In removing the theater and staging the play as one character's hallucination on the street, the fourth wall of realist theater dissolves into an uneasy intimacy with one character's schizophrenia. This departure from realism destabilizes the humanist perspective and enacts what Deleuze and Guattari, in their analysis of Kafka's minor literature, called "becoming-animal," or, in another context, the deterritorializing power of "the schizophrenic out for a walk."[77]

"The Snake" exploits the technical difference between reading fiction and spectating a play to make a political point about aesthetic experience: the absent theater is at once a regrettable historical fact of Japan in the late 1930s and a sign for the more general loss of the stability of realism. The story suggests that the synthesis of art and life within the new totalitarian environment takes the form of an extratheatrical but still performed hallucinatory interpenetration of dream and reality. Rather than acting the part of the proletariat who demands his humanity, the Satine role for which he was formerly typecast, the junkman instead identifies with the captive snake. As in many of Kim's texts, politics has become a matter of inclusion and exclusion, visibility and invisibility, hollow humanist ideas and animal existence, particularly as these problems converge within a fantasy about identity. Essentialist ideas of the human figure—from Satine's monologue to ancient Greek statues—are contrasted with the limits of the human in the near-death existence of the junkman and in the snake's eerily nonhuman gaze.

Kim Sa-ryang was aware that for his fiction to remain true to a dystopian period of mass mobilization for war, it had to take account of the failures that engaged realist art had experienced in attempting to bring forth a proletarian subject of history, even if he remained dedicated to cultural revolution. In accentuating the animal-like existence of the junkman actor, Kim works against prominent abstract notions of the human being by emphasizing the widespread experiences of abject poverty and mental instability in the everyday life of the empire. He situates the question of political and ethical action within a physiological and psychical world, challenging the implicit metaphysics in the notion of empire as a humanizing project. Bringing out the incommensurability of performance and context required a certain break from the conventions of social realism, the estrangement of its methods through the literary depiction of a failed theatrical performance. Many of Kim's stories similarly dramatize how the concepts and concerns of social realism are haunted by the extinction of cultural practices that could actualize those concepts and concerns in a socially meaningful theater.

Gorky's play is suitable for playing out this tension between the idea of the human being and the animal existence that also conditions action, because it saturates the figure of the human with such emotional intensity and historical import. By 1940, the recuperated Gorky had become a cultural celebrity in the Soviet Union, and despite his still contentious relation with Stalin, his humanism served the spectacle of Stalin-era socialist realism and its own masking of political terror.[78] Kim Sa-ryang seems aware of these contemporary political problems with Gorky's realism in the Soviet Union, but was equally concerned with the fate of realist literature in his more immediate context. He was concerned with the nation-state's new monopoly over the realist avant-garde, the effort of imperialist intellectuals to bring the art/life nexus out of the proletarian literature project and completely into the fold of the absolutist politics of the imperial state.

In many of Kim's stories, it is also not the proletariat who is the primary subject of colonization, but rather the displaced subaltern peasant or subproletariat—the slash-and-burn farmer, the junk salesman, the migrant prostitute, the imprisoned peasant rebel, the elder opium addict.[79] What these various characters have in common, in Kim's fictionalization at least, is that they are not in the position of becoming imperial subjects. As Marx reminds us, such surplus male populations could become resources for the industrial reserve army (after the volunteer soldier system was introduced into the colonies in 1939). As for such female populations, they were certainly at the greatest risk of being mobilized for military sexual slavery.[80] What many of Kim's stories present, therefore, are the excluded subjectivities that the dictates on imperial practice attempt to include through a moralistic, state-centered philosophy. They are in the most vulnerable position among the vulnerable because they exist at the margins of the system of abstract labor and the colonial economy, and are therefore not necessary for the production and reproduction of society. The deaths of the cave-dwellers, the self-immolation of the ex-convict, the incorporation of the slash-and-burn farmers by the murderous leader of the "white-white" religious cult, the psychosis of the junk salesman, and the failed attempts on the part of the opium addict to convince the suicidal to forgo their plans and smoke with him—all of this death and mental anguish are presented, sometimes explicitly and sometimes implicitly, as effects of colonization.[81]

These characters are unable to commit to the practices of the imperial subject, because they constantly confront the material, physical, and psychological limits to their actions, the dire historical and social circumstances within which the demands of imperial subjectification are made. Characters that do come to think of themselves as imperial subjects do so as a last resort. Their grave, disjointed, and deranged experiences of colonial relations lead them to desire a disturbingly comic salvation. "Tenma," another of Kim's Japanese-language stories, describes an outcast writer who wanders colonial Seoul attempting to track down a famous novelist visiting from Tokyo.[82] The story contains classic urban scenes of the writer waiting in a hotel lobby, engaging in disjointed conversation at a café, and wandering the streets aimlessly after he embarrasses himself in front of the Japanese writer and the Korean guide. At the end of the story, rejected by the visiting novelist and left without the possibility of cultural fame, the writer is no longer capable of social interaction. He begins to communicate with animals, particularly frogs that mock him with the racial epithet *yobo*. Kim surrealizes, or rather derealizes, both colonial racism and the writer's responses to it, using speaking animals to emphasize that racial and national identities are fantasy structures, not something written transparently on the human body. He also compares himself to a mythical flying horse (Tenma). He declares his loyalty to the Japanese spirit, calling to the sky for the emperor to take him to heaven—he stutters, "Make me a Japanese *(naichijin)!*"[83] By the time he has declared his political loyalty, he is already a nonperson; he stands outside the normative political discourse to the degree that no one can recognize his performance of Japanese nationalism. Rather than the writer's profession of loyalty to Japan guaranteeing his return to society and the world of national literature, it is rather a sign of his psychological instability and his inability to mold himself into an acceptable imperial subject.

Written at the margins of Japanese national identity, Kim's minor literature turns to such invisible, anonymous, and tragically alienated performances of political belief, performances that he situates within the impoverished social context and contrasts with the abstract ideas of practice that presume the moral and political efficacy of correct action. The invisibility of Kim's characters' performances of imperial subjectivity to the society of the diegesis also accentuates the absurd effectiveness of colonial discourse. Colonial discourses about world history and the fulfillment of humanity's ultimate purpose cause his characters to overidentify with a mode of practice that is materially, culturally, and psychologically untenable under conditions of empire. By portraying these characters' invisible performances of political faith, Kim reveals the absurd and ironic aspect of idealist nationalism, similarly to the way that his literary hero, Heinrich Heine, had parodied German idealism from a minority Jewish perspective.[84] In many ways, this technique of estrangement was a more effective method for conveying the function of ideology than proletarian literature's garnering of sympathy for the purely oppressed, because it broke more completely from the illusion that shared experiences of victimization lead directly and organically to the formation of correct ideas and correct practices (a perspective that fascist melodrama shared with proletarian realism).

Thus every expression of political identity in Kim's stories is framed by an acknowledgment of the invisibility or caricatured presence of colonial subjects within the dominant culture, as well as the spatial and social relations out of which a desire for identity emerges. Ideological fantasy and political identity both remain contingent and precarious, in contrast to the discourse of people's literature, in which individuals are supposed to actualize the national subject through their fully conscious acts of human will. The result of Kim's technique is not a cynical satire of colonial subjects' desire for proletarian class identity or Japanese national identity, but rather an inquiry into the contingency of performance and the enunciation of identity, the gap between the subject of enunciation and the subject that is enunciated. His characters' acting out of identity is never true or necessary as an internalized code of national practice, as in the "people's standpoint." The representation of contingency by way of a contrast between performance and context allowed Kim's art to push against the nation-state's subsumption of performance into abstract notions of political and moral practice in the project of people's literature. It also transformed the representation of class dynamics and the relation of class to nations during a time when the idea of a unified international proletariat was collapsing along with the left avant-garde that had articulated it.

Kim Nam-ch'ŏn's linked novellas "Management" (1940) and "Barley" (1941) also deal with the friction between contingent performance and abstract ideas of practice in the aftermath of severe police repression.[85] Although Kim wrote these stories in Korean, they can be considered minor literature akin to Kafka's works in the sense that they appropriate and allegorize the language of empire, bureaucracy, and the law, exposing the surreal, yet real and concrete, juridical apparatus through which the colonial intellectual was forced to speak the spiritual language of humanism and the world-historical state. Through the estrangement of the language and everyday experience of the law and the discourses on world history, these stories show that the philosophical idea of "historical actuality," which was central to philosophical claims about correct practice at the time, was not simply an idea about the historical present, but also a discourse spoken within a context. Kim's stories show, through irony, satire, and an attention to the everyday, that the actions dictated through the concept of "historical actuality" were always also situated performances.[86]

"Management" focuses on the quotidian life of a philosopher, O Si-hyŏng, and a clerk at the Yamato Inn, Ch'oe Mu-gyŏng, who gives him a room to stay in at the boardinghouse. The story describes Si-hyŏng's life as he prepares for his trial, including his giving up on the study of economics (that is, Marxism) and his embrace of both the discipline of philosophy and a multiple modernities perspective on world history (in this way, Si-hyŏng's life story and intellectual trajectory are very similar to the real philosopher Sŏ In-sik). The two stories explore the problem of philosophical detachment by depicting the everyday, mundane circumstances under which imperialist philosophers in colonial Korea articulated their idealist conceptions of human culture, society, and history. At the end of "Management," Si-hyŏng leaves for Pyongyang with his father. In "Barley," philosophical conversations about world history, Europe, and the East continue between Mu-gyŏng and a new boarder, Kwan-hyŏng, who is a lecturer at the Imperial University. The detachment of the imperial philosopher from the everyday economic and political circumstances of Korea comes through in scenes in which Si-hyŏng gives his philosophical justification for converting to Pan-Asianism or Kwan-hyŏng explains his own more Eurocentric views on history. Despite her intellectual interest in the men and their ideas, Mu-gyŏng's uncertainty about each of them, including their everyday habits and ethics, provides a contrapuntal perspective to their grand philosophical narratives of culture and world history.[87]

Kim's background in the proletarian arts movement certainly encouraged him to give attention to the everyday conditions that governed intellectual choices in the late 1930s. However, at a time when the more macrohistorical discourses of Marxism remained prominent and were often compatible with the modernizing impulse of imperialism, his concern with the everyday apartment life of the philosopher-boarder also provided a way to work against the complicity of the grand narratives of humanism with the imperial project. From the somewhat eerie contrast between Si-hyŏng's ideas about practical action and the contained everyday movements of the characters, one senses the concrete limits to the idea of subjective freedom in narratives of alternative modernization (for example, Hegelian ideas of East Asian Community).

In addition to viewing the philosophers from Mu-gyŏng's perspective, the stories also highlight the institutional and bureaucratic contexts within which philosophical viewpoints were assumed. The final scene of "Barley" takes place in a courtroom, where the defendant Si-hyŏng makes a statement to the judge to convince him that he has renounced his political activism and has committed himself to the Japanese empire. As in Kim Sa-ryang's stories, the scene plays on the discord between performance and context. Imagining that he must prove he is dedicated to Japan's "revolt against the West," Si-hyŏng argues against the Europeans' emanationist and stagist views of history and claims that historical actuality has revealed the plurality of world history to him:

> "I think Europeans have one belief concerning history. They believe that it is like flowing water or like a ladder with various steps. They think that the European

nations are leading the way and that the primitive nations are in the middle, undergoing a process that the European nations have already experienced.... I think we must shatter this illusion about history if we are to establish, with our own hands, a pluralistic world history. Historical actuality is revealing this to me."

The judge asked, "With these thoughts of yours, defendant, how do you comprehend the present tendencies of world history and the ongoing war?" The defendant stopped talking to recover his breath. After a moment he seemed ready to speak again.

"If I look at my intellectual path, I feel I have moved from Dilthey's humanism toward Heidegger. What left a deep impression on me was the fact that Heidegger came to admire Hitlerism out of an examination of the human being. I think that one recent tendency in our philosophical world is for philosophy to take up new problems out of the situations that presently surround it. Current events are very noticeable in Dr. Watsuji's historical observations on climate and Dr. Tanabe's investigations into the state, the nation, and the people. My excitement to purge the thoughts of the past and construct a new order arose from scholarly paths like these."

A satisfied smile came to the judge's lips.[88]

In the earlier story, "Management," Si-hyŏng tells Mu-gyŏng that he had no access to economics books in prison (for example, Marx's *Capital*) and could only read philosophy (particularly ancient Greek philosophy). This turn from political economy to philosophy continues as he prepares for his courtroom appearance. By the time of his trial, he explains world history no longer as the history of global capitalism, but rather as a Hegelian World History made up of the Western and Eastern worlds.

Si-hyŏng mentions the *humanism* and *engagement* of the philosophers who have influenced him because he feels compelled to present the empire as a cosmopolitan endeavor based on a superior mode of practice, no matter how inhuman the empire's modes of governing have become. The defendant iterates a pluralist historical model in order to connect his political practice to the totality called human history, and even though he bifurcates this history into the East and the West for political reasons, the unity of humanity itself and the idea that it ultimately has a shared cosmopolitan purpose are not questioned. In acting human, Si-hyŏng presents himself as both a passive observer of historical actuality and a willful subject who is morally and politically free to act in accordance with these objective conditions. He visualizes empire as an unavoidable historical process, but one to which he contributes voluntarily. In this scene, acting human requires both understanding the objective conditions of human history and acting freely to actualize these very conditions—the anthropomorphizing of the state that we found in the works of An Ham-kwang and other imperial intellectuals eventually becomes a matter of the individual human's capacity to act in the interests of the totality.

However, within the story, Si-hyŏng's narrative of his scholarly path is an elegant fabrication that has less to do with the content of the philosophies he mentions and more to do with trying to prevent his prosecution. His professed move from Wilhelm Dilthey's humanism to Martin Heidegger's Nazism and his assertion that Heidegger's support of Hitler was an outcome of his analysis of *Dasein* are both interesting in their implications. What brings together Dilthey's life philosophy and Heidegger's fundamental ontology is less the concrete lineage of German intellectual history, but rather the fact that each is a humanist, and that the latter has derived a philosophy of practice from his humanism. The mention of Watsuji Testurō's philosophy of climate and Tanabe Hajime's philosophy as examples of engaged philosophy elides the differences between Watsuji's ethnic nationalism and Tanabe's multiethnic nationalism, but unifies them under the concepts of humanism and practice. However, the story represents the point of Si-hyŏng's philosophical education as solely a matter of being able to defend his practice to the court. There is no expectation in the setting of the courtroom that Si-hyŏng will elaborate on the conceptual details of his personal intellectual path. The whole narrative is detached from the intricacies of what he has studied so rigorously for the occasion. It is only necessary for him to avoid any reference to economics, to include the correct names of philosophers, and to connect these names to his political support of the revolt against European colonialism and Japan's war in Asia. The courtroom is the very material context in which he proclaims to witness the meaning of the historical present, and where he is forced to see his subjection to the law as an expression of historical necessity and his own will. In this sense, his statement is a kind of pure ideology because he pieces together his narrative for the sole purpose of creating for himself an imaginary relation to history and an imaginary relation to his own intellectual practice that will potentially be affirmed by those who have control over his life and death.

Kim Nam-chŏn contrasts the dominant philosophies of practice of the time, which asserted the subject's free actualization of the laws of morality and history, with the quotidian and legal circumstances that conditioned life practices in late colonial Korea. As in Kim Sa-ryang's stories, the performance of the colonial subject in "Barley" remains contingent and precarious, because there is no guarantee that Si-hyŏng's professions of intellectual faith will earn him recognition as a Japanese national subject acting in the interests of the nation-state. Si-hyŏng can assert his humanity and national subjectivity in an act of will, but the degree to which he belongs to these categories is open to the interpretation of the judge and to his own existential uncertainty in the space where he proclaims his newfound ethics. Tanabe and other philosophers discussed historical actuality as the dialectical unity of contingency and necessity, which was a way of conceptualizing culture and history as a dialectical movement.[89] The courtroom scene in "Barley" intervenes into this imaginary unity of History by depicting a much more uncertain institutional relation between history and the laws of necessity. There is a point where the destruction implicit in the idea of World History meets its material limit in the body of the politically accused. Kim Nam-chŏn's tragic and ironic treatment of intellectual conversion questions the institutional languages of both philosophy and law, as coherently and realistically as any of Kafka's representations of bureaucracy.

Kim Sa-ryang and Kim Nam-chŏn both addressed the limits of humanism because they recognized that notions of humanistic moral practice allowed imperialist discourse to present its dehumanizing political project as a cosmopolitan undertaking. In their stories they show how the rhetoric of liberating the human, of enlivening the freedom of the subject through the mediation of the nation-state, entailed the actual domination of national and colonial subjects. Kim Sa-ryang's writer in "Tenma" is an outcast of official culture, no matter how close to the center he imagines himself to be. In describing the mental deterioration of this character as he gradually comes to embrace Japanese identity, Kim suggests that the liberation offered by identification with Japan is a desperate act of imagination and that the desire for liberation is better considered a symptom of the impoverishment of social life in colonial Korea, not a local or regional expression of universal human will. Kim Nam-chŏn's Sihyŏng claims to free himself from Marxism and to embrace a different view of history that historical actuality reveals to him, but the story describes the terror and incarceration that lead him to view history and freedom in this way. The prisons and the courts institute the concept of historical actuality through the violence of the law.

Particularly in their pragmatic application within national and colonial governmentality, idealist notions of the human are intimately tied to ontology, to how subjects relate to their existence and to their mortality. The colonial writer in Kim Sa-ryang's "Tenma" embraces the Japanese state's imperial mission at the moment of his furthest isolation, when he realizes that he can only remain a member of the human community by displaying his fanatical belief in the national spirit. Kim Nam-chŏn's philosopher, O Si-hyŏng, turns to philosophy and the cosmopolitan project of the East Asian Community when his communist political practice is no longer possible, when he can continue to live and write as a humanist philosopher of empire or otherwise not at all. In each case, a humanist discourse is empowered by the nation-state and the subject assimilates this discourse after confronting finite existence, entering a kind of waking dream that perhaps accompanies the anticipation or direct experience of war. The observations that critics have made of Kim Nam-chŏn's portrayals of prominent cultural figures of the time—that they too readily mimicked thinkers of Japan proper, that their ideas about culture and humanity were too divorced from the circumstances of colonial Korea, and that their philosophies reflected a petit-bourgeois or aristocratic worldview—are applicable to the psychology of "pro-Japanese intellectuals" *(ch'inilp'a)* or the Korean "converts" *(chŏnhyangja)* to Japanese nationalism in the 1930s and 1940s. However, reading the late 1930s and early 1940s as the period of the "pro-Japanese" does not adequately encapsulate what was involved in writing at the limits of humanism, in depicting a proletarian actor's homelessness and psychosis, a thwarted colonial writer's suicidal and anonymous dedication to the ethical norms of empire, and a former communist, released from prison, turning to the utopian ideas of East Asian Community, even as his life becomes the object of totalitarian governance.

AMBIGUOUS IDENTITIES: "INTO THE LIGHT"

"Into the Light" (1939) is the story of Kim Sa-ryang's that deals most directly with the dynamic between minority identity and imperial subjectivity.[90] While this story seems to address the question of minority identity in rather familiar terms, it is also possible to read it as a transitional text between a minority literature that displaces the concrete of the social into the ontology of the personal and a minor literature that allegorizes the social in a nonmetaphorical manner. An U-sik explains how Kim was initially pleased and inspired by the reception of the story as one that showed the "painful fate of an ethnic community."[91] However, in a published statement explaining his decision not to choose "Into the Light" for the Akutagawa Prize, Kawabata Yasunari wrote that the text touched on "large issues for the emotions of a nation," and that it was very well written, but that he was not satisfied with the lack of complex characterization.[92] Although Kawabata felt compelled to give the prize to a minority, he was not satisfied with the way that the characters seemed to stand in for ideas. However, Kawabata's reading depended on a certain understanding of the "national" as both minority identity and national Japanese identity. When minority literature is discussed in terms of a personal identity struggle, there is little difference, under the discourse of imperial subjectification, between becoming one identity (a Japanese national subject) and being another (Korean minority). However, in his celebratory biography, An U-sik also reduces Kim's motivations to a "responsibility toward the [Korean] nation."[93]

Why did both Japanese imperial nationalists and Korean nationalists in postwar Japan read the story as primarily about the internal struggle to become national? Besides losing the competition, why was Kim dissatisfied with Kawabata's reading and why did he no longer write stories so directly focused on the problem of minority and national identity?[94] First of all, the story does not deal with identity through the rubric of imperial subjectification, because the "national" of both Korean and Japanese is not framed as an internal identity struggle. The aspect of the story that Kawabata did not appreciate, which is the allegory that results from the dispersal of identity into multiple characters metonymically related to one another, is actually one of the story's virtues—it takes identity out of the interiority of the subject and situates it within the concrete social conditions of colonial modernity and immigrant communities.

The most obvious reason that the story cannot be read simply as a description of an internal identity struggle is that in the final scene it is not the narrator who asserts that his name (南) is the Korean name "Nam" rather the Japanese "Minami." Rather, Yamada Shunsuke, the young boy helped by Nam, recognizes him as Korean and thus is able to find a certain resolution, for the moment, to *his* internal conflict over identity. Although the text is written in the first person, it is necessary to distinguish between the traces of the narrative voice (the enunciating subject) and the main character (the subject enunciated). Because a productive disjuncture is maintained between these two, it would be reductive to read it solely in terms of the narrator's and the author's individual identity struggle. Instead of having a central locus of subjective reference for identity, the story is rather a layered and multivocal text in which various identity formations occur in relation to one another, and specifically according to asymmetrical relationships determined by class, gender, and colonialism.

"Into the Light" uses the metaphorical problems often found in *kōminka* literature: Which pronunciation will *stand in* for the narrator/teacher? What is the ethnic identity of each character? However, it also calls attention to metonymical relations in a way that makes the text a more complex allegory for imperial subjectification. The formation of identity in the story is primarily metonymical and relational, rather than symbolic and representational; all the identities in the story are defined only in relation to others. Furthermore, identities are not sites for the resolution of conflict, but rather traces of violent confrontations that have occurred in the past and that are visible only in the acts of violence and self-identification depicted in the narrative present. Shunsuke's violence against his classmate, which is the teacher's first clue that Shunsuke is part Korean, is a repetition of his father's violent outbursts toward his wife (Shunsuke's mother). The father's violence begins to emerge during his incarceration at the detention center, more than likely a racially motivated imprisonment, and from the anxiety over his hybridity, which is contrasted to the "purer" Koreanness or Japaneseness attributed to other characters. Shunsuke's mother is Korean in relation to the teacher, whom she considers to be Japanese *(naichijin)*, and to the husband who beats her in part out of self-hatred over his half-Koreanness. Shunsuke is able to accept that he is Korean by recognizing the teacher and his mother by way of the teacher as both Korean. Yi, the driver and a student of Minami, asserts his Korean identity partially as a class statement against his seemingly assimilated teacher. Finally, until the very end of the story, the narrator (南, Nam, Minami) shifts between signifiers fluidly, eschewing the question of his own identity and framing identity as a problem for the young (Yi and Shunsuke), the deranged (Habei), and women (Yi's and Shunsuke's mothers).

One is forced to discard a reading that remains within the idea of a dialectical struggle between minority identity and imperial subjectivity insofar as representation, despite the first-person narrative, becomes decentered and relational. However, it is possible to locate a point around which the various identities, as traces of violence, circulate. One might expect that Shunsuke's reconciliation with his mother at the end of the story would have been the climactic scene where he accepts his mother's Koreanness and makes a tentative return to the imaginary of mother and nation. His mother is a victim with no possibility of agency; she is only *subjected* to identities that she comes to despise. She is marked as purely Korean and yet herself has no place to which to return. She refuses to return home to Korea to escape her abusive relationship (the suggestion of Yi's mother), she cannot be a Japanese national subject (her image of the teacher), and she cannot assert her Korean identity as a political statement (Yi). Her conversation with Yi's mother in the hospital room is the only extensive section of the story marked as Korean language and it appears reported and translated into Japanese by the teacher, who listens in as he leaves the room out of politeness. This gendered translation, whereby the teacher conveys the two mothers' Korean speech to the reader in Japanese, figures feminine speech as a passive original and masculine speech as active, translational, and public. Yet, despite these various acts of locating and translating the feminine in the story, they do not lead to a return to the feminine as a point of ethnic or national origin. At the moment when the imagination of such a return could have been given representation, the narrator does not relate the scene. We do not see the son reconcile with his mother by bringing her tobacco leaves to serve as bandages. Instead, following the teacher's assertion to Shunsuke's mother that Yamada had been transferring his love for her on to him, the story ends with the scene between the boy and the teacher.

While Shunsuke's mother is the character whose ethnic and gender identity is the most violently and painfully inflicted, she is not the object or point around which identities as traces of violence circulate, or, of course, the source of any violence (her criticism of the teacher is self-debasing rather than aggressive). Shunsuke's male hybrid father (Habei) is rather the source of all of the extreme violence in the story, including his son Shunsuke's repetitions. If identities, as traces of violence, are figured in the story in relation to other identities, then Habei, as the origin of the violence, is responsible for many of the figurations of identity that occur, particularly within his family. Shunsuke's mother becomes a locus of Korean identity through the violence he inflicts, Yi's mother is marked as Korean by her conversation with Shunsuke's mother at the hospital, Shunsuke's Korean identity becomes apparent to the teacher through the repetition of his father's violence, and even the man that Shunsuke's mother goes to visit to get food is marked as Korean by virtue of Habei's anger about the visit. As for the teacher, he only becomes Korean again, to Shunsuke at least, through the whole process of witnessing Habei's and Shunsuke's violence and his attempts to encourage Shunsuke's reconciliation with his mother.

It is necessary to pause and ask why the hybrid father and the hybrid son are both the sources of violence and the figures around which identity formations emerge. There is a line of escape from the dialectical internal struggle into an allegorical structure of mourning centered on an originary colonial violence of which the hybrids are both the products and the agents of repetition. Stuart Hall has discussed the Caribbean as a territory of the "primal scene" of colonial violence between Euro-American power and black Africa.[95] The Korean communities in Tokyo at the time were also hybrid territories where colonial domination had its direct and immediate effects, but was also at a certain distance from the site of primitive accumulation. Colonialism proper was something happening back in Korea, where one could not easily return, though it was also occurring, in a different form, in the metropole. With so much forced migration to Japan proper during the time when this story was written, Tokyo and its minority communities were the site of a displaced colonial relationship.[96] There the effects of the external colonialism of the empire confronted the internal stratifications at the center. In these communities, no one would have been, simply, a colonized or excluded other. Colonial violence would have been felt as a trace or memory that, through an experience of the pressure for assimilation at the center, could be transformed into a minority identity. At a time when the technology of imperial subjectification was making the entire territory of the empire a site where colonial and class antagonisms were displaced into subjective struggles over identity, Kim's depiction of scenes in the minority community in Tokyo was very timely. After all, it is in these communities where colonialism had already been a displaced and personalized phenomenon for many years previous. Kim also would have been familiar with the politics of identity in Japan proper through his experiences working for Korean-language journals and theatre.

As Hall points out, the effect of colonialism was to make the colonized see himself as other. What imperial subjectification did was to make subjects recognize the other within not as an effect of colonialism, but as the content of an identity that could be preserved through its sublation into the imperial order. In my reading, by inserting the hybrid into the story as the initiator of violence and the catalyst for the formation of various identities, Kim was not calling for the purification or attainment of national identity, but rather bringing the trace of colonial violence to the surface and showing how this violence marks people with identities. He displaced the metaphorics of imperial identity formation into an allegory of the social that resituated the question of national identity within the concrete material and psychological context of the colonial relationship and its violence.

This approach differed from many of the earlier attempts of proletarian literature to represent imperialism in that it critiqued, and even satirized, the new conditions of national identity formation that existed in the logic of imperial subjectification. However, it also owed something to the attempts of proletarian literature to represent the dire effects of imperialism. Kim's "dangerous hybrid" was construed with reference to the colony as a site of primitive accumulation, a theme in his earlier works. Before the proletarian journal *Teibō* was suppressed in 1936, Kim published a story there, "Dosonran," which depicts the lives of cave dwellers on the outskirts of Pyongyang. The story describes the troubled lives of the cave dwellers and their attempts to make it into the urban wage labor system. The original story ends with the destruction of the caves by the Japanese colonial authority, which builds a highway through the area. Afterward, the main character, an old man named Wŏnsami, commits suicide because his home and his hopes of becoming a wage earner are both destroyed. Perhaps because of concerns of censorship, the end of the second version of the story published in *Bungei shuto* in February 1940 was changed so that a violent storm comes and washes away the caves.

Despite such capitulations and rewriting, in the context of imperial subjectification, Kim's stories served to remind the urban literati of the rapacity of colonization and to give an image to those who were being excluded, or violently included, in the process of rapid urbanization, militarization, and the imperial expansion of industrial capital. When Japanese national literature and culture and its ontology of the personal were called on to mediate between the world-historical state and its internal ethnic and cultural differences, Kim diagnosed the need to address these social issues with an attention to the processes of inclusion and exclusion and by articulating an alternative politics of the personal. This politics of the personal described the ambiguous and metonymic construction of ethnic identity and exposed the impossibility of fully actualizing the idea of total integration that underpinned the metaphorics of imperial nationalism.

6

Modernism without a Home
Cinematic Literature, Colonial Architecture, and Yi Sang's Poetics

Temporality—or historicity by way of popular thought.
—YI SANG

Yi Sang's poem "The Infinite Hexagon of Architecture," published in 1932, begins with a philosophical reflection on post-Euclidean geometry and twentieth-century visuality, particularly in poetry after the advent of cinema: "A square inside a square inside a square inside a square inside a square / A square circle of a square circle of a square circle. A person sees through the scent of soap from a vein where soap passes. The Earth imitates a globe imitates the Earth."[1] The image expresses a *mise en abyme*—two mirrors are facing each other, framing smaller and smaller frames of infinitesimal sizes, infinitely. In the aftermath of Albert Einstein's visit to Japan and brief travel through Korea in 1922, Yi Sang reflected on the recursivity of the *mise en abyme* with an added sense derived from popularized versions of the theory of relativity. The infinite lines bending around a singular point are not the extensive, straight lines of Cartesian geometry, but rather lines that curve in space-time (the notion of a square circle conveying this paradoxical space). As in most of Yi's poems and fiction, the perspective at the center of this infinite recursivity is a "person" *(hito)*. However, the person, or subject, is not constituted through the expressive causality of state-centered dialectics found in Tanabe Hajime's philosophical texts, which also drew from the theory of relativity; the person is rather a singular intensive point, or frame of reference, around which space-time curves. Finally, this recursivity is a matter of mimesis, but mimesis as an infinite mirroring rather than as the means toward a total artwork that could reconcile self and other dialectically. There is no original object called the "world" to be subsumed into a subject, but a globe that transforms and is transformed by the being of the Earth.

This chapter explores Yi's linking of the space-time of the theory of relativity to literary modernism and modern subjectivity, but in order to see fully what was at stake in Yi's poetics, and to evaluate the claims he made for another, more cinematic colonial architecture, it is necessary to discuss the ecstatic temporality of the modernist subject (or the modern human's constant projecting of itself outside of itself) more broadly in the context of fascism and imperialism. This discussion will focus on how space is reincorporated into ecstatic time differently between dialectical philosophy and Yi Sang's minor literature.

When read in the aesthetic contexts of both colonial architecture and literary modernism, it is clear that Yi's writings were political in their concern with vision, social space, architecture, and cinema. A series of Yi's most famous poems, "Bird's-Eye View," presents the other side of modern visuality from the *mise en abyme*, the image of the ground from the sky. Although it is normally said that Yi began the series of fifteen Korean-language poems in 1934, the first poem actually bearing this title appeared, not accidentally, in the Japanese-language colonial architecture journal *Korea and Architecture*.[2] In the most famous installment, Yi presents an image of frightened children viewed from above: "The first child says that he is frightened. / The second child also says that he is frightened. / The third child also says that he is frightened."[3] The poem continues in discrete, voiceless lines until the fifteenth child is documented. From the bird's-eye view, each child appears faceless and enumerated on the page, and yet the fear professed by each suggests the violence and power of the poem's abstract perspective. As a kind of spatial double-consciousness, Yi's poems contain references both to the plan seen from the bird's-eye view and to the infinite regress of the modern subject's vision. Yi Sang subverted the architectonic images of the colony, both through concrete images of the violence of the "bird's-eye view" and through his appropriations of the theory of relativity.

In order to see how the new geometries of postcinematic cultural life could be valued politically and socially in multiple ways, including fascism and imperialism, it will be necessary to take a somewhat long excursion into the problem of ecstatic temporality and cinematic literature, before returning to one of Yi Sang's most powerful poems dealing with the politics of space and time, "Blueprint for a Three-Dimensional Shape."[4] By then it will be clear what is at stake in the minute distinctions between the expressive subject and osmotic space of Tanabe's philosophy and the intensive expression that we find in Yi Sang's cinematic poetics.

MODERNIST TEMPORALITY AND IMPERIALISM

The relation between culturalism and Japan's colonial project is apparent in the simultaneity of the culturalist boom in Japan proper and the administration of cultural policy in Korea. The idea of culture was central to the reformist political discourse of colonial bureaucrats as much as it was the primary concern of culturalist intellectuals. The connections between imperialism and Marxism were also fairly direct, although more internally contradictory, insofar as Marxism both provided models for unilinear modernization and colonial assimilation and opened up the possibility for representations that exposed the dire social effects of capitalist modernity and the expansion of the empire. In each of these cases, a concept of the human genus-being and a belief in culture's role in actualizing the general character of this being tended to legitimate the violence and exploitation of "development."

The relations between modernism, imperial expansion, and humanism are somewhat more complex, because in fiction and criticism that have been construed to be modernist we find a number of qualities that do not lend themselves as easily to a sociopolitical reading. The search for temporalities that could estrange that of cultural progress, explorations of the alienation, illness, and death of the modern subject, the hermetic artwork of "art for art's sake," and the self-reflexive focus on aesthetic, linguistic, and formal experimentation rather than on political engagement—all aspects associated with modernism in Korean and Japanese literature—constitute a field of writing seemingly opposed to the notion of history as a process of humanity fulfilling a teleological purpose.

Many of the basic tropes associated with modernism reflect experimentations with time that contradict the reduction of time to history that we find in both culturalism and the proletarian arts. James Joyce compressed the sprawling time of the epic into a single day, Marcel Proust wrote in the alternative temporality of involuntary memory, and W. B. Yeats concerned himself with mythic historical cycles rather than historical progress. In East Asia, Akutagawa Ryūnosuke wrote of the repetitive cogwheel of modern life, Yokomitsu Riichi applied the aesthetic of cinematic time to the novel, and Pak T'ae-wŏn tracked the peripatetics of a single day in the life of a writer.[5] Shu-mei Shih has explored the variety of experimentations with time in semicolonial China.[6] Many of these literary experiments exposed the division and nonidentity of the human subject to itself as an effect of the ecstatic temporality of modernity, the modern subject's constant movement outside of itself, through which it constructs the future, the present, and the past.[7] This is a powerful critique of the search for stasis in the teleological anthropologies, because it figures the human's alienation from itself as a permanently repeated condition that negates any moral or social teleology to history.

In addition to its narrative and visual experimentations with time, if we take modernism at its face value, it also seems more generally detached from the worldly political problems of empire. However, as Peter Bürger and Boris Groys have shown, the whole notion of a modernist avant-garde presupposes that at some point the separation of the artist from society will be overcome, and that aesthetic experimentation will be displaced again into social experimentation, into that moment of anthropological pragmatism that characterizes modern political authority.[8] One purpose of this chapter is to address the imperialist dimension of modernism, just as I have tried to show how culturalism, Marxism, and imperial nationalism were not just imperialist impositions, but universalist discourses that mediated and facilitated the colonial relation.

Although there is no way to generalize about the politics of modernism, there are several moments of confluence between European modernism and fascism that have been explored in detail: Wyndham Lewis's aggressive narratives and support for Hitler, Filippo Marinetti's and Ezra Pound's propaganda for Mussolini, Martin Heidegger's version of the *Führerprinzip,* and so on (the examples accumulate quickly).[9] Others have interpreted the colonial attitudes or blindnesses specific to European modernist works; Edward Said's reading of Albert Camus in *Orientalism* stands out in the way that it connects aesthetic and formal experimentation to the racial and cultural anxieties of the colonizer.[10] As Seiji Lippit and Alan Tansman have shown, in the case of the Japanese empire the politics and politicization of aesthetic modernism must be considered in relation to Japanese fascism and imperialism.[11]

Those who represented ecstatic temporality as a break from tradition could also return to an anthropocentric mode, and also to fascist and imperialist political programs, when they began to foresee the possibility for a new anthropocentric thought that would neither be a static historical philosophy like the philosophy of culturalism nor rely on the materialist view of historical development belonging to Marxism. For example, the iconoclastic New Sensationist Yokomitsu Riichi destroyed the essayistic form of the I-novel *(shishōsetsu)* through a kind of derealization of the literary aesthetic and literary subject, but he also stepped into the political realm in his colonial novel *Shanghai* and, with more blatantly imperialist rhetoric, advocated the volunteer soldier system in the colonies and the violent unification of Japan and Korea.[12] The Korean literary critic Ch'oe Chae-sŏ established himself with an essay comparing the cinema eye of the novelist in Pak T'aewŏn's "Riverside Scene" and Yi Sang's "Wings," and providing an incisive analysis of the objective, externally directed "camera" of the former and the subjective, internally directed "camera" of the latter.[13] However, as I showed in the last chapter, Ch'oe later argued that Japanese national literature could resolve the problem of modern alienation and fragmentation that he located in Yi Sang's fiction, reuniting consciousness and Being by establishing an authentic and organic poetics of the warring mass.

In order to analyze how the ecstatic temporality of modernist writing became political and politicized through spatial figures, I will compare two modernists who eventually supported a total war politics, Yokomitsu Riichi and Ch'oe Ch'ae-sŏ, with the bilingual fictional and poetic works of Yi Sang. My approach will address three primary factors that are significant for the way that modernism was able to question the anthropological universals prominent in the Japanese empire, but also the ways that many modernists eventually capitulated to the total war system of the 1940s:

1. How modernist philosophers and writers discussed ecstatic temporality and the self-alienation of the human in a way that undermined the static view of the human as the subject and object of historical development.
2. The relation between this ecstatic temporality and the reproducible images of cinema.
3. The ways that the modernist critique of the human as empirico-transcendental doublet was respatialized in fascist and imperialist turns in modernist writing.

The turn to ecstatic temporality, and the way that philosophers and writers in the Japanese empire used it to challenge culturalism, cannot be conflated with political fascism. Ecstatic temporality is exemplified by statements that are not in themselves locatable on a political spectrum—the "being-toward-death" of Heidegger's *Dasein*, Rimbaud's proclamation that "the I is somebody else," Yokomitsu's dissolution of naturalism and the "I-novel," and Yi Sang's schizophrenic subject. The political and ethical question that should be posed to these experimentations with time and a subject constantly moving outside of itself is, at what point does ecstasis reconnect with a spatial image of utopia and a poetic project of modernization? How is it that Heidegger's *Dasein* transmogrified, however briefly or obliquely, into a territorialized and ethnicized German national subject? How did Yokomitsu's avant-garde destruction of the novel through an engagement with cinematic time become compatible with an image of imperial Japan in which Japan and Korea would become linguistically and ideologically transparent to each other though the Japanization of the Korean peninsula? In my view, these are the questions of social space through which the politics of modernist texts of the Japanese empire can be interpreted in a manner that gives attention to the political ramifications of modernism while not assuming that it has any essential connection to fascism.

In a reading of Arthur Rimbaud that situates him in the space of both the Paris Commune and European empires, Kristin Ross proposes introducing Lefebvreian analyses of social space and the production of space as a Marxist's way out of two familiar types of readings of modernism: one that proclaims the mythic genius of the rebel modernist poet and the other argument that abstracting and derealizing the linguistic medium of literature are tantamount to a transformation of a world entirely constituted through discourse and counterdiscourse.[14] Lippit makes another kind of turn to space in his use of the category of topography. Although my own approach in this book has been spatial in the sense more of a Foulcauldian archaeology than of a fully developed literary or cognitive mapping, I have shown that in the case of realism, breaking with the humanism of culturalism and the more schematic Marxist social science was a matter of developing other chronotopes that worked against the spatiotemporality of cultural modernization. This was a matter not only of finding representations that were more adequate to the objective conditions of imperialism or colonial modernity, but also of reconsidering how the form of literature coded personal psychology into a political and social narrative. Jameson, drawing from Deleuze and Guattari, improved on the psychobiographic approach of psychoanalysis by referring to these two registers as the molecular and the molar of narrative, which intersect, according to Jameson, through what J.-F. Lyotard called the "libidinal apparatus."[15] Realist texts that expanded their form and complexified their chronotopes were able to relate the molecular and the molar differently from the proletarian allegories of class consciousness, in which personal psychology stands in typologically, and melodramatically, for a political or social position. Reimagining social space and the ways it is constructed through a kind of "desiring-production" was key to finding a different interface between the molecular and the molar for realist literature. The same could be said about both the subversive experimentations and the imperialist-fascist fantasies of modernism in the late Japanese empire. Insofar as cinema was the primary technology through which desire was deterritorialized and reterritorialized in the early twentieth century, examining cinematic space and time and their bearing on the architectonics of modernist literature makes it possible to recognize the significance of molecular modernist critiques of the anthropocentric space-time of culturalism and Marxist social science, while also clarifying the particular ways that these critiques of humanism eventually capitulated to imperialist and fascist ideologies in the register of the molar. I take up Ross's concern with modernism's connections to social space in the context of the early twentieth century, when cinematic metaphors and motifs allowed writers to question the self-identity of the human subject and the author function, but also created a mass culture whose transformation of space and time created a new moving-image of the collective political bodies of nations and empires.

Tanabe's reading of Heidegger, discussed in the previous chapter, provides a philosophical case in point of the problem of the return of social space. In articulating a passage from the "schema time" to the "schema world," Tanabe reintroduced space into ecstatic temporality. While he does not discuss cinema directly in the essay, there are many analogies one finds between his concept of the world and the world-making power of cinema. More or less contemporaneously with Yi Sang's references to Einsteinian physics (1931–33), discussed later in this chapter, Tanabe states that the theory of relativity has transformed modern humanity's worldview from that of "three spatial dimensions plus the fourth dimension of time" into one in which four dimensional space-time unifies the past, present, and future into a single spatiotemporal world, a unity symbolized in the human sciences as the process of world history. In arguing for the spatiotemporal unity of the world and world history against what he saw as Heidegger's overly localized and temporal self-affection, Tanabe arrived at the problem of what the cultural mediation might be between the subject's present moment of futural projection and the past lives that are made past by this very projection. He posited "expression" as the mediation between ecstatic temporality and the spatial difference from the past and the past self. Expression was the mediation that allowed for the unity of the subject in the spatiotemporal unity of the world, an idea that repressed issues of translation in the negotiation of ethnic differences. Tied to the mediation of expression was the state, which was the particular agent of world history that connected the general to the individual.

THE ECSTATIC TIME OF CINEMATIC LITERATURE: CH'OE CHAE-SŎ AND YOKOMITSU RIICHI

As a regulative idea, the genus-being remains in a kind of stasis, the thing-in-itself of human history that is never entirely present, but that does not itself transform in time. In neo-Kantianism, history is the actualization of moral universality, but moral universality itself is transhistorical. In Marxist social science, history is made up of the economic stages of the genus-being, but productive labor itself is transhistorical. In Gilles Deleuze's philosophical reading of modern temporality, he makes a Nietzschean break from the time of human history (that is, Hegel) through a conceptualization of repetition and difference. He pinpoints the need to discuss regulative ideas, or simply Kantian Ideas, not as static norms for knowledge, but rather as differential problems. Ideas change differentially in time, and therefore cannot guide History.[16]

In Deleuze's work this philosophical insight into time and knowledge is associated with the experience of time for the subject of cinema, and critical work on cinematic literature in the Japanese empire was in some respects working through the transition from movement-image to time-image, as reflected in the shift from a stable realist sense of the human type to representations of experience emerging out of ecstatic temporality.[17] In literary criticism of colonial Korea, the temporal estrangement of the human from itself was thought to originate in a division between the subject of representation and the self that is represented. As in Deleuze's work, this division was conceptualized through the apparatus of cinema, or what Ch'oe Chae-sŏ called "cameric spirit" and "cameric existence."[18] In "The Expansion and Deepening of Realism" (1936), Ch'oe discusses Pak T'ae-wŏn's "Riverside Scene" and Yi Sang's "Wings" as two stories that, respectively, expanded and deepened literary realism in Korea. Cinema creates the potential for a much more pervasive and psychologically complex mode of mimesis, not only for cinema, but also for literature. Ch'oe argues that the two stories are comparable, despite their very different content, because each author writes as though through the machine of the camera (the term *k'amera* could also mean the photographic camera, but he uses the example of the cinematic spectator and the film director when he discusses our perception of the existence of the camera in reading a story). According to Ch'oe, Pak T'ae-wŏn directs his cameric spirit objectively, toward the external world, whereas Yi Sang directs his subjectively, toward the interior self, one enacting an expansion of realism and the other deepening it. Whereas Pak's engagement with cinema remains within the realm of simple, typological representation, Yi's directing of the film camera toward the interiority of the subject is both pathological and epiphanic:

> With this camera the novelist can face the external world from his psychological type or face his own internal world. In the former case the situation is comparatively simple and in the latter case it is extremely strange, because the relation between the observer and the observed is internal to the same person. There is no problem in the case of a self-descriptive poet or an autobiographical novelist who expresses his life and feelings candidly. However, if we differentiate to an extent between the writer of "Wings," or the artist who observes his own interior, and the human who is observed (as a living person), the observation and analysis of the interior of the self from the position of the artist may be pathological, but it is also the highest summit yet attained by human wisdom. This is the development of a consciousness of self, which is premised on a division of consciousness. It is not a healthy state. However, if the division of consciousness is the status quo for modern people, then the work of the true artist is to express this state of division faithfully.[19]

Ch'oe questions the simplicity and lack of subjectivity in Pak's use of the cinematic eye, stating further along in the essay that refusing to turn the camera inward means that Pak has not sufficiently dealt with questions of the truth and ethicality of his descriptions. Pak explores only the mechanical reproduction of external, objective reality and not the way that the camera functions also as an apparatus for the modern person's construction of an internal subjectivity. However treacherous a proposition turning the camera inward might be, and however pathological the resulting images, this is an unavoidable condition for modern people and the artists who represent them. Ch'oe defends Yi's concern with cinema's technological break with natural representation and his taking up of the position of the director in order to represent the material of internal consciousness. Embedded in Ch'oe's admittedly reductive binary between Pak's objective approach and Yi's subjective approach is an important insight about representation and the human: after the emergence of the cinematic eye, it is anachronistic to return to either the philosophy of culturalism or the optics of omniscient realist narration and description, both of which rely on a typology of human individuals whose external cultural life and internal consciousness reflect each other. Culturalism assumes but also represses this same division, because the empirico-transcendental doublet is a structure of identity between the experience of culture and the transcendentals that should govern culture, as well as the center of a teleological philosophy in which the human should eventually return to its moral essence. However, Ch'oe's reading shows that after cinema the historical genus-being can no longer function as a stable mediator between the transcendentals of the self-conscious subject and the empirical signs of this interiority in the national, ethnic, or class type of the individual. Ch'oe critiques Pak T'ae-wŏn's use of the camera spirit only to represent the world from the perspective of his type *(t'aip)*, because in the era of cinema types can no longer adequately stand in for subjectivity. The project of seeking the origins of the transcendental in an empirical identity runs into the problem of the division between the external and the internal enacted by the cinematic apparatus. Ch'oe shows that in cinematic modernist literature, the worldview of culturalism is reversed and fragmented; rather than the internal self-consciousness and morality of the individual being the source for the unity of representation of the external world, this internal world, as Yi Sang's works show, is a world of division, mirrors, pathologies, and discontinuity. Conversely, the external world appears continuous in Pak's story only because the human will is completely subtracted and reproduction becomes an entirely mechanical operation of the camera.

The problem of interiority and exteriority in culturalism is how to locate the origins of transcendental subjectivity in the empirical object of the human. In cinematic modernism, the temporal interior of the human becomes fragmentary and discontinuous because of the intervention of the visual machine that usurps the transcendental subject's ability to schematize the world. Suddenly, it is not the interior of the human but rather the mechanically reproduced external world that appears to the spectator as an ideal whole, whereas the internal time of the subject is the time of a radical dissolution, an abyssal and curved regression that Yi signifies with the image of two mirrors reflecting each other, shrinking into and encasing infinitely smaller squares.[20] As with light in the theory of relativity, if we were to extend this reflection infinitely, it would eventually curve around a singular point, forming a circle. This was Yi's image of both the space-time of cinema and the poetic subject. He was so enamored with the image of infinitely reflecting screen surfaces that in 1932, while publishing his poems in *Korea and Architecture*, he chose the penname "box" *(Sang)*. The "box" of his name is a reference not to space as the empty container of Euclidean geometry, but rather to the screen upon which Sergei Eisenstein's "filmic fourth dimension" is projected; this box is both a technology and a mode of subjectivity. This mode of subjectivity cannot be static, because it is constantly reflected and reflected upon, projected and projected upon.[21] As in Tanabe's philosophy of the imperial subject, cinematic subjectivity is ecstatic, constantly projected in time and therefore constantly alienated from its past selves.[22]

Ch'oe did not fully endorse the schizophrenia that resulted from Yi Sang's image of the subject as an ecstatic screen constantly transformed through reflection and projection. Even though he saw in "Wings" a valid reproach to the traditions of melodrama and realism in modern Korean literature and a necessary step toward the deepening of realism, he was concerned about the nihilistic implications of Yi's affective and fragmentary poetics. He guarded against the possibility that the age of mechanical reproducibility might be the age when the aesthetic disorientation of the fragmented and artificial human also entails a loss of capacity for moral judgment. Adumbrating his later turn to a theory of state literature, Ch'oe's concern at the end of "The Expansion and Deepening of Realism" is how truth and morality can be reestablished after the cinematic division of the human subject. Lacking a practical ideology connected to truth and morality, Yi's internal cinematic consciousness can only muster a series of artificially and loosely connected affects:

> The author [Yi Sang] connects each episode to the next, but has only an artificial method of doing so. This work was not constituted through the "-ism" of a living self that is steeped in everyday life, but rather connects each scene artificially. What is the main reason that the work is deprived of artistic elegance and faithfulness? Because the unnatural bursts of laughter and the unpleasant ridicule that appear occasionally in the work do not emerge from the morals of the author, but rather the artificial motivations of the surface. Won't the acquisition of morals be the main problem that permeates this author's future?[23]

The ramifications of Ch'oe's questioning of the lack of a practical ideology, or "-ism," in "Wings" extend well beyond the field of literary criticism into the philosophical and social science discourses of imperial nationalism. The human subject is irreversibly divided by the space-time of cinema—all of the external world becomes reproducible by the machine, with little need for human intervention, and at the same time the human interior becomes a hall of mirrors in which the schizophrenic writer never arrives at a stable image of the human's place in this infinitely reproducible world. External representations of everyday cultural life come to lack internal consciousness; the exploration of internal consciousness leads to a discontinuous, artificial, and ultimately pathological subject that loses any sense of the transcendentals that might organize representation. In *Korean Literature in a Time of Transition,* Ch'oe would eventually surmise that as the ecstatic subject of cinema loses any sense of order or organic cohesion, the individual life of the cosmopolitan modernist becomes pathological and void of meaning. In turning to Japanese national literature as the organic totality that could organize the spatiotemporal ecstasis unleashed by cinema, Ch'oe, in his reactionary modernist mode, sought to reinvigorate culture without assuming a priori the kind of continuous cosmopolitan world that naïve culturalists had envisioned.

In arguing for a literature that could unite the mass culture of everyday life (including, prominently, film) with the elite culture of the cosmopolitan individual, Ch'oe did not seek a romantic return to anything that preceded the historical present. After all, Koreans were not Japanese in the past, so the past offered no image for the utopian reconciliation to be brought about by people's literature. He sought instead to overcome the aesthetic chaos and artificiality of the fragmented modern individual by inventing a new ethical order for the organization of representation, a practical "-ism" that could unite the dispersed affects and associations we find in Yi's stories and poetry. In other words, Ch'oe's modernism turns to fascism not in the antihumanist parts of his discussion of modernity—the parts in which he recognizes that the human is fundamentally divided and irreconcilable to itself— but rather in the humanist part, in his search for a new moral continuity in the ecstatic space-time of cinematized life. This moral continuity was for him very much a narrative and spectacular continuity, a matter of creating a new story and a new image through which the fragments of modern life could be pieced together again according to a moral principle. As I showed in the last chapter, Japan's world-historical mission to unify East Asia into a single nation-state would become that story and that image through which to imagine a new morality and a new spatio-temporal existence no longer troubled by division, perhaps best exemplified by the attempt to unify mechanical reproduction and expressive interiority that we find in the fascist film aesthetic (particularly fascist melodrama).[24] Again, in Kōyama's words, Ch'oe found in the aesthetic of national literature and imperial film a means toward a subjective culture, "the fundamental quality of which lies in breaking from anthropocentrism, even as one returns to anthropocentrism."[25]

Yokomitsu Riichi's New Sensationist literary works are similarly concerned with the way that the ecstatic temporality of life in the cinematic age creates a troubling but perhaps generative split within both the writer and his characters. In his works, the "external" representations of character are no longer cohesive with the "internal" time sense of the subject of writing or the subject of action. The I-novel relied on a sense of unity between the subject of enunciation and the subject enunciated. In titling his two most important short stories "Machine" and "Time," Yokomitsu pointed to his engagement with cinema and its ecstasis. Like Ch'oe, when Yokomitsu turned to the social space of literature in an avant-garde fusion of aesthetics and political life, he also reintroduced essentialist anthropology into his discussions of Korea and the volunteer soldier system.

"Time" opens with an abrupt break from the time of the official economy. The chairman of a boardinghouse absconds with the money in the cash box and the renters, eight men and four women, are forced to flee. They decide to leave on a rainy night, and are drenched in water for much of the story. They journey to an ocean cliff, where they search for food, shelter, and water. In this surreal landscape, the male characters flirt with progressively more grotesque acts of violence.

The violence begins when Sasa draws a knife and starts a fight with Takaki over a shared love interest, though the fight is subdued. One of the women, Namiko, is ill, and becomes both an object of hatred and the impetus for cooperation. The men are forced to take turns carrying her on their backs, and contemplate leaving her behind (though they never do). Eventually, the group finds a hut with a water source. Toward the end of the story, the group huddles together in the hut, "losing their individuality," and hitting one another in their sleep. The narrator wonders if this violence arises out of love, or rather instinct. The characters are bound together by survival, but are also entirely alienated from one another through their violence. At one point, the narrator enters a state of hallucinatory solipsism, in which he contemplates the beauty of the state between life and death, and imagines the possibility that his suicide would also annihilate the other characters. He emerges from this state and beats the person next to him in a fit of rage. The story ends with the narrator forcing Namiko, who is very near death, to drink water.

There are two main mentions of time in this story. In the first, the narrator is walking in the deepest darkness and the only thing he can feel is his stomach pangs. He states that time is nothing more than an empty stomach, an intense feeling of hunger. The second mention of time occurs when the narrator is describing his hallucinatory state between life and death. He says that the waves of color that undulate before the eyes in this state of near death are instances of time. Significantly, the story begins with an exit from the economy, and from a society that will not tolerate the impecunious. If we assume that the characters are workers or students of some kind, their exit from the house is a dramatic break with the everyday life of wage labor or studying. The group leaves society and enters a Hobbesian state of nature in which time is a matter of life and death, rather than the repetition of the monetary circuit. The allegorical quality of the story is set up by this return to tribal organization and its effects on the lived experience of time on the part of the characters. Yokomitsu took his characters out of the modern capitalist present (where they presumably work, study, and pay rent), and depicted them coming to grips with a more fundamental and authentic temporality in which actions are based on the violence of instinct and the immediate physical sense of impending death. The narrator muses that those sensations one feels at the finite limit of subjectivity are time. These sensations of time at the limits of life are at once depersonalizing and entirely individual. Everyone in the group is subject to the same existential limits; however, each must compete with the others for his or her survival, to the extent that the world itself may be nothing more than an individual hallucination. There is only a collective insofar as it is necessary for the survival of its parts, but this collective itself may be a product of individual imagination.

Yokomitsu discusses the fictionality of such an idea of time in a short essay, "The Novel and Time" (1932). In this short, impressionistic essay, Yokomitsu distinguishes essay writing and fiction writing. This distinction was meaningful because in the genre of the I-novel, there was not always a clear demarcation between fictional narrative and an essay. Yokomitsu claims that an essay is not written about reality directly because the subject who writes is self-reflexive (or, in his phrase, "measures its own mind"). In other words, because an essay is not simply an observation of objective reality, but also an observation of oneself and one's own thoughts, its form can never be a precise empirical description of experience. As in Ch'oe Chae-sŏ's reading of Pak T'ae-wŏn's objective exterior and Yi Sang's schizophrenic interior, the self-reflexivity of the modern subject creates a persistent temporal division between the observer and the observed. Essays and fiction are different media, but there is also a fictional aspect to essays. Therefore, he could write that a writer's essays are not necessarily better than his fictional works simply because they appear closer to the truth. Essays do not provide a more immediate representation of psychical reality and the value of writing cannot be derived from its degree of psychological realism. All representation is fictional in the sense that it is written out of an ecstatic state between perspective and internal intuition.

The argument made against the I-novel and its interpretative community is that psychological description is involved in a kind of paradoxical folly. The desire for the real in psychological description leads to the fictionalization of the self. The I-novelist is in a position of weakness in relation to his audience because he must expose the most mundane aspects of his daily life. However, Yokomitsu provides a different possibility for the ascetic novelist. In his detachment from the surrounding world, and in the progress of his training, he can assign value to himself by seeking what awakens his mind and senses. This image of the self-valuing writer is also a break from culturalism, because interpretative evaluation is no longer a matter of drawing the individual into relation with the social whole through a regulative concept of general cultural value and national culture. Instead, the relationship between the individual and society is itself a fiction, and therefore remains malleable to the writer and his own sense of meaning, art, and literary form. To take the time to write an essay is to sacrifice the more authentic and determinant time of novel writing, the time of fictionalizing rather than describing the self. It is this more authentic time of fiction writing in which the subject confronts the determination of his destiny, which is a matter of constantly confronting the possibility and inevitability of one's death. In "Time," he began with an exit from the imposed time of the monetary economy, contrasting the time of abstract labor with a more authentic existential time that passes outside the experiential subject. In this disoriented state, a new mode of perception was possible.

The loss of ethical bearings in this radical existential temporality appears at the end of the story "Machine," when the narrator, who has killed one of his colleagues, professes that, if asked, he cannot claim to know what he has done.[26] Reality has become a machine in which the subject has no control over his actions, at the same time as he decides who is to live and who is to die. Through the severing of the scene of fiction from the mundane passage of everyday life in modernity, Yokomitsu's narrators proclaim a more immediate and authentic relation to time and sensation. However, this was at the cost of a relationality that could recognize others as more than the effect of the individual's confrontation with death.

Yokomitsu's break with the temporality of the I-novel, signified by his rearticulation of the relation between determination and destiny and his critique of the perspective of psychological realism, is closely related to the potential of cinema, to that new "Machine" of "Time." With its rapid cutting to different perspectives and its capacity to reorder the perception of time, cinema was in many ways the sort of individual and collective experience that Yokomitsu imagined for the New Sensationist novel. The advent of cinema as mass spectacle exposed the fictionality of the stable and individuated perspective of the I-novel. With cinema's ability to restructure space and time, the image of the writer as a psychological type fully integrated into a spatiotemporal context no longer appeared natural. In *Shanghai*, and certainly in his short stories, Yokomitsu explored the potential to create cinematic sensations in fiction. His works aestheticize life and death by highlighting the interpenetration of fiction and reality, or, more particularly, the interpenetration of mechanical reproduction and everyday perception within the new ecstatic temporality of cinematized culture. Although he did not theorize the relation between cinema and modernist fiction as explicitly as Ch'oe, his critique of the I-novel and the imagery of his stories are in accord with Ch'oe's theory that the moving image, in both its objectivist and its expressionist uses, could deepen rather than displace the realism of fiction in the era of cinema. At the same time, in both "Time" and "Machine" there also appears a great deal of anxiety about this new integration of the human being with mechanical representation. In his thematization of antisocial and criminal acts of violence and scenarios of collective confrontations with death, the new sensations of modern ecstatic temporality not only come to enliven desire and possibility, but also threaten to overwhelm perception and to create a concomitant desire to return to stasis. In Freud's terms, the integration of human and mechanical representation creates new sensations and pleasures, but also a death-drive, the drive to return to an inorganic state.[27]

This death-drive had its colonial aspect. Particularly in Yokomitsu's later essays concerning Korea and China, he still imagined an alternative space and time to the mundane everyday life of psychological realism. However, this desire for another temporality now located ecstasis very conservatively in the historical progress of multiethnic Japanese state subjectivity, and simultaneously reified the depth of the authentic space and time of the colonial cultural artifact that reveals, transparently, the essence of the colonial other. In "Korean Things" (1943), Yokomitsu proclaims an exotic appreciation for the secret Korea that lies behind the façade of modern social life and behind the intermediaries of the tourist's interpreter and his monetary compensation. At the same time, the Japanese state's mobilization of Koreans into the military is a sign to him that the need for intermediaries would be eliminated, and the true, secret essence of the Korean people could be revealed:

> When I travel I always think, "What is it that is hidden in the greatest recesses of this land?" As long as I do not see this—what is breathing secretly in the furthest interior—travel is hardly different from a stroll in the mountains.
>
> However, what is hidden in the greatest recesses cannot be known only with a passing glance. One cannot know it even if one imagines it from the stories of the land's people, and it is not something that is easily understood through observation or writings. If so, how can the traveler know what lies in the inner recesses? These complex things always seem to remain unknown and are set aside and dismissed. Then, the interpreter *(tsūben),* who intervenes into this lack of guidance for his own profit, often causes confusion and disputes between him and the traveler, and goes from place to place of his own accord.
>
> The past history between the Korean peninsula and Japan proper has not escaped from this example. Those who have gained have been the interpreters and those who have lost have been the human beings of Japan proper and the peninsula who were left not knowing those secret things that lie hidden in the inner recesses of the others' daily lives. The first pioneer in Japan who noticed this was probably Shin-i Shiroishi.
>
> With the institution of conscription now occurring on the peninsula, the various incomprehensible gasps that have arrived for thousands of years across that short distance have become the swell of a large wave formed into a single breath, and one feels happy to have entered an age in which interpreters are no longer required.
>
> When I am at home looking at the pottery of ancient Korea, it is very pleasurable to listen to the sorrow of days gone by, to the murmuring of a secret and obscure beauty, to what lay at the innermost depth of the people who lived there. It allows me to see directly, without being misled by an interpreter, the true hidden desire, happiness, and sadness of the person who made the form, and it is, more than anything else, the essence of travel. However, from then on it has already become a stand-in, lacking in the feelings of travel.[28]

An exoticizing colonial gaze accompanies the alienation of the modern writer and his search for a time outside of modernity. Yokomitsu contrasts his distrust of the interpreter with ruminations about the connection he feels with ancient Koreans when viewing their pottery back home. Actual travel becomes inauthentic because one is subjected to the interpreter's disorienting mobility, his economic compensation, and his present view of the past. This mediation alienates one from the true essence of the other, which lies in the "deep recesses" inaccessible to the tourist. Viewing the art of the colonized from a distance (of both space and time) allows one a glimpse of their true past. This exotic view is accompanied by nostalgia for the context of the aesthetic object, its imagined time in history. He laments that the experience of viewing the pottery, while authentic in its lack of mediation, is detached from travel itself. The exoticization of Korea reinforces the feeling of sublime alienation from the present, but it also bridges the distance between the imperial subject and the colonial other. Still, the imperial subject's melancholic relation to the lost object is a feeling with a political and historical future, as military conscription promises to overcome interpreters and the fragmentation of the traveler's colonial gaze. Paradoxically, as Koreans assimilate into the Japanese nation, their difference will appear more freely and directly to the view of the traveler. Koreans will finally speak the same language and expose what has been lingering beneath the surface of their modern lives.

Lippit distinguishes between the experimental Yokomitsu of the 1920s and early 1930s, particularly of the novel *Shanghai*, and the ethnic nationalist Yokomitsu of the 1940s, while recognizing that there were both continuities and discontinuities between his modernist and ethnic nationalist writings.[29] It is tempting to imagine a cosmopolitan Yokomitsu interested in translating the methods of the European avant-garde and a nationalist Yokomitsu who withdrew into tradition and racist perspectives on the colonized. However, as in the case of other modernists who eventually took on a fascist aesthetic, the temporality of this turn to tradition was not the same as a Romantic nostalgia for a lost national past; nor was the original formulation of an avant-garde aesthetic entirely devoid of nationalism. More important is the way that the articulation of the ecstatic temporality of a literary I constantly moving outside of itself, as well as a spiritual vision of the machine as transformative of the human and its literary representation, eventually arrived at a new organic view of the social totality in which colonizer and colonized, human and machine, and the nation-state and its internal differences were all unified through an embrace of national culture, national language, and collective death. Imperial nationalists steeped in modernism could imagine that the deep time of the colonized was unified with the ecstasis of the imperial subject through a poetic national language and national spirit that erased the need for translation, and a shared sacrifice of life to the state that erased the political suspicion of the colonized that we find in *Shanghai*. The authentic Korea, existing outside the mechanical time of capitalism, merged with the ecstatic time of an imperial subject constantly moving outside of itself. In a cinematic image of simultaneity between the colonized and imperial subject, Yokomitsu's radical break from the I-novel and the mundane time of the literary essay connected with the aesthetic of fascism, which imagines a totality in which all the visual, cultural, and social crises of capitalism are overcome through the visualization of an alternative temporality and historical trajectory. This is not an aesthetic return to a past Japan, but rather a cinematic image of a society in which the temporal movement of the ecstatic subject forms a future community where colonial differences have been erased, or at least reduced to the reified, dead objects of Yokomitsu's "colonial kitsch."[30]

In connecting destiny and determination through ecstatic temporality, Yokomitsu broke from national literary and cultural tradition and developed a cinematic literature. However, like Ch'oe Chae-sŏ, he arrived at another imperialist notion of culture in his organic view of social space for which the temporal and spatial difference between metropole and colony would be overcome through the nationalization of Korea. Although he continued to discuss the "deep recesses" of Korean life, this anthropological view of Korea's otherness to modernity was a projection of sameness and a disavowal of difference, an identification of an outside to modernity in the primitive other and the illusory conflation of that outside with the social space of an imperial state supposedly going against the grain of Eurocentric world history.

CULTURALISM AND ARCHITECTURAL SPACE: *KOREA AND ARCHITECTURE*

From these few texts of modernism in the early 1930s, it is clear that writers and critics were concerned with the transformation in perspective undergone through the cinematization of daily life, from which they derived an understanding of time not as a progressive movement toward the genus-being, but rather as an ecstasis that constantly compromised the coherency of the human as the subject and object of modern thought. It is equally clear that for many modernists this fragmentation should not persist indefinitely—a new ethics and a new politics had to intervene to restore meaning to a subject disoriented and incapable of positioning itself in any ethically meaningful way. Despite their iconoclasm, modernists often accorded the capacity for this intervention to the world-historical state and its subjects. Ch'oe, Yokomitsu, and Tanabe each found in the multiethnic national community the potential to overcome or to sublate alienation and fragmentation through the individual's immersion in collective warfare. Becoming imperial almost always entailed a kind of imperial humanism, as suggested by Kōyama's call for a new anthropocentrism, Tanabe's discussions of the nation-state as the worldly representative of the human's genus-being, and the various searches for a new humanism in Korea. Modernism's particular way of becoming imperial was equally humanist, in the way that Ch'oe sought a new moral continuity in fragmentary representation and Yokomitsu sought to arrest the play of difference by making the military state the center of ecstasis, while at the same time reducing colonial culture to a static object. Was this the only possible political and social direction for modernism at the time? If not, then should we try to locate other political possibilities for aesthetic modernism?

I will approach this question through a reading of the poetry of Yi Sang, not to present him as a modernist untainted by fascism or imperialism, but rather to address the more specific problems of ecstatic temporality, cinema, and modernism's tendency in the 1930s to return to nationalized space and particular origins. Modernism became political through its representation of social space, the Japanese imperial version of which gave a picture of a state subject sublating all past identities and affiliations in its ecstatic projection toward an unprecedented future. In Tanabe's theory of expression as osmosis, in Ch'oe's attempt to transform Japanese national culture internally, and in Yokomitsu's celebration of the end of translation, there is a shared image of an ecstatic human subject constantly moving outside of itself but nonetheless constantly returning to an identity with itself—a poetic subject both ecstatic and completely immersed in the totality. If it is possible for the ecstatic and cinematic subject of modernism during this period to avoid this aesthetics and politics of territorialization and the imperial social space represented through it, then such a subjectivity might present another possibility for modernism in relation to the politics of imperial subjectification.

Because he died before the institution of the policy of imperial subjectification, it is difficult to know whether or not Yi Sang would have supported Japan-Korea unification, remained silent, or tried to negotiate between his individual artistic practice and the demands of imperialism. Although this remains an unknown, already in Ch'oe's reading of Yi we can see dissatisfaction with his schizophrenic writing style on the part of those who would eventually advocate national literature. In his critique of Yi's version of cinematic literature, Ch'oe lauded his willingness to turn the camera inward and to expose the fragmentation of the modern subject, but he also argued that Yi lacked a moral direction and that he tended to piece together series of affects and sensations with no clear moral purpose.[31] Although we cannot know how Yi would have responded to the politics of the late 1930s, if we take the fragmentation and experimentation of his works as a virtue rather than a shortcoming, his aesthetic can be seen to challenge the anthropocentric epistemology of culturalism without returning to another imperial mode of humanism in the manner of Kōyama's anti-anthropocentric anthropocentrism. Yi's aesthetic entails another kind of representation of the ecstasis of the cinematic subject in literature, one that imagines space and time outside the culturalist structure of the individual, the nation, and the world, but does not introduce an osmotic state formation as the solution to the crisis of representation in the modern era of aesthetic disorientation (analyzed symptomatically by Ch'oe Chae-sŏ in his analysis of the cinematic apparatus's effects on literature). In order to continue to read these political problems of modernism through the question of social space, I have chosen to focus on the four poems that Yi Sang published in Japanese in the colonial architecture journal *Korea and Architecture*. These poems are the most emblematic of a modernism that refuses to return to either tradition or empire, to the particular or the universal, and are therefore the most significant of his works for the present project (as well as a useful place to end this study).

Korea and Architecture was not only a trade journal for architects and surveyors working in colonial Korea, but also a forum for the introduction of modernist discourse. Many of the articles in the journal are concerned with how to transform the urban space of Seoul. However, other articles introduce art and architecture movements as diverse as Cubism, Futurism, and the modernism of Le Corbursier, as well as anthropological perspectives on architecture. *Korea and Architecture* gave colonial intellectuals like Yi Sang, who was studying to become a surveyor, access to European modernist art and architecture. Furthermore, even though the journal mostly adhered to culturalist principles and was concerned mainly with the pragmatics of colonial architecture and the colonial project in general, the genre of *manpitsu* (random jottings) allowed Yi to contribute quite experimental and radical poems to the journal. Perhaps unbeknownst to the editors of the journal, Yi's poems were nothing less than a complete dismantling of the dominant philosophical premises and spatiotemporal orientations of the journal, performed largely through a meditation on the relationship between the human subject, architectural planning, and cinema. At the same time, unlike the many Hegelian and state-centered critiques of cosmopolitan culturalism offered by imperial philosophers of time (including Tanabe's appropriation of Einsteinian physics and Bergsonian duration to articulate the practice of the Japanese imperial subject), Yi's forays into non-Euclidean geometry, the theory of relativity, and science fiction largely avoided any return to unity, identity, or stasis. In my comparison between Yi and Tanabe, I will focus in particular on the way that Yi's mode of expression, which I will term "intensive expression," differed in minute but important ways from Tanabe's view of expression as the unifying mediation between past and present selves, between the negated past and a positive future.

In order to interpret Yi's poems and their intensive expression, it is necessary to situate them within this original visual context and to see how they interacted with the other pages of the journal. While attempts have been made to transform Yi Sang into a national genius of Korean literature through the translation of his Japanese works into vernacular Korean, in these poems there is a great deal going on at the interstices between language and the concrete images of science and mathematics. In order to interpret them, it is necessary to recognize these poems as minor literature (that is, literature written in a second, hegemonic language), as well as visual artifacts with important connections to their original visual and discursive context. Before entering into a discussion of how Yi's cinematic poems engaged with and broke from the optics of the culturalist architecture project—while not succumbing to an overtly imperialist ideology of ecstatic temporality—it is necessary to define more clearly the discursive and visual context in which these poems appeared.

In *Korea and Architecture* there is a clear culturalist approach to questions of the relationship between space and time. For the inaugural issue the editors commissioned the Tokyo Imperial University professor and culturalist intellectual Kuroita Katsumi for an article, "Culture and Architecture," which began a tendency of the journal to criticize the overly abstract, modernist approach to architecture, because it too radically broke with any sense of the cultural past.[32] He argued that in Korea there would be a great deal of architecture that should be preserved and the theorists discussed the problem of finding public funding for these preservation projects. Even as architects discussed the need to preserve the past, the journal was an integral site for the exchange of ideas concerning the building of schools, department stores, and other modern infrastructure. It is difficult to characterize the general approach of a journal that was active for twenty years, and included many different perspectives on both architecture and art. However, the place of Korea in the journal, as object of perception and object of transformation, remained fairly consistent. As part of a modernizing colonial project, there was a concern for functionality and the modernization of subjectivity through architectural space in most of the building projects. However, the preservation of the Korean cultural past through museumification tempered this functionality with a concern for indigenous traditions, their interaction with Japanese culture, and the colonial fusion of Japanese and Korean design elements.

The reduction of indigeneity to tradition allowed many of the architects to see the time of the built environment through a dichotomy of modernity and tradition. In addition to discussions of architectural method, many geographical and anthropological studies appear in order to explain how the human being should inhabit a built space tailored to local cultural features that are assumed to be national features. The influence of Bauhaus, expressionism, and other European architectural movements is prominent in translated articles by figures like Peter Behrens, Adolf Behne, and Johannes Itten.[33] However, statements in the journal frequently claim that architecture is necessarily national and that one needs to be aware of the characteristics and culture of the national people who are going to occupy the built space. This was part of the journal's general critique of the abstract modernist style epitomized by Le Corbusier. For example, in the issue from October 1931, when Yi Sang began publishing his poems, an assistant professor in the Engineering Department of Tokyo Imperial University, Itō Tadahiro, wrote the following comment in the lead article, which was directed toward the advocates of a purely international style:

> Certainly, architects are free to build whatever they think up, but notwithstanding any other intervention, there is one condition. Japanese architects should not forget Japan, and, if the architecture is to be built in Korea, they should not forget Korea. When building for the Japanese, one must know Japan from various angles—land, climate, environment, as well as the interests, everyday conditions, and preferences

of the people. One must also know the origins of Japanese culture. In knowing Japan, research about Japan is by itself not enough. It is necessary to research the world as broadly as possible.[34]

Itō's criticism of modernist architecture is that it does not incorporate the past into the present through the preservation of national cultural characteristics. Incorporating international styles and techniques from the Bauhaus and Le Corbusier was acceptable as long as architects also remained conscious of their national contexts. These national contexts could be understood through the study not only of existing traditional architecture, but also of climate, environment, practices of habitation, and, ultimately, national character. Articles in geography and anthropology were prominent in the journal, because they could explain how national environments affect the dispositions of different peoples and contribute to their preferences in terms of spatial organization, design, and style. As part of a specifically colonial architectural project, the idea of national tradition allowed the architects and theorists to reify the Korean past—particularly through preservation and museumification projects in Kyŏngju and Seoul—even as they sought to make Korean tradition compatible with both Japanese culture and functional modern structures. The goal of a cultural approach was to recognize and preserve tradition, while at the same time developing a sense of the national character of Japanese and Korean architecture that would inform the production of new structures.

In order to better define how anthropological discourse affected the theories and practices of architecture in *Korea and Architecture,* I will give four examples from the journal of construction projects, focusing on the way that the culturalist mode of architecture, despite its concern with local national difference, became an imposition of an abstract spatial model of modernity that simultaneously transformed, erased, and recoded the local contexts of lived space. These projects are the construction of monumental architecture, the preservation of ancient Korean architecture, the hybrid fusion of Japanese and Korean styles for political purposes, and the program for cultural housing *(bunka jūtaku).*

Example 1

Monumental public architecture is represented in the journal through sketches of public buildings that are objects unto themselves, imposed onto central spatial contexts. Modern public and financial buildings such as banks, post offices, and government buildings were typical of monumental architecture in colonial Seoul and architectural plans and sketches of such monuments appear frequently in *Korea and Architecture.* These include plans and sketches for the original Bank of Chosŏn, the Offices of the Governor-General of Korea, the Seoul Train Station, and the New Diet Building in Tokyo. Many of the designs were based on late-nineteenth-century German models and have a neoclassical design. For monumental public buildings, discussions of habitation and the location of the building within the larger urban space are largely occluded. These buildings became important monuments in the urban space of Seoul as signs of both the modernity of Japan's colonial rule and nodal points for the urban "psychogeography."[35] However, as an image for colonial Seoul, they give the sense of being set off and autonomous from the local landscape. It was this image of modernity and modern architecture as an abstract imposition of neoclassical design that the modernist, internationalist architects and the culturalist architects in the journal tried to temper.

Example 2

Therefore, the preservation of ancient Korean architecture was a prominent theme in many of the discussions of culture, cultivation, and Korean national consciousness. A large portion of the issue from May 1931 was dedicated to "A Roundtable Discussion concerning the Preservation of Ancient Korean Architecture" and articles like "The Educational Value of Preserving Ancient Architectural Artifacts," both of which were typical of the discourse of preservation and considered the importance of preserving traditional Korean architecture in order to cultivate and educate Korean and colonial Japanese schoolchildren about Korea's ancient past.[36] The preservation of the many beautiful temples and other older buildings in Kyŏngju was a primary concern of the journal, and the legacy of this effort is felt today, as Kyŏngju remains a tourist destination for those interested in traditional Korea.[37] These preservation projects were in some ways commendable efforts to restore some of the cultural legacy of traditional Korean architecture. On the other hand, these preservation projects also served to monumentalize the Korean past, and were another way of reducing lived time and space to isolatable cultural traditions and characteristics whose only connection to the modern present was as a pedagogical tool for nationalization.

Example 3

The case of the construction of the Itō Hirobumi temple provides an important and interesting example of the colonial dimension of architects' attempts to temper the modernist, internationalist impulse, which entered in a strong way in the 1930s, with a concern for national cultural traditions. In this case, the concern for tradition was related directly to politics and the attempt to sacralize the life and memory of Itō Hirobumi through a hybrid Japanese-Korean monument. Itō was the first resident general of Korea and was assassinated in Harbin, China, in 1909 by the Korean nationalist An Chung-gŭn. In the early 1930s, the governor-general started on plans for a monument to Itō that would educate the Korean people about his historical importance. As was the case with the Offices of the Governor-General, designed by Georg de Lalande and built on the site of Kyŏngbŏkkung Palace, the planners of the Itō Hirobumi temple explicitly chose a site valued by Koreans. Sasa Keiichi, an engineer working for the governor-general, writes,

> Of the possible sites for the construction of Hirobumi temple, the most suitable candidate was Samjŏngdong, particularly because of its importance for Koreans, and in order to give living Koreans an understanding of the merits of Itō Hirobumi. Even though the existing establishment of Japanese *(naichijin)* is in the south of Seoul, the desire to commemorate Itō Hirobumi is less among Koreans compared to Japanese; therefore, turning to the north of Seoul, we proposed a site where many Koreans reside. The interior of Samjŏngdong is also recommended because the hilly landscape and the beauty of the scenery are truly spectacular.[38]

The choice to build the temple in a place where many Koreans resided shows that monumental architecture was explicitly political. Even though the building was to be imposed upon the lived landscape, it was also supposed to instill a new historical and political consciousness in the residents. The architects and planners intended that residents would no longer think of Itō as a repressive colonial governor, but instead remember him as one of the founders of modern Korea. The problem of how the building related to the existing environment in Samjŏngdong came out in discussions about the style to be employed in the construction of the building. Saki wrote,

> In addition to determining the site, one of the most significant problems was the architectural style of the main building. Some were of the opinion that it must be constructed in the style of Korean temples, others said it would be ideal to construct a temple in the pure style of Japan proper, another group asked whether or not it would be better to use a newer, modern style; finally, there were various suggestions that these styles be tossed out or mixed, and that the temple be made in a style appropriate to Seoul.[39]

The architects finally decided on the style of a Japanese Zen Buddhist temple, but with as much "Korean color" as possible:

> With the guidance of various authorities, beginning with the chair of the commemoration committee, and after asking the advice of various teachers in Japan proper, we employed the architectural style of Zen Buddhist temples in Japan proper. However, because the temple was to be constructed in Korea, it was decided that a more appropriate style would include as much Korean color as possible and express the real harmony between Japan and Korea. The structure is made of inflammable materials, is fireproof and earthquake-proof, is equipped with heating and running water, and though we may have diverged too much from a traditional temple, our main objective was to construct a temple that took on the new demands for the establishment of cultural institutions.[40]

In the choice to make the temple in a Japanese Zen style with Korean color, the architects conflated stylistic harmony and political harmony. The inclusion of

Korean color and the choice to reference a religious tradition belonging to both Korea and Japan were supposed to allow for the building to blend into the environment of Seoul, while at the same time cultivating a harmonious political consciousness in the colonial population. The modern accoutrements of the temple were to allow it to serve as a "cultural institution" that would educate Korean subjects. Again, cultural anthropology played a role in defining the local cultural features. However, the hybridity of the monument is highly manufactured and still very much abstracted from the everyday processes of transculturation occurring in the city. I argue that such a monumental version of hybridity creates a spatial aesthetic of what Walter Benjamin referred to as "homogeneous empty time," a time in which the traditions of Japan and Korea can coalesce in the present, supposedly not through a dynamic and violent process of transculturation, but rather by way of quotation and the bringing together of static national elements. Yi Sang's introduction of a different kind of temporality in his poems will explicitly confront this harmonious version of colonial hybridity.

Example 4

Finally, in a more functional and modernist vein, the journal was concerned with transforming the everyday dwelling of Japanese migrants and bourgeois Koreans. In the 1930s, the concepts and practices of cultural housing *(bunka jūtaku)* were key to this transformation. In 1932, Asagawa Noritaka described the transition to cultural housing in the following way:

> The body of the human being is the dwelling for its soul. If a house is a dwelling for the body, we can say that it is also a dwelling for the soul.
>
> The problem of housing is based on food, clothing, and shelter, and there is a saying that "the home moves the heart." If the problem of dwelling is our most heartfelt problem, then I think it is a problem for which we must utilize the heart.
>
> The Japanese are a mysterious people, and with the introduction of new things, we have tried to invent dwellings appropriate to the age. . . .
>
> Mainland Japanese have lived in Seoul for thirty years, and if we look back at past changes, we can see here, too, some interesting phenomena in the changes in residences during that time. We can roughly divide these thirty years into three decades:
>
> 1. The period of reconstructing Korean houses.
> 2. The period of the Japanese "barracks."
> 3. The period of cultural housing.[41]

In Asagawa's statement about the historical development of housing in colonial Korea, he mentions a period when there was an attempt to rebuild Korean houses to suit the needs of Japanese colonials, a period when Japanese lived in a kind of "barracks" set off from the rest of the city, and, finally, cultural housing, which quickly became, in the 1930s, the most prominent style of housing for both Japanese colonials and Koreans.[42] Asagawa claims that cultural housing is

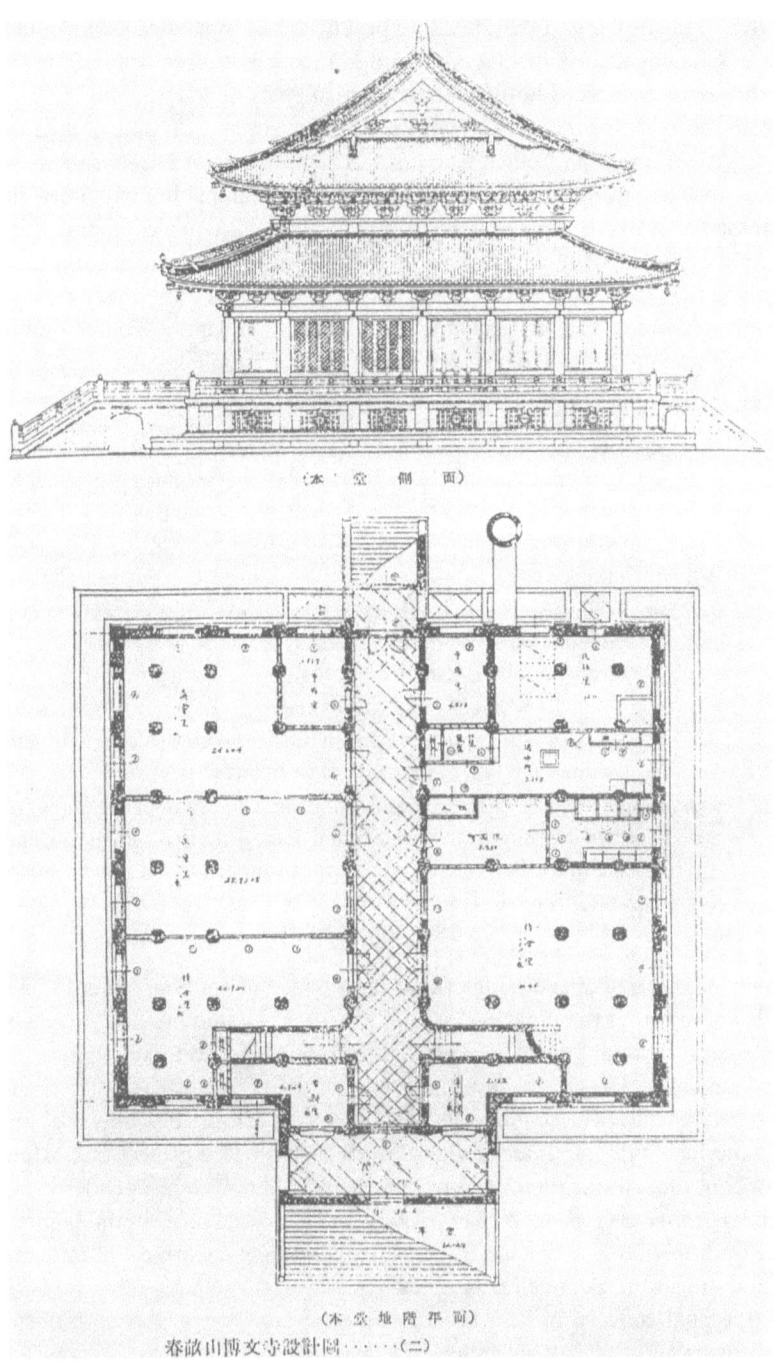

Architectural plan for the Itō Hirobumi Temple, *Korea and Architecture*, November 1932.

a matter of the heart, and that dwelling practices had to change as the demands of the soul changed. The spiritual demand in this case was really a need for cost-effective, mass-produced housing that was also pleasing to the "soul."

From the following discussion concerning the traditional division of the Korean house between inner and outer sections and the practice of husbands and wives sleeping in different rooms, we can see that the spiritual mission of cultural housing was a matter of creating more efficient and rationalized nuclear families. In the following discussion, in which a Korean architect also participated, the argument was made that modern women should be more visible, and the inner recesses of the house should not be off-limits to people outside the family. Houses should be integrated into an undivided, rational, and economic whole inhabited by modern individuals and modern families:

> *Mr. Sasa*: From now on the human being will mature, and if economic problems arise, and people are to live a daily life in which they occupy a small space and pay high rents, then this custom [husband and wife occupying different rooms] will have to be abolished.
>
> *Mr. Pak*: I think so, too.
>
> *Mr. Mori*: I think that there are various problems concerning customs, but the primary one is architecture. Because architecture is built every fifty or one hundred years, I think that if you change that, then other problems are greatly simplified.
>
> *Mr. Pak*: Then, in order to remove the division between the inner and outer sections, it is best to make a room without a barrier wall.
>
> *Mr. Nakamura*: As Mr. Pak says, the internal boundaries must be removed; if not, then the daily life of the inner and outer sections is split in half. Furthermore, because the equipment of the inner and outer sections is split in half, if we don't first end this practice, then we cannot facilitate the rationalization of daily life.[43]

In their insistence that the walls of the traditional Korean house should be broken down, and that the inner recesses of the house should become more visible to outsiders, these architects expressed the colonial desire to see the colonized more completely and to not have their view of daily life obstructed by the division of houses into two sections. The purpose was to "rationalize daily life," and to create modern individuals and modern nuclear families, a project that extended throughout most of the discourses of Japan's cultural policy. The gendered aspect of this will to see everything is clear in that it is the inaccessible, feminine interiors of the traditional house that are the most troubling for the project of rationalization and the creation of nuclear families.

In the dual concern in *Korea and Architecture* for the preservation of indigenous forms and the rationalization of everyday life, there was a certain instrumental application of the notion of cultural tradition, particularly in national

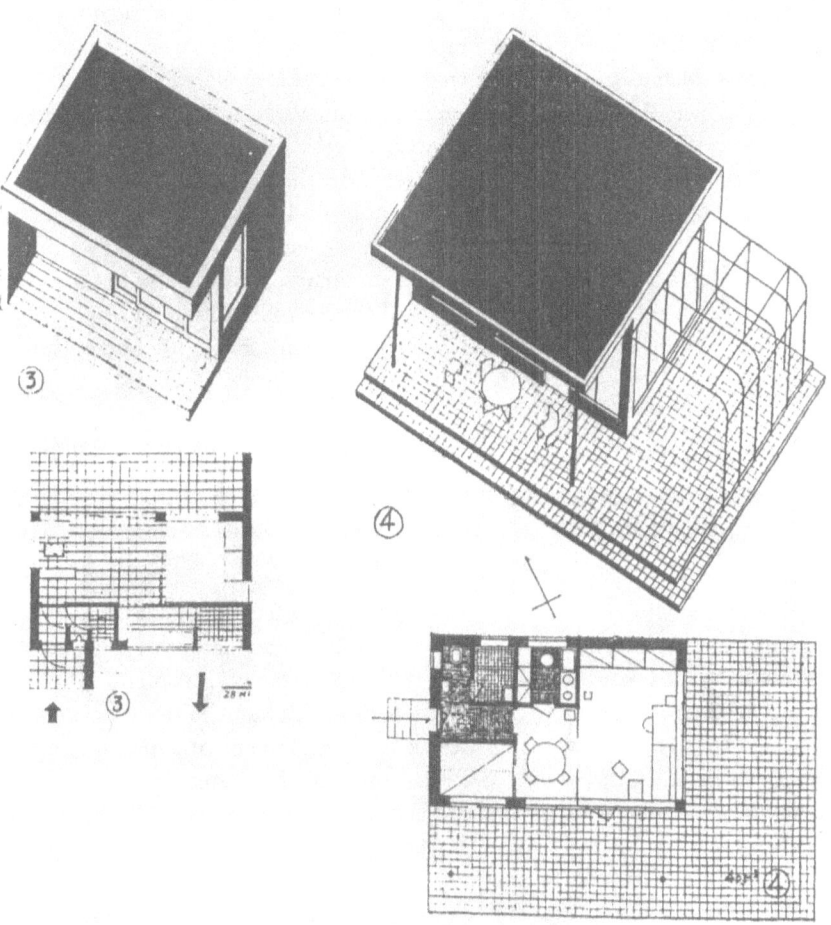

Architectural plan for cultural housing, *Korea and Architecture*, October 1931.

monumental architecture such as the Itō Hirobumi temple, an attempt to hybridize Japanese nationality in order to include within it aspects of Korean tradition. In cultural housing, there was a minimal attempt to reconcile existing architectural forms, such as the use of water-heating systems in Korean floors, with the economic efficiency and familial structure thought necessary for a modern society, but the emphasis was on what needed to be transformed or destroyed in order to produce nuclear families. In each case, there was a certain translation of spatial representations between contexts. In both cases, however, the instrumentality of this practice of architecture precluded any mode of construction and reconstruction performed by the inhabitants themselves, because it reduced the cultural agency of the colonized to a reified concept of tradition. The necessity of the nuclear family in Korea was determined through sociological and anthropological study and criteria. Cultural housing was built accordingly, and it was up to the colonial population to adjust to the historical necessity of cultural and spatial modernization, while preserving mostly fragments of their national cultural past.

YI SANG'S CINEPOETIC SPACE: "BLUEPRINT FOR A THREE-DIMENSIONAL SHAPE"

Yi Sang (born Kim Hae-gyŏng) was a trained architect and surveyor, but he is remembered now mostly for his literature. By the invitation of the publishers, he wrote a series of poems for *Korea and Architecture* between 1931 and 1933. They were published in the short-lived section titled "random jottings" *(manpitsu)*, dedicated to vignettes exploring the everyday experience of urban life. Of the works submitted in this genre, Yi clearly envisioned the greatest scope and potential for an architectural and imagistic poetry that reflected on the experience of urban space.

The visual elements in Yi Sang's poems, including numbers, graphs, and Chinese characters, make it quite difficult to reproduce the poems in translation without dramatically transforming the multiple relationships they create between word and image. Yi's architectural poems are not purely literary or linguistic, and are therefore from the outset difficult to canonize into the poetic tradition of either Japanese or Korean national literatures. With a similar concern for the context of practice that I described in the works of Kim Sa-ryang and Kim Nam-chŏn, Yi used concrete imagery in order to represent the performative context for the practice of bilingual writing; therefore, the inclusion of images is concretely related to the translation occurring in the writing. Furthermore, it was by combining linguistic and nonlinguistic elements in order to create a new language of space that Yi enacted a spatial and bodily practice that was counter to the dominant discourses of the architecture journal. Translating Yi's poems into a more literary format can erase the many reflections on space, spatial reasoning, and spatial practice that appear through his bringing together of language, writing, and image. In particular it can erase the way the poems engage with cinematic space-time, or Eisenstein's filmic fourth dimension, in order to articulate a subversive cinepoetic space.

In "Blueprint for a Three-Dimensional Shape," Yi is interested in the relationship between space, time, and light.[44] He takes the primary figure of Euclidean geometry, the three-dimensional shape, and temporalizes it, making various references to the transformation of space through cinematic space-time. He relates this space-time to the ecstatic becoming of a person constantly projecting himself into the future and confronting, through that projection, his past selves. Einstein's theories had been introduced into Japan and Korea and their popularization led to many artistic reflections on the new physics. Whatever physicists might think of the appropriation of the theory of relativity for cultural theory, writers and critics in the early twentieth century made various associations between the cinematic apparatus's imprintment and projection of light and the ramifications of four-dimensional space-time for the productive subject of poetry and fiction. The attempt to monumentalize the harmonious relationship between Japan and Korea in projects like the Itō Hirobumi temple instituted an anthropological homogeneous empty time in which national characteristics were appropriated and combined for the instrumental purposes of modernization. In "Blueprint for a Three-Dimensional Shape," Yi quotes popularized versions of Einstein's theory of relativity in order to put into question the Cartesian notion of space as pure extension. The poem is divided into seven "memos concerning the line," but just as the poem presents a number of significant challenges to the architectural ethos of the blueprint and the three-dimensional shape, each of these seven sections figures the line differently from the architectural plans and colonial anthropological discourse that appear in the journal.

Yi questions the way that architectural discourse initially subtracts time, particularly the time of habitation and lived space, from consideration. The result of this subtraction of time in the case of culturalist architectural discourse is that the time of lived space becomes history, particularly the uniform passage from tradition to modernity. It proposes that the space of Korea progresses at a constant rate out of a given national past toward modernity, and that the past should become an object of preservation. Like Tanabe in the same year, in "From Schema 'Time' to Schema 'World,'" Yi references the theory of relativity in order to throw into question the subject position from which homogeneous empty time, the uniformity of modernity, and the anthropological object of tradition are all perceived. Yi's poem does not present physics in any sort of systematic way, but rather uses tropes of physics (including science fiction themes of time travel) to provide us with a different image of the poetic subject. This subject's perspective, which is also a cinematic perspective, is referenced on the first page in the image of $3 + 1$ that turns 180 degrees and doubles as it is repeated across the page.[45] The matheme refers to the three dimensions of space plus a fourth dimension, time. The Euclidean notion of time is that it is a fourth dimension that is constant in relation to space. However, in Yi's poem, the matheme turns as it is repeated across the page in order to mimic another space-time, one that includes within it the Euclidean formula. What is this other dimension that neither the 3 nor the 1 can reference directly, but only when they rotate in repetition? On the one hand, this dimension is spatial, because without the series of rotating formulas spread on the page we could not register the time of the repetition. On the other hand, this dimension is temporal, because each instance of the rotating formula presents a movement that must happen in time. Yi combines the three dimensions of space and the fourth dimension, time, into a single "space-time," because the repeated, rotating image figures another dimension in which the formula for Euclidean space is itself temporalized as it is spatialized.

In this way, Yi conveys space-time through an image of repetition and difference that is evocative of a series of film cells that are both spatially and temporally sequential. However, in making the Euclidean geometric formula the recorded content of each film cell (so to speak), he points symbolically and concretely to a paradox in cinematic space-time (or Eisenstein's filmic fourth dimension). This paradox is that cinematic space-time is three-dimensional space plus time, transferred into two dimensions through the imprintation and projection of light. In physics as well, in the post-Einstein universe, light is the only constant and time is no longer constant in relation to space. Time is now relative to the space of reference and the speed of the perceiver, two factors that this poem relates metaphorically to the space-time of cinema. Through cinematic imprintation and projection, and depending on a number of formal factors, objects can be made to move faster or slower in time without the recorded object itself changing speed. According to Einstein, time is not independent of motion, but rather different velocities, relative to the speed of light, can change the speed at which time passes. For Yi as well, the rate of time can shift according to the velocity and coordinates of the object in motion. Through some basic precepts of the theory of relativity, cinematic metaphors, and science fiction reference to time travel, Yi challenges the idea that time passes at a constant rate, independently from spatial coordinates or the speed of objects (clarified in the first image of a grid of singular points represented by black dots). And yet without the mundane raw material of three-dimensional space and its objects, film could not transform space into space-time in this manner. Yi expresses this paradox in the line "Today, when Euclid has died, Euclid's point of focus burns the brain of humanity like dry hay."[46]

> (Through a convex lens a ray of sun is concentrated, it shines brightly at a single point, burns brightly at a single point. It is amusing to consider the luck of Genesis, that a layer of the heavens and another layer combined to make another, creating a convex lens; isn't geometry such a play of light? Today, when Euclid has died, Euclid's

point of focus burns the brain of humanity like dry hay. By enumerating a concentration, it stimulates the greatest concentration, it stimulates danger. A person despairs, a person is born, a person despairs, a person is born.)[47]

He might have stated that *with the advent of cinema*, Euclid is dead, but what remains is his intensive point of focus, the concentrated singular point of the convex lens of the camera or magnifying glass.

Representing the death and survival of Euclidean space through the rotation of the image of the formula as though in film cells is an ingenious artistic expression of transformations of space and time in the cinematic twentieth century. However, in addition to this aesthetic ingenuity, in its context, the ironically titled "Blueprint for a Three-Dimensional Shape" has an important discursive and political register as well. Yi's turn to cinematic space-time appears in an architecture journal that had a clear set of parameters concerning space, time, modernity, and tradition, one that imagined time historically as a passage from tradition to modernity, from the stagnant and petrified things of the cultural past to the formation of the modern cultural individual and his nuclear family.

In order to challenge the architectural notion of three dimensions of space plus the time of history, Yi rearticulates a fundamental element of geometry, the line. He introduces three points—A, B, and C—and writes three equations: $A + B + C = A$; $A + B + C = B$; $A + B + C = C$.[48] Whenever there is a line with three points, there is also an intensive point from which it is viewed. A line is never merely an extension in space, but also a perspective. When the points are added together, or synthesized, they can become equal to any one of the points on the line. This is a reflection on "spaces of reference" in Einsteinian physics. His discussion of the subject as a "ray of sun" means that he appropriated the new theories of light in order to think perspective as constituted by energy, rather than perspective as a res cogito for which a line is a mere extension in space. He writes, "Enjoy light, be saddened by light, laugh at light, cry at light. / Light is a person and a person is a mirror. / Wait for light."[49] The metaphor of the mirror enters into his view of the poetic subject, suggesting that in its intensive relation to space the subject enters into a kind of schizophrenic self-awareness in which the poetic "I" is akin to two mirrors facing each other, reflecting each other infinitely, as in the first image of "The Infinite Hexagon of Architecture."[50]

As in Tanabe's discussion of the dialectic and expression, Yi discusses this schizophrenic I as an ecstatic movement in time that brings the future I into contact with an alien past. For Tanabe, the osmotic expression of the dialectic allowed for identity between this future I and the past. Yi, on the other hand, figures this being outside of oneself through an intensive rather than osmotic relation to space. As in the Hegelian dialectic, the present, future, and past subjects remain forever nonidentical to one another in the constant "invention" of the person, but this is not the invention of a state subject and its world, but rather a singular intensive point of focus without a clear social determination. Yi refers to the popular idea after Einstein that if one travels faster than the speed of light then it might be possible to travel back in time. He refers to this movement faster than light as a "discarding of numbers," as the "invention of a person," and as a birth that happens "through the despair of three-dimensions":

>   MEMO 1 CONCERNING THE LINE
>
> (Outer space through curtains)
> (A person discards numbers)
> (Silently make me an electron's proton)
>
> Spectral
>
> Axis X Axis Y Axis Z
>
> The control of velocity, etc.; for example, if it is certain that light travels at 300,000 kilometers per second, then certainly the invention of a person can occur at 600,000 kilometers per second. Multiply this by tens, hundreds, thousands, tens of thousands, millions, billions, then can't a person see a reality that is tens, hundreds, thousands, tens of thousands, millions, billions of years in the ancient past? Or else is one destroyed? An atom is an atom is an atom is an atom. Do physiological functions mutate? An atom is not an atom is not an atom is not an atom. Is radiation destruction? When a person lives the eternal that is eternal . . . life is neither vitality nor existence, but rather light.
>
> The taste of smell and the smell of taste.
>
> (Birth through the despair for three dimensions)
> (Birth through the despair for movement)
> (When the globe is an empty nest, I long for the feudal period to the point of tears)[51]

Throughout the poem, Yi is concerned with how a person or a subject is constituted, and how this constitution might occur without the person being counted arithmetically, and without reducing subjectivity to the empty res cogito that observes a three-dimensional res extensa. Yi suggests that in viewing and occupying space in the manner of cultural housing, the "person" feels "despair," and that this despair leads the person to project himself, to "hypothesize" himself as a "phenomenon of dynamics" (as he writes later in the poem). For Yi, this invention occurs through light, and, indeed, at the speed of light. In this invention, life *(seimei)* is transformed into light, and is no longer "vitality" *(sei)* or "existence" *(mei)*—that is, the two common ways to describe the mere fact of living. This line is particularly difficult to translate, because Yi splits the character compound for *seimei*, playing with the relationship between the two characters. In my reading, *sei* refers to the biological fact of life, or "vitality," and *mei* refers to a person's mortal life, or "existence." Yi writes that as a combination of the biological fact of life *(sei)* and one's existence *(mei)*, the term *seimei* is more than the sum of its parts, and that "light" *(hikari)*, in a sense, is what brings together the biological body and one's mortal existence.

The only constant in the theory of relativity is the speed of light, which for Yi would constitute the poetic subject. However, the poetic subject is not purely light. He or she is at once caught in three-dimensional space and seeks to reinvent itself out of three-dimensional space by traveling at the speed of light. The activity of the poetic subject (or the "person") is precisely this sort of back and forth between the despair of three dimensions and a rebirth through light. The person still despairs, because of the power of architectonic space to condition life, and to treat the human being as the contents of a container. It is this denial of the temporality of life and lived space that leads to nostalgia for feudal life, when space was perhaps not subjected to such abstraction. In the first quotation, he writes, "If the globe is an empty nest, I long for the feudal period to the point of tears."[52] This longing for the feudal period is a sentimental and nostalgic response to modernity and the shock that accompanies the lived experience of abstract space.[53] Yi's mention of the globe as an "empty nest" seems directed at the architects of *Korea and Architecture*. In occupying the space of Korea, which architects take as an empty tableau upon which to actualize their structures, the poet desires to return to the feudal period, before this kind of abstract spatial imaginary was possible. However, the overall tenor of the poem is not to remain in this nostalgia, but rather to move ahead of the colonizer, in terms of both scientific progress and the imaginative possibilities for space. By thinking through advancements of physics by way of physical, bodily activity in space, Yi articulated a critical mode of spatial practice that could challenge the biopolitcal worldview of culturalism.

In the passage quoted, we get a sense of how the post-Einstein version of light is significant for Yi not only because it offers the possibility for rebirth or invention out of three dimensions, but also because it allows for a particular kind of vision. In the very first image of the poem, we are presented with a set of coordinates, and the suggestion is that according to the speed of any one coordinate, space-time will curve differently. As the poem progresses, it becomes clearer that for this poetic subject, space is not the container that allows us to view extended objects, but rather space is curved around singular points of intensity that have a gravitational pull. Metaphorically speaking, this gravitational pull is the person's vision, and ultimately the vision of the camera; it is included within space by traversing space at varying speeds that transform the frame of reference. The poetic subject and the cinematic subject are each one of these singular points through which the intensity of light is magnified and concentrated. The curvature of space both creates this singular point through its many layers and curves around it. This singular point that marks the position and speed of the subject is, for Yi, a perspective. It is not a Cartesian, Euclidean, or culturalist perspective, but an intensive perspective that is itself included in space, and around which space curves. In this sense, Yi was articulating a spatial perspective and a spatial practice that were quite different from an architectonic concept of space. His poetics was engaged with both the emergence of cinema and cinematic perspective, as well as the ecstatic temporality of a schizophrenic human subject constantly moving ahead of itself and outside of itself.

In his discussion of the singular point as a "convex lens," Yi refers to the way that cinema and cinematic perspective relate to space differently than a Euclidean geometry. Yi asks, "Isn't geometry such a play of light?" suggesting that spatial reasoning is now intimately connected to light and vision, rather than Euclidean abstract space.[54] We can imagine how this notion of geometry could greatly transform the perspective of the architect, and therefore the way that he or she actualizes structures. Monumental architecture is set off from the environment, and imposes its rational forms onto lived space. Cultural preservation reifies the past and the cultural hybridity of the Itō Hirobumi temple combines traditions with modernity for political purposes. If geometry is rather a "play of light" for which the subject is an ecstatic point of concentration, then the architect would have to imagine space from the perspective of the inhabitant, the person whose vision and activity will gradually transform the structure. In cinematic city spaces, the city is not a conglomeration of monuments; rather, the camera's angle, its proximity to the object, its relative speed and slowness all shape our vision of the city. In cinema, it is precisely light that registers these changes; it is the constancy relative to which various coordinates and perspectives can be arranged.

In reference to the popular or populist aspect of this cinematic perspective, Yi writes, "Temporality, or historicity by way of popular thought."[55] It was this sort of popularization of time in which he was ultimately interested. If history was the time of grand movements that allowed culturalist architects to contextualize their works in relation to the individual, the nation, and the world, "popular thought" was related to the everyday, temporal experience of space as a lived and intensive space. Yi appropriated a science fiction notion of time from the theory of relativity in order to articulate this popular, temporal relation to space. The question of the name for this popular aspect of the cinematic perspective comes through at the end of the poem, when he writes,

> Vision's name is numerical, or one point, that should live eternally along with the person. Vision's name does not move, but has only a course of movement.
>
> Vision's name has light and does not have light; because of vision's name, a person has no need to escape more quickly than light.
>
> Forget the names of vision.
> Preserve the names of vision.

A person conserves velocity, to escape faster than light, and selects the past in the future.[56]

In writing that "vision's name does not move, but has only a course of movement," Yi was juxtaposing the idea of movement through Euclidean space with a course of movement that itself curves and transforms space. Vision's name has no final locale in which to settle, and from which space would be present before it as a comprehensible externality. The person transcends the everyday, and becomes "eternal," but time is also not a "perpetual development," to use Kuwaki's phrase, but rather a variable dependent upon the poetic subject's speed and course.

Yi's poetic engagement with science and philosophy dramatically transformed the premises of space and time discussed by the architects of *Korea and Architecture*. From the position of a colonial intellectual and a bilingual writer, Yi saw the architectonic view of space as a kind of stasis that could only produce despair. This view comes through in the lines "a person is the eternal hypothesis that it is not a phenomenon of statics / a person casts off the objectivity of the person."[57] The political and social stakes of Yi's rewriting of personhood are evident. The architectonic space of cultural housing was a violent imposition represented by the "destruction of barriers" and the formation of individuals and modern nuclear families. It viewed the person as a single member of a cultural totality that had to be rationalized and modernized. This view of the individual person's relationship to the totality treated the person as "a phenomenon of statics." Yi's idea that the "person casts off the objectivity of the person" articulated a spatial practice that would not situate the human being as an object in space. The hypothesis of personhood is eternal; the refusal to be a mere object requires a persistent forward invention that draws the person out of the realm of objects. However, this movement is not the same as Kuwaki's practical subject setting itself off from phenomena so that it can become capable of applying the universal law to itself as an object. It is rather an entrance into an intensive and cinematic space-time enlivened through new relations between light, vision, and the possible social spaces to be created by a modernism that does not desire to return home. This intensive space does not lead Yi to the problem of morals, or of how to establish that condition in the series of perceptions that is itself unconditioned. After his critique of Yi, that unconditioned condition became the human and eventually the imperial state in Ch'oe Chae-sŏ's modernism. Yi's turn to temporality, or historicity by way of popular thought, suggests instead a critical spatial practice of persons as singular points of vision that never become subjects, objects, or individuals. It is possible that this practice, too, could constitute a genus-being.

There is a fine line between such a genus-being, constituted by intensive space and the *mise en abyme*, and a dynamic imperial subject mediated by the cinematic apparatus. If culturalism established the possibility for a continuous cosmopolitan world made up of individuals and nations, both imperial nationalism and minor literature sought to break with these ideal wholes and to present the spaces and times of modernity as ecstatic, relative, and caught in a circulation of metonymical images that never arrive at the kind of symbolic closure sought in culturalist allegories. The question then becomes not if one can continue to imagine a self-identical, general human subject at the center of knowledge, life, and politics, because clearly one cannot; it is rather a matter of how to confront permanent nonidentity and alienation. There is no absolute distinction between Tanabe's dialectical totality of singular individuals projecting themselves in time and Yi Sang's image of space curving around singular points of vision. However, by continuing to refer to the totality of these points as the social being of the state, and by maintaining the absolutely negative ideal of the genus as the center of world history, Tanabe kept alive a means to reterritorialize the human being. On the other hand, Yi Sang's poems and minor literature in general gesture toward a space and a time at once deeply contextualized and beyond any territory.

NOTES

INTRODUCTION

1. Kuwaki Gen'yoku, *Bunkashugi to shakai mondai* (Tokyo: Shizendō Shoten, 1920), 105.
2. Kuwaki, *Bunkashugi to shakai mondai* and *Bunka to kaizō* (Tokyo: Shimode Shoten, 1921).
3. Kuwaki, *Bunkashugi to shakai mondai*, 107.
4. Kuwaki, *Bunka to kaizō*, 30.
5. Kuwaki, *Bunkashugi to shakai mondai*, 108.
6. Nils Gilman, *Mandarins of the Future: Modernization Theory in Cold War America* (Baltimore: Johns Hopkins University Press, 2007), 24–71.
7. Johannes Fabian, *Time and the Other: How Anthropology Makes Its Object* (New York: Columbia University Press, 2014); Naoki Sakai, "'You Asians': On the Historical Role of the West and Asia Binary," in *Japan after Japan: Social and Cultural Life from the Recessionary 1990s to the Present,* ed. Tomiko Yoda and Harry Harootunian (Durham: Duke University Press, 2006), 167–69.
8. Kuwaki Gen'yoku, *Tetsugaku gaisetsu: Mono to ga* (Tokyo: Kaizōsha, 1940), 245.
9. "General culture" *(ippan bunka)* was a common phrase in writings about culturalism and cultural science. It referred to the unity of human culture under the rules and norms of transcendental values. Kuwaki Gen'yoku tended to use the more Hegelian term "absolute values."
10. Through research into Yi Kwang-su's letters, Michael D. Shin discovered the significance that Kuwaki Gen'yoku had for Yi's education. The connections between chapter 1 and chapter 2 are indebted to Shin's archival research into Yi's time as a student at Waseda University.
11. Naoki Sakai, *Translation and Subjectivity: On "Japan" and Cultural Nationalism* (Minneapolis: University of Minnesota Press, 1997), 156–57.

12. The cultural-anthropological perspective toward Japan stretches across innumerable works and disciplines in US area studies, but by "cultural anthropology," I am referring in particular to the views of national and ethnic cultures in the tradition of Ruth Benedict, *The Chrysanthemum and the Sword: Patterns of Japanese Culture* (Boston: Houghton Mifflin, 2005); and Benedict, *Patterns of Culture* (Boston: Houghton Mifflin, 1989).

13. Gilman, *Mandarins;* Benedict, *Chrysanthemum.*

14. For example, one can follow the postliberation careers of Im Hwa and Paek Nam-un, who were supporters of late imperial Japan. See Charles Armstrong, *The North Korean Revolution, 1945–1950* (Ithaca: Cornell University Press, 2004).

15. An Ho-sang studied philosophy in Germany and was a researcher at Kyoto Imperial University, publishing a text on Hegel's *Science of Logic* in the leading philosophy journal in Japan: An, "Heigeru ronrigaku ni okeru kyakkan-teki handan no mondai," trans. Takeuchi Yoshitomo, *Tetsugaku kenkyū* 26, no. 8 (1941): 677–716. He was the minister of culture under the Syngman Rhee regime and articulated a moral and historical philosophy for One-nationism *(ilminjuŭi)*, the ideology that legitimated Rhee's presidency and also the republic's moral and political right to the entirety of the peninsula. In *The Essence of One-Nationism,* published four months before the official onset of the Korean War, An refers to communists as foreign beasts, and the primary distinction he makes is a moral one: communists are trapped in their natural instincts and the material world and South Korean subjects have both culture and morality *(todŏk).* This distinction and his critique of materialism in general are very reminiscent of, if not directly indebted to, the philosophy of culturalism's statements about materialism. An Ho-sang, *Ilminjuŭi ŭi pon pat'ang* (Seoul: Chomunsa, 1950); An, *Yumullon pip'an* (Seoul: Munhwadang, 1947). Hwang Chang-yŏp's philosophical education was not as elite, but he was an exchange student in Japan who read Kant and Hegel as a young student. He was an important government figure in the Democratic People's Republic of Korea during the 1960s, which he called the "golden era" of Juche thought, before it became an ideology of dictatorship. Since defecting to the South in 1996, he has been known as the philosopher who developed the humanist aspects of Juche thought, including the idea that "man is the master of all things." Hwang Chang-yŏp, *Na nŭn yoksa ŭi chilli rŭl pwatta: Hwang Chang-yŏp hoegorok* (Seoul: Hanul, 1999).

16. Charles R. Bambach, *Heidegger, Dilthey, and the Crisis of Historicism* (Ithaca: Cornell University Press, 1995).

17. Guy Oakes, "Introduction: Rickert's Theory of Historical Knowledge," in *The Limits of Concept Formation in the Natural Sciences: An Introduction to the Historical Sciences,* by Heinrich Rickert, ed. Guy Oakes (Cambridge: Cambridge University Press, 1986), vii–xxx.

18. Tanabe Hajime, "Shu no ronri to sekai zushiki," in *Tanabe Hajime zenshū,* vol. 6 (Tokyo: Chikuma Shobō, 1963), 169–264; Naoki Sakai, "Subject and Substratum: On Japanese Imperial Nationalism," *Cultural Studies* 14, nos. 3, 4 (2000): 462–530.

19. Foucault demarcates a break between the taxonomic table of the classical period and the anthropocentrism of modern thought in Foucault, *The Order of Things: An Archaeology of the Human Sciences* (New York: Vintage, 1973). However, the discussion of this transition in terms of genus-being is my own.

20. Simon Skempton, *Alienation after Derrida* (London: Continuum, 2010), 99–104.

21. Tanabe, "Shu no ronri no sekai zushiki," 232–33; Sŏ In-sik, "Chisŏng ŭi sidaejŏk sŏngkyŏk," in *Sŏ In-sik chŏnjip,* vol. 1 (Seoul: Yŏngnak, 2006), 109.

22. Peter Osborne, *How to Read Marx* (London: Norton, 2006); Skempton, *Alienation*. They prefer the translation "generic-being," whereas I have chosen "genus-being" to suggest the genitive rather than adjectival construction of *Gattungswesen*.

23. Miki Kiyoshi, *Pasukaru ni okeru ningen no kenkyū* (Tokyo: Iwanami Shoten, 1980); Watsuji Testurō, *Ningen no gaku to shite no rinrigaku* (Tokyo: Iwanami Shoten, 2007); Naoki Sakai, *Translation and Subjectivity*, 75–77.

24. Etienne Balibar, "Racism as Universalism," in *Masses, Classes, Ideas: Studies on Politics and Philosophy before and after Marx*, trans. James Swenson (London: Routledge, 1994), 191–204; Sakai, *Translation and Subjectivity*, 153–76; Takashi Fujitani, *Race for Empire: Koreans as Japanese and Japanese as Americans in World War II* (Berkeley: University of California Press, 2011).

25. Patricia Fara, *Sex, Botany, and Empire: The Story of Carl Linnaeus and Joseph Banks* (New York: Columbia University Press, 2004), 20.

26. Ibid., 102. Kant posits the "stem-genus" *(Stammgattung)* of white European man as the mythical origin of humanity in "On the Different Races of Man," in *Race and the Enlightenment: A Reader*, ed. Emmanuel Chukwudi Eze (London: Wiley-Blackwell, 1997), 38–48. He discusses Europe as the teleology of history when he states, in "Idea for a Universal History with a Cosmopolitan Purpose," that Europe will "probably legislate eventually for all other continents." In Kant, *Kant: Political Writings*, ed. H. S. Reiss (Cambridge: Cambridge University Press, 1991), 52.

27. Foucault, *Order of Things*, 217–20. Kant worked on the cusp of this transition from the "classical" to the "modern," and therefore his anthropological and historical works utilize both natural-historical, physiological categories of race and cultural-historical notions of national and cosmopolitan character.

28. Ibid., 157–65.

29. Andre Schmid, *Korea between Empires, 1895–1919* (New York: Columbia University Press, 2002).

30. Ibid.

31. Mark Driscoll, *Absolute Erotic, Absolute Grotesque: The Living, Dead, and Undead in Japan's Imperialism, 1895–1945* (Durham: Duke University Press, 2010), 119.

32. Bruce Cumings, *Korea's Place in the Sun: A Modern History* (New York: Norton, 2005), 142.

33. Kuwaki, *Tetsugaku gaisetsu*, 244.

34. Saitō Makoto, "Nendai ni saishite," in *Chōsen sōtoku yūkoku kunji shūsei*, vol. 3, ed. Naoki Mizuno (Tokyo: Ryokuin Shobō, 2001), 224.

35. Yoshino Sakuzō, ed., *Meiji bunka kenkyū zenshū*, vol. 1 (Tokyo: Nihon Hyōronsha, 1928).

36. Yoshino Sakuzō, *Mimponshugiron* (Tokyo: Kigensha, 1948).

37. Yoshino, *Chūgoku, Chōsenron* (Tokyo: Heibonsha, 1970).

38. Sōda Kiichirō, *Bunka kachi to kyokugen gainen* (Tokyo: Iwanami Shoten, 1972), 231.

39. Yi Kwang-su, "Minjok gaejoron," in *Yi Kwang-su chŏnjip*, vol. 10 (Seoul: Usinsa, 1979), 116–17.

40. Terry Eagleton, *The Idea of Culture* (Oxford: Blackwell, 2000), 2.

41. Foucault, *The Birth of Biopolitics: Lectures at the Collège de France, 1978–1979*, trans. Graham Burchell (New York: Palgrave MacMillan, 2008).

42. Foucault, *Order of Things*, 318.
43. Immanuel Kant, *Anthropology from a Pragmatic Point of View*, trans. Robert B. Louden (Cambridge: Cambridge University Press, 2006).
44. Foucault's second dissertation was a translation of and introduction to Kant's *Anthropology*, which eventually became *The Order of Things*. Foucault, *Introduction to Kant's Anthropology*, trans. Roberto Nigro and Kate Briggs (Los Angeles: Semiotext[e], 2008).
45. Kant, *Anthropology*, 3, emphasis in the original.
46. Theodor Adorno discusses the complexity of Kant's search for the "laws of freedom" in his lectures on Kant's moral philosophy: Adorno, *Problems of Moral Philosophy*, trans. Rodney Livingstone (Stanford: Stanford University Press, 2000), 80.
47. Foucault, *Introduction*, 52.
48. Mills, *The Racial Contract* (Ithaca: Cornell University Press, 1999), 41–61.
49. Kant, *Anthropology*, 183–238.
50. Kant, "On the Different Races of Man," 47–48.
51. Watsuji, *Ningen no gaku to shite no rinrigaku*, 76.
52. Ibid.
53. Watsuji Tetsurō, *Fūdō: Ningengaku-teki kōsatsu* (Tokyo: Iwanami Bunko, 1979).
54. Sakai, *Translation and Subjectivity*, 136–39.
55. Yi, "Minjok gaejoron," 116–17.
56. Sōda Kiichirō, *Geld und Wert* (Tübingen: Mohr, 1909), iii–iv.
57. Yi Kwang-su, "Chorŏpsaeng ŭl saenggak hago," in *Yi Kwang-su chŏnjip*, 10:295; Ch'oe Nam-sŏn, "Chosŏn kwa segye ŭi kongt'ongŏ: Chosŏnŏ rosŏ chŭngmyŏng hal wŏnsi munhwa ŭi haeksim," in *Yuktang Ch'oe Nam-sŏn chŏnjip*, vol. 9 (Seoul: Yŏngnak, 2003), 315–17.
58. Leo T. S. Ching, *Becoming Japanese: Colonial Taiwan and the Politics of Identity Formation* (Berkeley: University of California Press, 2001), 126.

1. CULTURALISM AND THE HUMAN

1. Saitō, "Nendai ni saishite," 224.
2. Ariyoshi Chūichi, "Kokumin no dai ichi no shimei," in *Chōsen sōtoku yūkoku kunji shūsei*, vol. 3, ed. Mizuno Naoki (Tokyo: Ryokuin Shobō, 2001), 202–3.
3. Kyoko Inoue, *Individual Dignity in Modern Japanese Thought: The Evolution of the Concept of Jinkaku in Moral and Educational Discourse* (Ann Arbor: University of Michigan Center for Japanese Studies, 2001), 5.
4. Kant introduces the concept of the "kingdom of ends," his moral version of the social contract, in Kant, *Groundwork for the Metaphysics of Morals*, trans. Mary Gregor (Cambridge: Cambridge University Press, 1998), 41.
5. Kuwaki Gen'yoku, *Kanto to gendai no tetsugaku*, 3rd ed. (Tokyo: Iwanami Shoten, 1932), 177–78.
6. Sōda, *Bunka kachi*, 250.
7. Kuwaki, *Kanto to gendai no tetsugaku*, 178.
8. Mills, *The Racial Contract*, 41–61.
9. Kuwaki, *Kanto to gendai no tetsugaku*, 179.

10. Giorgio Agamben, *Homo Sacer: Sovereignty and Bare Life,* trans. Daniel Heller-Roazen (Stanford: Stanford University Press, 1998), 1–5.

11. Michel Foucault, "Governmentality," in *The Foucault Effect: Studies in Governmentality,* ed. Graham Burchell, Colin Gordon, and Peter Miller (Chicago: University of Chicago Press, 1991), 93.

12. The original uses the translation "conduct" for a term prevalent in discussions of practice in modern Japanese philosophy (行為): "'行' 或は '行為' (Conduct) という."

13. Kuwaki, *Tetsugaku gaisetsu,* 206.

14. Such empirical studies would include Yanagita Kunio's folklore studies and Kon Wajirō's modernology. Harry Harootunian, *History's Disquiet: Modernity, Cultural Practice, and the Question of Everyday Life* (New York: Columbia University Press, 2002).

15. Kant, *Groundwork,* 31.

16. Kuwaki, *Tetsugaku gaisetsu,* 219.

17. Kuwaki, *Bunkashugi to shakai mondai,* 113.

18. Kuwaki, *Tetsugaku gaisetsu,* 242–43.

19. Ibid., 245.

20. Saitō, "Nendai ni saishite," 224.

21. Edward Said, *Orientalism* (New York: Vintage, 1978), 222.

22. Kuwaki, *Kanto to gendai no tetsugaku,* 262.

23. Ibid., 277.

24. Kuwaki uses the term *seishin kagaku,* which is a translation of *Geisteswissenschaft* and literally means "the spiritual sciences." The direct translation is misleading because it suggests a direct relation with theology. *Geisteswissenschaft* is often translated as the "humanities," but because Kuwaki includes disciplines that would now be considered social sciences, I have decided upon "human sciences."

25. Kuwaki, *Bunkashugi to shakai mondai,* 409–11.

26. Gilman, *Mandarins,* 100–103.

27. These criticisms are interspersed throughout Kuwaki, *Bunkashugi to shakai mondai.*

28. Kant, *Groundwork,* 41–46.

29. Sōda, *Bunka kachi,* 5–11.

30. Nishida's critique, in which he challenges Sōda's neo-Kantian conflation of self-awareness with objective knowledge, appears in Nishida, "Sōda hakase ni kotau," in *Nishida Kitarō zenshū,* vol. 4 (Tokyo: Iwanami Shoten, 1965), 290–323. In his critique, Tanabe, who remained neo-Kantian, attempts to improve upon Sōda's philosophy of individual causality by thinking of internal causality as freedom and external causality as necessity, and Kant's categorical imperative and his teleological judgment as the synthesis of these. This critique appears in Tanabe, "Kobetsu-teki inkaritsu no ronri ni tsukite Sōda Kiichirō no kyō wo kou," reprinted in Sōda Kiichirō, *Bunka kachi,* 191–201.

31. Sōda Kiichirō, *Sōda Kiichirō zenshū,* vol. 1 (Tokyo: Iwanami Shoten, 1930–31).

32. Sōda Kiichirō, *Die logische Natur der Wirtschaftsgesetze* (Stuttgart: Verlag von Ferdinand Enke, 1911). These texts were read globally, as evidenced by Carl E. Parry, review of *The Logical Nature of Economic Laws* by Sōda Kiichirō, *American Economic Review* 2, no. 3 (1912): 607–8.

33. Sōda, *Geld und Wert,* vi.

34. Georg Simmel, *Philosophy of Money*, trans. David Frisby (New York: Routledge, 2004).
35. Ibid., 90–91.
36. Sōda, *Bunka kachi*, 271–72.
37. Sōda, "Kobetsu-teki inkaritsu no ronri," in *Bunka kachi*, 149–90.
38. Ibid.
39. Alan Kim, "Paul Natorp," *Stanford Encyclopedia of Philosophy*, Fall 2008 edition, ed. Edward N. Zalta, http://plato.stanford.edu/archives/fall2008/entries/natorp. I am drawing from Theodor Adorno's discussion of the "block" between cognition and things-in-themselves, which appears in his lectures: Adorno, *Kant's* Critique of Pure Reason, trans. Rodney Livingstone (Stanford: Stanford University Press, 2001).
40. Kim, "Paul Natorp."
41. Kuwaki, *Kanto to gendai no tetsugaku*, 177–78.
42. Jean-François Lyotard, *The Postmodern Condition: A Report on Knowledge*, trans. Geoff Bennington (Minneapolis: University of Minnesota Press, 1984), 78–79.
43. Sōda, *Bunka kachi*, 231.
44. Ibid., 59.
45. Ibid., 52–53.
46. Gayatri Spivak, *The Critique of Postcolonial Reason* (Cambridge, MA: Harvard University Press, 1999), 21–37.
47. Sōda, *Geld und Wert*, iii–iv.
48. Kim Kyŏng-mi, "Pot'ong hakkyo chedo ŭi hwangnip kwa hakkyo hunyuk ŭi hyŏngsŏng," in *Ilche ŭi singminji chibae wa ilsangsaenghwal* (Seoul: Hye-an, 2004), 487–48.
49. Heinrich Rickert, *Das Eine, Die Einheit, und die Eins* (Tübingen: Verlag, 1924).
50. Ibid., viii–ix.
51. Hannah Arendt traces National Socialism to colonial regimes in Africa, particularly the Boer War in South Africa, in Arendt, *Origins of Totalitarianism* (New York: Harvest, 1973).
52. Kim, "Pot'ong hakkyo," 487–91.
53. Ibid., 495–98.
54. Karatani Kōjin, "Nationalism and Écriture," *Surfaces* 5 (1995): 5–25.
55. Gauri Viswanathan, *Masks of Conquest: Literary Study and British Rule in India* (New York: Columbia University Press, 1989).
56. Antoine Berman analyzes Martin Luther's translation of the Bible as a foundation for German national language and literature in Berman, *The Experience of the Foreign*, trans. S. Heyvaert (Albany: SUNY Press, 1992), 23–34.
57. Yi Kwang-su, "Yesugyo ŭi Chosŏn e chun ŭnhye," in *Yi Kwang-su chŏnjip*, 10:19.
58. Yi, "Chosŏn minjongnon," in *Yi Kwang-su chŏnjip*, 10:216–17.
59. The "regime of translation" is Naoki Sakai's term. Through a reading of Ogyu Sorai and other eighteenth-century national studies scholars, Naoki Sakai discusses the very regime of translation that Yi Kwang-su covets for Korean modernity in this passage. Sakai, *Voices of the Past: The Status of Language in Eighteenth-Century Japanese Discourse* (Ithaca: Cornell University Press, 1991), 218–20.

60. Mills, *The Racial Contract*, 40–61; Gilman, *Mandarins*; Benedict, *Chrysanthemum*.

61. Chizuko T. Allen, "Northeast Asia Centered around Korea: Ch'oe Nam-sŏn's View of History," *Journal of Asian Studies* 49, no. 4 (1990): 787–806.

62. Ch'oe Nam-sŏn, "Chosŏn kwa segye ŭi kongt'ongŏ: chosŏnŏ rosŏ chŭngmyŏng hal wŏnsi munhwa ŭi haeksim," in *Yuktang Ch'oe Nam-sŏn chŏnjip* (Seoul: Yŏngnak, 2003), 315–17.

63. Kitagawa Sukehito, ed., *Chōsen koyūshoku jiten* (Seoul: Seiko Hakkōjo, 1932), i.

64. Arai Tetsu, "Kenchiku no majutsu," in *Arai Tetsu no zenshigoto* (Tokyo: Sojusha, 1983), 33–34.

2. THE COLONY AND THE WORLD

1. Yi Kwang-su, "Maybe Love," trans. John Whittier Treat, *Azalea: Journal of Korean Literature and Culture* 4 (2011): 321–27; Yi, "Yun Kwang-ho," in *Kubo ssi ŭi ŏlgul* (Seoul: Bookfolio, 2004), 24–42.

2. I use the term "landscape," derived from the work of Karatani Kojin, with reference to Michael D. Shin, "Interior Landscapes: Yi Kwang-su's *The Heartless* and the Origins of Modern Literature," in *Colonial Modernity in Korea*, ed. Gi-Wook Shin and Michael Robinson (Cambridge, MA: Harvard University Asia Center, 1999).

3. Yi Kwang-su, "Saengsagwan," in *Yi Kwang-su chŏnjip*, 10:260.

4. Yi Kwang-su, "Sinsaenghwallon," in *Yi Kwang-su chŏnjip*, 10:328.

5. Yi, "Minjok kaejoron," 126.

6. Ibid., 116–17.

7. Kim Hyŏn-ju, *Yi Kwang-su wa munhwa ŭi kihoek* (Seoul: T'aehaksa, 2005); Hwang Chong-yŏn, "Sin ŏmnŭn chayŏn," in *Munhak kwa kwahak*, vol. 1 (Seoul: Somyŏng, 2013).

8. For a study of the idea of "self-strengthening" in the work of An Chaehong, and its relationship to cultural nationalism, see Lee Ji-won, "An Chaehong's Thought and the Politics of the United Front," in *Landlords, Peasants, and Intellectuals in Modern Korea*, ed. Pang Kie-chung and Michael D. Shin (Ithaca: Cornell East Asia Series, 2005).

9. Yi, "Minjok kaejoron," 116–47.

10. Yi Kwang-su, "Sungmyŏngnonjŏk insaenggwan esŏ chiryŏngnonjŏk insaenggwan e" (1918), in *Yi Kwang-su chŏnjip*, 10:48. Thank you to Paul Rouzer for assistance with this translation.

11. Yi, "Minjok kaejoron," 116.

12. Ibid.

13. Yi Kwang-su, "Pisangsi ŭi pisangin," in *Yi Kwang-su chŏnjip*, 10:213.

14. Yi, "Minjok kaejoron," 127–28.

15. Ibid., 117.

16. Ibid., 128.

17. Ibid., 118.

18. Yi's Christian disagreement with Socrates follows a consistent pattern of the turn to the pastoral in modern politics. Foucault, *Security, Territory, Population: Lectures at the Collège de France, 1977–1978*, trans. Graham Burchell (New York: Palgrave Macmillan, 2007), 147–48.

19. Yi, "Minjok kaejoron," 118–19.
20. In referring to the "subject of judgment," Yi was using a Kantian framework of aesthetic and teleological judgment to articulate the need for a nation to have self-conscious purpose in order to be civilized and modern. Ibid., 117–19.
21. Yi Kwang-su, "What Is Literature?," trans. Jooyeon Rhee, *Azalea: Journal of Korean Literature and Culture* 4 (2011): 293.
22. There are numerous examples of these kinds of comparisons in Yi's essays, including Yi's discussions of the Russian Revolution, the American Revolution, and the Meiji Restoration as examples of reconstruction in "Minjok gaejoron."
23. Yi, "Sinsaenghwallon," 328.
24. Yi, "Minjok kaejoron," 117–19.
25. Yi, "Sungmyŏngnonjŏk insaenggwan," 48.
26. Yi Kwang-su, "Yesul kwa insaeng: Sinsegye wa Chosŏn minjok ŭi samyŏng," in *Yi Kwang-su chŏnjip*, 10:359–69.
27. Ibid., 360–61.
28. Yi, "Sinsaenghwallon," 325–51.
29. Martin Heidegger, "The Question concerning Technology," in *The Question concerning Technology, and Other Essays,* trans. William Lovitt (New York: Harper and Row, 1977), 10.
30. Yi, "Sinsaenghwallon."
31. Yi Kwang-su, *The Heartless,* trans. Ann Sung-hi Lee, in *Yi Kwang-su and Modern Korean Literature: Mujong* (Ithaca: Cornell East Asia Series, 2005).
32. Ibid., 136.
33. Ibid., 139.
34. Ibid., 250–53, 165–66.
35. Yi Kwang-su, "Minjok e kwanhan myŏt kaji saenggak," in *Yi Kwang-su chŏnjip*, 10:221.
36. Yi, "Sinsaenghwallon," 326.
37. Ibid.
38. Yi refers to purpose in many writings, but most forcefully at the beginning of "Reconstruction," 117.
39. Sōda, "Kobetsu-teki inkaritsu no ronri."
40. Yi, "Kyoyukka chessi ege," 50–51.
41. Ibid., 52–53.
42. Kim, "Pot'ong hakkyo," 487–88.
43. "Mechanism" was the term Arnold used to describe older ideas of education, and the description had appeared earlier in the work of J. G. Fichte and others. Matthew Arnold, *Culture and Anarchy* (Oxford: Oxford University Press, 2006); J. G. Fichte, *Addresses to the German Nation,* trans. R. F. Jones and J. H. Turnbull, ed. George Armstrong Kelly (New York: Harper and Row, 1968).
44. Yi, "Sinsaenghwallon," 328.
45. Yi Kwang-su, "Kaein ŭi ilsangsaenghwal ŭi hyŏksin i minjokjŏk palhŭng ŭi kŭnbon ida," in *Yi Kwang-su chŏnjip*, 10:268–71.
46. "Temperament" and "sentiment" appear with English translations in the original.
47. Yi, "Kaein ŭi ilsangsaenghwal," 271.
48. Saitō, "Nendai ni taishite," 224.

49. Yi Kwang-su, "Munhak kwa 'purŭ wa 'puro,'" in *Yi Kwang-su chŏn-jip*, vol. 10.
50. I have taken this language—"to make live" or "let die"—from Foucault's lectures: Foucault, *Society Must Be Defended*, trans. David Macey (New York: Palgrave MacMillan, 2003).
51. Yi Kwang-su, "Chorŏpsaeng ŭl saenggak hago," in *Yi Kwang-su chŏnjip*, 10:295.
52. Yi, "Chosŏn minjongnon," 215.
53. Etienne Balibar, "The Nation Form: History and Ideology," trans. Chris Turner, in *Race, Nation, Class: Ambiguous Identities* (London: Routledge, 1991), 96–100.
54. Yi, "Chosŏn minjongnon," 215.
55. Ibid., 216–17.
56. Fujitani, *Race for Empire*, 329.
57. Yi, "What Is Literature?" 297–99.
58. Yi, "Yesul kwa insaeng," 361.
59. Yi Kwang-su, "Munhak kwa 'purŭ' wa 'p'uro,'" in *Yi Kwang-su chŏnjip*, 10:440–41.
60. Ibid., 441.
61. Ibid.
62. Yi, "Sinsaenghwallon," 339.
63. Ibid.
64. Yi, "What Is Literature?" 295–96.
65. Yi Kwang-su, "Chosŏn minjongnon," in *Yi Kwang-su chŏnjip*, 10:217.
66. Martin Heidegger, "Question concerning Technology," 10; Yi, "Chosŏn minjongnon," 217.
67. Walter Benjamin, *The Origin of German Tragic* Drama, trans. James Osborne (London: Verso, 2009); Paul de Man, "The Rhetoric of Temporality," in *Blindness and Insight: Essays in the Rhetoric of Contemporary Criticism* (Minneapolis: University of Minnesota Press, 1983); Andrea Mirabile, "Allegory, Pathos, and Irony: The Resistance to Benjamin in Paul de Man," *German Studies Review* 35, no. 2 (2012): 319–33.
68. Hong Hye-wŏn examines the space and time of Yi's narratives in *Yi Kwang-su sosŏl ŭi iyagi wa tamron* (Seoul: Ehwa Women's University Press, 2002).
69. Yi, "Maybe Love"; Shin, "Interior Landscapes"; John Whittier Treat, "Introduction to Yi Kwang-su's 'Maybe Love' (*Ai ka*, 1909)," *Azalea: Journal of Korean Literature and Culture* 4 (2011): 315–20.
70. Yi, "Minjok kaejoron," 119.
71. Yi, "Yun Kwang-ho," 25.
72. Ibid., 42.
73. Ibid., 29.
74. Kwŏn Bodŭrae describes popular and literary ideals of romantic love in great detail in Kwŏn, *Yŏnae ŭi sidae: 1920-nyŏndae ch'oban munhwa wa yuhaeng* (Seoul: Hyŏnsil munhwa yŏn'gu, 2003).
75. Benedict Anderson, *Imagined Communities: Reflections on the Origins and Spread of Nationalism* (London: Verso, 2006).
76. Yi Kwang-su, *Kaech'ŏkja* (Seoul: Ilsinsŏjŏk, 1995), 18–19.
77. Ibid., 41.
78. Sin Ch'ae-ho, "Chosŏn hyŏngmyŏng sŏnŏn," in *Han'guk kŭndae riŏllijŭm pip'yŏng sŏn-jip*, ed. Kim Yun-sik (Seoul: Seoul National University Press, 1988), 4.

79. Yi Kwang-su, *Hyŏngmyŏngga ŭi anae: Ch'unwŏn ŭi tanp'yŏnsŏn* (Seoul: Sŏnghan, 1991).
80. Yi Kwang-su, *Maŭit'aeja* (Seoul: Ilsin Sŏjŏk, 1995); Yi Kwang-su, *Tanjong aesa* (Seoul: Ilsin Sŏjŏk, 1995).
81. Benjamin, *Origins*, 52.
82. An Ham-gwang, "Nongmin munhak munje chaeron," in Kim, *Han'guk kŭndae riŏllijŭm pip'yŏng sŏnjip*, 69–73.
83. Yi Kwang-su, *Hŭk* (Seoul: Tong'a, 1995), 14.
84. Chŏng Sŏn-t'ae, "'Hail Hit'ŭllŏ' e chungdok toen Chosŏn," *Hankyŏre 21*, March 11, 2004, http://h21.hani.co.kr/arti/culture/culture_general/10464.html.
85. Yi Kwang-su (Kayama Mitsurō), *"Hei ni nareru," Sin Taiyō*, November 1943, reprinted in *Kindai Chōsen bungaku Nihongo sakuhinshū: 1939–1945, Sōsakushū*, vol. 5, ed. Masuo Ōmura and Toshihiro Hotei (Tokyo: Ryokuin Shobō, 2002), 115–22.
86. Fujitani, *Race for Empire*.
87. Sin Ch'ae-ho, *Chosŏn sanggosa* (Seoul: Pibong, 2008), 24–29.
88. Sin, "Chosŏn hyŏngmyŏng sŏnŏn," 4.
89. Carl Schmitt, *The Concept of the Political*, trans. George Schwab (Chicago: University of Chicago Press, 2007), 7–13.
90. Michael Robinson, "National Identity and the Thought of Sin Ch'ae-ho: *Sadaejuŭi* and *Chuch'e* in Thought and History," *Journal of Korean Studies* 5 (1984): 127.
91. Andre Schmid, "Rediscovering Manchuria: Sin Ch'aeho and the Politics of Territorial History in Korea," *Journal of Asian Studies* 56, no. 1 (1997): 26–46; Hyun Ok Park, *Two Dreams in One Bed: Empire, Social Life, and the Origins of the North Korean Revolution in Manchuria* (Durham: Duke University Press, 2005).
92. Im Chŏng-jae, "Munsa chegun ege hŭng hanŭn ilmun," in Kim, *Han'guk kŭndae riŏllijŭm pip'yŏng sŏnjip*, 14.
93. Yŏm Sang-sŏp, *Mansejŏn* (Seoul: Ch'angjaksa, 1987); Sunyoung Park, "The Colonial Origin of Korea Realism and Its Contemporary Manifestation," *positions: east asia cultures critique* 14, no. 1 (Spring 2006): 176–77.
94. Im Hwa disucusses "transplantation" in *Kaesŏl sinmunhaksa* (1939), in *Im Hwa munhak yesul chŏnjip*, vol. 2 (Seoul: Somyŏng, 2009), 15–16.
95. Kōtoku Shūsui, *Teikokushugi* (Tokyo: Iwanami Shoten, 1964).
96. Aono Suekichi, "Geijutsu no kakumei to kakumei no geijutsu," in *Nihon puroretaria bungaku hyōronshū*, vol. 3 (Tokyo: Shin nihon, 1990), 208–9.

3. LABOR AND BILDUNG IN MARXISM AND THE PROLETARIAN ARTS

1. Giorgio Agamben, *Man without Content*, trans. Georgia Albert (Stanford: Stanford University Press, 1999), 79–80.
2. George Lukács, *History and Class Consciousness*, trans. Rodney Livingstone (Cambridge, MA: MIT Press, 1971), 345.
3. Kim Yun-sik, "Isik munhangnon pip'an," in Kim, *Han'guk kŭndae riŏllijŭm pip'yŏng sŏnjip*, 223–41; Im Hwa, *Kaesŏl sinmunhaksa*, in *Im Hwa munhak yesul chŏnjip*, vol. 2 (Seoul: Somyŏng, 2009), 21.

4. Chŏng Sŭng-un, *Nakano Shigeharu to Chōsen* (Tokyo: Shinkansha, 2002).
5. Ibid., 16–19.
6. Ibid., 18–20.
7. For the lines that were not censored in Japanese, I have used Miriam Silverberg's translation: Silverberg, *Changing Song: The Marxist Manifestoes of Nakano Shigeharu* (Princeton: Princeton University Press, 1990), 161–62.
8. Im Hwa, "Usan padŭn Yokkohama ŭi pudu," in *Im Hwa munhak yesul chŏnjip*, vol. 1 (Seoul: Somyŏng, 2009), 70–73.
9. Karen Laura Thornber, *Empire of Texts in Motion: Korean, Chinese, and Taiwanese Transculturations of Japanese Literature* (Cambridge, MA: Harvard University Asia Center, 2009).
10. Silverberg, *Changing Song*, 160–61.
11. Michael Robinson, *Cultural Nationalism in Colonial Korea* (Seattle: University of Washington Press, 1989).
12. Nakano Shigeharu, *Three Works by Nakano Shigeharu*, trans. Brett de Bary (Ithaca: Cornell East Asia Series, 1979), 8–14.
13. Im, "Usan," 70–71.
14. Im Hwa, "Negŏri ŭi Suni," in *Im Hwa chŏnjip*, 1:52–54.
15. Zenovia A. Sochor, *Revolution and Culture: The Bogdanov-Lenin Controversy* (Ithaca: Cornell University Press, 1988).
16. V. I. Lenin, *Materialism and Empirio-Criticism: Critical Notes concerning a Reactionary Philosophy*, trans. David Kvitko, in *Collected Works of V. I. Lenin*, vol. 13 (New York: International Publishers, 1927).
17. V. I. Lenin, "On Proletarian Culture," in *V. I. Lenin Complete Works*, vol. 3 (Moscow: Progress Publishers, 1965), 316–17.
18. Leon Trotsky, *Literature and Revolution*, trans. Rose Strunsky (Chicago: Haymarket, 2005), 155.
19. Alexander Bogdanov, *Essays in Tektology, The General Science of Organization*, trans. George Gorelik (Seaside, CA: Intersystems Publications, 1984).
20. Ibid., xiii.
21. Lenin, *Materialism and Empirio-Criticism*, 189–95.
22. Lukács, *History and Class Consciousness*, 345.
23. Harootunian, *History's Disquiet*.
24. Leon Trotsky, *Permanent Revolution & Results and Prospects* (London: International Marxists Group, 2007), 132–33.
25. Aono Suekichi, "Mokuteki ishikiron," in *Gendai Nihon bungaku zenshū*, vol. 78 (Tokyo: Chikuma Shobō, 1957), 77–78.
26. Hirabayashi Hatsunosuke, "Bungaku hōhōron," in *Gendai Nihon bungaku zenshū*, vol. 78 (Tokyo: Chikuma Shobō, 1957), 19.
27. Karl Marx, "Theses on Feuerbach," in *The Marx-Engels Reader,* ed. Robert C. Tucker (New York: Norton, 1978).
28. Agamben, *The Man without Content*, 79–80.
29. Kurahara Korehito, "Puroretaria geijutsu no naiyō to keishiki," in *Gendai Nihon bungaku zenshū*, vol. 78 (Tokyo: Chikuma Shobō, 1957), 182.

30. Park, "Colonial Origin," 177.
31. Pak Yŏng-hŭi, "'Sin'gyŏnghyangp'a' munhak kwa 'musanyu' ŭi munhak," in Kim, *Han'guk kŭndae riŏllijŭm pip'yŏng sŏnjip*.
32. Ibid., 53.
33. Ibid., 48.
34. Heather Bowen-Struyk, "Guest Editor's Introduction: Proletarian Arts in East Asia," *Positions: East Asia Cultures Critique* 14, no. 2 (2006): 251–78.
35. Kim Ki-jin, "P'ŭromŭnadŭ sangt'imangt'al," *Kaebyŏk* 37 (July 1923); quoted in Kim, *Han'guk munhak pip'yŏng nonjaengsa*, 50.
36. Kim Ki-jin, "Chibae ŭi kyohwa wa p'ijibae ŭi kyohwa," in *Kim Ki-jin munhak chŏnjip*, 1:492–3. Quoted in Kim, *Han'guk munhak pip'yŏng nonjaengsa*, 52.
37. Nikolai Bukharin, *Historical Materialism: A System of Sociology* (Ann Arbor: Ann Arbor Paperbacks, 1969).
38. Nakano Shigeharu, "Puroretaria geijutsu to wa nanika?," in *Kōki puroretaria bungaku hyōronshū*, vol. 1 (Tokyo: Shin Nihon, 1990), 57.
39. Ibid.
40. Ibid., 58.
41. Ibid., 59.
42. Ibid.
43. Ibid., 60.
44. Joseph Stalin, "Concerning Questions of Leninism" (1926), in *Works*, vol. 8 (Moscow: Foreign Language Publishing House, 1954).
45. Joseph Stalin, "Marxism and the National Question" (1913), in *Works*, vol. 2. (Moscow: Foreign Language Publishing House, 1954).
46. Barbara Foley, *Radical Representations: Politics and Form in U.S. Proletarian Fiction, 1929-1941* (Durham: Duke University Press, 1993), 170–212.
47. Evgeny Dobrenko, *Political Economy of Socialist Realism*, trans. Jesse M. Savage (New Haven: Yale University Press, 2007).
48. Kim, "Isik munhangnon pip'an."
49. Im, *Kaesŏl sinmunhaksa*, 21.
50. Im Hwa, "Sinmunhaksa ŭi pangbŏp," in *Im Hwa munhak yesul chŏnjip*, vol. 3 (Seoul: Somyŏng, 2009), 647–63.
51. Kim, *Han'guk munhak pip'yŏng nonjaengsa*, 437–54.
52. Maxim Gorky, "Soviet Literature," in *Soviet Writers' Congress 1934* (London: Lawrence and Wishart, 1977).
53. Dobrenko, *Political Economy of Socialist Realism*.
54. Yi Hyŏn-sik, "'Kwadogi' tasi ilgi," in *Han Sŏrya munhak ŭi chaeŭisik* (Seoul: Somyŏng, 2000), 57.
55. Im Hwa, "Yugwŏl chung ŭi ch'angjak," in *Im Hwa munhak yesul chŏnjip*, 1:246–68; Kim Nam-ch'ŏn, "Im Hwa-jŏk ch'angjakp'yŏng kwa chagi pip'an," in Kim, *Han'guk kŭndae riŏllijŭm pip'yŏng sŏnjip*, 89–98.
56. This interpretation is my way of connecting Im's simultaneous work on both new literature as "transplanted literature" and the gradual sublation of literary forms culminating in his version of humanism and socialist realism, found in *The Logic of Literature (Munhak ŭi nolli)*, *Im Hwa munhak yesul chŏnjip*, vol. 3.

57. Kim, *Han'guk munhak pip'yŏng nonjaengsa*, 459–68.
58. Im Hwa, "Hyumŏnijŭm nonjaeng ŭi ch'onggyŏlsan" (1938), in *Im Hwa yesul chŏnjip*, 3:177.
59. Kim, *Han'guk munhak pip'yŏng nonjaengsa*, 477–79.
60. Im Hwa, "Hyŏndae pup'ae ŭi p'yojing in in'gan t'amgu wa komin ŭi chŏngsin: Paek Chŏl kun ŭi soron e taehan pip'yŏng" (1936), in *Im Hwa munhak yesul chŏnjip*, 1:629.
61. Im, "Hyumŏnijŭm nonjaeng ŭi ch'onggyŏlsan," 181.
62. Im Hwa, "Nangmanjŏk chŏngsin ŭi hyŏnsiljŏk kujo: Sin ch'angjak iron ŭi chŏngdang han ihae rŭl wi hayŏ" (1934), in *Im Hwa munhak yesul chŏnjip*, 3:13–29; Im Hwa, "Widae han nangmanjŏk chŏngsin: irossŏ chagi rŭl kwanch'ŏl hara!" (1936), in *Im Hwa munhak yesul chŏnjip*, 3:30–45.
63. Im Hwa, "Sasiljuŭi ŭi chaeinsik: Saeroun munhakjŏk t'amgu e ki hayŏ," in *Im Hwa munhak yesul chŏnjip*, 3:79–80.
64. Im Hwa, "Chuch'e ŭi chaegŏn kwa munhak ŭi segye," in *Im Hwa munhak yesul chŏnjip*, 3:46–63.
65. Im Hwa, "Ilbon nongmin munhak ŭi tonghyang: T'ŭkhi 't'o ŭi munhak' ŭl chungsim ŭro," in *Im Hwa munhak yesul chŏnjip*, 3:630–43; Kang Kyŏng-ae, *In'gan munje*, in *Kang Kyŏng-ae chŏnjip* (Seoul: Somyŏng, 1999), 135–413; Kang Kyŏng-ae, *From Wonso Pond*, trans. Samuel Perry (New York: Feminist Press at CUNY, 2009).
66. An Ham-gwang, "Nongmin munhak."
67. Michael D. Shin and Pang Kie-jung, eds., *Landlords, Peasants, and Intellectuals* (Ithaca: Cornell University Press, 2004).
68. Paek Nam-un, *Chosŏn sahoe kyŏngjesa*, translated from Japanese by Sim U-sŏng (Seoul: Tongmunsŏn, 2004). Paek's application of stage theory to national history leading up to the establishment of the DPRK appears in *Chosŏn minjok ŭi chillo: Chaeron* (Kyŏnggi-do P'aju-si: Pŏmu, 2007), originally published in 1947.
69. Paek Nam-un, "Kwahak paljŏn ŭi p'ilyŏnsŏng," in *Paek Nam-un chŏnjip*, vol. 4, ed. Ha Il-sik (Seoul: Iron kwa Silch'ŏn, 1991), 73.
70. Paek, *Chosŏn sahoe kyŏngjesa*.
71. Paek, "*Chosŏn sahoe kyŏngjesa* ch'ulp'an e taehan sogam," in Ha, *Paek Nam-un chŏnjip*, 4:85.
72. Ibid., 84.
73. Paek Nam-un, "Tōsei keizai no rinrisei," *Tōyō no hikari* 4–6 (June 1942), reprinted as "T'ongje kyŏngje ŭi yullisŏng," trans. Ha Il-sik, in *Paek Nam-un chŏnjip*, 4:278–92.
74. See notes 77 and 78.
75. Karl Marx, "The German Ideology," in *The Marx-Engels Reader*, ed. Robert C. Tucker (New York: Norton, 1978), 151–55.
76. Charles Armstrong, *The North Korean Revolution, 1945–1950* (Ithaca: Cornell University Press, 2005), 29.
77. Paek, *Chosŏn minjok ŭi chillo, chaeron*, 41–91.
78. Sŏ In-sik, "'Chisŏng' ŭi chayŏnsŏng kwa yŏksasŏng," in *Sŏ In-sik chŏnjip*, vol. 1 (Seoul: Yŏngnak, 2006), 48.
79. Sŏ In-sik, "Yŏksa e issŏsŏ ŭi haengdong kwa kwansang: Yŏksa wa yŏngung ŭl malham," in *Sŏ In-sik chŏnjip*, 1:175.
80. Im, "Ilbon nongmin munhak"; Kang Kyŏng-ae, *From Wonso Pond*.

4. OTHER CHRONOTOPES IN REALIST LITERATURE

1. Yoshino Sakuzō, ed., *Meiji bunka kenkyū zenshū*, vol. 1 (Tokyo: Nihon Hyōronsha, 1928).
2. Nakanishi Inosuke, *Shokeishū no jinseikan* (Tokyo: Etsuzando, 1924). Andre Haag discusses Nakanishi's criticisms of the discourse of "outlaw Koreans" around the time of the Great Kantō earthquake of 1923 in "Nakanishi Inosuke to Taishōki nihon no 'futei senjin' e no manazashi: Taishū disukūru to coroniaru gensetsu no tenpuku," *Ritsumeikan gengo bunka kenkyū* 22, no. 3 (2011): 81–97. In the aftermath of the earthquake, rumor and speculation about rioting and looting Koreans and Chinese led to the killing and injuring of hundreds of minorities in Japan proper. Nakanishi shows in his critiques of Kantian philosophy that such popular colonial racism was not in contradiction with the cosmopolitan and assimilationist rhetoric of Japan's cultural policy, despite the latter's claims to universality.
3. Miki Kiyoshi, *Jinseiron nōto* (Tokyo: Sōgensha, 1941); Watsuji, *Ningengaku to shite no rinrigaku*.
4. Nakanishi, *Shokeishū no jinseikan*, 16–17.
5. Nishida Kitarō, "Sōda Kiichirō ni kotau," in *Nishida Kitarō zenshū*, vol. 1 (Tokyo: Iwanami Shoten, 1965), 290–323.
6. Nakanishi, *Shokeishū no jinseikan*, 38–39.
7. Kang, *From Wonso Pond*.
8. Mikhail Bakhtin, "Forms of Time and of the Chronotope in the Novel," in *The Dialogic Imagination: Four Essays* (Austin: University of Texas Press, 1981), 85.
9. Nakanishi Inosuke, *Manshū* (Tokyo: Ōzorasha, 1998).
10. G. W. F. Hegel, "The Oriental World," in *The Philosophy of History*, trans. J. Sibree (New York: Dover, 1956), 111–222.
11. Whatever attempt Fredric Jameson or other critics made to give a specific spatial location (that is, Third World) to national allegory, the national allegorical mode of representing and reading can be taken up in imperial nations and colonized nations, on the political left as well as the political right. Jameson, "Third-World Literature in the Era of Multinational Capitalism," *Social Text* 15 (1986): 65–88.
12. Many leftist texts were written in direct reponse to Yi Kwang-su's work. For example, Yi Ki-yŏng published the back-to-the-land novel *Hometown* (1934) just one year after Yi's *Soil*.
13. The criticism of naturalism appeared in cultural nationalist texts and in numerous KAPF texts.
14. Kim, *Han'guk munhak pip'yŏng nonjaengsa*, 14–21.
15. Pak Yŏng-hŭi, "Sanyanggae," in *Pak Yŏng-hŭi chŏnjip*, vol. 1 (Kyŏngbuk Kyŏngsan-si: Yŏngnam University Press, 1997); Kim Ki-jin, "Pulgŭn chwi," in *Kim Ki-jin munhak chŏnjip*, vol. 4 (Seoul: Munhak kwa Chisŏngsa, 1988), 11–25.
16. Kim Yun-sik, *Pak Yŏng-hŭi yŏn'gu* (Seoul: Yŏrŭmsa, 1989).
17. Pak, "'Sin'gyŏnghyangp'a' munhak."
18. Kim, "Pulgŭn chwi," 19–20.
19. Ibid., 21.
20. Ibid., 22.
21. Ibid., 23.

22. Ibid., 25.
23. Kim Ki-jin, "Chŏlmŭn isangjuŭija ŭi sa," in *Kim Ki-jin munhak chŏn-jip*, 4:26–39.
24. Kim, *Han'guk munhak pip'yŏng nonjaengsa*, 65–76.
25. Yi Ki-yŏng, *Kohyang* (Seoul: Munhak sasangsa, 1994).
26. Kang, *From Wonso Pond*, 269.
27. Kobayashi Takiji, *Kani Kōsen*, Tōseikatsusha (Tokyo: Shinkosha, 2003); Kobayashi Takiji, *The Crab Cannery Ship, and Other Novels of Struggle*, trans. Željko Cipriš (Honolulu: University of Hawai'i Press, 2013).
28. Hayashi Fusao, "Ringo," *Bungei sensen* (February 1926); Sata Ineko, "Kyarameru kōjō kara," in *Sata Ineko zenshū*, vol. 1 (Tokyo: Kōdansha, 1977), 21–31.
29. Kobayashi, *Kani Kōsen*, Tōseikatsusha.
30. Foley, *Radical Representations*.
31. Yamada Moritarō, *Yamada Moritarō chosakushū* (Tokyo: Iwanami Shoten, 1983–85).
32. Kobayashi, *The Crab Cannery Ship*, 19.
33. Ibid., 53.
34. Kobayashi states, "Koreans were treated most cruelly of all." Ibid., 54.
35. Ibid., 44.
36. Ibid., 45.
37. Hayashi Fusao, *Tairiku no hanayome* (Tokyo: Yumani Shobō, 2004); Kubokawa (Sata) Ineko, *Josei no kotoba; zoku, josei no kotoba* (Tokyo: Yumani Shobō, 2002), 167–85. Page numbers refer to the original pagination of *Zoku, josei no kotoba*.
38. Sata, *Zoku, josei no kotoba*, 184–85.
39. Pak Yŏng-hŭi, "Ch'oegŭn munye iron ŭi sinpalgae wa kŭ kyŏnghyang," in Kim, *Han'guk kŭndae riŏllijŭm pip'yŏng sŏnjip*, 127–46; "Chŏnjaeng kwa Chosŏn munhak," *Pak Yŏng-hŭi chŏnjip*, vol. 4.
40. In Chŏng-sik, "Naissen-ittai no bunka-teki rinen," *Quadrante* 7 (2005): 316–19; "Naissen-ittai to gengo," *Quadrante* 7 (2005): 331–32.
41. An, "Nongmin munhak," 69.
42. Ch'oe Sŏ-hae, *T'alch'ulgi: Ch'oe Sŏ-hae tanp'yŏnsŏn*, ed. Kwak Kŭn (Seoul: Munhak kwa Chisŏngsa, 2004), 422.
43. Kwak Kŭn, "Ch'oe Sŏ-hae ŭi chakp'um segye," in *T'alch'ulgi*, 410.
44. Ibid., 412.
45. Pak, "'Sin'gyŏnghyangp'a' munhak."
46. Yi Hyŏn-sik, "'Kwadogi' tasi ilgi," in *Han Sŏrya munhak ŭi chaeŭishik* (Seoul: Somyŏng Ch'ulp'an, 2000), 57.
47. Munhaksa wa Pip'yŏng Hakhoe, *Ch'oe Sŏ-hae munhak ŭi chaejomyŏng* (Seoul: Kukhak Ch'aryowŏn, 1987); Kwŏn, *Yŏnae ŭi sidae*.
48. Ch'oe Sŏ-hae, "Paekkŭm," in *T'alch'ulgi*, 88–111; Ch'oe Sŏ-hae, "Chŏn'asa," in *T'alch'ulgi*, 207–36.
49. Park, *Two Dreams in One Bed*.
50. Ibid., 124–61.
51. Ch'oe Sŏ-hae, "Koguk," in *T'alch'ulgi*, 7.
52. Ibid., 11.
53. Ibid.
54. Ch'oe Sŏ-hae, "T'alch'ulgi," in *T'alch'ulgi*, 15–28.

55. Kwŏn Bodŭrae, "Yŏnae p'yŏnji ŭi segyesang," in *Munhaksa wa Pip'yŏng Hakhoe, Ch'oe Sŏ-hae munhak ŭi chaejomyŏng,* 23.
56. Kwŏn, *Yŏnae sidae.*
57. Kwŏn, "Yŏnae p'yŏnji ŭi segyesang," 24.
58. Ch'oe Sŏ-hae, "Hongnyŏm," in *T'alch'ulgi,* 237–62.
59. Ch'oe Sŏ-hae, "Kia wa saryuk," in *T'alch'ulgi,* 49–66.
60. Kobayashi Takiji, *Absentee Landlord,* in *"The Factory Ship" and "Absentee Landlord,"* trans. Frank Motofuji (Seattle: University of Washington Press, 1973).
61. Louis Althusser, "Ideology and Ideological State Apparatuses," in *Lenin and Philosophy, and Other Essays* (New York: Monthly Review Press, 2001).
62. Paek, "Tōsei keizai no rinrisei."
63. Im, "Ilbon nongmin munhak."
64. Karl Marx, "So-Called Primitive Accumulation," in *Capital: Volume One,* trans. Ben Fowkes (London: Penguin, 1992), 873–942.
65. Rosa Luxemburg, *The Accumulation of Capital* (London: Routledge, 2003).
66. Ruth Barraclough, "Tales of Seduction: Factory Girls in Korean Proletarian Literature," *positions: east asia cultures critique* 14, no. 2 (Fall 2006): 345–71.
67. Maria Mies, *Patriarchy and Accumulation on a World Scale: Women in the International Division of Labor* (London: Zed Books, 1998).

5. WORLD HISTORY AND MINOR LITERATURE

1. An Ham-gwang, "Chōsen bungaku no tokushitsu to hōkō ni tsuite," *Kokumin bungaku* 3, no. 1 (January 1943): 42; facsimile, *Kokumin bungaku,* vol. 5 (Tokyo: Ryokuin Shobō, 1997–98).
2. An, "Nongmin munhak," 69–73.
3. G. W. F. Hegel, *The Phenomenology of Spirit,* trans. A. V. Miller (Oxford: Oxford University Press, 1977), 291.
4. Giovanni Gentile, *Origins and Doctrine of Fascism: With Selections from Other Works,* trans. A. James Gregor (New Brunswick, NJ: Transaction, 2004). In the colonial context, Sŏ In-sik critiques both liberalism and the organicist "culture of totalism" of National Socialism in "Munhwa ŭi kujo rŭl nonsul ham," in *Sŏ In-sik chŏnjip,* 1:63. He critiques the historical view of Giovanni Gentile and other fascist philosophers in "Chŏnch'ejuŭi ŭi yŏksagwan" (1939), in *Sŏ In-sik chŏnjip,* 1:165–68.
5. An, "Nongmin munhak," 73.
6. Sŏ In-sik, "'Chisŏng' ŭi chayŏnsŏng kwa yŏksasŏng," in *Sŏ In-sik chŏnjip: Yŏksa kwa munhwa* (Seoul: Yŏngnak, 2006).
7. An, "Chōsen bungaku," 43.
8. Tanabe Hajime, "Shu no ronri to sekai zushiki," in *Tanabe Hajime zenshū,* vol. 6 (Tokyo: Chikuma Shobō, 1963); Sŏ In-sik, "Chisŏng ŭi sidaejŏk sŏngkyŏk," in *Sŏ In-sik chŏnjip,* vol. 1 (Seoul: Yŏngnak, 2006).
9. Naoki Sakai, "Subject and Substratum: On Japanese Imperial Nationalism," *Cultural Studies* 14, nos. 3, 4 (2000), 462–530.
10. Sŏ, "Chisŏng ŭi sidaejŏk sŏngkyŏk," 109.
11. Kōsaka Masaaki, *Minzoku no tetsugaku* (Tokyo: Iwanami Shoten, 1942), 32.

12. Kōsaka Masaaki, Nishitani Keiji, Kōyama Iwao, and Suzuki Shigetaka, *Sekaishi-teki tachiba to Nihon* (roundtable discussion) (Tokyo: Chūōkōron, 1943).
13. Tanabe Hajime, "Bunka no genkai," in *Tanabe Hajime zenshū*, vol. 8 (Tokyo: Chikuma Shobō, 1963).
14. Sŏ In-sik, "Hyŏnje ŭi kwaje 2: Chŏnhyŏnggi ŭi chesang," in *Sŏ In-sik chŏnjip*, vol. 1 (Seoul: Yongnak, 2006), 154–64.
15. Kōyama Iwao, *Bunka ruikeigaku kenkyū* (Tokyo: Kōbundō, 1941).
16. Kim, *Han'guk munhak pip'yŏng nonjaengsa*, 459–68.
17. Im, "Ilbon nongmin munhak."
18. Kōyama, *Bunka ruikeigaku kenkyū*, 23–137. In "The Oriental World" chapter of *The Philosophy of History*, Hegel discusses the continuities between the divine, the human, and nature in both China and India in similar terms to Kōyama. Hegel, *The Philosophy of History*, 111–222.
19. Kōyama, *Bunka ruikeigaku kenkyū*, 126–27.
20. Ibid., 23–137.
21. Ching, *Becoming Japanese*, 126.
22. Gilles Deleuze and Félix Guattari, *Kafka: Toward a Minor Literature*, trans. Dana Polan (Minneapolis: University of Minnesota Press, 1986).
23. Park, *Two Dreams in One Bed*, 24.
24. Gilles Deleuze, *Difference and Repetition*, trans. Paul Patton (New York: Columbia University Press, 1994), 42–43.
25. Fredric Jameson, *The Political Unconscious: Narrative as a Socially Symbolic Act* (Ithaca: Cornell University Press, 1982), 24–30.
26. Hegel's discussion of ethical substance appears in the "Ethical Order" section of *Phenomenology of Spirit*, 266–94.
27. G. W. F. Hegel, *Science of Logic*, trans. George di Giovanni (Cambridge: Cambridge University Press, 2015), 51. Theodor Adorno quotes this passage in his discussion of the problem of positive identity within a dialectics that insists on a "standpoint" in *Negative Dialectics*, trans. E. B Ashton (New York: Continuum, 1973), 3–6.
28. Tanabe Hajime, "Zushiki 'jikan' kara zushiki 'sekai' e," in *Tanabe Hajime zenshū*, vol. 6 (Tokyo: Chikuma Shobō, 1963), 1–50.
29. Sakai, "Subject and Substratum."
30. Tanabe, "Shu no ronri no sekai zushiki," 232–33.
31. Tanabe, "Zushiki 'jikan' kara," 28.
32. Ibid., 26.
33. Ibid., 31.
34. Tanabe, "Shakai sonzai no ronri," in *Tanabe Hajime zenshū*, 6:151–67.
35. Immanuel Kant, *The Critique of Judgment*, trans. Werner S. Pluhar (Indianapolis: Hackett, 1987).
36. Tanabe, "Zushiki 'jikan' kara," 38.
37. Ch'oe Chae-sŏ, *Tenkanki no Chōsen bungaku* (Seoul: Jinbunsha, 1943), 59–61.
38. Ch'oe Chae-sŏ, "Riarijŭm ŭi hwaktae wa simhwa," in Kim, *Han'guk hyŏndae modŏnijŭm pip'yŏng sŏnjip*, 161–71.
39. Niizeki Ryōzō, *Kokumin bungaku to sekai bungaku* (Tokyo: Kawade Shobō, 1941).
40. Ibid., 40.

41. Ibid., 40–48.
42. Tokieda Motoki, *Kokugo genron: Gengo kateisetsu no seiritsu to sono tenkai* (Tokyo: Iwanami Shoten, 1974).
43. Ch'oe, *Tenkanki no Chōsen bungaku*, 74.
44. T. S. Eliot, *Christianity and Culture* (San Diego: Harcourt, 1976), 153.
45. Ch'oe Chae-sŏ, *Tenkanki no Chōsen bungaku*, 140–50, 37.
46. Ibid., 6.
47. Ibid., 8.
48. Nicos Poulantzas, *Fascism and Dictatorship: the Third International and the Problem of Fascism*, trans. Judith White (London: Verso, 1979), 241.
49. Ch'oe, *Tenkanki no Chōsen bungaku*, 16–18.
50. Ibid., 1–9.
51. Ibid., 59–61.
52. Kim Sa-ryang, "Dōitsu no aikoku bungaku," translated from Korean by Yi Hak-jun, in *Kim Sa-ryang zenshū*, vol. 4 (Tokyo: Kawade Shobō Shinsha, 1973), 31–35; Kim Sa-ryang, "Dōitsu no taisen bungaku," translated from Korean by Yi Hak-jun, in *Kim Sa-ryang zenshū*, vol. 4. (Tokyo: Kawade Shobō Shinsha, 1973), 36–40.
53. Ch'oe, *Tenkanki no Chōsen bungaku*, 60.
54. Ibid., 47.
55. Martin Heidegger, *Being and Time*, trans. John MacQuarrie and Edward Robinson (New York: Harper, 1962), 274–341.
56. Ch'oe, *Tenkanki no chōsen bungaku*, 182–83. I have consulted Janet Poole's translation of the end of this passage in *When the Future Disappears: The Modernist Imagination in Late Colonial Korea* (New York: Columbia University Press), 154.
57. "Chōsen bundan no saishuppatsu wo kataru" (roundtable discussion), *Kokumin bungaku* 1, no. 1 (November 1941): 78–79; facsimile, *Kokumin bungaku*, vol. 1 (Tokyo: Ryokuin Shobō, 1997–98).
58. One significant example is an exchange between Kikuchi Kan and Ch'oe Chae-sŏ in *People's Literature*. Although he asserted the need for Korean writers to overcome their nostalgic ethnic nationalism, during this discussion he willingly took up the position of the native informant, explaining in self-ethnographic terms the current state of Korean culture and letters. "Shin hantō bungaku e no yōbō" (roundtable discussion), *Kokumin bungaku* 3, no. 3 (March 1943): 2–14; facsimile, *Kokumin bungaku*, vol. 6 (Tokyo: Ryokuin Shobō, 1997–98).
59. Susan Buck-Morss, "Aesthetic and Anaesthetic: Walter Benjamin's Artwork Essay Reconsidered," in *October: The Second Decade, 1986–1996*, 375–86 (Cambridge, MA: MIT Press, 1997).
60. Kim Sa-ryang's master's thesis at Tokyo Imperial University was titled *Heinrich Heine, der letzte Romantiker* (*Heinrich Heine, the last Romantic*). An U-sik, *Kim Sa-ryang: Sono teikō no shōgai* (Tokyo: Iwanami Shoten, 1972), 89–92.
61. Deleuze and Guattari, *Kafka*, 23–25.
62. Kim Sa-ryang, "Chōsen bunka tsūshin," in *Kim Sa-ryang zenshū*, vol. 4 (Tokyo: Kawade Shobō Shinsha), 29.
63. Walter Benjamin, "The Translator's Task," trans. Steven Rendall, in *The Translation Studies Reader*, 3rd ed., ed. Lawrence Venuti (London: Routledge, 2012), 75–83.

64. Roman Jakobson, "On the Linguistic Aspects of Translation," in Venuti, *The Translation Studies Reader*, 126–31.

65. Jacques Derrida, "Des Tour de Babel," in *Difference in Translation*, ed. Joseph F. Graham (Ithaca: Cornell University Press, 1985), 199.

66. Kim, "Chōsen bunka tsūshin," 27.

67. Kim Yun-sik, *Han-il kŭndae munhak ŭi kwallyŏn yangsang sillon* (Seoul: Seoul National University Press, 2001), 13–14.

68. Goh Byeong-gwon, "R ŭl ssŭnda," in *Sosusŏng ŭi chŏngch'ihak*, 4–9 (Seoul: Gurin B, 2007).

69. Ching, *Becoming Japanese*, 92–132.

70. In South Korea, the study of pro-Japanese intellectuals began in 1966 with Im Chong-guk's study *Sillok ch'inilp'a* (Seoul: Tolbagae, 1991). The basic stance of this text is that anyone who wrote in Japanese was pro-Japanese and therefore a traitor to the Korean nation.

71. Kim Sa-ryang, "Hebi," in *Kim Sa-ryang zenshū*, vol. 1.

72. An, *Kim Sa-ryang*, 42–77.

73. A monologue containing words very close to these lines appears in the English version of *The Lower Depths*: Maxim Gorky, *The Lower Depths*, in *Gorky Plays: 1: The Lower Depths, Summerfolk, Children of the Sun, Barbarians, Enemies* (London: Bloomsbury Methuen, 1988), 79–81.

74. Kim, "Hebi," 105–6.

75. Ibid., 110.

76. Julio Cortázar, "Axolotl," in *Blow-Up, and Other Stories*, trans. Paul Blackburn (New York: Pantheon, 1985), 3–9.

77. Deleuze and Guattari, *Kafka*, 13; Deleuze and Guattari, *Anti-Oedipus: Introduction to Schizoanalysis*, trans. Robert Hurley, Mark Seem, and Helen R. Lane (Minneapolis: University of Minnesota Press, 1983), 2.

78. "The Gorky Factor," in *Soviet Culture and Power: A History in Documents, 1917–1953*, ed. Katerina Clark, Evgeny Dobrenko, Andreï Artizov, and Oleg V. Naumov (New Haven: Yale University Press, 2007), 179–93.

79. These characters belong to the following stories: the cave dwellers appear in *"Dosonran,"* the slash-and-burn farmers in "Kusa fukashi," a junk salesman in "Hebi," and the migrant prostitute and ex-convict in "Kija Sanrin," in *Kim Sa-ryang zenshū*, vol. 1. The opium addict appears in "Chigimi," *Samch'ŏlli* 149 (April 1941).

80. For demographics concerning the disproportionate number of peasant women who became comfort women, see Yoshimi Yoshiaki, *Comfort Women: Sexual Slavery in the Japanese Military during World War II*, trans. Suzanne O'Brien (New York: Columbia University Press, 2000).

81. This sentence refers to the climaxes of each of the stories listed in note 76.

82. Kim Sa-ryang, "Tenma," in *Kim Sa-ryang zenshū*, vol. 1.

83. Ibid., 103.

84. An, *Kim Sa-ryang*, 91.

85. Kim Nam-ch'ŏn, "Kyŏngyŏng" and "Maek," in *Maek: Kim Nam-ch'ŏn ch'angjakjip* (Seoul: Ŭryu Munhwasa, 1988).

86. Sunyoung Park draws our attention to everydayness in Kim Nam-chŏn's works in "Everyday Life as Critique in Late Colonial Korea: Kim Nam-chŏn's Literary Experiments, 1934–1943," *Journal of Asian Studies* 68, no. 3 (2009): 861–93.

87. Sŏn Chu-wŏn, "Tamron chuch'e ŭi t'ajasŏng ilggi wa sosŏl kyoyuk: Kim Nam-chŏn ŭi 'Kyŏngyŏng' kwa 'Maek' rŭl chungsim ŭro," *Hyŏndae Munhak Yŏn'gu* 22 (2004): 561–87.

88. Kim, "Maek," 333–34.

89. Tanabe Hajime, *Rekishi-teki genjitsu* (Tokyo: Kobushi Shobō, 2001).

90. Kim Sa-ryang, "Hikari no naka ni," in *Kim Sa-ryang zenshū*, vol. 1.

91. An, *Kim Sa-ryang*, 95.

92. Ibid., 99–100.

93. Ibid., 101.

94. Ibid., 100.

95. Stuart Hall, "Cultural Identity and Diaspora," in *Identity and Difference*, ed. Kathryn Woodward (London: Sage, 1997), 51–59.

96. Bruce Cumings estimates 1.4 million Koreans were in Japan proper, most of them brought there forceably to work in construction, manufacturing, and mining. Cumings, *Korea's Place in the Sun: A Modern History* (New York: Norton, 2005), 171.

6. MODERNISM WITHOUT A HOME

1. Yi Sang, "Kenchiku mugen rokumen kakutai," *Chōsen to kenchiku* 11, no. 7 (July 1932): 25; facsimile, *Chōsen to kenchiku*, vol. 20 (Seoul: Arŭm, 1995).

2. Yi Sang, "Chōkanzu," *Chōsen to kenchiku* 10, no. 8 (August 1931): 10–13; facsimile, *Chōsen to kenchiku*, vol. 18 (Seoul: Arŭm, 1995).

3. Yi Sang, "Chogamdo," *Chosŏn Chungang Ilbo*, July 24, 1934.

4. Yi Sang, "Sanjikaku sekkeizu," *Chōsen to kenchiku* 10, no. 10 (October 1931): 29–31; facsimile, *Chōsen to kenchiku*, vol. 18.

5. Yokomitsu Riichi, "Jikan," in *Teihon Yokomitsu Riichi zenshū*, vol. 4 (Tokyo: Kawaide Shobō Shinsha, 1981), 178–92; Akutagawa Ryūnosuke, "Cogwheels," in *The Essential Akutagawa: Rashomon, Hell Screen, Cogwheels, a Fool's Life, and Other Short Fiction*, trans. Seiji Lippit (New York: Marsilio, 1999); Pak T'ae-wŏn, *Sosŏlga Kubo Ssi ŭi iril* (Seoul: Munhak kwa Chisŏngsa, 1998).

6. Shu-mei Shih, *The Lure of the Modern: Writing Modernism in Semi-Colonial China, 1912–1937* (Berkeley: University of California Press, 2000).

7. This formulation of ecstatic temporality is derived from Heidegger's discussion of *ékstasis* in *Being and Time*. Thank you to Pedro Erber for emphasizing to me this aspect of Heidegger's thinking.

8. Peter Bürger, *Theory of the Avant-Garde* (Minneapolis: University of Minnesota Press, 1984); Boris Groys, *The Total Art of Stalinism: Avant-Garde, Aesthetic Dictatorship, and Beyond*, trans. Charles Rougle (London: Verso, 2011).

9. Wyndham Lewis, *Hitler* (London: Chatto and Windus, 1931); Ernesto Ialongo, "Filippo Tomaso Marinetti: The Futurist as Fascist, 1929–1937," *Journal of Modern Italian Studies* 18, no. 4 (2013): 393–419; Matthew Feldman, *Ezra Pound's Fascist Propaganda, 1935–1945* (London: Palgrave Macmillan, 2013); Charles Bambach, *Heidegger's Roots: Nietzsche, Nationalism Socialism, and the Greeks* (Ithaca: Cornell University Press, 2003), 88.

10. Said, *Orientalism*, 312–13.

11. Alan Tansman, *The Aesthetics of Japanese Fascism* (Berkeley: University of California Press, 2009); Seiji Lippit, *Topographies of Japanese Modernism* (New York: Columbia University Press, 2002).

12. Yokomitsu Riichi, *Shanghai: A Novel*, trans. Dennis Charles Washburn (Ann Arbor: University of Michigan Center for Japan Studies, 2001); Yokomitsu Riichi, "Shanhai," in *Teihon Yokomitsu Riichi zenshū*, vol. 3 (Tokyo: Kawaide Shobō Shinsha, 1981), 3–246.

13. Ch'oe, "Riarijŭm ŭi hwaktae wa simhwa," 162.

14. Kristin Ross, "Rimbaud and the Transformation of Social Space," *Yale French Studies* 97 (2000): 36–54.

15. Fredric Jameson, *Fables of Aggression: Wyndham Lewis, the Modernist as Fascist* (Berkeley: University of California Press, 1979).

16. Deleuze, *Difference and Repetition*, 68–221.

17. Deleuze, *Cinema 1: The Movement-Image*, trans. Hugh Tomlinson and Robert Galeta (Minneapolis: University of Minnesota Press, 1986); Deleuze, *Cinema 2: The Time-Image*, trans. Hugh Tomlinson and Barbara Habberjam (Minneapolis: University of Minnesota Press, 1989).

18. Ch'oe, "Riarijŭm ŭi hwaktae wa simhwa," 164–66.

19. Ibid., 164.

20. Yi, "Kenchiku mugen rokumen kakutai," 25.

21. Sergei Eisenstein, "The Filmic Fourth Dimension," in *Film Form: Essays in Film Theory*, ed. and trans. Jay Leyda (San Diego: Harcourt, 1977), 64–71.

22. This ecstasis is apparent in Yi Sang's references to relativity theory and the "invention of the person" in "Sanjikaku sekkeizu," *Chōsen to kenchiku* 10, no. 10 (October 1931): 29–31; facsimile, *Chōsen to kenchiku*, vol. 18.

23. Ch'oe, "Riarijŭm ŭi hwaktae wa simhwa," 171.

24. Travis Workman, "Stepping into the Newsreel: Melodrama and Mobilization in Colonial Korean Film," *Cross-Currents: East Asian History and Culture Review* 3, no. 1 (2014): 153–84.

25. Kōyama, *Bunka ruikeigaku kenkyū*, 126–27.

26. Yokomitsu Riichi, "Kikai," in *Teihon Yokomitsu Riichi zenshū*, vol. 3 (Tokyo: Kawaide Shobō Shinsha, 1981), 378.

27. Sigmund Freud, *Beyond the Pleasure Principle*, trans. James Strachey (New York: Norton, 1990), 46–49.

28. Yokomitsu, "Chōsen no koto," in *Teihon Yokomitsu Riichi zenshū*, 14:275–76.

29. Lippit, *Topographies*, 201–5.

30. Nayoung Aimee Kwon analyzes "local color" as "colonial kitsch" in "Collaboration, Coproduction, Code-Switching," *Cross-Currents: East Asian History and Culture Review* 2, no. 1 (2013): 10–40.

31. Ch'oe, "Riarijŭm ŭi hwaktae wa simhwa," 168–71.

32. Kuroita Katsumi, "Bunka to kenchiku," *Chōsen to kenchiku* 1, no. 1 (June 1922): 13–9; facsimile, *Chōsen to kenchiku*, vol. 1 (Seoul: Arŭm, 1995).

33. Johannes Itten, "Zuan kyōiku no ichi hōkoku," trans. Kojima Takashi, *Chōsen to kenchiku* 11, no. 8 (August 1932): 8–13; facsimile, *Chōsen to kenchiku*, vol. 20 (Seoul: Arŭm, 1995).

34. Itō Tadahiro, "Keishū ni tsuite," *Chōsen to kenchiku* 10, no. 10 (October 1931): 3; facsimile, *Chōsen to kenchiku,* vol. 18.

35. I take the term "psychogeography" from Guy Debord, "Introduction to a Critique of Urban Geography" (1955) in *Situationist International Anthology,* trans. and ed. Ken Knabb (Berkeley: Bureau of Public Secrets, 2006), 8. Debord states that an "illiterate Kabyle" first suggested the term.

36. "Chōsen hoson ni kansuru zadankai" (roundtable discussion), *Chōsen to kenchiku* 10, no. 5 (May 1931): 2–20; Fukushi Matsunosuke, "Kokenchikubutsu hoson no kyoiku-teki kachi," *Chōsen to kenchiku* 10, no. 5 (May 1931): 21–29; facsimiles, *Chōsen to kenchiku,* vol. 17 (Seoul: Arŭm, 1995).

37. Robert Oppenheim, *Kyongju Things* (Ann Arbor: University of Michigan Press, 2008).

38. Sasa Keiichi, "Shunbosan hakubunji shinchiku kōji ni tsuite," *Chōsen to kenchiku* 11, no. 11 (1932): 6; facsimile, *Chōsen to kenchiku,* vol. 20.

39. Ibid., 7.

40. Ibid.

41. Asagawa Noritaka, "Kenchiku ni taisuru sokumenkan," *Chōsen to kenchiku* 11, no. 8 (August 1932): 2; facsimile, *Chōsen to kenchiku,* vol. 20.

42. Kim Sŏng-u, "Tosi chut'aek ŭi hyŏngsŏng kwa saenghwal ŭi pyŏnhwa," in *Ilche ŭi singminji chibae wa ilsangsaenghwal* (Seoul: Hyean, 2004).

43. "Chōsen shiki jūtaku kenchiku kaizen zadankai" (roundtable discussion), *Chōsen to kenchiku* 10, no. 10 (October 1931): 13; facsimile, *Chōsen to kenchiku,* vol. 18.

44. Yi, "Sanjikaku sekkeizu."

45. Ibid., 29.

46. Ibid.

47. Ibid.

48. Ibid.

49. Ibid.

50. Yi, "Kenchiku mugen rokumen kakutai," 25.

51. Yi, "Sanjikaku sekkeizu," 29.

52. Ibid.

53. "Abstract space" is a term of Henri Lefevbre, *The Production of Space,* trans. Donald Nicolson Smith (London: Blackwell, 1991), 229–91.

54. Yi, "Sanjikaku sekkeizu," 29.

55. Ibid., 30.

56. Ibid., 31.

57. Ibid., 30.

APPENDIX

OPENING AN UMBRELLA ON YOKOHAMA PIER/IM HWA

Woman of the harbor! Woman of another country!
Do not come running on the *dock,* the *dock* is wet with rain
My heart burns with the sorrow of leaving and the grief of being pursued
Oh, you are the woman of *Yokohama* whom I love!
Do not come running on the *dock,* the railings are wet with rain

"What if the weather were fine today?"
No, no. These are only your poor, useless words
When it rains in your country, we depart from the *dock*
And poor you, you cry until your voice is cracked
Do not hold back this treasonous young man from another country
Poor woman of the harbor—do not cry

Your man knows that this ticket he carries is his banishment
And if you return now on this road
To that house where we spent every day in the midst of the laughter and the
   unyielding passion
     of those courageous men,
Now, there would be nothing to greet you but the clumps of dirt from the shoes
   that once trod
     inside
I know this better than anyone
Woman of the harbor!—you must know, too
Those people who now lie sleeping "inside a birdcage"—they have not lived in the

embrace of your country's love
Nor have they lived in your beautiful heart

And yet—
I for you, and you for me
The others for you, and you for them
Why have we promised our lives?
Why have we stayed up together so many snowy nights?

We had no reason to do so
We did not share the same fate
You are a woman from another country and I am a man of the colonies
Yet—there was one reason
You and I—we were siblings who labored
At the same task
Two lives from different countries ate the same food
And we came to live in love

Oh, woman of Yokohama whom I love
The rain falls upon the sea and the waves are like the wind
I am leaving everything behind on this land
I am departing on the Pacific Ocean
To return to the country of my mother and father
If I do not see a flock of long-winged seagulls on the sea
Yokohama woman, you who entered my heart will also disappear today

You, the bird of *Yokohama*—
You mustn't feel lonely. Doesn't the wind blow?
What if your paper umbrella were to break
Go back
The sound of your *geta* and the sound of the rain are buried in each other and fade
   away
Go, go
I am being hunted down, but those brave fellows,
Aren't they sitting behind iron bars and wearing clothes wet with sweat?
At the factory where you work, aren't there men from the Northern continent who
   long for their
      sisters and mothers?
You must wash the clothes of those men
Shouldn't you hold them against your chest?
Go! Go! You must return!
Already, the siren has cried out thrice
And the black clothes have tugged at my hand
Now we must go, you must go and I must go

Woman of another country!
Do not shed tears
I am not in the *demo* that flows through the streets, and many of the others have already fallen—
You must not be sad
When you come out of the factory, I will no longer be waiting for you behind the electrical pole
But the waves of other young workers swell your heart
And the hands of those starved for love await you

And again proclamations from the mouths of the young
Ignite a flame in the minds of working people

Return! Return quickly
The rain falls upon the *dock* and the wind strikes the *deck*
The umbrella may break—
With this umbrella that today bid farewell to a pursued young man from another country, you will tomorrow welcome those fellows
Shouldn't you walk the Kyōbin road making the sound of your *geta*?

Oh, you are the woman of the harbor whom I love
You are not one to sink into sorrow for sending me off
Or petty thoughts about parting with the man you love
The man you love, am I not chased from this land?
Those fellows are imprisoned and do not know I am pursued. That thought, that regrettable truth
Will be dyed in scarlet upon your dove-like chest
When your flesh becomes hot and you cannot bear it
Hold their faces and heads tight against your heart

By then, I, who am now leaving you, will have passed through Pusan, and Tokyo, and
    returned to *Yokohama* with a comrade
Bury your beautiful, weary head in my chest
And cry, and laugh
You are my woman of the harbor!
Do not come running on the *dock*

The rain falls on your gentle back and the wind blows your umbrella.

BLUEPRINT FOR A THREE-DIMENSIONAL SHAPE/YI SANG

三次角設計圖

金 海 卿

◇線に關する覺書 1

```
  0 9 8 7 6 5 4 3 2 1
1 ● ● ● ● ● ● ● ● ● ●
2 ● ● ● ● ● ● ● ● ● ●
3 ● ● ● ● ● ● ● ● ● ●
4 ● ● ● ● ● ● ● ● ● ●
5 ● ● ● ● ● ● ● ● ● ●
6 ● ● ● ● ● ● ● ● ● ●
7 ● ● ● ● ● ● ● ● ● ●
8 ● ● ● ● ● ● ● ● ● ●
9 ● ● ● ● ● ● ● ● ● ●
0 ● ● ● ● ● ● ● ● ● ●
```

(宇宙は羃に依る羃に依る)
(人は數字を捨てよ)
(靜かにオレを電子の陽子にせよ)

十倍百倍何千倍何萬倍何億倍何兆倍すれば人は數十年數百年數千年數萬年數億年數兆年の太古の事實が見れるぢやないか、それを又絶えず崩壞するものとするか、原子は原子であり原子であり原子である、生理作用は變移するものである、原子は原子でなく原子である、放射は崩壞であるか、人は永劫である永劫を生き得ることは生命は生でもなく命でもなく光であることである。

臭殼の味覺と味覺の臭殼

(立體への絶望に依る誕生)
(運動への絶望に依る誕生)
(地球は空巣である時封建時代は涙ぐむ程懐かしい)
一九三一、五、三一、九、一一

◇線に關する覺書 2

スペクトル
軸X 軸Y 軸Z

速度etcの統制例へば光は秒毎
三〇〇〇〇〇キロメートル逃げる
ことが確かなら人の發明は秒毎
〇〇〇〇〇キロメートル逃げられ
ないことはキツトない。それを何

線上の一點			C B A
線上の一點			C B A
線上の一點			C B A
二線の交點	A+B+C	A+B+C	C B A
三線の交點	A+B+C	A+B+C	
數線の交點			

```
1+3
3+1
1+3   3+1   1+3
1+3   3+1   1+3
1+3   3+1   1+3
      3+1   1+3
      3+1
```

(太陽光線は、凸レンズのために
收斂光線となり一點において嚇々
と光り嚇々と燃えた、太初の僥倖
は何よりも大氣の屑と屑との屑を
して凸レンズたらしめなかつた)

◇線に關する覺書 3

```
3 2 1     1 2 3
● ● ●     ● ● ●
● ● ●     ● ● ●
● ● ●     ● ● ●
```

$$\therefore \, _nP_h = n(n-1)(n-2)\cdots\cdots(n-n+1)$$

(腦髓は扇子の樣に圓迄開いた、
そして完全に廻轉した)
一九三一、九、一一

たこゝにあることを思ふさゞ樂し
い、幾何學は凸レンズの樣な火遊
びではなからうか、ユウクリトは
死んだ今日ユウクリトの焦點は到
る處において人文の腦髓を枯草の
樣に燒却する收斂作用を羅列する
ここに依り最大の收斂作用を營む
危險を促す、人は絶望せよ、人は
誕生せよ、人は絶望せよ、人は絶
望せよ)
一九三一、九、一一

◇線に關する覺書 4
（未定稿）

彈丸が一圓壔を走つた（彈丸が一直線に走つたにおける誤謬らの修正）

正六砂糖（角砂糖のこと）

湯筒の海綿質増充（瀑布の文學的解説）一九三一、九、一二

◇線に關する覺書 5

人は光よりも迅く逃げるここる人は光を見るか、人は光を見る。過去の眞空において二度結婚する。三度結婚するか、人は光よりも迅く逃げるこさである。

未來へ逃げて過去を見る、過去へ逃げて未來を見るか、未來へ逃げることは過去へ逃げることさ同じことでもなくオレへ逃げることが過去へ逃げることである。擴大する宇宙を憂ふ人よ、光よりも迅く未來へ逃げよ、光よりも迅く過去へ逃げよ。

人は再びオレを迎へる、人は若いオレに少くさも相會す、人より若いオレに少くさも相會す、人は全等形の體操の技術を習へ

は三度オレを迎へる、人は若いオレに少くさも相會す、人は癇寛に待てよ。そしてファウストはオレにあるのでもなくオレであるのメフィストはオレにあるのでもなくオレである。

速度を調節する朝人は過去を集める、オレらは語らない、過去らに傾聽する現在をしすることは間もない、繰返される過去、過去らに傾聽する過去、現在は過去をのみ印刷し過去の複数の場合においても同じである。

聯想は處女にせよ、過去を現在らす知る、人は古いものを新しいものをする、健忘よ、永遠の忘却は忽敷を皆敷ふ。

來るひは故に無慈悲に人に一致し人よりも迅くオレに逃げしい未來は過去へ逃げることさ同じ、人は光を廻り起し未來において過去を待ち伏す、先づ人は愛撫し過去からして再びその過去に生きる、童心よ、童心の童心に至るここはない永遠の童心。

思考の破片を食べよ、さもなければ新しいものは不完全である。聯想を殺せよ、一つを知ること三つを知ることを已めよ、一つを知ることの次は一つのことを知ることをあらしめよ。

人は一度に一度逃げよ、最大に××される前に祖先の祖先の星雲の星雲の星雲の太初に逃げよ、人は二度分娩される前に逃げることを發控へよ、人は迅く逃げて過去に生き過去を未來に生きる、人は静力學の現象しないことる、人は人の客観を拾てる主觀の詩系の收敛と收敛の假設に依

4 × ＋
4 ＋ ｒ
4 ＋ ｒ
ｒ ＋ 4
ｒ ＋ 4
etc

◇線に關する覺書 6

一九三一、九、一二

4 第四世

4 凸レンズ。

4 一千九百三十一年九月十二日生。

4 陽子核さしての陽子さ陽子さの聯想を選擇。

数字の力學

数字の方位學

時間性（通常思考に依る歴史性）

速度と座標と速度

よ、さもなければ人は過去のオレのバラバラを如何にするか。

(31)……三次角設計圖

原子構造としてのあらゆる運算の研究。

方位と構造式と質量としての數字の性狀性質に依る解答と解答の分類。

數字を代數的であることにする。ここから數字を數字的であることにする。ここから數字を數字である。ここにすることから數字を數字であることにすることへ（1234567890の疾愚の究明と詩的である情緖の乘塲

數字のあらゆる性狀　數字のあらゆる性質　このことさらに依る數字の語尾の活用に依る數字の滑減）

算式は光と光よりも迅く逃げる人さに依り運算せられること。

人は星、天體、星のために犧牲を惜むことは無意味である、星と星との引力圖と引力圖との相殺に依る加速度函數の變化の調査を先づ作ること。一九三一、九、一二

◎線に關する覺書 7

空氣構造の速度と音波に依り速らしくて三百三十メートルを摸倣する（何んと光に比しての拙だしき劣り方だらう）

光を染めよ、光を悲しめよ、光を笑へよ、光を泣けよ。

光が人であると人は鏡である。

光を持てよ。

———

視覺のナマヱを持つことは計算の嚆矢である。視覺のナマヱを發表せよ。

□　オレノナマヱ。

△　オレの妻のナマヱ（既に古い過去においてオレのAMOUREUSEは斯くの如く聰明である）

———

ソラは視覺のナマヱについてのみ存在を明らかにする（代表のオレは代表の一例を擧げること）

蒼空、秋天、蒼天、青天、長天一天、弩穹（非常に窮屈な地方色ではなからうか）ソラは視覺のナマヱを發表した。

視覺のナマヱは人と共に永遠に生きるべき數字的である或る一點である、視覺のナマヱは運動しないで運動のコヲスを持つばかりである。

———

視覺のナマヱは光を持つ光を持たない、人は視覺のナマヱのために光よりも迅く逃げる必要はない。

視覺のナマヱらを健忘せよ。

視覺のナマヱを節約せよ。

———

人は光よりも迅く逃げる速度を

調節し度々過去を未來において淘汰せよ。一九三一、九、一二

SELECTED BIBLIOGRAPHY

SOURCES IN KOREAN AND JAPANESE

An Ham-gwang. "Chōsen bungaku no tokushitsu to hōkō ni tsuite." *Kokumin bungaku* 3, no. 1 (January 1943): 38–48. Facsimile, *Kokumin bungaku*, vol. 5. Tokyo: Ryokuin Shobō, 1997.
———. "Nongmin munhak munje chaeron." In *Han'guk kŭndae riŏllijŭm pip'yŏng sŏnjip*, edited by Kim Yun-sik, 68–88. Seoul: Seoul Taehakkyo Ch'ulp'anbu, 1988.
An Ho-sang. "Heigeru ronrigaku ni okeru kyakkan-teki handan no mondai." Translated from German by Takeuchi Yoshitomo. *Tetsugaku kenkyū* 26, no. 8 (1941): 677–716.
———. *Ilminjuŭi ŭi pon pat'ang*. Seoul: Chomunsa, 1950.
———. *Yumullon pip'an*. Seoul: Munhwadang, 1947.
An U-sik. *Kim Sa-ryang: Sono teikō no shōgai*. Tokyo: Iwanami Shoten, 1972.
Aono Suekichi, "Geijutsu no kakumei to kakumei no geijutsu." In *Nihon puroretaria bungaku hyōronshū*, 3:206–12. Tokyo: Shin nihon, 1990.
———. "Mokuteki ishikiron." In *Gendai nihon bungaku zenshū*, 78:77–81.Tokyo: Chikuma Shobō, 1957.
Arai Tetsu (Uchino Kenji). "Kenchiku no majutsu." In *Arai Tetsu no zenshigoto*, 33–34. Tokyo: Sojusha, 1983.
Asagawa Noritaka. "Kenchiku ni taisuru sokumenkan." *Chōsen to kenchiku* 11, no. 8 (August 1932): 2–4. Facsimile, *Chōsen to kenchiku*, vol. 20 (Seoul: Arŭm, 1995).
Ch'oe Chae-sŏ. "Riarijŭm ŭi hwaktae wa simhwa." In *Han'guk hyŏndae modŏnijŭm pip'yŏng sŏnjip*, edited by Kim Yun-sik, 161–71. Seoul: Seoul Taehakkyo Ch'ulp'anbu, 1988.
———. *Tenkanki no chōsen bungaku*. Seoul: Jinbunsha, 1943.
Ch'oe Nam-sŏn. "Chosŏn kwa segye ŭi kongt'ongŏ: Chosŏnŏ rossŏ chŭngmyŏng hal wŏnsi munhwa ŭi haeksim." In *Yuktang Ch'oe Nam-sŏn chŏnjip*, 9:315–17. Seoul: Yŏngnak, 2003.
Ch'oe Sŏ-hae. "Chŏn-asa." In *T'alch'ulgi: Ch'oe Sŏ-hae tanp'yŏnsŏn*, 207–36.

———. "Hongnyŏm." In *T'alch'ulgi: Ch'oe Sŏ-hae tanp'yŏnsŏn*, 237–62.
———. "Koguk." In *T'alch'ulgi: Ch'oe Sŏ-hae tanp'yŏnsŏn*, 7–14.
———. "Paekkŭm." In *T'alch'ulgi: Ch'oe Sŏ-hae tanp'yŏnsŏn*, 88–111.
———. "T'alch'ulgi." In *T'alch'ulgi: Ch'oe Sŏ-hae tanp'yŏnsŏn*, 15–28.
———. *T'alch'ulgi: Ch'oe Sŏ-hae tanp'yŏnsŏn*, Edited by Kwak Kŭn. Seoul: Munhak kwa chisŏngsa, 2004.
Cho Hae-ok. *Yi Sang si ŭi kŭndaesŏng yŏn'gu: Yukch'e ŭisik ŭl chungsim ŭro*. Seoul: Somyŏng, 2001.
Chŏng Sŏnt'ae. "'Hail Hit'ŭllŏ' e chungdok toen Chosŏn." *Hankyŏre 21*, March 11, 2004. http://h21.hani.co.kr/arti/culture/culture_general/10464.html.
Chŏng Sŭng-un. *Nakano Shigeharu to Chōsen*. Tokyo: Shinkansha, 2002.
"Chōsen bundan no saishuppatsu wo kataru" (roundtable discussion). *Kokumin bungaku* 1, no. 1 (November 1941): 70–90. Facsimile, *Kokumin bungaku*, vol. 1. Tokyo: Ryokuin Shobō, 1997–98.
"Chōsen kokenchiku hoson ni kansuru zadankai" (roundtable discussion). *Chōsen to kenchiku* 10, no. 5 (May 1931): 2–20. Facsimile, *Chōsen to kenchiku*, vol. 17. Seoul: Arŭm, 1995.
"Chōsen shiki jūtaku kenchiku kaizen zadankai" (roundtable discussion). *Chōsen to kenchiku* 10, no. 10 (October 1931): 7–24. Facsimile, *Chōsen to kenchiku*, vol. 18. Seoul: Arŭm, 1995.
Fukushi Matsunosuke. "Kokenchikubutsu hoson no kyoiku-teki kachi." *Chōsen to kenchiku* 10, no. 5 (May 1931): 21–29. Facsimile, *Chōsen to kenchiku*, vol. 17. Seoul: Arŭm, 1995.
Goh Byeong-gwon. "R ŭl ssŭnda." In *Sosusŏng ŭi chŏngch'ihak*, 4–9. Seoul: Gurin B, 2007.
Haag, Andre. "Nakanishi Inosuke to Taishōki Nihon no 'futei senjin' e no manazashi: Taishū disukūru to coroniaru gensetsu no tenpuku." *Ritsumeikan gengo bunka kenkyū* 22, no. 3 (2011): 81–97.
Hayashi Fusao. "Ringo." *Bungei sensen* (February 1926).
———. *Tairiku no hanayome*. Tokyo: Yumani Shobō, 2004.
Hirabayashi Hatsunosuke. "Bungaku hōhōron." In *Gendai Nihon bungaku zenshū*, 78:16–26. Tokyo: Chikuma Shobō, 1957.
Hong Hye-wŏn. *Yi Kwang-su sosŏl ŭi iyagi wa tamron*. Seoul: Ehwa Taehakkyo Ch'ulp'anbu, 2002.
Hwang Chang-yŏp. *Na nŭn yoksa ŭi chilli rŭl pwatta: Hwang Chang-yŏp hoegorok*. Seoul: Hanul, 1999.
Hwang Chong-yŏn. "Sin ŏmnŭn chayŏn." In *Munhak kwa kwahak*, 1:19–56. Seoul: Somyŏng, 2013.
Im Chong-guk. *Ch'inil munhangnon: Ch'inil inmyŏng sajŏn p'yŏnch'an wiwŏnhoe ch'ulbŏm kinyŏmbon*. Seoul: Minjok Munje Yŏn'guso: 2002.
Im Chŏng-jae. "Munsa chegun ege hŭng hanŭn ilmun." In *Han'guk kŭndae riŏllijŭm pip'yŏng sŏnjip*, 11–20. Seoul: Seoul Taehakkyo Ch'ulp'anbu, 1988.
Im Hwa. "Chuch'e ŭi chaegŏn kwa munhak ŭi segye." In *Im Hwa munhak yesul chŏnjip*, 3:46–63.
———. "Hyŏndae pup'ae ŭi p'yojing in in'gan t'amgu wa komin ŭi chŏngsin: Paek Chŏl kun ŭi soron e taehan pip'yŏng." In *Im Hwa munhak yesul chŏnjip*, 1:628–50.
———. "Hyumŏnijŭm nonjaeng ŭi ch'onggyŏlsan." In *Im Hwa yesul chŏnjip*, 3:172–91.

———. "Ilbon nongmin munhak ŭi tonghyang: T'ŭkhi 't'o ŭi munhak' ŭl chungsim ŭro." In *Im Hwa munhak yesul chŏnjip*, 3:630–43.
———. *Im Hwa munhak yesul chŏnjip*. Seoul: Somyŏng, 2009.
———. *Kaesŏl sinmunhaksa*. In *Im Hwa munhak yesul chŏnjip*, 2:9–346.
———. "Nangmanjŏk chŏngsin ŭi hyŏnsiljŏk kujo: Sin ch'angjak iron ŭi chŏngdang han ihae rŭl wi hayŏ." In *Im Hwa munhak yesul chŏnjip*, 3:13–29.
———. "Negŏri ŭi Suni." In *Im Hwa chŏnjip*, 1:52–54.
———. "Sasiljuŭi ŭi chaeinsik: Saeroun munhakjŏk t'amgu e ki hayŏ." In *Im Hwa munhak yesul chŏnjip*, 3:64–85.
———. "Sinmunhaksa ŭi pangbŏp." In *Im Hwa munhak yesul chŏnjip*, 3:647–63.
———. "Usan padŭn Yokkohama ŭi pudu." In *Im Hwa munhak yesul chŏnjip*, 1:70–73.
———. "Widae han nangmanjŏk chŏngsin: Irossŏ chagi rŭl kwanch'ŏl hara!" In *Im Hwa munhak yesul chŏnjip*, 3:30–45.
———. "Yugwŏl chung ŭi ch'angjak." In *Im Hwa munhak yesul chŏnjip*, 1:246–68.
In Chŏng-sik. "Naissen-ittai no bunka-teki rinen." *Quadrante* 7 (2005): 316–19.
———. "Naissen-ittai to gengo." *Quadrante* 7 (2005): 331–32.
Itō Tadahiro. "Keishū ni tsuite." *Chōsen to kenchiku* 10, no. 10 (October 1931): 2–6. Facsimile, *Chōsen to kenchiku*, vol. 18. Seoul: Arŭm, 1995.
Itten, Johannes. "Zuan kyōiku no ichi hōkoku." Translated by Kojima Takashi. *Chōsen to kenchiku* 11, no. 8 (August 1932): 8–13. Facsimile, *Chōsen to kenchiku*, vol. 20. Seoul: Arŭm, 1995.
Kang Kyŏng-ae. *In'gan munje*. In *Kang Kyŏng-ae chŏnjip*, 135–413. Seoul: Somyŏng, 1999.
Kang Man-gil, ed. *Ilbon kwa sŏgu ŭi singmin t'ongch'i pigyo*. Seoul: Sŏn'in Comparative Cultural History Series, 1998.
Kim Hyŏn-ju. *Yi Kwang-su wa munhwa ŭi kihoek*. Seoul: T'aehaksa, 2005.
Kim Ki-jin. "Chibae ŭi kyohwa wa p'ijibae ŭi kyohwa." In *Kim Ki-jin munhak chŏnjip*, 1:479–93.
———. "Chŏlmŭn isangjuŭija ŭi sa." In *Kim Ki-jin munhak chŏnjip*, 4:26–39.
———. *Kim Ki-jin munhak chŏn-jip*. Seoul: Munhak kwa Chisŏngsa, 1988.
———. "Pulgŭn chwi." In *Kim Ki-jin munhak chŏnjip*, 4:11–25.
———. "P'ŭromŭnadŭ sangt'imangt'al." *Kaebyŏk* 37 (July 1923). Reprinted in *Kim Ki-jin munhak chŏn-jip*, 1:409–26.
Kim Kyŏng-mi. "Pot'ong hakkyo chedo ŭi hwangnip kwa hakkyo hunyuk ŭi hyŏngsŏng." In *Ilche ŭi singminji chibae wa ilsangsaenghwal*, 487–88. Seoul: Hyean, 2004.
Kim Nam-ch'ŏn. "Im Hwa-jŏk ch'angjakp'yŏng kwa chagi pip'an." In *Han'guk kŭndae riŏllijŭm pip'yŏng sŏnjip*, edited by Kim Yun-sik, 89–98. Seoul: Seoul Taehakkyo Ch'ulp'anbu, 1988.
———. "Kyŏngyŏng." In *Maek: Kim Nam-ch'ŏn ch'angjakjip*, 223–79. Seoul: Ŭryu Munhwasa, 1988.
———. "Maek." In *Maek: Kim Nam-ch'ŏn ch'angjakjip*, 280–341. Seoul: Ŭryu Munhwasa, 1988.
Kim Sa-ryang. "Chigimi." *Samch'ŏlli* 149 (April 1941).
———. "Chōsen bunka tsūshin." In *Kim Sa-ryang zenshū*, 4:21–30.
———. "Dōitsu no aikoku bungaku." Translated from Korean by Yi Hak-jun. In *Kim Sa-ryang zenshū*, 4:31–35.
———. "Dōitsu no taisen bungaku." Translated from Korean by Yi Hak-jun. In *Kim Sa-ryang zenshū*, 4:36–40.

———. "Dosonran." In *Kim Sa-ryang zenshū*, 1:37–66.
———. "Hebi." In *Kim Sa-ryang zenshū*, 1:105–10.
———. "Hikari no naka ni." In *Kim Sa-ryang zenshū*, 1:11–36.
———. *Kim Sa-ryang zenshū*. Tokyo: Kawade Shobō Shinsha, 1973.
———. "Kusa fukashi." In *Kim Sa-ryang zenshū*, 1:145–69.
———. "Tenma." In *Kim Sa-ryang zenshū*, 1:67–103.
Kim Sŏng-u. "Tosi chut'aek ŭi hyŏngsŏng kwa saenghwal ŭi p'yŏnhwa." In *Ilche ŭi singminji chibae wa ilsangsaenghwal*, 387–441. Seoul: Hyean, 2004.
Kim Tong-in. *Kamja: Kim Tong-in tanp'yŏnsŏn*. Seoul: Munhak kwa Chisŏngsa, 2004.
Kim Yŏng-min. *Han'guk munhak pipy'ŏng nonjaengsa*. Seoul: Han'gilsa, 1992.
Kim Yun-sik, ed. *Han'guk hyŏndae modŏnijŭm pip'yŏng sŏnjip*. Seoul: Seoul Taehakkyo Ch'ulp'anbu, 1988.
———, ed. *Han'guk kŭndae riŏllijŭm pip'yŏng sŏnjip*. Seoul: Seoul Taehakkyo Ch'ulp'anbu, 1988.
———. *Han-il kŭndae munhak ŭi kwallyŏn yangsang sillon*. Seoul: Seoul Taehakkyo Ch'ulp'anbu, 2001.
———. *Ilche malgi Han'guk chakka ŭi ilbonŏ kŭlssŭgiron*. Seoul: Seoul Taehakkyo Ch'ulp'anbu, 2003.
———. "Isik munhangnon pip'an." In *Han'guk kŭndae riŏllijŭm pip'yŏng sŏnjip*, 223–41. Seoul: Seoul Taehakkyo Ch'ulp'anbu, 1988.
———. *Pak Yŏnghŭi yŏn'gu*. Seoul: Yŏrŭmsa, 1989.
Kitagawa Sukehito, ed. *Chōsen koyūshoku jiten*. Seoul: Seiko Hakkōjo, 1932.
Kobayashi Takiji. *Kani Kōsen, Tōseikatsusha*. Tokyo: Shinkosha, 2003.
Kōsaka Masaaki. *Minzoku no tetsugaku*. Tokyo: Iwanami Shoten, 1942.
Kōsaka Masaaki, Nishitani Keiji, Kōyama Iwao, and Suzuki Shigetaka. *Sekaishi-teki tachiba to Nihon* (roundtable discussion). Tokyo: Chūōkōron, 1943.
Kōtoku Shūsui. *Teikokushugi*. Tokyo: Iwanami Shoten, 1964.
Kōyama Iwao. *Bunka ruikeigaku kenkyū*. Tokyo: Kōbundō, 1941.
Kurahara Korehito. "Puroretaria geijutsu no naiyō to keishiki." In *Gendai nihon bungaku zenshū*, 78:180–87. Tokyo: Chikuma Shobō, 1957.
Kuwaki Gen'yoku, *Bunkashugi to shakai mondai*. Tokyo: Shizendō Shoten, 1920.
———. *Bunka to kaizō*. Tokyo: Shimode Shoten, 1921.
———. *Kanto to gendai no tetsugaku*. 3rd ed. Tokyo: Iwanami Shoten, 1932.
———. *Tetsugaku gaisetsu: Mono to ga*. Tokyo: Kaizōsha, 1940.
Kwak Kŭn. "Ch'oe Sŏ-hae ŭi chakp'um segye." In *T'alch'ulgi: T'alch'ulgi: Ch'oe Sŏ-hae tanp'yŏnsŏn*, 410–20. Seoul: Munhak kwa Chisŏngsa, 2004.
Kwŏn Bodŭrae. *Yŏnae ŭi sidae: 1920-yŏndae ch'oban ŭi munhwa wa yuhaeng*. Seoul: Hyŏnsil Munhwa Yŏn'gu, 2003.
Miki Kiyoshi. *Jinseiron nōto*. Tokyo: Sōgensha, 1941.
———. *Pasukaru ni okeru ningen no kenkyū*. Tokyo: Iwanami Shoten, 1980.
———. "Shin nihon no shisō genri." In *Miki Kiyoshi zenshū*, 19:507–33. Tokyo: Iwanami Shoten, 1967.
Mizuno Naoki, ed. *Chōsen sōtoku yūkoku kunji shūsei*, vol. 3. Tokyo: Ryokuin Shobō, 2001.
Munhaksa wa Pip'yŏng Hakhoe, ed. *Ch'oe Sŏ-hae munhak ŭi chaejomyŏng*. Seoul: Kukhak Charyowŏn, 1987.
Nakanishi Inosuke. *Manshū*. Tokyo: Ōzorasha, 1998.

———. *Shokeishū no jinseikan*. Tokyo: Etsuzando, 1924.
Nakano Shigeharu. "Puroretaria geijutsu to wa nanika." In *Kōki puroretaria bungaku hyōronshū*, 1:55–70. Tokyo: Shin Nihon, 1990.
Niizeki Ryōzō. *Kokumin bungaku to sekai bungaku*. Tokyo: Kawade Shobō, 1941.
Nishida Kitarō. "Kōi-teki chokkan." In *Nishida Kitarō zenshū*, 8:541–71. Tokyo: Iwanami Shoten, 1965.
———. "Sōda Kiichirō ni kotau." In *Nishida Kitarō zenshū*, 1:290–323.
O Sŏg-yun. "Nak'ano Sigeharu si e nat'anan Han'gukkwan." *Ilbonhak* 22 (2003): 141–59.
Paek Nam-un. *Chosŏn minjok ŭi chillo, chaeron*. Kyŏnggi-do P'aju-si: Pŏmu, 2007.
———. *Chosŏn sahoe kyŏngjesa*. Translated from Japanese by Sim U-sŏng. Seoul: Tongmunsŏn, 2004.
———. "*Chosŏn sahoe kyŏngjesa* ch'ulp'an e taehan sogam." In *Paek Nam-un chŏnjip*, 4:85–88. Seoul: Iron kwa Silchŏn, 1991.
———. "Kwahak paljŏn ŭi p'ilyŏnsŏng." In *Paek Nam-un chŏnjip*, 4:71–79. Seoul: Iron kwa Silchŏn, 1991.
———. "T'ongje kyŏngje ŭi yullisŏng." Translated from Japanese by Ha Il-sik. In *Paek Nam-un chŏnjip*, 4:278–92. Seoul: Iron kwa Silchŏn, 1991.
Pak T'ae-wŏn. *Sosŏlga Kubo Ssi ŭi iril*. Seoul: Munhak kwa Chisŏngsa, 1998.
Pak Yŏng-hŭi. "Ch'oegŭn munye iron ŭi sinpalgae wa kŭ kyŏnghyang." In *Han'guk kŭndae riŏllijŭm pip'yŏng sŏnjip*, 127–46. Seoul: Seoul Taehakkyo Ch'ulp'anbu, 1989.
———. "Chŏnjaeng kwa Chosŏn munhak." In *Pak Yŏng-hŭi chŏnjip*, vol. 4. Kyŏngbuk Kyŏngsan-si: Yŏngnam Taehakkyo Ch'ulp'anbu, 1997.
———. "Sanyanggae." In *Pak Yŏng-hŭi chŏnjip*, vol. 1. Kyŏngbuk Kyŏngsan-si: Yŏngnam Taehakkyo Ch'ulp'anbu, 1997.
———. "'Sin'gyŏnghyangp'a' munhak kwa 'musanyu' ŭi munhak." In *Han'guk kŭndae riŏllijŭm pip'yŏng sŏnjip*, 46–54. Seoul: Seoul Taehakkyo Ch'ulp'anbu, 1989.
Pang Kie-jung, ed. *Ilcheha chisigin ŭi p'asijŭmch'eje insik kwa taeŭng*. Seoul: Hyean, 2005.
Sasa Keiichi. "Shunbosan hakubunji shinchiku kōji ni tsuite." *Chōsen to kenchiku* 11, no. 11 (November 1932): 6–9. Facsimile, *Chōsen to kenchiku*, vol. 20. Seoul: Arŭm, 1995.
Sata Ineko. *Josei no kotoba; zoku, josei no kotoba*. Tokyo: Yumani Shobō, 2002.
———. "Kyarameru kōjō kara." In *Sata Ineko zenshū*, 1:21–31. Tokyo: Kōdansha, 1977.
"Shin hantō bungaku e no yōbō" (roundtable discussion). *Kokumin bungaku* 3, no. 3 (March 1943): 2–14. Facsimile, *Kokumin bungaku*, vol. 6. Tokyo: Ryokuin Shobō, 1997–98.
Sin Ch'ae-ho. "Chosŏn hyŏngmyŏng sŏnŏn." In *Han'guk kŭndae riŏllijŭm pip'yŏng sŏnjip*, edited by Kim Yun-sik, 1–10. Seoul: Seoul Taekhakkyo Ch'ulp'anbu, 1988.
———. *Chosŏn sanggosa*. Seoul: Pibong, 2008.
Sin Ch'un-ho. *Ch'oe Sŏ-hae: Kungp'ip kwa ŭi munhakjŏk ssaum*. Seoul: Kŏn'guk Taehakkyo Ch'ulp'anbu, 1994.
Sōda Kiichirō. *Bunka kachi to kyokugen gainen*. Tokyo: Iwanami Shoten, 1972.
———. *Sōda Kiichirō zenshū*, vol. 1–5. Tokyo: Iwanami Shoten, 1930–31.
Sŏ In-sik. "'Chisŏng' ŭi chayŏnsŏng kwa yŏksasŏng." In *Sŏ In-sik chŏnjip*, 1:18–50.
———. "Chisŏng ŭi sidaejŏk sŏngkyŏk." In *Sŏ In-sik chŏnjip*, 1:96–113.
———. "Chŏnch'ejuŭi ŭi yŏksagwan." In *Sŏ In-sik chŏnjip*, 1:165–68.
———. "Hyŏndae ŭi kwaje 2: Chŏnhyŏnggi ŭi chesang." In *Sŏ In-sik chŏnjip*, 1:148–64.
———. "Munhwa ŭi kujo rŭl nonsul ham." In *Sŏ In-sik chŏnjip*, 1:51–66.

———. *Sŏ In-sik chŏnjip*. Seoul: Yŏngnak, 2006.

———. "Yŏksa e issŏsŏ ŭi haengdong kwa kwansang: Yŏksa wa yŏngung ŭl malham." In *Sŏ In-sik chŏnjip*, 1:173–89.

Sŏn Chu-wŏn, "Tamron chuch'e ŭi t'ajasŏng ilggi wa sosŏl kyoyuk: Kim Nam-ch'ŏn ŭi 'Kyŏngyŏng' kwa 'Maek' ŭl chungsim ŭro." *Hyŏndae Munhak Yŏn'gu* 22 (2004): 561–87.

Tanabe Hajime. "Bunka no genkai." In *Tanabe Hajime zenshū*, 8:263–305.

———. "Kobetsu-teki inkaritsu no ronri ni tsukite Sōda Kiichirō no kyō wo kou." Reprinted in Sōda Kiichirō, *Bunka kachi to kyokugen gainen*, 191–201.

———. *Rekishi-teki genjitsu*. Tokyo: Kobushi Shobō, 2001.

———. "Shakai sonzai no ronri." In *Tanabe Hajime zenshū*, 6:151–67.

———. "Shu no ronri to sekai zushiki." In *Tanabe Hajime zenshū*, 6:169–264.

———. *Tanabe Hajime zenshū*. Tokyo: Chikuma Shobō, 1963.

———. "Zushiki 'jikan' kara zushiki 'sekai' e." In *Tanabe Hajime zenshū*, 6:1–50.

Tokieda Motoki. *Kokugo genron: gengo kateisetsu no seiritsu to sono tenkai*. Tokyo: Iwanami Shoten, 1974.

Watsuji Testurō. *Fūdō: Ningengaku-teki kōsatsu*. Tokyo: Iwanami Bunko, 1979.

———. *Ningen no gaku to shite no rinrigaku*. Tokyo: Iwanami Shoten, 2007.

Yi Hyŏn-sik. "'Kwadogi' tasi ilgi." In *Han Sŏrya munhak ŭi chaeŭisik*. Seoul: Somyŏng, 2000.

Yi Ki-yŏng. *Kohyang*. Seoul: Munhak Sasangsa, 1994.

Yi Kwang-su. *Chaesaeng*. Seoul: Munhwa Sanŏp Yon'guso, 2005.

———. "Chorŏpsaeng ŭl saenggak hago." In *Yi Kwang-su chŏnjip*, 10:293–98.

———. "Chosŏn minjongnon." In *Yi Kwang-su chŏnjip*, 10:215–19.

——— (Kayama Mitsurō). "*Hei ni nareru*." *Sin Taiyō* (November 1943). Reprinted in *Kindai Chōsen bungaku Nihongo sakuhinshū: 1939–1945, Sōsakushū*, vol. 5, edited by Masuo Ōmura and Toshihiro Hotei, 115–22. Tokyo: Ryokuin Shobō, 2002.

———. *Hŭk*. Seoul: Tong-a, 1995.

———. *Hyŏngmyŏngga ŭi anae: Ch'unwŏn ŭi tanp'yŏnsŏn*. Seoul: Sŏnghan, 1991.

———. *Kaech'ŏkja*. Seoul: Ilsin sŏjŏk, 1995.

———. "Kaein ŭi ilsangsaenghwal ŭi hyŏksin i minjokjŏk palhŭng ŭi kŭnbon ida." In *Yi Kwang-su chŏnjip*, 10:268–71.

———. "Kyoyukka chessi ege." In *Yi Kwang-su chŏnjip*, 10:49–62.

———. *Maŭi t'aeja*. Seoul: Ilsin sŏjŏk, 1995.

———. "Minjok kaejoron." In *Yi Kwang-su chŏnjip*, 10:116–47.

———. "Minjok e kwanhan myŏt kaji saenggak." In *Yi Kwang-su chŏnjip*, 10:219–22.

———. *Mujŏng*. Seoul: Munhak Sasangsa, 1993.

———. "Munhak kwa 'purŭ' wa 'p'uro.'" In *Yi Kwang-su chŏnjip*, 10:440–41.

———. "Pisangsi ŭi pisangin." In *Yi Kwang-su chŏnjip*, 10:213–14.

———. "Saengsagwan." In *Yi Kwang-su chŏnjip*, 10:259–62.

———. "Sinsaenghwallon." In *Yi Kwang-su chŏnjip*, 10:325–51.

———. "Sungmyŏngnonjŏk insaenggwan esŏ chiryŏngnonjŏk insaenggwan e." In *Yi Kwang-su chŏnjip*, 10:47–49.

———. *Tanjong aesa*. Seoul: Sŏngkong Munhwasa, 1993.

———. "Yesugyo ŭi Chosŏn e chun ŭnhye." In *Yi Kwang-su chŏnjip*, 10:17–19.

———. "Yesul kwa insaeng: Sin segye wa Chosŏn minjok ŭi samyŏng." In *Yi Kwang-su chŏnjip*, 10:359–69.

―――. *Yi Kwang-su chŏnjip*. Seoul: Usinsa, 1979.
―――. "Yun Kwang-ho." In *Kubo ssi ŭi ŏlgul*, 24–42. Seoul: Bookfolio, 2004.
Yi Kyŏng-ran. "1930-nyŏndae nongmin sosŏl ŭl t'onghae pon 'singminji kŭndaehwa' wa nongminsaenghwal." In *Ilche ŭi singminji chibae wa ilsangsaenghwal*. Seoul: Hyean, 2004.
Yi Sang (Kim Hae-gyŏng). "Chogamdo." *Chosŏn Chungang Ilbo*, July 24, 1934.
―――. "Chōkanzu." *Chōsen to kenchiku* 10, no. 8 (August 1931): 10–13. Facsimile, *Chōsen to kenchiku*, vol. 18. Seoul: Arŭm, 1995.
―――. "Kenchiku mugen rokumen kakutai." *Chōsen to kenchiku* 11, no. 7 (July 1932): 25–7. Facsimile, *Chōsen to kenchiku*, vol. 20. Seoul: Arŭm, 1995.
―――. "Nalgae." In *Yi Sang munhak t'anpyŏnsŏn*. Seoul: Munhak kwa chisŏngsa, 2005. 268–300.
―――. "Sanjikaku sekkeizu." *Chōsen to kenchiku* 10, no. 10 (October 1931): 29–31. Facsimile, *Chōsen to kenchiku*, vol. 18. Seoul: Arŭm, 1995.
Yokomitsu Riichi. "Chōsen no koto." In *Teihon Yokomitsu Riichi zenshū*, 14:275–77. Tokyo: Kawaide Shobō, 1982.
―――. "Jikan." In *Teihon Yokomitsu Riichi zenshū*, 4:178–92.
―――. "Kikai." In *Teihon Yokomitsu Riichi zenshū*, 3:350–78.
―――. "Shanhai." In *Teihon Yokomitsu Riichi zenshū*, 3:3–246.
―――. "Shōsetsu to jikan." In *Teihon Yokomitsu Riichi zenshū*, 14:166–67.
Yŏm Sang-sŏp. *Mansejŏn*. Seoul: Ch'angjaksa, 1987.
Yoshino Sakuzō. *Chūgoku Chōsenron*. Tokyo: Heibonsha, 1970.
―――, ed. *Meiji bunka kenkyū zenshū*, vol. 1. Tokyo: Nihon Hyōronsha, 1928.
―――. *Mimponshugiron*. Tokyo: Shin Kigensha, 1947.
―――. *Yoshino Sakuzō henshū*. Tokyo: Chikuma Shobō, 1976.

SOURCES IN ENGLISH AND OTHER LANGUAGES

Adorno, Theodor. *Kant's Critique of Pure Reason*. Translated by Rodney Livingstone. Stanford: Stanford University Press, 2001.
―――. *Problems of Moral Philosophy*. Translated by Rodney Livingstone. Stanford: Stanford University Press, 2000.
Adorno, Theodor, and Max Horkheimer. *Dialectic of Enlightenment*. Translated by John Cumming. New York: Continuum, 1991.
Agamben, Giorgio. *Homo Sacer: Sovereignty and Bare Life*. Translated by Daniel Heller-Roazen. Stanford: Stanford University Press, 1998.
―――. *The Man without Content*. Translated by Georgia Albert. Stanford: Stanford University Press, 1999.
Akutagawa Ryūnosuke. "Cogwheels." In *The Essential Akutagawa: Rashomon, Hell Screen, Cogwheels, a Fool's Life, and Other Short Fiction*. Translated by Seiji Lippit. New York: Marsilio, 1999.
Allen, Chizuko. "Northeast Asia Centered around Korea: Ch'oe Nam-sŏn's View of History." *Journal of Asian Studies* 49, no. 4 (1990): 787–806.
Althusser, Louis. *Lenin and Philosophy, and Other Essays*. New York: Monthly Review Press, 2001.

Anderson, Benedict. *Imagined Communities: Reflections on the Origins and Spread of Nationalism.* London: Verso, 2006.
Arendt, Hannah. *The Origins of Totalitarianism.* New York: Harcourt, Brace, Jovanovich, 1973.
Armstrong, Charles. *The North Korean Revolution, 1945–1950.* Ithaca: Cornell University Press, 2004.
Bakhtin, Mikhail. "Forms of Time and of the Chronotope in the Novel." In *The Dialogic Imagination: Four Essays.* Austin: University of Texas Press, 1981.
Balibar, Etienne. *Masses, Classes, Ideas: Studies on Politics and Philosophy before and after Marx.* Translated by James Swenson. London: Routledge, 1994.
Balibar, Etienne, and Immanuel Wallerstein. *Race, Nation, Class: Ambiguous Identities.* Translated by Chris Turner. New York: Verso, 1991.
Bambach, Charles. *Heidegger, Dilthey, and the Crisis of Historicism.* Ithaca: Cornell University Press, 1995.
———. *Heidegger's Roots: Nietzsche, Nationalism Socialism, and the Greeks.* Ithaca: Cornell University Press, 2003.
Barraclough, Ruth. "Tales of Seduction: Factory Girls in Korean Proletarian Literature." *positions: east asia cultures critique* 14, no. 2 (2006): 345–71.
Benedict, Ruth. *The Chrysanthemum and the Sword: Patterns of Japanese Culture.* Boston: Houghton Mifflin, 2005.
———. *Patterns of Culture.* Boston: Houghton Mifflin, 1989.
Benjamin, Walter. *The Origin of German Tragic Drama.* Translated by James Osborne. London: Verso, 2009.
———. "The Translator's Task." Translated by Steven Rendall. In *The Translation Studies Reader,* edited by Lawrence Venuti, 3rd ed., 75–83. London: Routledge, 2012.
———. "The Work of Art in the Age of Its Mechanical Reproducibility: Second Version." In *Walter Benjamin, Selections,* vol. 3, *1935–1938,* edited by Howard Eiland and Michael W. Jennings. Cambridge, MA: Belknap Press of Harvard University, 2006.
Berman, Antoine. *The Experience of the Foreign: Culture and Translation in Romantic Germany.* Translated by S. Heyvaert. Albany: SUNY Press, 1992.
Bogdanov, Alexander. *Essays in Tektology: The General Science of Organization.* Seaside, CA: Intersystems Publications, 1984.
Bowen-Struyk, Heather. "Guest Editor's Introduction: Proletarian Arts in East Asia." *Positions: East Asia Cultures Critique* 14, no. 2 (2006): 251–78.
Buck-Morss, Susan. "Aesthetic and Anaesthetic: Walter Benjamin's Artwork Essay Reconsidered." In *October: The Second Decade, 1986–1996,* 375–86. Cambridge, MA: MIT Press, 1997.
Bukharin, Nicolai. *Historical Materialism: A System of Sociology.* Ann Arbor: Ann Arbor Paperbacks, 1969.
Bürger, Peter. *Theory of the Avant-Garde.* Translated by Michael Shaw. Minneapolis: University of Minnesota Press, 1984.
Ching, Leo T.S. *Becoming Japanese: Colonial Taiwan and the Politics of Identity Formation.* Berkeley: University of California Press, 2001.
Cortázar, Julio. "Axolotl." In *Blow-Up, and Other Stories,* translated by Paul Blackburn, 3–9. New York: Pantheon, 1985.

Cumings, Bruce. *Korea's Place in the Sun: A Modern History.* New York: Norton, 2005.
Debord, Guy. "Introduction to a Critique of Urban Geography." In *Situationist International Anthology,* translated and edited by Ken Knabb, 8–11. Berkeley: Bureau of Public Secrets, 2006.
Deleuze, Gilles. *Cinema 1.* Translated by Hugh Tomlinson and Robert Galeta. Minneapolis: University of Minnesota Press, 1986.
———. *Cinema 2.* Translated by Hugh Tomlinson and Barbara Habberjam. Minneapolis: University of Minnesota Press, 1989.
———. *Difference and Repetition.* Translated by Paul Patton. New York: Columbia University Press, 1995.
Deleuze, Gilles, and Félix Guattari. *Anti-Oedipus: Introduction to Schizoanalysis.* Translated by Robert Hurley, Mark Seem, and Helen R. Lane. Minneapolis: University of Minnesota Press, 1983.
———. *Kafka: Toward a Minor Literature.* Translated by Dana Polan. Minneapolis: University of Minnesota Press, 1986.
De Man, Paul. *Aesthetic Ideology.* Minneapolis: University of Minnesota Press, 2002.
———. *Blindness and Insight: Essays in the Rhetoric of Contemporary Criticism.* Minneapolis: University of Minnesota Press, 1983.
Derrida, Jacques. "Des Tour de Babel." In *Difference in Translation,* edited by Joseph F. Graham, 165–207. Ithaca: Cornell University Press, 1985.
Dobrenko, Evgeny. *Political Economy of Socialist Realism.* Translated by Jesse Savage. New Haven: Yale University Press, 2007.
Driscoll, Mark. *Absolute Erotic, Absolute Grotesque: The Living, Dead, and Undead in Japan's Imperialism, 1895–1945.* Durham: Duke University Press, 2010.
Eagleton, Terry. *The Idea of Culture.* Oxford: Blackwell, 2000.
———. *The Ideology of the Aesthetic.* Cambridge, MA: Basil Blackwell, 1990.
Elias, Norbert. *The Civilizing Process: Sociogenetic and Psychogenetic Investigations.* London: Blackwell, 2000.
Fabian, Johannes. *Time and the Other: How Anthropology Make Its Object.* New York: Columbia University Press, 2014.
Feldman, Matthew. *Ezra Pound's Fascist Propaganda, 1935–1945.* London: Palgrave Macmillan, 2013.
Fichte, J. G. *Addresses to the German Nation.* Translated by R. F. Kelly and J. H. Turnball. Edited by George Armstrong Kelly. New York: Harper and Row, 1968.
———. *Foundations of Transcendental Philosophy (Wissenschaftslehre) Novo Methodo (1796/99).* Translated by Daniel Brazeale. Ithaca: Cornell University Press, 1992.
Foley, Barbara. *Radical Representations: Politics and Form in U.S. Proletarian Fiction, 1929–1941.* Durham: Duke University Press, 1993.
Foucault, Michel. *The Birth of Biopolitics: Lectures at the Collège de France, 1978–1979.* Translated by Graham Burchell. Basingstoke, UK: Palgrave Macmillan, 2008.
———. "Governmentality." In *The Foucault Effect: Studies in Governmentality,* edited by Graham Burchell, Colin Gordon, and Peter Miller, 87–104. Chicago: University of Chicago Press, 1991.
———. *Introduction to Kant's* Anthropology. Translated by Robert Nigro and Kate Briggs. Los Angeles: Semiotext(e), 2008.

———. *The Order of Things.* New York: Vintage, 1973.
———. *Security, Territory, Population: Lectures at the Collège de France, 1977–1978.* Translated by Graham Burchell. Basingstoke, UK: Palgrave Macmillan, 2007.
———. *Society Must Be Defended: Lectures at the Collège de France, 1975–1976.* Translated by David Macey. Basingstoke, UK: Palgrave Macmillan, 2003.
Freud, Sigmund. *Beyond the Pleasure Principle.* Translated by James Strachey. New York: Norton, 1990.
Fujitani, Takashi. *Race for Empire: Koreans as Japanese and Japanese as Americans in World War II.* Berkeley: University of California Press, 2011.
Gentile, Giovanni. *Origins and Doctrine of Fascism: With Selections from Other Works.* Translated by A. James Gregor. New Brunswick, NJ: Transaction, 2004.
Gilman, Nils. *Mandarins of the Future: Modernization Theory in Cold War America.* Baltimore: Johns Hopkins University Press, 2003.
"The Gorky Factor." In *Soviet Culture and Power: A History in Documents, 1917–1953*, edited by Katerina Clark, Evgeny Dobrenko, Andreï Artizov, and Oleg V. Naumov, 179–93. New Haven: Yale University Press, 2007.
Gorky, Maxim. *Gorky Plays.* Vol. 1, *The Lower Depths, Summerfolk, Children of the Sun.* London: Bloomsbury Methuen, 1988.
———. "Soviet Literature." In *Soviet Writers' Congress 1934*, 25–69. London: Lawrence and Wishart, 1977.
Groys, Boris. *The Total Art of Stalinism: Avant-Garde, Aesthetic Dictatorship, and Beyond.* Translated by Charles Rougle. London: Verso, 2011.
Hall, Stuart. "Cultural Identity and Diaspora." In *Identity and Difference*, edited by Kathryn Woodward, 51–59. London: Sage, 1997.
Harootunian, Harry D. *History's Disquiet: Modernity, Cultural Practice, and the Question of Everyday Life.* New York: Columbia University Press, 2000.
———. *Overcome by Modernity: History, Culture, and Community in Interwar Japan.* Princeton: Princeton University Press, 2000.
Harvey, David. "Cosmopolitanism and the Banality of Geographical Evils." *Public Culture* 12, no. 2 (2000): 529–64.
Hegel, G. W. F. *The Phenomenology of Spirit.* Translated by A. V. Miller. Oxford: Oxford University Press, 1977.
———. *The Philosophy of History.* Translated by J. Sibree. New York: Dover, 1956.
———. *Science of Logic.* Translated by George di Giovanni. Cambridge: Cambridge University Press, 2015.
Heidegger, Martin. *Being and Time.* Translated by John MacQuarrie and Edward Robinson. New York: Harper, 1962.
———. *The Question concerning Technology, and Other Essays.* Translated by William Lovitt. New York: Harper and Row, 1977.
Henry, Todd. *Assimilating Seoul: Japanese Rule and the Politics of Public Space in Colonial Korea, 1910–1945.* Berkeley: University of California Press, 2014.
Ialongo, Ernesto. "Filippo Tomaso Marinetti: The Futurist as Fascist, 1929–1937." *Journal of Modern Italian Studies* 18, no. 4 (2013): 393–419.
Inoue Kyoko. *Individual Dignity in Modern Japanese Thought: The Evolution of the Concept of Jinkaku in Moral and Educational Discourse.* Ann Arbor: University of Michigan Center for Japanese Studies, 2001.

Jakobson, Roman. "On the Linguistic Aspects of Translation." In *The Translation Studies Reader*, edited by Lawrence Venuti, 3rd ed., 126–32. London: Routledge, 2012.
Jameson, Frederic. *Fables of Aggression: Wyndham Lewis, the Modernist as Fascist.* Berkeley: University of California Press, 1979.
———. *The Political Unconscious: Narrative as a Socially Symbolic Act.* Ithaca: Cornell University Press, 1982.
———. *A Singular Modernity: Essay on the Ontology of the Present.* London: Verso, 2002.
———. "Third World Literature in the Era of Multinational Capitalism." *Social Text* 15 (1986): 65–88.
Kang Kyŏng-ae. *From Wonso Pond.* Translated by Samuel Perry. New York: Feminist Press at CUNY, 2009.
Kant, Immanuel. *Anthropology from a Pragmatic Point of View.* Translated by Robert B. Louden. Cambridge: Cambridge University Press, 2006.
———. *The Critique of Judgment.* Translated by Werner S. Pluhar. Indianapolis: Hackett, 1987.
———. *The Critique of Practical Reason.* Translated by Werner S. Pluhar. Indianapolis: Hackett, 2002.
———. *The Critique of Pure Reason.* Translated by Werner S. Pluhar. Indianapolis: Hackett, 1998.
———. *Education.* Translated by Annette Charton. Ann Arbor: University of Michigan Press, 1960.
———. *Groundwork of the Metaphysics of Morals.* Translated by Mary Gregor. Cambridge: Cambridge University Press, 1998.
———. "Idea for a Universal History with a Cosmopolitan Purpose." In *Kant: Political Writings*, edited by H. S. Reiss, 41–53. Cambridge: Cambridge University Press, 1991.
———. "On the Different Races of Man." In *Race and the Enlightenment: A Reader*, edited by Emmanuel Chukwudi Eze, 38–48. London: Wiley-Blackwell, 1997.
———. "Perpetual Peace: A Philosophical Sketch." In *Kant: Political Writings*, edited by H. S. Reiss, 93–130. Cambridge: Cambridge University Press, 1991.
Karatani Kōjin. "Nationalism and Écriture." *Surfaces* 5 (1995): 5–25.
———. *Origins of Modern Japanese Literature.* Edited by Brett de Bary. Durham: Duke University Press, 1993.
Kim, Alan. "Paul Natorp." *Stanford Encyclopedia of Philosophy*, Fall 2008 edition, edited by Edward N. Zalta. http://plato.stanford.edu/archives/fall2008/entries/natorp.
Kim, John Namjun. "On the Brink of Universality: German Cosmopolitanism in Japanese Imperialism." *Positions: East Asia Cultures Critique* 17, no. 1 (2009): 73–95.
Kim Sa-ryang. *Heinrich Heine als Romantiker.* Graduation thesis, Tokyo Imperial University, 1939.
Kim Yun-sik. "KAPF Literature in Modern Korean Literary History." Translated by Yoon Sun Yang. *Positions: East Asia Cultures Critique* 14, no. 2 (2006): 405–25.
Kobayashi Takiji. *"The Factory Ship" and "Absentee Landlord."* Translated by Frank Motofuji. Seattle: University of Washington Press, 1973.
Kwon, Nayoung Aimee. "Collaboration, Coproduction, Code-Switching." *Cross Currents: East Asian History and Culture Review* 2, no. 1 (2013): 10–40.
Le Bon, Gustav. *The Crowd: A Study in the Popular Mind.* Mineola, NY: Dover, 2002.
———. *The Psychology of Socialism.* New Brunswick, NJ: Transaction, 2003.

Lee Ji-won. "An Chaehong's Thought and the Politics of the United Front." In *Landlords, Peasants, and Intellectuals in Modern Korea*, edited by Pang Kie-chung and Michael D. Shin. Ithaca: Cornell East Asia Series, 2005.

Lenin, V. I. *Imperialism: The Highest Stage of Capitalism*. New York: International Publishers, 1939.

———. *Materialism and Empirio-Criticism: Critical Notes concerning a Reactionary Philosophy*. Translated by David Kvitko. In *Collected Works of V. I. Lenin*, vol. 13. New York: International Publishers, 1927.

———. "On Proletarian Culture." In *Collected Work*s, 4th ed., 31:300–13. Moscow: Progress Publishers, 1965.

Lefevbre, Henri. *The Production of Space*. Translated by Donald Nicolson Smith. London: Blackwell, 1991.

Lewis, Wyndham. *Hitler*. London: Chatto and Windus, 1931.

Lippit, Seiji. *Topographies of Japanese Modernism*. New York: Columbia University Press, 2002.

Lukács, Georg. *History and Class Consciousness*. Translated by Rodney Livingstone. Cambridge, MA: MIT Press, 1971.

Luxemburg, Rosa. *The Accumulation of Capital*. London: Routledge, 2003.

Lyotard, Jean-François. *The Postmodern Condition: A Report on Knowledge*. Translated by Geoff Bennington. Minneapolis: University of Minnesota Press, 1984.

Marx, Karl. "The German Ideology." In *The Marx-Engels Reader*, edited by Robert C. Tucker, 146–200. New York: Norton, 1978.

———. *Grundrisse: Foundations of the Critique of Political Economy*. Translated by Martin Nicolaus. New York: Vintage, 1973.

———. "So-Called Primitive Accumulation." In *Capital: Volume One*, translated by Ben Fowkes, 873–942. London: Penguin, 1992.

———. "Theses on Feuerbach." In *The Marx-Engels Reader*, edited by Robert C. Tucker, 143–15. New York: Norton, 1978.

Menger, Anton. *Right to the Whole Produce of Labor: The Origin and Development of the Theory of Labour's Claim to the Whole Product of Industry*. Translated by M. E. Tanner. New York: A. Kelley, 1962.

Mies, Maria. *Patriarchy and Accumulation on a World Scale: Women in the International Division of Labor*. London: Zed Books, 1998.

Mills, Charles. *The Racial Contract*. Ithaca: Cornell University Press, 1999.

Mirabile, Andrea. "Allegory, Pathos, and Irony: The Resistance to Benjamin in Paul de Man." *German Studies Review* 35, no. 2 (2012): 319–33.

Nakano Shigeharu. *Three Works by Nakano Shigeharu*. Translated by Brett de Bary. Ithaca: Cornell East Asia Series, 1979.

Oakes, Guy. "Introduction: Rickert's Theory of Historical Knowledge." In *The Limits of Concept Formation in the Natural Sciences: An Introduction to the Historical Sciences*, by Heinrich Rickert, edited by Guy Oakes, vii–xxx. Cambridge: Cambridge University Press, 1986.

Oppenheim, Robert. *Kyongju Things*. Ann Arbor: University of Michigan Press, 2008.

Osborne, Peter. *How to Read Marx*. London: Norton, 2006.

Ozaki Makoto. *Individuum, Society, and Humankind: The Triadic Logic of Species according to Hajime Tanabe*. Boston: Brill, 2001.

Park, Hyun Ok. *Two Dreams in One Bed: Empire, Social Life, and the Origins of the North Korean Revolution in Manchuria*. Durham: Duke University Press, 2005.
Park, Sunyoung. "The Colonial Origins of Korea Realism and Its Contemporary Manifestation." *Positions: East Asia Cultures Critique* 14, no. 1 (2006): 165–92.
———. "Everyday Life as Critique in Late Colonial Korea: Kim Nam-ch'ŏn's Literary Experiments, 1934–1943." *Journal of Asian Studies* 68, no. 3 (2009): 861–93.
Parry, Carl E. Review of Sōda Kiichirō's *The Logical Nature of Economic Laws*. *American Economic Review* 2, no. 3 (1912): 607–8.
Poole, Janet. *When the Future Disappears: The Modernist Imagination in Late Colonial Korea*. New York: Columbia University Press, 2014.
Poulantzas, Nicos. *Fascism and Dictatorship: The Third International and the Problem of Fascism*. Translated by Judith White. London: Verso, 1979.
Rickert, Heinrich. *Das Eine, die Einheit, und die Eins: Bemerkungen zur Logik der Zahlbegriffs*. Tübingen: Mohr, 1924.
———. *Kant als Philosoph der Modernen Kultur*. Tübingen: Mohr, 1924.
———. *Kulturwissenschaft und Naturwissenschaft*. Freiburg: J. C. B. Mohr, 1899.
———. *The Limits of Concept Formation in the Natural Sciences: A Logical Introduction to the Historical Sciences*. Translated by Guy Oakes. London: Cambridge University Press, 1986.
Robinson, Michael. *Cultural Nationalism in Colonial Korea*. Seattle: University of Washington Press, 1989.
———. "National Identity and the Thought of Sin Ch'ae-ho: *Sadaejuŭi* and *Chuch'e* in Thought and History." *Journal of Korean Studies* 5 (1984): 121–42.
Ross, Kristin. "Rimbaud and the Transformation of Social Space." *Yale French Studies* 97 (2000): 36–54.
Said, Edward. *Orientalism*. New York: Vintage, 1979.
Sakai, Naoki. "Subject and Substratum: On Japanese Imperial Nationalism." *Cultural Studies* 14, nos. 3, 4 (2000): 462–530.
———. *Translation and Subjectivity: On "Japan" and Cultural Nationalism*. Minneapolis: University of Minnesota Press, 1997.
———. "Translation and the Figure of the Border: Toward the Apprehension of Translation as a Social Action." *Profession* (2010): 25–34.
———. *Voices of the Past: the Status of Language in Eighteenth-Century Japanese Discourse*. Ithaca: Cornell University Press, 1992.
———. "'You Asians': On the Historical Role of the West and Asia Binary." In *Japan after Japan: Social and Cultural Life from the Recessionary 1990s to the Present*, edited by Tomiko Yoda and Harry Harootunian, 167–94. Durham: Duke University Press, 2006.
Schmid, Andre. *Korea between Empires, 1895–1919*. New York: Columbia University Press, 2002.
———. "Rediscovering Manchuria: Sin Ch'aeho and the Politics of Territorial History in Korea." *Journal of Asian Studies* 56, no. 1 (1997): 26–46.
Schmitt, Carl. *The Concept of the Political*. Translated by George Schwab. Chicago: University of Chicago Press, 2007.
Shih, Shu-mei. *The Lure of the Modern: Writing Modernism in Semi-Colonial China, 1912–1937*. Berkeley: University of California Press, 2000.

Shin, Gi-wook, and Michael Robinson, eds. *Colonial Modernity in Korea*. Cambridge, MA: Harvard University Press, 1999.
Shin, Michael D., and Pang Kie-jung, eds. *Landlords, Peasants, and Intellectuals*. Ithaca: Cornell East Asia Series, 2004.
Silva, Denise Ferreira da. *Toward a Global Idea of Race*. Minneapolis: University of Minnesota Press, 2007.
Silverberg, Miriam. *Changing Song: The Marxist Manifestoes of Nakano Shigeharu*. Princeton: Princeton University Press, 1990.
Simmel, Georg. *Philosophy of Money*. Translated by David Frisby. New York: Routledge, 2004.
Skempton, Simon. *Alienation after Derrida*. London: Continuum, 2010.
Sochor, Zenovia A. *Revolution and Culture: The Bogdanov-Lenin Controversy*. Ithaca: Cornell University Press, 1988.
Sōda Kiichirō. *Geld und Wert*. Tübingen: Mohr, 1909.
———. *Die logische Natur der Wirtschaftsgesetze*. Stuttgart: Verlag von Ferdinand Enke, 1911.
Spivak, Gayatri. *The Critique of Postcolonial Reason: Toward a History of the Vanishing Present*. Cambridge, MA: Harvard University Press, 1999.
Stalin, Joseph. "Concerning Questions of Leninism" (1926). In *Works*, 8:13–96. Moscow: Foreign Language Publishing House, 1954.
———. "Marxism and the National Question" (1913). In *Works*, vol. 2. Moscow: Foreign Language Publishing House, 1954.
Sternhell, Zeev. *Neither Right nor Left: Fascist Ideology in France*. Translated by David Maisel. Princeton: Princeton University Press, 1995.
Suh, Serk-Bae. *Treacherous Translation: Culture, Nationalism, and Colonialism in Korea and Japan from the 1910s to the 1960s*. Berkeley: Global, Area, and International Archive, 2013.
Tansman, Alan. *The Aesthetics of Japanese Fascism*. Berkeley: University of California Press, 2009.
Thornber, Karen Laura. *Empire of Texts in Motion: Korean, Chinese, and Taiwanese Transculturations of Japanese Literature*. Cambridge, MA: Harvard University Asia Center, 2009.
Treat, John Whittier. "Choosing to Collaborate: Yi Kwang-su and the Moral Subject in Colonial Korea." *Journal of Asian Studies* 71, no. 1 (February 2012): 81–102.
———. "Introduction to Yi Kwang-su's 'Maybe Love' (*Ai ka*, 1909)," *Azalea: Journal of Korean Literature and Culture* 4 (2011): 315–20.
Trotsky, Leon. *Literature and Revolution*. Translated by Rose Strunsky. Chicago: Haymarket, 2005.
———. *Permanent Revolution & Results and Prospects*. London: International Marxists Group, 2007.
Wall-Romagna, Christophe. *Cinepoetry: Imaginary Cinemas in French Poetry*. New York: Fordham University Press, 2013.
Workman, Travis. "Sŏ In-sik's Communism and the East Asian Community." *positions: asia critique* 21, no. 1 (2013): 133–60.

———. "Stepping into the Newsreel: Melodrama and Mobilization in Colonial Korean Film." *Cross-Currents: East Asian History and Culture Review* 3, no. 1 (2014): 153–84.

Yi Kwang-su. "Maybe Love." Translated by John Whittier Treat. *Azalea: Journal of Korean Literature and Culture* 4 (2011): 321–27.

———. "What Is Literature?" Translated by Jooyeon Rhee. *Azalea: Journal of Korean Literature and Culture* 4 (2011): 293–313.

———. *Yi Kwang-su and Modern Korean Literature: Mujong*. Translated by Ann Sung-hi Lee. Ithaca: Cornell East Asia Series, 2005.

Yokomitsu Riichi. *Shanghai*. Translated by Dennis Washburn. Ann Arbor: University of Michigan East Asia Series, 2001.

Yoshimi Yoshiaki. *Comfort Women: Sexual Slavery in the Japanese Military during World War II*. Translated by Suzanne O'Brien. New York: Columbia University Press, 2000.

INDEX

Absentee Landlord, The (Kobayashi), 161
"absolute values," 4, 249n9
Adorno, Theodor, 252n46, 254n39, 265n27
"Advice to the Litterateurs" (Im Chŏng-jae), 94–95
aesthetics, 52, 63, 70, 179; "cooperative beauty" and, 189; developmental models and, 99; experience of unity and, 80; Marxist, 108; nineteenth-century realist, 126; politics and morality collapsed into, 83; self-legislated morality and, 64
Agamben, Giorgio, 99
Akutagawa Ryūnosuke, 215
alienation, 85, 92, 216, 248; of the colonial intellectual, 84; of colonial modernity, 193; human essence as laborer and, 130; human self-alienation, 25, 217; of labor, 9, 166; of modern writer, 227; as permanent condition, 215, 248; from the present, 228; proletariat and, 128, 131; sublated through immersion in warfare, 229
allegory, literary, 82, 84–92, 137, 139–140, 262n11; ambiguous identity and, 208, 210–11; chronotopes and, 140–42, 145–47; in cinematic literature, 224; in proletarian literature, 148, 149, 152; translation and, 196
Althusser, Louis, 161, 176
anarchism, 94, 113, 114, 146
An Chung-gŭn, 234
An Ham-gwang, 90, 126, 128, 153, 205; "On the Characteristics and Direction of Korean Literature," 167; inclusive Japanese nation-state and, 169
An Hosang, 6, 250n15
anthropocentrism, 6, 7, 250n19; break from and return to, 167, 174, 223; cultural values and, 47; human as subject-object of knowledge, 19; Kantian, 174; Linné's binomial taxonomy and, 11; literature and, 108; transcendentality of, 21; Western worldview associated with, 173–74; world history and, 19
anthropology, 8, 12–13, 20, 38, 46, 139, 233; biopolitics and, 65; center–periphery relation and, 153; colonial Other and, 12, 13; cultural, 5, 17, 19, 56, 236, 250n12; of culturalism, 60; essentialist, 223; ethnology distinguished from, 11; genus-being and, 84; imperial space and, 190; Korean nation connected to world through, 64; Marxism and, 111; non-West as object of empirical knowledge, 3; "originary anthropology," 21; philosophical, 134, 135, 173; world-historical state and, 171
Anthropology from a Pragmatic Point of View (Kant), 19, 20–21, 37, 135–36, 170
An U-sik, 208
Aono Suekichi, 96, 98–99, 113, 142, 143
"Apple" (Hayashi Fusao), 148
Arai Tetsu (Uchino Kenji), 23, 31, 57, 58, 60–61; "The Magic of Architecture," 58–59

293

architecture, 57, 58–60, 121, 214; cinepoetic space of Yi Sang and, 240–48; culturalism and architectural space, 229–240, 237, 239
area studies, 57, 61
Arendt, Hannah, 254n51
Ariyoshi Chūichi, 29, 30, 33, 34, 39
Arnold, Matthew, 76, 256n43
"Art and Life: The New World and the Mission of the Korean Nation" (Yi Kwang-su), 70–71, 72
Asagawa Noritaka, 236
"Asiatic Mode of Production" (AMP), 128, 139
assimilation, 28, 40, 188; cosmopolitan, 58; genus-being and, 66; modernization and colonial assimilation, 215; osmotic expression of, 176–180; status of ethnic minorities in Japanese empire and, 65, 85
"Axolotl" (Cortázar), 200

Bakhtin, Mikhail, 134, 138
Balibar, Etienne, 11, 79
Barbusse, Henri, 119
"Barley" (Kim Nam-ch'ŏn), 203, 204–206
Bauhaus, 232, 233
Beginnings of Art, The (Grosse), 117
Behne, Adolf, 232
Behrens, Peter, 232
Being and Time (Heidegger), 137, 188
Benedict, Ruth, 250n12
Benjamin, Walter, 84, 139, 194, 236
Bildung (subject formation), 20, 116, 117; bourgeois idea of, 98; proletarian, 24, 101, 108, 113, 121, 127
bilingual writing, 58, 59, 60, 192–96, 240, 247
biology, 38
biopolitics, 22, 30, 72, 77, 87; cosmopolitan humanism and, 65; of culturalism, 41, 71, 74–75, 245; culture and, 78; neo-Kantianism and, 91
"Bird's-Eye View" (Yi Sang), 214
"Bloody Flames" (Ch'oe Sŏ-hae), 158
"Blueprint for a Three-Dimensional Shape" (Yi Sang), 241–48
Bogdanov, Alexander, 109, 110–11, 113
bourgeoisie: art and personhood in relation to, 94–95; colonial, 88, 94; individualism of, 93, 96; proletariat opposed to, 104; urban petit-bourgeoisie, 90
Brothers Karamazov (Dostoevsky), 159
Buddhism, architecture and, 235–36
Bukharin, Nikolai, 121, 122
Bungei sensen (journal), 148
Bungei shuto (journal), 212
Bürger, Peter, 215
Byron, Lord, 183

Camus, Albert, 216
Capital (Marx), 145, 205
capitalism, 4, 7, 24, 47, 161; allegorical literature and, 144; conflict between bourgeoisie and proletariat, 117–18; division of labor and, 110; estranged labor and, 10; fascism and, 91; imperialist phase of, 149, 150; individualism and, 183; internationalism and, 184; limit of, 43; mechanical temporality of, 228; modernization of, 88; philosophy of money and, 42–43; political economic critique of, 96; primitive accumulation and, 162; progressive dialectic of history and, 105; "second nature" of, 47; stage theory of history and, 23, 128, 129, 131; theory of surplus value, 145; transition from feudal relations to, 100–101; transition to socialism from, 122, 123; "uneven development" in, 111–12; world history and, 205
Capital News, 15
categorical imperative, 34, 35
causality, 43, 44, 116, 253n30; culturalist, 71, 75; expressive, 176, 213; in history of literature, 115; mechanistic, 176; in natural science, 48; nature–culture divide and, 75
Chang Hyŏk-ju, 192
China, 80, 120, 163, 215, 226; Kando border region and, 156; Korea's independence from, 15; Yanbian Korean autonomous prefecture, 154
Ching, Leo, 24, 174–75, 196, 197
Ch'oe Chae-sŏ, 175, 180–193, 216, 229, 247, 266n58; "The Expansion and Deepening of Realism," 219–222; *Korean Literature in a Time of Transition*, 181, 222; "people's standpoint" theory of, 24, 180–82, 186, 188, 196, 197; reactionary modernism of, 222–23; "What Is Poetic?," 188–89
Ch'oe Nam-sŏn, 23, 56–57, 124, 129
Ch'oe Sŏ-hae, 24, 125, 142, 153–160
Ch'oe Sŏ-hae, works of: "Bloody Flames," 158; "The Death of Pak Dol," 159; "Farewell," 156; "Native Land," 157; "Paekkŭm," 156; "Record of Escape," 157–58; "Starvation and Slaughter," 158–59
Chŏng Chin-sŏp, 124
Chŏng Sŭng-un, 102
Chosŏn period (1392–1897), 55, 63, 78, 89; feudal class relations of, 81, 129; literature of, 193
Christianity, 79, 182; Christian ethics, 76; *han'gul* writing in Korea and, 54; Korean national language and, 54–55; secularized Christian humanism, 78

chronotopes, 84, 101, 148, 218; allegorical literature and, 140–42, 145–47, 152; in Ch'oe Sŏ-hae stories, 153, 156, 160; of frontier expansion, 161; gender and, 165; humanism and, 134–39; stage theory of history and, 162
cinema, 24–25, 218; cinepoetic space of Yi Sang, 240–48; death of Euclidean space and, 243; ecstatic time of cinematic literature, 219–229
citizenship (*kokuseki*), 188
city–country divide, 105
civilization, discourse of, 13–18, 65, 69–70, 73, 164; imperialism and, 145; Japan's place in world civilization, 75
Clarté movement, 119
class, social, 14, 81, 92, 127, 128, 209
class consciousness, 7, 96, 97, 123, 148; allegories of, 218; proletarian arts movements and, 101
Climate and Culture (Watsuji), 21
Cold War, 5, 6
collectivism, 29
colonialism, 7, 13, 27, 63, 131, 175; colonial education, 54, 75–76; German colonialism in Africa, 52, 254n51; hybridity and colonial violence, 211; identity formations and, 209; Japan at war with European colonialism, 206; self–other dichotomy and, 93; settler colonialism in Hokkaido, 150
communism, 43, 100, 103, 112, 146, 199; African American struggles in American South and, 123; Comintern, 122, 131; in Japanese proletarian literature, 149–152; Korean communists in Japan, 103; stage theory of history and, 128
Confucianism, 55, 63, 73, 82, 87; collapse of Confucian social order, 141; Confucian schools as "natural education," 76; male–female relationships freed from dictates of, 88; morality without free will, 81
consciousness, 185, 188, 216, 220; as object of historical arts and sciences, 114; spontaneous, 113, 143, 149, 160. *See also* class consciousness
consciousness, purposive, 7, 110, 113, 114, 118; allegorical literature and, 146; in colonial Korea, 142; fate contrasted to, 68; Kant's teleology and, 115; as Marxist-Leninist idea, 110; New Tendency Group and, 155, 159; proletarian literature and, 143, 144; "proletarian nation" concept and, 96–97; role of vanguard intellectual and, 151; "spontaneous consciousness" distinguished from, 113, 149; spontaneous revolts and, 145

"Consciousness of Nature" (Kim Hwan), 140
conservatism, 36
"Content and Form of Proletarian Art, The" (Kurahara), 117
Continent Bride (Hayashi), 152
Cortázar, Julio, 200
cosmopolitanism, 4, 21, 65, 66, 83, 136; abstract and ahistorical, 8; Christian, 16; cultural science and, 37; denationalized, 183; in Germany, 42, 52; Korean national self-consciousness and, 23; liberal Japanese reformers and, 26; minority's selfhood and, 85; nation-state and, 181; role of literature and, 80–83; as technology of colonial rule, 22; as unification of humanity, 27
Crab Cannery Ship, The (Kobayashi), 134, 147–152
Creation (journal), 140
Crime and Punishment (Dostoevsky), 159
Criticism (journal), 119
Critique of Judgment (Kant), 179
Critique of Pure Reason (Kant), 44–45, 138
Cubism, 231
cultural housing (*bunka jūtaku*), 236, 238, 240, 247
culturalism, 2, 4, 12–13, 167, 250n15; anthropocentric space-time of, 218; architectural space and, 229–240, 237, 239; biopolitics and, 41, 71, 74–75, 245; cinematic literature and, 220–21; colonial dimension of, 18, 39, 137, 214–15; cosmopolitanism of, 6, 24, 40, 56, 168, 247–48; critiques of, 92–97; cultural policy and, 26–31; culture of daily life and, 184; external borders as internal borders, 59; genus-being (*Gattungswesen*) and, 13; geographical determinism of, 129; intertextuality with proletarian arts, 113, 115; Japanese imperial project and, 53; limits of, 23, 43, 61; moralistic governmentality of, 106; national language and, 49; nations in, 17; neo-Kantianism and, 6–7, 21; "new woman" and, 88; shift from model of civilization, 14; teleology of, 98
Culturalism and Social Problems (Kuwaki), 1, 3, 4, 36, 37
cultural nationalism, 16, 40, 56, 129; center-periphery relation and, 153; compatibility with Japanese colonial rule, 66; modernization project of, 155; nation (*minjok*) concept in, 69
cultural policy, in Korea, 8, 14, 56, 135; architecture and, 238; cosmopolitanism and colonial rule, 22; critiques of, 93; culturalism and, 26–31; institution of (1919), 66; Korean language banned in schools, 54; philosophical origin of, 33

cultural science, 34, 110, 114; colonized Korean intellectuals and, 54; cosmopolitan ethos and, 37; epistemological divide with natural science, 116; limit concept in, 43, 45; neo-Kantianism and, 2, 6–7, 42, 68
Cultural Value and the Limit Concept (Sōda), 44, 45
"Cultural Value as Limit Concept" (Sōda), 46
culture, 7, 8, 22, 30, 55, 67, 179; bourgeois, 126, 146; cultural preservation as reification of the past, 246; economies and, 42; higher unity of, 97; labor conflated with, 127; mass view of, 94–95; in neo-Kantian philosophy, 32; self-determination and, 192; Soviet debates on, 108–12; teleological principle and, 47; universal and national, 125. *See also* general culture; nature–culture divide; world culture
Culture and Reconstruction (Kuwaki), 36
Cumings, Bruce, 268n96

Dante Alighieri, 53
Darwin, Charles, 38
Dasein, of Heidegger, 177, 188, 217
"Death of a Young Idealist" (Kim Ki-jin), 145
"Death of Pak Dol, The" (Ch'oe Sŏ-hae), 159
De Bary, Brett, 105
Debord, Guy, 270n35
Deleuze, Gilles, 175, 176, 200, 218, 219
De Man, Paul, 84, 139
democracy/democratization, 41, 66; imperialism and, 67; of Taishō period, 6, 16, 37
Derrida, Jacques, 194
dialectic, 176, 177, 192, 209, 243
Dictionary of the Intrinsic Colors of Korea, The, 57
Difference and Repetition (Deleuze), 176
differences: architecture and national difference, 233; equivalence-in-difference, 194, 195; ethnic difference, 24; genus-being as evacuation of, 9; Hegelian philosophy and, 176; internal ethnic and cultural, 212; myth and social difference, 61; national language and, 50; spatiotemporal unity of the world and, 219
Dilthey, Wilhelm, 205, 206
Dobrenko, Evgeny, 124
"Dosonran" (Kim Sa-ryang), 212
Dostoevsky, Fyodor, 159

Eagleton, Terry, 17
East Asian Community, 109, 130, 162, 189; as cosmopolitan project, 207; differentiated from European fascism, 170; Hegelian ideas and, 204; proletarian culture and, 132–33; shared cultural tradition of, 173; universality of, 11

Economic History of Korean Society, The (Paek Nam-un), 128
education, 67, 78; colonial education in Korea, 54, 75–76; mechanism in, 76, 256n43; natural and cultural, 75, 76; of women, 73–74
ego: boundary with nonego, 180; Fichtean, 62, 67, 70; of past and present, 178–79
Einstein, Albert, 213, 241
Eisenstein, Sergei, 221
Eliot, T. S., 181, 188
emotions, 55, 64, 81, 106; "common emotion ", 82; educational process and, 71; freed from Confucian hierarchies, 81; modernization of, 88; moral training and, 77; socialization of, 121; world human community and, 67
empiricism, 33
empirico-transcendental doublet, 32, 35, 65–66, 99, 221; allegory and, 84; chronotopes and, 134, 138, 139; European representations of Asia and, 37; fascism and, 168; genus-being (*Gattungswesen*) and, 19, 20; limits of, 22; literature and, 125; Marxism and, 100
Empirio-Monism (Bogdanov), 110
Enlightenment, 176, 187
epistemology, 42, 48; anthropocentric, 99, 108, 230; humanist, 110; Kantian, 19; limit concept and, 49; natural science versus cultural science, 68; natural-scientific, 39, 40; subjectivity and, 126–27; transcendental, 41
Era of Love, The (Kwŏn Bodŭrae), 155
Essence of One-Nationism (An), 250n15
Ethics as the Study of the Human (Watsuji), 21, 134
ethnicity, 127, 128, 171
ethnic nationalism, 28, 37, 68, 129, 228, 266n58; Cold War view of, 6; fascism compared with, 169; formation after World War II, 5; in Germany, 52; Korean, 40
ethnocentrism, 28, 169, 187
ethnology, 11
Eurocentrism, 21, 204
Europe, 5, 12, 22; antifascist movements in, 126; fascism in, 131, 169, 170
Evergreen (Sim Hun), 90
evolution, theory of, 38
"Expansion and Deepening of Realism, The" (Ch'oe Chae-sŏ), 219–222
expressionism, 232

"Faces Change" (Yi Kwang-su), 80
"Farewell" (Ch'oe Sŏ-hae), 156
Farrar, Geraldine, 1, 2

fascism, 65, 78, 97, 167, 203; aesthetic of blood and soil, 90, 187; aesthetics and, 83; ecstatic temporality and, 214, 217; ethnocentric state and, 169; Italian Fascism, 168, 169; melodrama and, 199, 203, 223; modernism and, 216, 217, 223, 228; moral humanist aesthetic of, 198, 199; nationalist rural nostalgia and, 163; organicist ideology of, 169; as petit-bourgeois anticapitalism, 184; planned economy and, 131. *See also* National Socialism
feminism, 133
feudal society, 81, 88, 128, 131, 146; maintained by Japanese colonial rule, 163; nostalgia for, 245; primitive accumulation and, 166; Renaissance humanism and, 183
Feuerbach, Ludwig, 9, 98, 99
Fichte, Johann Gottlieb, 62, 67, 70, 73, 76, 256n43
Foley, Barbara, 123, 148
folklore studies, 253n14
Foucault, Michel, 12, 13–14, 32; on anthropocentrism in modern thought, 250n19; on "governmentality," 18, 34, 78; on Kant's *Anthropology*, 20, 46; on knowledge and the human, 19; *The Order of Things*, 12, 22
free will, 35, 81
Freud, Sigmund, 226
"From the Caramel Factory" (Sata Ineko), 148
"From the Schema of 'Time' to the Schema of 'World'" (Tanabe), 177, 241
From Wonso Pond [*Human Problems*] (Kang Kyŏng-ae), 138, 146–47, 164–66
Fuchs, Carl Johannes, 43, 50, 51
Futurism, 231

Gattungswesen. See genus-being (*Gattungswesen*)
gender, 5, 9, 72, 92, 127; identity formations and, 209; same-sex relations, 100
general culture (*ippan bunka*), 4, 9, 81, 249n9; organicist theory of, 35; unity of Japanese and Korean culture within, 39
Gentile, Giovanni, 168
genus-being (*Gattungswesen*), 17, 18–19, 30, 116, 126, 247; assimilation and, 66; as cosmopolitan subject, 79; cultural formation of proletarian class subject and, 123; culturalism and, 39; Feuerbach's abstract essentializing of, 98; ideologies of practice and, 18, 19; industrial proletariat and, 99; Linnaean taxonomy and, 170; logic of, 6–13; of morality, 31; nation-state as worldly representative of, 229; nation-state subjectivity and, 18, 128, 167; race as "stem-genus" (*Stammgattung*),

20–21, 251n26; self-legislated morality and, 34, 41; "species-being" versus "genus-being," 10–11, 251n22; stage theory of history and, 23, 128–132, 162; transcendental philosophy of culture and, 46, 84; violence and exploitation legitimated by, 215
geography, 21, 56, 129, 233
geometry: Cartesian, 213; Euclidean, 213, 221, 231, 241, 242–43, 246
German idealist philosophy, 16, 67, 127, 131, 202. *See also* life philosophy (*Lebensphilosophie*); neo-Kantianism
"German Ideology, The" (Marx), 131
German language, 52, 191; Japanese intellectuals' writings in, 23, 42, 50; Luther's translation of the Bible and, 54, 254n56; status as world scientific language, 50
Germany, 1, 37, 42; cultural relativists in, 51–52; neo-Kantian liberals in, 27–28; socialist and communist movements in, 43
Gide, André, 126
Goebbels, Josef, 186
Goethe, Johann Wolfgang, 12, 42, 187
Gorky, Maxim, 126, 199, 200, 201
governmentality, 18, 22, 34, 40; colonial, 19, 182; human genus-being and, 68; individual ethics and, 78
Great Chain of Being, 12
Greater East Asian Co-Prosperity Sphere, 109, 130, 131
Grimm, Hans, 187
Grosse, Ernst, 117
Groys, Boris, 215
Guattari, Félix, 175, 200, 218

Hall, Stuart, 211
Hani Gorō, 129
Hayashi Fusao, 148, 152, 187
Heartless, The (Yi Kwang-su), 75, 82–83, 85, 86, 87, 91, 107–8; allegorical novels contrasted with, 145; Ch'oe Sŏ-hae inspired by, 154; education of women in, 72–73
Hegel, G.W.F., 9–10, 110, 139, 168, 219, 250n15; difference incorporated into philosophy of, 176; *The Philosophy of History*, 173, 265n18; *The Science of Logic*, 176
Heidegger, Martin, 84, 177, 217, 218, 219; *Being and Time*, 137, 188; Nazism of, 205, 216
Heine, Heinrich, 187, 192, 202
Hemp-Clad Prince, The (Yi Kwang-su), 88–89
Hirabayashi Hatsunosuke, 113, 115–17
historical materialism, 37, 125, 216

Historical Materialism (Bukharin), 121
historicism, 36, 163
historiography, 93, 131
history, 3, 21, 36, 139–140; as ceaseless war, 63; dialectical laws of, 144; Eurocentric view of, 21; Hegel's philosophy of, 168; historical materialism, 37, 125, 216; literary form and, 148; Marxist-Leninist view of, 113, 142, 147, 153; "proletarian nation" as subject of, 97; proletariat as subject of, 93, 140; race theory and, 12; Social Darwinist view of, 15; stage theory of, 23, 99, 111, 121; time reduced to, 215; universal, 24, 104, 130, 149–150; world culture and, 27
History of Japan, The (Kaempfer), 37
Hitler, Adolph, 64, 91, 206, 216
Hokkaido, 149, 150, 153, 161
Home Village (Yi Ki-yŏng), 90, 146, 163–64, 165, 262n12
"Hound, The" (Pak Yŏng-hŭi), 142, 143–44, 145, 149
House in the Village, The (Nakano), 105
human, the: existence in History, 12; as liminal and mediating figure, 11; limits of, 22–25, 200; Linné's binomial taxonomy and, 11–12; as object of anthropological knowledge, 18, 19, 20; origins of transcendental subjectivity and, 221; teleological form of, 39; totality of humanity, 30. *See also* empirico-transcendental doublet
human community, 22, 29, 49, 67, 83, 207
humanism, 3, 27, 56, 70, 95, 174; antifascist, 173; bourgeois, 109; chronotope and, 134–39; crisis of, 180–191; discursive formation of, 11; of European Renaissance, 126, 183; genus-being and, 132; imperial expansion and, 215; of Juche philosophy in North Korea, 6; limits of, 207; Marxism and, 101, 125, 133; "new humanism," 126, 146, 173, 198; questioned in minor literature, 198–208; secularized Christian humanism, 78; socialist realism and, 131, 158; spatiotemporal limit of, 23; stage theory of history and, 130; totality of knowledge and, 136; transcendental, 127
human sciences, 2, 23, 39, 112, 253n24; evolution and, 38; Foucault's archaeology of, 13–14, 19; relations between culture and labor, 132; Soviet, 122; transcendental human, 57
Hwang Chang-yŏp, 6, 250n15
Hwang Chong-yŏn, 65
hybridity, 83, 209, 236
Hyŏn Chin-gŏn, 154

identities: anthropological, 23; dialectic and, 176, 243, 265n27; genus-being (*Gattungswesen*) and, 12, 13; Japanese national identity, 91; Korean national identity, 89, 91; minority identity and imperial subjectivity, 208–12; multiple, 120; turn from proletarian to national identity, 152
imagined community, 87
Im Chong-guk, 267n70
Im Chŏng-jae, 93, 96, 118, 120; "Advice to the Litterateurs," 94–95; personhood theorized by, 121, 128
Im Hwa, 23–24, 95, 108, 155, 250n14; critique of new humanism, 126; East Asian Community and, 162; inclusive Japanese nation-state and, 169; as leader of KAPF, 124–25; "Method of the History of New Literature," 124; on "new Korean literature," 124; "Opening an Umbrella on Yokohama Pier," 103, 106–108; peasant literature and, 132–33; on proletarian culture, 100; "The Reconstruction of the Subject and the World of Literature," 127; turn to socialist realism, 125–26, 140, 260n56
imperialism, 5, 13, 16, 97, 214; anticolonial revolution as response to, 105; British imperialism in India, 53; democracy and, 67; discourse of civilization, 145; ecstatic temporality and, 231; effects on Korean economic development, 128; European, 170; human genus-being and, 8; Korean protests against, 26; Lenin's theory of, 96; limits of the human and, 24; linguistic, 51; in Manchuria, 94; modernist temporality and, 214–19; modernization and, 101; proletarian revolution against, 104; universalizing discourse of, 8; as war between the powerful and the weak, 94; world history and, 7
imperial nationalism, 8, 18, 149, 212, 248; anthropology and, 13; fascism compared with, 168; nation-state subjectivity and, 14; social science discourses of, 222
imperial subjectification (*kōminka*), 24, 174, 175, 197, 202, 211, 230; ambiguous identity and, 208, 211; "ontology of the personal" and, 196, 198
imperial subjectivity, 124, 126, 175, 176, 177; ethnic identity and, 175, 194; minority identity and, 198, 202, 208, 209; performance of, 176
In Chŏng-sik, 153
Independent News, 15
individualism, 29, 30, 33, 186; abstract internationalism and, 183–84; of bourgeoisie, 93, 96; cosmopolitan, 185; crisis of, 182; Italian

Renaissance humanism and, 183; overcoming of, 181–82
industrialization, 146, 184
"Infinite Hexagon of Architecture, The" (Yi Sang), 213, 243
Inoue Tetsujirō, 31
internationalism: abstract, 184; citizenship and, 188; Marxism and, 103; proletarian, 107, 152
International Writers' Conference in Defense of Culture (Paris, 1935), 126
intertextuality, 27
"Into the Light" (Kim Sa-ryang), 208–11
Itō Tadahiro, 232–33
Itō Hirobumi temple, 234–35, 246
Itten, Johannes, 232

Jakobson, Roman, 194
Jameson, Fredric, 176, 218, 262n11
Japan: capitalist stage of development in, 105; indexical notion of, 2; Korean students in, 85–86, 154; Marxist thought in, 10; national exceptionalism, 58; postwar, 5; proletarian literature in, 96; racist attacks on Koreans and Chinese after Kanto earthquake, 134, 262n2; world-historical mission of, 223
Japanese empire, 19, 29, 99, 189, 198; biopolitics of, 65; from civilization to culture, 13–18; culturalism as hegemonic ideology of, 6; economic and political order of, 148; expansion of, 154; fascism and, 126, 168, 218; Korean intellectuals in support of, 131, 133; possibility of socialist revolution in, 125; proletarian literature of, 155; state projects of crisis management, 162; universality and, 1–6, 145
Japanese-Korean unification (naisen-ittai), 153, 174, 175, 230
Japanese language, 10–11, 24, 153; Chinese characters and, 55; compulsory in Korean schools, 51, 53; Koreans writing in, 85, 181, 197; Taiwanese and Koreans as nonnative speakers, 54; as world language of science, 23, 53
Japaneseness, 3, 4, 37, 40, 209
Japan-Korea Annexation Treaty (1910), 53
Jesus, 71, 77, 78
Joyce, James, 184, 215
Juche philosophy, 6, 250n15

Kaempfer, Engelbert, 37
Kafka, Franz, 175, 200, 203, 207
Kando Convention (1909), 156

Kang Kyŏng-ae, 24, 147, 154; as radical feminist writer, 133; *From Wonso Pond*, 138, 146–47, 164–66
Kant, Immanuel, 3, 30, 33, 42, 70, 250n15; *Anthropology from a Pragmatic Point of View*, 19, 20–21, 135–36, 170; categorical imperative of, 35; "cooperative beauty" and, 189; *Critique of Judgment*, 179; *Critique of Pure Reason*, 44–45, 138; debates among Russian Marxists and, 110; Japan viewed by, 37–38; on "kingdom of ends," 31, 41, 252b4; modern anthropocentric thought and, 100; moral philosophy of, 19–20, 32, 252n46; on race and history, 12, 20–21, 37, 251nn26–27; on schematism, 177; teleological view of nature, 47, 115; on thing-in-itself, 45; three critiques of, 82
Kant and Contemporary Philosophy (Kuwaki), 32, 37, 45
Kanto earthquake (1923), racist attacks following, 103, 134, 262n2
KAPF (Korea Artista Proleta Federacio), 94, 100, 119, 153, 154; allegorical literature and, 142, 146; Ch'oe Sŏ-hae criticized by, 160; disbanding of, 127; founding of, 118; New Tendency Literature and, 159; peasant novel and, 163, 164; police crackdowns on, 126; "transplanted literature" and, 124–25
Karatani Kojin, 53, 255n2
Kawabata Yasunari, 208
Keijō Imperial University (Seoul), 182, 193
Kim Ho-yong, 102
Kim Hwan, 140, 141
Kim Hyŏn-ju, 65
Kim Ki-jin, 96–97, 113, 119–120, 146, 155; "Death of a Young Idealist," 145; "The Red Mouse," 142, 144, 145, 154, 164
Kim Kyŏng-mi, 53, 76
Kim Nam-ch'ŏn, 24, 125, 175, 197–98, 206–207, 240; "Barley," 203, 204–206; "Management," 203–204, 205
Kim O-sŏng, 126
Kim Sa-ryang, 23, 24, 144, 175, 187, 240; critique of humanism in minor literature of, 196–203, 267n79; "Dosonran," 212; "Into the Light," 208–11; "The Snake," 199–201; "Tenma," 202, 207; translation as tactic and, 191–95
Kim Tong-in, 140, 141, 145, 159; "Potatoes," 141
Kim Tu-yong, 126
Kim Yun-sik, 124, 195
Kitagawa Sukehito, 57, 58
Kobayashi Takiji, 24, 134, 142, 147; *The Absentee Landlord*, 161; death of, 149–150; "Life of a

Party Member," 148; proletarian literature and, 148
Komaki Oki, 119
Kon Wajirō, 253n14
Korea, colonial, 4, 5, 38, 63, 122; assimilation in, 52, 65; culturalist discourse in, 75; as cultural/literary region in Japanese empire, 56–61; cultural reconstruction in Yi's thought, 66–70; human life formed through culture and education in, 70–80; Kando as rural frontier region, 153–54, 156–160, 164; Korean students in Japan, 85–86; limit of transcendental Japan and, 30; literary criticism of, 219; Marxist social science in, 129; massive social transformations in, 142; modern world and, 6; national liberation of, 104; nation-building under, 18; proletarian culture as modernization in, 120; as "proletarian nation," 119, 155; from state of nature to world of culture, 56, 60, 66–67; transformation into "world cultural nation," 78–79, 88, 92; transition from feudal relations to capitalism, 100–101. *See also* cultural policy, in Korea; March First Movement
Korea, dynastic: Koryŏ kingdom, 89, 193; Later Three Kingdoms period (892–936), 89; Silla kingdom (668–935), 89; Unified Silla, 129. *See also* Chosŏn period (1392–1897)
Korea, North (DPRK), 5–6, 91, 128, 132; *juche* philosophy in, 6, 250n15; "national communism" in, 161; nationalism in, 94; socialist realist aesthetics in, 127
Korea, South (Republic of Korea), 5, 53, 91, 94, 267n70
Korea and Architecture (journal), 25, 214, 221, 229–240, 237, 239; nostalgic response to modernity and, 245; space and time discussed in, 247
"Korea and the Common Language of the World" (Ch'oe), 57
Korean empire (1894–1910), 14, 15, 39, 78
Korean language, 10–11, 23, 210; banned in schools, 54; Christianity and, 54–55; dialects and hybrid writing systems, 83; *han'gul* writing, 54, 55; Korean Language Research Group, 54; vernacular literature, 124, 159, 231. *See also* language, national
Korean Literature in a Time of Transition (Ch'oe Chae-sŏ), 181, 182, 222
Korean nation, 63, 78, 80, 93, 108, 208; blood lineage of, 79; brought into the world through anthropology, 64, 71; "common emotion" and, 82; "converts" to Japanese nationalism, 207; cultural improvement of, 154; culturalism and, 94; cultural policy and, 56; differences internal to, 64; education of, 78–79; intellectuals' rejection of, 65; Koreans in Japan, 211, 268n96; life philosophy and, 92; mobilized for Japan's war effort, 91–92, 188, 227; reconstruction of, 66, 73; as stateless people, 17; Tan'gun origin myth, 93; transcendental subject in context of, 125; writing in Japanese as treason to, 267n70
"Korean Things" (Yokomitsu), 227
"Korean World of Ideas, The" (Kuwaki), 38
Koryŏ kingdom, in Korea, 89, 193
Kōsaka Masaaki, 171, 172, 192
Kōtoku Shūsui, 96
Kōyama Iwao, 173, 265n18; anthropocentrism of, 229, 230; on break from and return to anthropocentrism, 167, 174, 223
Kurahara Korehito, 113, 117
Kuroita Katsumi, 232
Kuwaki Gen'yoku, 1–4, 6, 31–41, 49, 66, 247, 249n9; culturalism and, 74, 135; cultural reconstruction and, 93; on culture–nature distinction, 57, 172; on Japanese culture as world-historical development, 85; "The Korean World of Ideas," 38; limit of humanism and, 30; national language and, 23; neo-Kantianism and, 28, 31–32, 34, 38; personalism of, 85; politicization of cultural science and, 7; on progress and development, 15; as student in Germany, 1, 28, 37; Yi Kwang-su as student of, 5, 31, 63, 66, 249n10
Kuwaki Gen'yoku, works of: *Culturalism and Social Problems*, 1, 3, 4, 36, 37; *Culture and Reconstruction*, 36; *Kant and Contemporary Philosophy*, 32, 37, 45; "On the Notion of 'Japanese'" (Kuwaki), 1, 2; *Outline of Philosophy: The Thing and the I*, 34
Kwak Kŭn, 154–55
Kwŏn Bodŭrae, 155, 156, 158
Kyŏngbŏkkung Palace, 234
Kyoto School, 21, 171, 180

labor, productive, 7, 18, 146; alienation of labor, 9, 166; division of labor, 110, 111; genus-being (*Gattungswesen*) as, 23, 105; universality of, 124
Labor-Peasant School, 128, 161
labor theory of value, 43, 48
Lalande, George de, 234
language, national, 41, 49–56, 60, 79; cosmopolitan person and, 64; discursive subject

of, 186; humanism transmitted through, 83; imperialization and minor literature, 197; imperial subjectivity and, 176; language of Japan proper (*naichigo*), 192, 194, 195; multiethnic national culture and, 180; "regime of translation," 55, 59, 254n59; self-consciousness and, 68; transcendental subject of modernity and, 22–23; translation and, 197, 231; translation as tactic, 191–96; as universalizing medium, 80; world culture and, 173

Later Three Kingdoms period (892–936), in Korea, 89

Le Bon, Gustav, 67, 68

Le Corbusier, 231, 232, 233

Lectures School, 128, 161, 162

Lenin, V. I., 69, 110, 113; *Materialism and Empirio-Criticism*, 109; "On Proletarian Culture," 109; "What Is to Be Done?," 114

Lewis, Wyndham, 216

liberalism, 29–30, 117

"Life of a Party Member" (Kobayashi), 148

life philosophy (*Lebensphilosophie*), 2, 34, 63, 92, 144

"Limits of Culture, The" (Tanabe), 172–73

Linné, Carl von, 11–12

Lippit, Seiji, 216, 217, 228

literary criticism, 24, 84, 140–41, 219, 222

"Literary Methodology" (Hirabayashi), 115

literature, 35, 57, 67, 121; back-to-the-land novels, 90, 91, 262n12; *Bildungsroman* genre, 95, 148, 154; bourgeois, 118, 125, 140; Chinese literary culture, 55; cinematic, 219–229, 230; epistolary novel, 158; I-novel (*shishōsetsu*), 147, 185, 216, 217, 223, 226, 228; Japanese national literature, 152–53, 240; Korean national literature, 62, 69, 240; minor, 175, 191, 196–208; modernist, 183, 184, 214; "new literature," 95, 124; pedagogical function of, 120; *shudai* (treatment of subjects), 186, 187; Western, 125. See also allegory, literary; proletarian literature

"Literature and 'Bourgeois'/'Proletariat'" (Yi Kwang-su), 81

Literature and Revolution (Trotsky), 109

Logical Nature of Economic Laws, The (Sōda), 42

"Logic of Individual Causality, The" (Sōda), 44

Logic of Literature, The (Paek Chŏl), 126

"Logic of Species, The" (Tanabe), 177

Lower Depths, The (Gorky), 199, 200

Lukács, Georg, 99, 100, 111, 131

Lunarcharsky, Anatoly, 109

Luther, Martin, 54, 254n56

Luxembourg, Rosa, 162

Lyotard, J.-F., 218

"Machine" (Yokomitsu), 223, 225–26

Madame Butterfly (Puccini opera), 1–2, 37, 38, 50, 85

"Magic of Architecture, The" (Arai), 58–59

"Management" (Kim Nam-chŏn), 203–204, 205

Manchuria, 139, 152, 160, 163, 176; Japanese puppet state in, 156; Kando region, 164; as part of Korean territory, 94

Manchuria (Nakanishi), 139

"Manifesto for Korean Revolution" (Sin), 93

Mansejŏn (Yŏm), 95

March First Movement (Korea), 4, 14, 16, 144; cultural policy and, 26; as natural event, 68; self-conscious subject and, 64

Marinetti, Filippo, 216

Marx, Karl, 9, 43, 98, 99; break from German idealism, 131; *Capital*, 145, 205; critique of transcendental humanism, 127; *Gattungswesen* concept, 10–11; "The German Ideology," 131; on industrial reserve army, 201; on nature of proletariat, 109; on primitive accumulation, 162; "Theses on Feuerbach," 116

Marxism, 4, 9, 18, 37, 167, 168; anthropology and, 12–13, 116; colonial dimension of, 10; empirico-transcendental doublet in, 100; genus-being (*Gattungswesen*) and, 14, 99; humanism in, 101, 125; Japanese-Korean unification and, 153; literary criticism and, 90; modernization and, 204, 215; particularities of Japanese capitalism/imperialism and, 96; proletarian culture concept and, 7; social science and, 24, 136, 138, 218, 219; view of universal history, 104

Marxism-Leninism, 108, 109, 113, 132, 142, 143, 155; developmental allegory of history, 160; as modernizing project, 173

masculinity, 107, 164, 210

Materialism and Empirio-Criticism (Lenin), 109

"Maybe Love" (Yi Kwang-su), 62, 85, 87

Meiji Culture Research Group, 134

Meiji period, 13–14, 15, 16, 38, 40, 53

Meiji Restoration, 69, 128, 256n22

melodrama, 87, 89, 90, 106, 160, 222; colonized nationalism and, 137; contrast of spirit and material, 88; fascist aesthetics and, 199, 203, 223; moral allegory and, 141–42, 218; naturalism and, 145; suffering and struggle, 103

Menger, Anton, 41

"Method of the History of New Literature" (Im Hwa), 124

Mies, Maria, 165

Miki Kiyoshi, 11, 134, 173

Mills, Charles, 20, 33, 56
mimesis, 105, 142, 213, 219
mimponshugi theory, 16, 69
Mizuno Naoki, 102
modernism, aesthetic, 24–25, 214–19
modernity, 4, 12, 166, 179, 183; cosmopolitan, 187; crisis of, 181, 182; culture as site for subject of, 8; fascist responses to, 91; human as subject-object of knowledge, 12, 19; spatiotemporality and, 241; spiritual cultivation of, 63; transcendental subject of, 23, 80; universality and, 124
Modernity (journal), 140
modernization, 14, 88, 155, 217; aesthetic, 108; cultural, 24; development of productive relations and, 123; nation-building project and, 15; proletarian culture and, 120
modernization theory, 3, 5, 19, 39, 56, 110
Money and Value (Sōda), 42, 50
morality, 12, 20, 35, 65, 146; cultural life and, 35; emotion and, 82; fascist ideology and, 168; freedom and, 19; as free individual activity, 32; grounding in the universal, 4; ideologies of practice and, 18; modernization of, 88
morality, self-legislated, 8, 17, 20, 21; anthropological identity and, 23; as demand on colonial subjects, 34; as formal essence of the human, 28, 31; genus-being and, 30, 41; moral law and, 32; nation-state formation and, 33; telos of the person (*in'gyŏk*) and, 63
music, 121
Mussolini, Benito, 216

Nakanishi Inosuke, 24, 166, 262n2; *Manchuria*, 139; *The View of Life and Death Row Inmates*, 134–37
Nakano Shigeharu, 23, 100, 102–108, 112, 117, 120–21, 125; allegorical narrative and, 140; on class and emotions, 121; *The House in the Village*, 105; theory of proletarian art, 161; "What Is Proletarian Art?," 104, 121–22. See also "Shinagawa Station in the Rain"
NAPF (Nippona Artista Proleta Federacio), 100, 146
Narodnik movement, in Russia, 89
national culture, 2, 64, 85, 185, 191; as anthropological category, 127, 176; capitalism and, 88; culturalism and, 66; disappearance of social classes and, 77; geographical determination of, 129; individual disconnected from, 183; Japanese, 7, 172, 182, 183; Korean, 69, 196; in Marxist discourse, 152; mediating role of, 7, 24, 172, 181; multiethnic, 7, 180; species and, 171; translation and, 194; universal history and, 125
nationalism, 11, 23, 136; anticolonial, 39; antistate, 186; blood nationalism, 64; imperial Japanese, 127, 202, 207; Korean, 85, 94, 186; multiethnic, 206; nostalgia and, 153. See also cultural nationalism; ethnic nationalism; imperial nationalism
nationality, 106, 107; assimilation in colonies and, 4; cosmopolitan view of, 55; Japanese, 65; Korean, 66, 82, 105; morality as foundation of, 64
national liberation, 104, 105, 157, 163
National Socialism, 168, 169, 186, 187, 264n4. See also fascism
national social type, 111–12
national studies (*kokugaku*), 53, 254n59
nation-building, 14, 15, 53; in colonial Korea, 18, 63; in the Soviet Union, 104
nation-state, 28, 32, 36, 170; autonomy of international economy from, 184; collective planning and formation of, 65; imperial nationalism and, 14; individual sacrificed to, 92; relation between individual and totality, 63; world-historical, 176
nation-state subjectivity, 10, 13, 146, 191; ethnic difference and, 172; genus-being and, 18, 128, 167; highter unity of culture and, 97; imperial nationalism and, 8, 14; turn from proletarian to national identity, 152
"Native Land" (Ch'oe Sŏ-hae), 157
Na To-hyang, 154
Natorp, Paul, 45
naturalism, 126, 143, 145, 155, 159, 217
natural laws, 39–40, 47, 72, 92
natural rights, 40, 41
natural science, 6, 34, 38, 168; epistemological divide with cultural science, 116; limit concept in, 45; mechanical causality of, 48; neo-Kantianism and, 68
nature, 30, 39, 45, 126, 143, 180; assimilation as liberation from, 66; in back-to-the-land novels, 90; "countries belonging to nature," 33; free will and, 35; human conquest of, 110, 111; patriarchy and, 165; teleological view of, 47
nature–culture divide, 17–18, 33; education and, 75, 76; individual versus mechanical causality, 75; Korean movement from nature to culture, 56, 60, 66–67, 79, 82; neo-Kantianism and, 67, 68; proletarian class consciousness and, 113, 114
Negative Dialectics (Adorno), 265n27

neo-Kantianism, 2, 5, 17, 54, 64, 114; biopolitics and, 91; on causality, 115; cosmopolitan-national community and, 27–28; critique of natural-scientific ideologies and, 38–39; cultural science and, 6; cultural value formation and, 38, 128; economics and, 42; history as moral universality, 219; moral action and, 32; on nature–culture divide, 67, 68, 116
New Sensationism, 25, 216, 223, 226
New Tendency Group, 94, 96, 118, 125, 142, 154; allegorical literature and, 143; KAPF and, 159; Pak Yŏng-hŭi's criticism of, 155
nihilism, 85, 144
Niizeki Ryōzō, 181
Nishida Kitarō, 135
Notes on Human Life (Miki Kiyoshi), 134
Notes on Life (Miki), 173
"Novel and Time, The" (Yokomitsu), 224–25
nuclear family, housing and, 238, 240, 243, 247

Ogyu Sorai, 254n59
One, the Unity, and the Oneness, The (Rickert), 51–52
One-nationism (*ilminjuŭi*), 250n15
"On Linguistic Aspects of Translation" (Jakobson), 194
"On Proletarian Culture" (Lenin), 109
"On the Characteristics and Direction of Korean Literature" (An Ham-gwang), 167
"On the Korean Nation" (Yi Kwang-su), 55, 79–80, 83
"On the New Life" (Yi Kwang-su), 74
"On the Notion of 'Japanese'" (Kuwaki), 1, 2
"On the Reconstruction of the Nation" (Yi Kwang-su), 17, 22, 63, 66–67, 79, 93, 114
"ontology of the personal," 24, 174–75, 196
Opening, The (KAPF journal), 94–95, 117, 119
"Opening an Umbrella on Yokohama Pier" (Im Hwa), 103, 106–108
Order of Things, The (Foucault), 12, 22
Orientalism, 1–2, 37, 38, 50, 51, 85; anthropocentric epistemologies of, 173; dismantling of representational structure of, 3
Orientalism (Said), 216
Orwell, George, 126
Osborne, Peter, 10, 251n22
Other/otherness, 57, 177, 229; genus-being (*Gattungswesen*) and, 13; Orientalist view of, 37; racialized or ethnicized, 12

Paek Chŏl, 126, 173, 190
"Paekkŭm" (Ch'oe Sŏ-hae), 156

Paek Nam-un, 127, 138, 161, 169, 250n14; *The Economic History of Korean Society*, 128; primitive accumulation and, 162–63; stagist histories of Korea, 23, 128–132, 162, 261n68
Pak T'ae-wŏn, 215, 219, 220, 221, 225
Pak Yŏng-hŭi, 96–97, 113, 118–19, 120, 154; "The Hound," 142, 143–44, 145, 149; New Tendency Group criticized by, 155; Proletkult supported by, 146; recantation of proletarian literature, 152; urban Marxism-Leninism of, 155
Pan-Asianism, 15, 204
Park, Hyun-ok, 156, 176
Patriarchy and Accumulation on a World Scale (Mies), 165
peasantry, 100, 101, 120, 161; displacement of, 145, 201; Japanese peasant literature, 127–28; Korean, 59; peasant literature, 153, 164, 169; primitive accumulation and, 165; role in proletarian revolution, 104; unity with proletariat, 128
People's Literature (journal), 173, 192, 266n58; crisis of humanism and, 181, 182, 184–87, 189–191; state-centered culture and, 167
People's Literature and World Literature (Niizeki), 181
"people's standpoint" (*kokumin-teki tachiba*), 180–82, 186, 188, 196, 197, 203
People without Land (Grimm), 187
performance, 121, 197; of imperial subjectivity, 176; of inherited moral dictates, 82; of Japanese nationalism, 202; ontology of the personal and, 175
personhood, 8, 34, 47, 121, 147; critiques of cultural personhood, 92–97; cultural human and, 26; economics and, 43; female, 74
Philosophy of History (Hegel), 173, 265n18
Philosophy of Money (Simmel), 42
Philosophy of the Nation (Kōsaka), 171, 172
Pioneers (Yi Kwang-su), 87–88
Plato, 52
poetry, 114, 140; of Arai Tetsu, 31, 58, 60; of Pak Yŏng-hŭi, 125, 142; of Yi Sang, 25, 213, 214, 230, 240–48
political economy, 31, 41, 43, 94, 163, 205; cultural modernization and, 120; German idealist philosophy and, 42; historical uncertainty and, 48; Marxist, 148, 149
Political Unconscious, The (Jameson), 176
Polo, Marco, 37
Portsmouth, Treaty of (1905), 53
"Potatoes" (Kim Tong-in), 141
Poulantzas, Nicolas, 184

Pound, Ezra, 216
"Primary Mission of the Nation, The" (Ariyoshi), 29
primitive accumulation, 6, 97, 133, 149; peasants expelled from land by, 101; proletarian literature and, 160–66; in the Soviet Union, 104
progress, 15, 16, 39, 66
proletarian arts, 121–22, 132; center–periphery relation and, 153; chronotype of nation form and, 23; colonial dimension of, 10; conflict with culturalism, 96; gendering of proletarian subject and, 108; genus-being (*Gattungswesen*) and, 14; intertextuality with culturalism, 113, 115; modernization project of, 155; proletarian culture concept and, 7; Russian Revolution and, 109, 110; suppressed by Japanese police state, 126; theater, 199; as trivial mass culture, 24; universality of, 117. *See also* KAPF (Koreana Artista Proletaria Federacio)
proletarian culture, 7, 100, 101, 117, 132–33
proletarian literature, 96, 115, 117, 127, 138, 140; dominance in representing experience of colonial modernity, 158; in Japan, 148, 152; peasant novel and, 164; primitive accumulation and, 160–66
proletariat, 9, 93, 140, 163; as class bringing end of social classes, 109; cultural formation of national proletariat, 113–128; genus-being (*Gattungswesen*) and, 13, 105; industrial mode of production and, 111; internationalization of, 107; national, 18, 24; "proletarian nation," 97, 119; as subject/object of history, 99, 100, 111; as unified national-international subject, 7; unity with peasantry, 128
Proletkult, 109, 110, 120, 146
Proust, Marcel, 215
psychoanalysis, 183, 218
psychogeography, 234, 270n35
Puccini, Giacomo, 1, 37, 38

race, 21, 37; fascist ideology and, 168; genus-being (*Gattungswesen*) and, 12, 20–21; Kantian taxonomy of, 170; "norming of space" and, 33
racism, 11, 80, 134, 149, 170
"Rat Fire" (Yi Ki-yŏng), 125
realism, literary, 139, 146, 218, 222; loss of stability for, 200; psychological realism, 225, 226
"Record of Escape" (Ch'oe Sŏ-hae), 157–58
"Red Mouse, The" (Kim Ki-jin), 142, 144, 145, 154, 164
Reformation, in Germany, 54

"Reform of the Individual's Daily Life Is the Basis for National Power, The" (Yi Kwang-su), 76–77, 80–81
Reillumination of Ch'oe Sŏ-hae's Literature, The (anthology), 155
"Relation between Life and Death, The" (Yi Kwang-su), 63
relativity, theory of, 25, 213–14, 218–19, 221, 241–44
Renaissance, European, 126, 183
Research Group on Meiji Culture, 16
Research on the Typology of Culture (Kōyama), 173
Rhee, Syngman, 250n15
Ricardo, David, 12, 42
Richards, I. A., 181, 189
Rickert, Heinrich, 6–7, 44, 49, 51–52, 55
Rimbaud, Arthur, 217
"Riverside Scene" (Pak T'ae-wŏn), 216, 219
Romanticism, 54, 84, 181; German, 192; individualism and, 183; revolutionary romanticism of socialist realism, 126–27, 140
Ross, Kristin, 217
Ruins (journal), 140
Russian Revolution, 29, 30, 69, 109, 149, 256n22
Russo-Japanese War, 16

Sad History of Tanjong, The (Yi Kwang-su), 89
Said, Edward, 37, 216
Saitō Makoto, 16, 27, 28, 36, 39; culturalism and, 30; on world culture, 26–27
Sakai, Naoki, 11, 171, 254n59
Sasa Keiichi, 235, 238
Sasaki Takamaru, 119
Sata Ineko, 148, 152
Schmid, Andre, 14
Schmitt, Carl, 94
science, 23, 45, 110, 247; "Asian science," 51; national language and, 50, 53; as systematization of thought, 121
Science of Logic, The (Hegel), 176
self-consciousness, 4, 17, 67; active transformation of phenomena and, 70; in Kant's thought, 64; Korean national, 23; nature–culture divide and, 68; universality of, 4
self-determination, 17, 64, 172, 192
self-other dichotomy, 93, 94
Shanghai (Yokomitsu Riichi), 216, 226, 228
Shelley, Percy Bysshe, 183
"Shinagawa Station in the Rain" (Nakano), 102, 103, 104, 118, 122, 123
Shu-mei Shih, 215
Silla Kingdom (668–935), in Korea, 89

INDEX 305

Silverberg, Miriam, 103
Sim Hun, 90
Simmel, Georg, 42, 43
Sin Ch'ae-ho, 66, 93–94, 129, 144–45, 156
Sino-Japanese War, First (1895–96), 14, 16
Skempton, Simon, 10, 251n22
Smith, Adam, 12, 42
"Snake, The" (Kim Sa-ryang), 199–201
Social Darwinism, 15, 36–37, 38, 39
socialism, 7, 42, 43, 88; proletarian revolution and, 99; stage theory of history and, 128; Stalin's "socialism in one country," 104, 111–12, 122; transition from capitalism to, 122, 123
socialist realism, 95, 110, 113, 131, 155; as aestheticization of socialism, 123; formation at First Soviet Writers' Congress, 125; humanism of, 131, 158, 173; political terror and, 201; revolutionary romanticism of, 126–27, 140
social sciences, 8, 35, 68, 101; genus-being (*Gattungswesen*) and, 13; imperial nationalism and, 222; Marxist, 24, 136, 138, 218, 219; "national economy studies," 41; neo-Kantianism and, 128
Socrates, 68, 69, 255n18
Sōda Kiichirō, 6, 7, 16–17, 93, 172, 253n30; culturalism and, 74–75, 134, 135; on culture-nature distinction, 57; on general cultural value, 31, 32–33; limit concept of, 41–49; limit of humanism and, 30; national language and, 23, 49–56; on natural human versus cultural human, 26; neo-Kantianism and, 28, 31, 32; as student in Germany, 28, 42
Sōda Kiichirō, works of: *Cultural Value and the Limit Concept*, 44, 45; "Cultural Value as Limit Concept," 46; *The Logical Nature of Economic Laws*, 42; "The Logic of Individual Causality," 44; *Money and Value*, 42, 43, 50
Soil (Yi Kwang-su), 89–91, 163, 165, 262n12
Sŏ In-sik, 9–10, 11, 130, 132, 170; critique of fascism, 169–171, 264n4; inclusive Japanese nation-state and, 169
Southwest Baden School of Neo-Kantianism, 6
sovereignty, popular, 17, 18, 41, 63, 69
Soviet Union, 29, 104, 108–12, 117, 133; aestheticization of socialism in, 123; First Soviet Writers' Congress (1934), 125; in Japanese proletarian literature, 149–152; national minorities in, 122
spatiotemporality: allegory and, 84, 139–140; of cultural modernization, 218; of cultural/social development, 9; of Hegelian world history, 104; imperial subjectivity and, 177; limit

of humanism and, 22–24; unity of time and space, 178, 179. *See also* chronotopes; relativity, theory of; time/temporality
Spencer, Herbert, 38
Spengler, Oswald, 184
Spivak, Gayatri, 48
stage theory, 23, 99, 111, 121, 204; appropriated by Marxist social scientists, 136; genus-being and, 128–132
Stalin, Joseph, 112, 122, 201
Stalinism, 108–9, 122, 125
"Starvation and Slaughter" (Ch'oe Sŏ-hae), 158–59
subjectivity, 4, 16, 24, 65, 156, 189; architectural space and, 232; cinematic, 221; cosmopolitan, 93; epistemological versus practical, 126–27; Korean national subjectivity, 60, 67; moral, 46; nation-state subjectivity, 14, 18; premodern political, 113; proletarian, 103, 104, 110, 120, 147, 148; relativity theory and, 214; of the state, 132; time and limit of, 224; universal moral practice and, 81; women's education and, 74; world-historical, 145. *See also* imperial subjectivity; transcendental subject
syndicalism, 42
Systema Naturae (Linné), 11
systems theory, 110

Taft-Katsura agreement (1905), 15
Tagore, Rabindranath, 71, 77
Taishō period, 6, 14, 15, 16, 37
Takashi Fujitani, 11, 92
Tanabe Hajime, 8, 9–10, 11, 170, 171, 177–180, 229; Hegelian dialectic of, 25, 213, 248; imperial subjectivity and, 221; Kyoto School and, 21; "The Limits of Culture," 172–73; "The Logic of Species," 177; multiethnic nationalism of, 206; as neo-Kantian, 178, 253n30; philosophy of expression, 196, 230; physics appropriated by, 231; on relativity theory, 218–19; "From the Schema of 'Time' to the Schema of 'World'", 177, 241
Tan'gun origin myth, 93, 129
Tansman, Alan, 216
technology, 18, 22, 110, 117, 221
Teibō (journal), 211–12
Tektologia (Bogdanov), 110
"Tenma" (Kim Sa-ryang), 202, 207
territorialization, 196, 197, 230
"The Red Mouse" (Kim Ki-jin), 142, 144
"Theses on Feuerbach" (Marx), 116
"Time" (Yokomitsu), 223–24, 225, 226

time/temporality, 52, 136, 213; in back-to-the-land novels, 91; of *Dasein*, 177; "ecstatic," 25, 214–229, 230, 268n7; Euclidean notion of, 242; imperialism and, 214–19; linguistically defined territory and, 57; Marxist theories of historical development and, 112; nature-culture divide and, 115; science fiction and, 241, 246. *See also* spatiotemporality
Tokieda Motoki, 182
Tokugawa period, 53
Tokyo Imperial University, 232
Tolstoy, Lev, 64
transcendental philosophy, 41, 43, 45, 46, 70
transcendental subject, 3, 30, 58, 79, 125; hypothetical unity of national language and, 60; Kant's aesthetic philosophy and, 82; limits of, 137; local anthropological identity and, 23, 50; a priori categories of, 135; translation between national languages and, 41, 59
"Translator's Task, The" (Benjamin), 194
Trotsky, Leon, 109–10, 111, 112, 113, 146; *Literature and Revolution*, 109; on nonexistence of proletarian culture, 119

underdevelopment, 77, 131
United States, 1, 6; American Revolution, 69, 256n22; Korean students in, 154; modernization theory in, 19, 39; New Deal in, 131
universality, 11, 35; Japanese empire and, 1–6, 145; modernity and, 124; moral, 15, 21; of self-consciousness, 4
urbanization, 142, 184, 212
utilitarianism, 38

"Value of Literature, The" (Yi Kwang-su), 82
View of Life and Death Row Inmates, The (Nakanishi), 134–37
Viswanathan, Gauri, 53
Voltaire, 37, 41

Waseda University (Tokyo), 4, 16, 31
"Water" (Kim Nam-chŏn), 125
Watsuji Tetsurō, 11, 129, 205, 206; *Climate and Culture*, 21; *Ethics as the Study of the Human*, 21, 134
"What Is Literature?" (Yi Kwang-su), 81, 82
"What Is Poetic?" (Ch'oe Chae-sŏ), 188–89
"What Is Proletarian Art?" (Nakano), 104, 121–22
"What Is to Be Done?" (Lenin), 114
White Birch Group (Shirakaba), 64
White Tide [*Paekjo*] (journal), 95, 142
"Wife of a Revolutionary" (Yi Kwang-su), 88

Wilson Doctrine, 17, 64
Windelband, Wilhelm, 6
"Wings" (Yi Sang), 216, 219, 220, 222
women, 13, 145, 152; bound to national identity, 107; education of, 73–74; liberation of, 66, 88; "new woman" in Yi's fiction, 88; primitive accumulation and, 164–66
Words of Women, The (Sata), 152
world culture (*sekai bunka*), 9, 15, 27, 28, 137, 194
world history, 7, 10, 40, 130, 206–207; anthropocentric view of, 19; ethnic origin and, 93; Eurocentric, 229; genus-being at center of, 248; Hegelian, 139, 177; Japanese state as subject of, 190, 219; plurality of, 204–205; proletariat as primary subject of, 100, 110–11; world-historical state, 167–175
World War I, 27, 28, 29
World War II (Pacific War), 91, 167

Yamada Moritarō, 148
Yanagita Kunio, 253n14
Yeats, W. B., 215
Yi Ha-yun, 124
Yi Hyo-sŏk, 195
Yi In-jik, 124
Yi Ki-yŏng, 24, 125, 139; *Home Village*, 146, 163–64, 165, 262n12; view of Korea's distant historical past, 88–89
Yi Kwang-su, 4, 16, 53, 62–66, 93, 124, 154; allegorical narrative and, 140, 141; allegorical representation of colonized nation, 137; anthropological view of Korea, 153; biopolitics and, 62–63; on Christianity and Korean national language, 54–55; critique of Socrates, 68, 255n18; culturalism and, 144; debate with Sin Ch'ae-ho, 144–45; development of modern vernacular and, 159; on education, 78–79; on emotions, 76–77, 81–82; experience of alienation and, 84–85; fascism and, 64, 90, 91; Japanese identity embraced by, 78, 86; name change to Kayama Mitsurō, 65, 91; national language and, 23, 49; people's literature and, 181; politicization of cultural science and, 7; primitive accumulation and, 163; "reconstruction" (*kaejo*) term of, 64, 66–70; schizophrenic subject of, 246; as student of Kuwaki Gen'yoku, 5, 31, 63, 66, 249n10; teleological principle in, 95; women's education supported by, 73–74
Yi Kwang-su, works of: "Art and Life: The New World and the Mission of the Korean

Nation," 70–71, 72; "Faces Change," 80; *The Hemp-Clad Prince*, 88–89; "On the Korean Nation," 55, 79–80, 83; "Literature and 'Bourgeois'/'Proletariat'," 81; "Maybe Love," 62, 85, 87; "On the New Life," 74; *Pioneers*, 87–88; "On the Reconstruction of the Nation," 17, 22, 63–64, 66–67, 79, 93, 114; "The Reform of the Individual's Daily Life Is the Basis for National Power," 76–77, 80–81; "The Relation between Life and Death," 63; *The Sad History of Tanjong*, 89; *Soil*, 89–91, 163, 165, 262n12; "The Value of Literature," 82; "What Is Literature?," 81, 82; "Wife of a Revolutionary," 88; "You Can Be a Soldier," 91–92, 188; "Yun Kwang-ho," 62, 85, 87. See also *Heartless, The*

Yi Puk-man, 96–97, 102, 118

Yi Sang (Kim Hae-gyŏng), 25, 181, 213–14, 217, 236; "Bird's-Eye View," 214; "Blueprint for a Three-Dimensional Shape," 241–48; cinepoetic space of, 240–48; "The Infinite Hexagon of Architecture," 213, 243; theory of relativity and, 218; schizophrenic subject of, 217, 222, 225, 230, 243; "Wings," 216, 219, 220, 222

Yokomitsu Riichi, 25, 215, 216, 223–29; "Korean Things," 227; "Machine," 223, 225–26; "The Novel and Time," 224–25; *Shanghai*, 226, 228; "Time," 223–24, 225, 226

Yŏm Sang-sŏp, 95, 140–41, 154

Yoshino Sakuzō, 16, 17, 69

"You Can Be a Soldier" (Yi Kwang-su), 91–92, 188

"Yun Kwang-ho" (Yi Kwang-su), 62, 85, 87

Zweig, Stefan, 183

STUDIES OF THE WEATHERHEAD EAST ASIAN INSTITUTE
Columbia University

Selected Titles

(Complete list at: http://www.columbia.edu/cu/weai/weatherhead-studies.html)

The Age of Irreverence: A New History of Laughter in China, by Christopher Rea. University of California Press, 2015

The Nature of Knowledge and the Knowledge of Nature in Early Modern Japan, by Federico Marcon. University of Chicago Press, 2015

The Fascist Effect: Japan and Italy, 1915–1952, by Reto Hoffman. Cornell University Press, 2015

The International Minimum: Creativity and Contradiction in Japan's Global Engagement, 1933–1964, by Jessamyn R. Abel. University of Hawai'i Press, 2015

Empires of Coal: Fueling China's Entry into the Modern World Order, 1860–1920, by Shellen Xiao Wu. Stanford University Press, 2015

Casualties of History: Wounded Japanese Servicemen and the Second World War, by Lee K. Pennington. Cornell University Press, 2015

City of Virtues: Nanjing in an Age of Utopian Visions, by Chuck Wooldridge. University of Washington Press, 2015

The Proletarian Wave: Literature and Leftist Culture in Colonial Korea, 1910–1945, by Sunyoung Park. Harvard University Asia Center, 2015.

Neither Donkey Nor Horse: Medicine in the Struggle Over China's Modernity, by Sean Hsiang-lin Lei. University of Chicago Press, 2014.

When the Future Disappears: The Modernist Imagination in Late Colonial Korea, by Janet Poole. Columbia University Press, 2014.

Bad Water: Nature, Pollution, & Politics in Japan, 1870–1950, by Robert Stolz. Duke University Press, 2014.

Rise of a Japanese Chinatown: Yokohama, 1894–1972, by Eric C. Han. Harvard University Asia Center, 2014.

Beyond the Metropolis: Second Cities and Modern Life in Interwar Japan, by Louise Young. University of California Press, 2013.

From Cultures of War to Cultures of Peace: War and Peace Museums in Japan, China, and South Korea, by Takashi Yoshida. MerwinAsia, 2013.

Imperial Eclipse: Japan's Strategic Thinking about Continental Asia before August 1945, by Yukiko Koshiro. Cornell University Press, 2013.

The Nature of the Beasts: Empire and Exhibition at the Tokyo Imperial Zoo, by Ian J. Miller. University of California Press, 2013.

Public Properties: Museums in Imperial Japan, by Noriko Aso. Duke University Press, 2013.

Reconstructing Bodies: Biomedicine, Health, and Nation-Building in South Korea Since 1945, by John P. DiMoia. Stanford University Press, 2013.

Taming Tibet: Landscape Transformation and the Gift of Chinese Development, by Emily T. Yeh. Cornell University Press, 2013.

Tyranny of the Weak: North Korea and the World, 1950–1992, by Charles K. Armstrong. Cornell University Press, 2013.

The Art of Censorship in Postwar Japan, by Kirsten Cather. University of Hawai'i Press, 2012.

Asia for the Asians: China in the Lives of Five Meiji Japanese, by Paula Harrell. MerwinAsia, 2012.

Lin Shu, Inc.: Translation and the Making of Modern Chinese Culture, by Michael Gibbs Hill. Oxford University Press, 2012.

Occupying Power: Sex Workers and Servicemen in Postwar Japan, by Sarah Kovner. Stanford University Press, 2012.

Redacted: The Archives of Censorship in Postwar Japan, by Jonathan E. Abel. University of California Press, 2012.

Empire of Dogs: Canines, Japan, and the Making of the Modern Imperial World, by Aaron Herald Skabelund. Cornell University Press, 2011.

Planning for Empire: Reform Bureaucrats and the Japanese Wartime State, by Janis Mimura. Cornell University Press, 2011.

Realms of Literacy: Early Japan and the History of Writing, by David Lurie. Harvard University Asia Center, 2011.

Russo-Japanese Relations, 1905–17: From Enemies to Allies, by Peter Berton. Routledge, 2011.

Behind the Gate: Inventing Students in Beijing, by Fabio Lanza. Columbia University Press, 2010.

Imperial Japan at Its Zenith: The Wartime Celebration of the Empire's 2,600th Anniversary, by Kenneth J. Ruoff. Cornell University Press, 2010.

www.ingramcontent.com/pod-product-compliance
Lightning Source LLC
Chambersburg PA
CBHW030522230426

43665CB00010B/734